"Elder of the Jews"

"Elder
of the Jews"

JAKOB EDELSTEIN
OF THERESIENSTADT

RUTH BONDY

*Translated from the Hebrew
by Evelyn Abel*

GROVE PRESS
New York

Published by Grove Press
a division of Wheatland Corporation
841 Broadway
New York, N.Y. 10003

Library of Congress Cataloging-in-Publication Data

Bondy, Ruth.
    "Elder of the Jews".

    Translation of: Edelshtain neged ha-zeman.
    Bibliography: p.
    Includes index.
    1. Edelstein, Jakob, d. 1944.   2. Jews—Czechoslovakia—Biography.   3.
Terezin (Czechoslovakia : Concentration camp)   4. Holocaust, Jewish (1939–
1945)—Czechoslovakia.
    I. Title.
DS135.C97E34213   1989   940.53'15'039240437   88-37751
ISBN 0-8021-1007-X

Designed by Irving Perkins Associates

Manufactured in the United States of America

This book is printed on acid-free paper.

First Edition 1989

10   9   8   7   6   5   4   3   2   1

To Tali and her generation

ACKNOWLEDGMENTS

This book could never have been written without the great help of many individuals and institutions that stood by my side all through the many and difficult years I gave to the biography of Jakob Edelstein. My thanks go, first of all, to the Memorial Foundation for Jewish Culture in New York and to the Tel Aviv Foundation for Literature and the Arts, which helped me to finance the research. I am grateful to all those I interviewed, who gave freely of their time; to the archivists who have been my support; to the former inmates of the Theresienstadt ghetto who answered my many questions; to everybody who read and commented on various parts of the manuscript. Special thanks are due to Professor Leny Yahil, who has been my patient adviser and a constant source of encouragement; to my original publishers, Zmora, Bitan, Modan of Tel Aviv; to Evelyn Abel, who translated the book from Hebrew into English; and to everybody at Grove Press who toiled for the American edition.

Ramat Gan, February 1989   R.B.

CONTENTS

ix

CONTENTS

Illustrations follow page 210

PREFACE

Jakob Edelstein was not one of the great spiritual leaders of European Jewry swept away by the Holocaust. He was neither a visionary nor a war hero. Had not fate—or he himself—decided that he would lead Czechoslovakian Jewry after the Munich Pact, had he rejected the responsibility and emigrated to Palestine before the gates were closed, he would no doubt have numbered among the top ranks of the Israeli Labor Party, served as a mayor, perhaps, or a cabinet minister; and his life would have warranted little more than a footnote in the annals of the State of Israel. What set him apart was the time and the place, his function as "Elder of the Jews" in the Theresienstadt ghetto, his determination to save the Jews of Bohemia and Moravia until the Nazi storm had passed, and his desperate race against time—which, in the end, he lost.

I have been writing this book in my mind for thirty years, ever since I came to Israel and heard the accusations hurled against the survivors of the Holocaust by the people of Israel: Why didn't you fight back? Why didn't you defend yourselves? This lack of understanding of what had happened in Europe under Hitler found true expression in the popular summation "they went as sheep to the slaughter," and in the disproportionate emphasis accorded armed warfare in the chapter of history remembered in Israel on the day known as "Holocaust and Heroism." And while the Israeli public may have been ambivalent in its attitude toward the helpless gray multitude led to destruction, they were even less kind to the Jewish leaders who had represented European Jewry vis-à-vis the Germans. These were summarily dismissed, convicted without trial.

The Judenräte, the Jewish councils appointed by the Germans, did not all come from the same mold. There were essential differences in their composition and in the way they operated. They

xi

varied from place to place, indeed from stage to stage as the work of destruction advanced. The Councils of Elders reflected conquered European Jewry, their world view, their patterns of thought, their hopes and illusions. It requires an arrogance devoid of compassion—for a people lost—to reach a sweeping verdict, as did Hannah Arendt, on the Jews who collaborated in their destruction. The six million dead, and the Jewish leaders among them, must be allowed the basic right to be seen as individuals, not to be lumped together as a dim and formless mass.

I wanted the generation born after the Holocaust to know as much of the facts as possible before they judged, and I wanted to clarify for myself the progression of events from Hitler's rise to power to the death machines at Auschwitz. But I needed thirty years of writing experience and a store of strength before I could tackle the subject not as a witness of the period but as a researcher. From the factual point of view, it makes absolutely no difference that I went through the Theresienstadt ghetto, that I was at Birkenau. I lived through the period cut off from facts about the war, as if outside the flow of time, absorbed in myself, my immediate vicinity, my friends in the youth movement, the struggle to survive. I, too, had to learn the facts from the beginning.

I chose Jakob Edelstein precisely because he was no giant, but a man like all men, who knew both courage and fear. I chose him out of loyalty to my roots, to the Jews of Prague—out of a sense that we who survived by the grace of fate owe our friends from the youth movements and the Zionist organization who headed the Theresienstadt ghetto and the family camp at Birkenau at least the kindness of knowing the facts—even if only in an attempt to balance the scale between courage in arms and the courage required to preserve one's humanity: to educate the young, anywhere, anyhow, as a surety for the generations to come.

While working on the book, I arrived at the surprising conclusion that the Jews in the Diaspora and the Jews in Eretz-Israel (Palestine) were not so different, not such opposites, as it had seemed in the general exhilaration following Israel's victory in her War of Independence. The reactions of the two groups to the danger of the German Reich's expansion had been basically similar, and the essential difference between them stemmed from the lesson of the Holocaust itself. Neither had ever imagined that people could be fed by conveyor belt into a mechanized system of destruction. Here lies the dividing line, not only between different generations of

Jewry, but in human history as a whole. Here was man's second fall. The student of Jewish behavior under German conquest must never lose sight of one simple fact: *they did not know that death factories were possible.* The Jews acted on the basis of their historical experience of riots, persecution, and pogroms: these had flared up and died down, had taken their toll of victims, but had nonetheless permitted the majority to flee and survive. Though they might not have been able to articulate it, even those Jews of Central Europe who had been assimilated for two or three generations, and were far removed from tradition, still somehow carried the faith in their hearts that "Israel is eternal." The guiding line in their relations with the Germans was not a sense of imminent death but a stubborn faith in the possibility of survival.

The Jewish institutions in conquered Europe under the Nazi regime were a natural, logical extension of the separate community organization Jews had built up over generations. They were established not with the thought of total annihilation in mind but in adherence to life, to meet the basic requirements necessary for continued existence, for educating the young, providing shelter for the old, employment for those deprived of work, vocational training for potential emigrants. They were established out of a sense of responsibility in a common destiny, and in the delusion that the world of yesterday still existed.

Jakob Edelstein's life gains significance only against the background of his period, and therefore, even though my story really begins with the partition of Czechoslovakia and the German entry into Prague, I felt it necessary to return to his roots. To shed light on the mentality and world view of the Jews, on their attitude to the events of their time, I had to go back to the Austro-Hungarian monarchy and the beginning of the new Czechoslovakian republic under the leadership of Thomas G. Masaryk. This is not a full biography of Edelstein, and not simply because of the lack of material (he did not keep a diary and only a scant number of his personal letters remain). It is an attempt to illuminate an entire period through the life of an individual. Though I devoted more than three years to collecting material, I could not rely on documentary evidence alone. Much material from the Reich archives has disappeared, still waiting to be found, perhaps, in some dark cellar. I drew on personal accounts but, where possible, always tried to substantiate them with the aid of documents. And still the story of Edelstein's life remains sketchy, full of questions no one can answer.

On his stay in the punishment bunker at Auschwitz I have only three short testimonials. On his thoughts during the six months he waited to die I have nothing.

If I were to try and resolve the question of Edelstein's chief error, I would say that it lay in his logic. He, like all the Jews—true to their education and reasoning—assumed that the Germans needed as much manpower as they could get in their war against the three great allied powers, Britain, Russia, and the United States. It never dawned on them that the hatred Hitler and his Nazi ideologues bore the Jews, and their desire to destroy them once and for all, took precedence even over their desire to win the war, and only increased as all hope of victory diminished. Edelstein, like all the Jews, believed wholeheartedly in Hitler's inevitable defeat, and the Allies' certain victory. It was merely a question of time. They had to hold out another day, another week, another month, until the spring, the winter, next year. Had the war ended in 1943, as the British General Staff had anticipated, or even in 1944—as indeed it might well have—the stubborn optimism shown by the Jews would not have seemed so painful or so naïve.

Ramat Gan, May 1981   R.B.

"Elder of the Jews"

1

THE BEGINNING

ON DECEMBER 4, 1941, Jakob Edelstein and his colleagues journeyed by regular train to the Theresienstadt ghetto. They carried small suitcases, had no police escort, and, as far as appearances went, might have been ordinary tourists. The group consisted mainly of Edelstein's friends from Hehalutz ("The Pioneer," a federation of Zionist youth movements), and they joked and told stories on the short trip from Prague. Their chief worry was that they would not be able to find their way to Terezin itself, about an hour's walk from the train station. They did in fact get lost, had to ask directions, and arrived rather tired at the fortress town where, for the Czech population, life still continued as usual. Only one of the town's many barracks had been set aside for the Jewish advance unit, come to prepare what they considered a city of refuge for the Jews of Bohemia and Moravia until German rule disappeared from Europe.

When the Czech policeman closed the barracks gate behind Edelstein and his colleagues who had come to lead the ghetto, a veteran resident with ten long days of experience as a ghetto inmate told them: "And now, gentlemen, you're in shit." Hans Günther, one of Eichmann's underlings and head of the "Center for Jewish Emigration," summarized the situation in a similar manner when Edelstein complained that the Germans had not kept their promises: "Now, Jews, when you're *im Dreck,* let's see what you can do." The Jews accepted the challenge. They'd show the Germans, they'd

3

show the world, what Jews were capable of. Despite the obstacles, despite the harsh beginnings, despite German domination, here they would build a model Jewish city.

And here, in fact, the real story begins. But before we can take up the threads we must make a long detour in search of an answer to the question of whether Jakob Edelstein's character, education, and views led him on a direct route to ghetto leadership. Is man born an Elder of the Jews? And so we must begin at Horodenka.

The Jews in Horodenka (Gorodenka), a small town in Eastern Galicia (in what is now the western Ukraine, not far north of the Rumanian border), were divided in outlook between orthodox and liberal traditionalists, *hasidim* and *mitnagdim*, Zionists and Bundists. With respect to the emperor, Franz Josef, however, they were unanimous. To them he symbolized permanence, security, a safe haven that had stood firm for almost fifty years and dispelled all fear of distant wars. His Majesty the Emperor, whom the Jews affectionately called Froim Yossel, was their protector. He was their guarantee that no harm would come to them from the Polish nobility who ruled huge territories, entire provinces containing cities, towns, and villages; from the Polish civil servants who resented Jewish penetration of local government offices; from Ukrainian nationalists who tried to free their people of their dependence on Jewish trade.

Such was the population breakdown in Horodenka, as in all the towns of Eastern Galicia, under the Austro-Hungarian monarchy. The Poles, Catholics, filled clerical positions. The Ukrainians, Greek Orthodox, worked the land. The Jews dealt in commerce. In times of danger to their lives or livelihood, the Jews always felt that they could appeal directly to Vienna, to the monarchy, and seek redress. Should their hopes be dashed, it was surely not the fault of His Majesty the Emperor, but of his hardhearted officials. For it was common knowledge that the emperor often praised the Jews for their devotion to family life and their ready philanthropy; he had even bestowed noble titles on a select few, and he knew very well how to show his appreciation of their loyalty to the monarchy.

The many nationalities who made up the Hapsburg realm (including Hungarians, Serbs, Croats, Poles, Czechs, Slovaks, Italians, Ukrainians) were all intoxicated with nineteenth-century nationalism and dreamed of self-rule or national unity. The Jews, however, in a curious alliance—of which no one seemed aware—with the

Austrian army, the nobility, the government administration, and the Catholic Church, were devotees of the monarchy and sought to preserve its unity. Love of the monarchy did not necessarily demand Austrian nationalism of the Jews, but rather loyalty to the Hapsburg dynasty and the aging emperor who had come to the throne after the revolution of 1848. This loyalty the Jews gave wholeheartedly. On August 18, the emperor's birthday, Horodenka's synagogues all said special prayers, attended by representatives of the monarchy. Schoolchildren marched in parade to the city square, where a festive ceremony was held, with government officials in traditional dress and black two-cornered hats. A brass band played marching songs. The monarchy's black and yellow flags, and Austria's double-headed eagle, swayed in the wind. It was the chief annual holiday, the only one shared by all religions.

Also present at the ceremony were pupils of the Baron Hirsch school, including Jakob Edelstein, all decked out in holiday clothes, not a hair out of place. It was the emperor, after all, who had allowed Baron Maurice de Hirsch, that well-known philanthropist, to open Jewish schools in Bukovina and Galicia, primarily for the poor. Baron Hirsch, it was said in Horodenka, kept company with kings and counts. He had been friend to poor Rudolf, the heir to the Austrian throne who had committed suicide at Mayerling; he was friend to the Prince of Wales, Queen Victoria's son. And when the emperor wanted to reward Baron Hirsch for his many noble deeds—so the pupils of the school were told—the baron asked only permission to build and finance special schools for Jews who were not prepared to put their children through the regular school system.

The Baron Hirsch school in Horodenka had four grades and stood at the edge of town, a single-story building with a spacious yard that served as a playground during recess. Many of the pupils came from poor homes, and the baron's money bought them boots and warm jackets for winter and even provided them with a hot meal when it was cold. At home the children spoke Yiddish, but in school the language of instruction was German. The teachers were not locals. They hailed from Austria and Moravia and had come to inculcate in Galician children the superior German culture and language, a policy dating back to the days of Emperor Josef II which aimed at uniting the many nationalities in the Hapsburg realm.

The same Josef II, by a decree of 1785, had ordered Jews to take surnames, and six years later a few Edelsteins already featured in a list of Jewish heads of families, drawn up for tax purposes: Yeruham Edelstein and Mordko Edelstein, Leib Edelstein and Meir Edelstein. Mottel Edelstein, Jakob's father, came from Czortkov, a largely Jewish town about thirty miles from Horodenka across the Dniester river. Its spiritual life revolved around the Czortkov rabbi, Israel Friedmann, sought out by hasidim from miles away for blessings, counsel, and consolation. Another Jakob Edelstein was among the members of the Horodenka Jewish community who, according to a protocol dated July 13, 1792, informed the Viennese authorities that the sum they were asked to pay for residence tax was incorrect, since they had already paid the state treasury a tolerance and protection levy. The annexation of Galicia to the Austro-Hungarian monarchy in 1772, after the first partition of Poland, did away with certain discriminatory practices: Jews were now allowed to own real estate and acquire a general education. But at the same time they lost certain privileges. They could no longer have their own law courts, nor could the community determine how the tax burden was to be divided; in fact, as far as taxation was concerned, all semblance of equality vanished. While Christians paid an average annual tax of little more than one florin per head, Jews were asked to pay six florins: protection tax, property and occupation tax, marriage tax, kosher-meat tax, Sabbath-candle tax.

Mottel Edelstein was a God-fearing man and easygoing in his relations with mortals. He had a wide flat face, thick lips, and curly hair, which he passed on to his son Jakob, fondly known as Yankele. The dominant personality in the family was his wife Mattel, or Mathilda in German, who came of distinguished Horodenka stock. She was the daughter of Menahem Mendel Koch, owner of the Einfuhrhaus, a large inn on the main street for wagoners and carriage drivers. Horodenka's Jews were clearly stratified according to wealth. At the top were a few rich men who owned real estate, flour mills, and quarries. Then came an extensive middle class of merchants and businessmen, followed by craftsmen, and finally the poor: the peddlers, the laborers, the drifters. Somewhat removed from all these were the intelligentsia: Dr. Kanafas, the town's only Jewish physician, and Myron Luria, the pharmacist. Whether to save lives, or because he was a freethinker, he kept the pharmacy open on the Sabbath. All other Jewish shops were of course closed that day, and the real day of business was Tuesday, market day, eagerly anticipated by all. According to a charter of residence granted by Count Potocki at the beginning of the eighteenth century, Horodenka's Jews, like all the Jews on his lands, were promised that market day would not fall on the Sabbath.

On market day noise and uproar reigned as the town filled up with people, wagons, and livestock. The main street was tumultuous, the bells above shop doors clanged continuously. From the dozens of villages in Horodenka county sheepskin-clad Ukrainian peasants thronged to town. They came to sell their goods: wheat, vegetables, fruit, eggs, poultry, beef; to down a few drinks; and to stock up on those few articles they could not produce at home—salt, matches, soap, herring, tools. Horodenka, accordingly, boasted two types of groceries, those which met the needs of the villagers, and those which catered to more urban tastes, providing not only quality merchandise but also imported goods.

Mottel and Mattel Edelstein owned a *Delicatessen* (a candy store, in those days), distinguished by the installation of the town's first automat: a coin was inserted through one side, and from the other emerged a paper-wrapped chocolate bar. Their handsome shop was located in a building owned by Velvel Seidman, a man said to be rich in both property and learning. He and his family resided on the second floor of the stone house, while the ground floor housed the shops, including Seidman's own textile store. Only the wealthy lived in stone houses; other people's homes were built of wood and clay. And though shopkeepers generally lived in two rooms behind their business, the Edelsteins occupied a separate apartment near the courthouse, in keeping with their middle-class standing.

Menahem Mendel Koch was a pillar of the Jewish community and member of the Czortkov rabbi's old synagogue. It was a low building with thick walls, austere and imposing. Because of his father-in-law, Mottel Edelstein, sometimes with his son Yankele, also prayed with that illustrious line of Czortkov hasidim—and in Horodenka lineage was no small matter among the Jews. It decided one's place of prayer in the synagogue, and bestowed the honor of reciting certain prayers; it determined the education chosen for sons, the marriages contracted for daughters. Menahem Mendel Koch was among the strictly pious, but his two sons were already modern, and were leaders in the Zionist movement. His daughters belonged to Tzeirei Zion ("Young Zion"), a club started by young people in the area who found the general Zionist association, set up in 1897, too adult in taste and conservative in outlook.

As in all Galician towns, Theodor Herzl's political Zionism found a much more enthusiastic following in Horodenka than in neighboring Russia. Dr. Herzl after all was one of them, a subject of the Austro-Hungarian realm who lived in its capital, Vienna, and spoke the Viennese German which linked Jews to the world. But perhaps they were fired by the Zionist idea because hope of the messiah's coming was never far from their hearts. Horodenka's Jews had remained loyal to the false messiah Shabbetai Zevi long after most Jews had already turned their backs on that shattered dream. And perhaps their love of Zion was enhanced by the personal stake they had there: the gravesite of Rabbi Nahman of Horodenka, one of the followers of the Ba'al Shem Tov who had been privileged to learn Torah with the Ba'al Shem Tov himself. Rabbi Nahman had immigrated to Eretz-Israel with a group of his students in 1764, and settled in Tiberias. There he lived, and there he died.

Very few Jews in Horodenka were anti-Zionists, though the community included both the strictly orthodox and Bundists. On the other hand, there were many active Zionists, members of the Zionist congregation who spoke the new Hebrew. Most Jews, however, were like Mottel Edelstein, who loved and supported Eretz-Israel without committing their souls. Mottel was a religious man who scrupulously observed the commandments, but, unlike his elders, he wore modern garb and sported a starched white collar, in keeping with the dictates of fashion which arrived—somewhat belatedly—from Vienna. What the monarchy had failed to achieve at the beginning of the nineteenth century, when it had tried to force the Jews to leave off traditional dress and speed up their assimilation into the general population, the spirit of the times now brought about naturally.

Life in Horodenka's Jewish community still followed the Jewish calendar, with rejoicing on festivals and fasting on solemn holy days. The days of the week, with their long working hours, were merely a necessary bridge from Sabbath to Sabbath, from Rosh Hashanah to Sukkot, from Sukkot to Hannukah and the thread which joined all, weaving its way through working days and holidays, was the hasidic melody, heard as a hum in the kitchen at nightfall, a life force, a cry of joy on Sabbath eve, an intoxicant in the shadow of the rabbi.

Since there were no automobiles in Horodenka, and carriages were used only to and from the train station, people were not pressed by time, even when they worked from dawn until dusk to provide for their families. Children spent mornings at the Baron Hirsch school or the Polish school, and afternoons at the *heder*, receiving religious instruction. Lessons sometimes stretched past nightfall, and they returned home carrying small candle lamps. Horodenka at the beginning of the twentieth century had no street lights, since there were few real streets with paved sidewalks. Only the main street had sewage canals concealed beneath the sidewalk; everywhere else canals were open and water rushed along them when it rained. Only the main street was meticulously swept and in summer even sprayed with water from an iron cask hauled by a wagon. Only the main street had kerosene lamps hung on wooden poles, and in the evening a policeman with a ladder passed from one to another to light them.

Most boys went to *heder* even before they reached school age, and over the years they passed through the hands of various religious instructors, according to their age and understanding. The very young were taught to read from clear large letters; sometimes they joined the rabbi's prayer at a newborn's cradle to ward off evil spirits. At the age of five they were initiated into the Pentateuch, and in their last year they were introduced to Gemorrah. In 1913, after Jakob Edelstein finished four years at the Baron Hirsch school, he enrolled at the Polish high school, which occupied an ancient monastery. Ongoing disputes took place between parents and children, grandparents and grandchildren, about enrollment at the Polish school, where classes were held on the Sabbath (though Jewish children were excused from writing that day). With a heavy heart, parents sometimes gave in, for high school led to higher education and the coveted doctoral degree. This was only one of the concessions exacted by the times; another was the first Hebrew school, which opened in Horodenka in 1907. Children sometimes attended regular school in the morning, *heder* in the late afternoon, and Hebrew school in between. They were taught Hebrew only in Hebrew, though not enough to speak it. However, as beginners they could recite Bialik, and when more advanced they could read newspapers at the Tzeirei Zion club, so that by the age of eleven Horodenka youngsters, who for the most part never left their immediate neighborhood, could read and write Yiddish, German, Polish, and Hebrew, and to some extent carry on a conversation in Ukrainian.

There were several Jewish districts in Horodenka, but never a separate ghetto. Oddly enough, the town's beautiful churches, the Greek Orthodox, and the Catholic with its clock tower and bells which measured time at quarter-hour intervals, were surrounded by Jewish homes. On Sundays and Christian holidays churchgoers passed beneath their windows. The Jewish prayer houses, the great synagogue, the learning academies (*batei-midrash*), the small synagogue (*kloiz*), all faced back, away from the street—and the evil eye—hiding modestly in alleyways behind the main street. Jews and Christians did not quarrel, nor did they come to blows. Both were conscious of the sharp line dividing them and, despite the periodic efforts to oust them from commerce, there was a general feeling among the Jews that they were vital to Horodenka, and that the Watchman of Israel stood guard, both in Vienna and in heaven.

For the Jews in the surrounding villages, Horodenka, with its eleven thousand citizens (about a third of whom were Jewish), its courthouse and county offices, its municipal park and train station, was the big city. The few kilometers that separated them from Horodenka constituted a much more insurmountable distance than the miles between Horodenka and Lvov (Lemberg), Galicia's old capital. In the villages people lived off the land and were close to one another. In Horodenka, people lived off people, wrote Alexander Granach, the town's native son and a famous Jewish actor. By 1914, Granach had played in Max Reinhardt's theater in Berlin and made a name for himself throughout Germany.

Who thought of war in the spring of 1914? Since 1867 Franz Josef had preserved the peace, at least with respect to external foes. To European thinkers and diplomats the Austro-Hungarian monarchy, attached by alliance to expansionist Germany, may have appeared a tottering giant, a weary realm reflecting its aged emperor, surrounded by enemies who sought to subdue it and tear it to pieces. But to Horodenkans, the monarchy seemed very strong. Viennese socialists might consider it a "dictatorship sweetened by negligence"; to the Jews it was nevertheless a warm home, in contrast to tsarist Russia with its reign of terror, pogroms, and pale of settlement. When, in June 1914, following the assassination of Archduke Franz Ferdinand and his wife Sophie at Sarajevo, the eighty-four-year-old emperor delivered an ultimatum to the Serbs and, on July 28, declared war against them, the Jews were as confident as the general staff in Vienna that it would be a short and decisive punitive campaign. Horodenka's young men were mobilized, Jews and Christians alike. Mothers and sweethearts wept at the railroad station while the soldiers, hungry for adventure, joked or at least tried to put on a brave face: what was there to cry about? It would all be over in a few weeks. The emperor's proclamation was posted all over town: "It has been my great wish to devote the years which God in His kindness has been pleased to grant me to strengthening peace and protecting my people from the heavy burden and sacrifices of war. But fate has decreed otherwise. . . . I put my faith in the Austro-Hungarian army, in its courage and unquestioning loyalty; I put my faith in God, may He grant our forces victory. Signed: Franz Josef."

On the first day of the war with Serbia, Russia ordered a general call-up. The next day Germany declared war on Russia. On August 2, Germany delivered an ultimatum to Belgium demanding free passage for her forces, and on August 3, she declared war on France. A day later, the British prime minister sent an ultimatum to Berlin, demanding an immediate reply. By August 4 this had failed to materialize, and all Europe was plunged in war. Most of the news was about the western front in Flanders and France. Details of the long, terrible, exhausting battles fought by Russia and Austria along a fifteen-hundred-kilometer front—where two million men were caught in a horrible struggle—were known mainly to the citizens of the battle regions.

A few weeks after fighting broke out, Horodenka received its first shock: the Russians had managed to penetrate Austrian lines near the Dniester and take the city. Not many Jews fled as the Russians advanced. Most tried to keep a low profile, stay alive, and guard their daughters and property. There were only a few cases of rape and pillage, and the Jews were convinced that this was merely a temporary local victory and that the Austrian heavy artillery and other excellent weaponry would still triumph. And indeed, in the early spring of 1915 the Russians were pushed back across the river and the Austrians returned to Horodenka, followed by the Jews. They danced on tables, raised their cups in joy, and offered up prayers of thanks. Crown Prince Karl visited Horodenka and was received by a delegation of the town's distinguished citizens, including its rabbis. The Jews breathed more easily. But not for long. The Russians soon returned. This time, most of the Jews had fled in fear even before the Russian and Cossack soldiers, inflamed by battles where life was worthless, reached the outskirts of the town.

This time the Russians spent their passion on the Jews. Nine Jews were hanged in the city square, accused of lighting fires to warn the Austrians. The Russians burned, pillaged, raped, and wrecked, and when the Austrians returned to Horodenka a month later, followed by the Jews who had waited out the horrors in neighboring towns and villages, they found the great synagogue and several homes destroyed, the shops looted. And who could be sure whether it was the soldiers or their good neighbors who had wreaked the havoc?

This time there was no rejoicing, only fear of what was to come. When the Russians advanced a third time, all the Jews fled in panic, together with the retreating Austrian army. A stream of wagons, weapons, horses, and soldiers of the emperor's defeated army moved along the roads. The Jews walked at the roadsides carrying bundles in their arms or on their backs, or pushing handcarts. Children were tied to their mother's clothing or to the carts so as not to be lost in the human flow. First they fled to nearby Kolomea, not yet taken, and from there, by train, sometimes in open flatbed cars, they moved inland, to Hungary, Moravia, Bohemia, and Austria proper.

Mottel and Mattel Edelstein locked up their home—as if locks and bolts could deter fire and pillage—took some clothing and valuables, and together with their children, Jakob, aged twelve, and Dora, ten, joined the human exodus, as frightened as everybody else. The Austrian authorities scattered Jews all along the railroad line. Every town was given a quota of refugees in an effort to keep as many as possible from reaching Vienna. They did not want to swell the capital's already large Jewish population, nor did they want throngs of witnesses to the emperor's defeat descending on the city. The authorities asked few questions: the Edelsteins were put off the train at Brünn (Brno), the capital of Moravia, a six-hour journey from Vienna.

Gone was the security and steady rhythm of life in Horodenka. Gone the sense of belonging. The death of the emperor at the age of eighty-six in November 1916 marked the end of an era. It was clear that a new Europe was to rise out of the ashes of the Great War. But not many people, including those national leaders who regarded the conflagration as a golden opportunity to attain self-rule, envisaged the utter disintegration of the Hapsburg monarchy that had controlled the heart of Europe for more than six hundred years.

In wartime children mature quickly, and refugee children doubly so. The local German and Czech population of Bohemia and Moravia was not enthusiastic about the refugees augmenting their numbers and competing for food. Provisions were becoming scarce, and most people lived on cornbread, boiled turnips, and millet. In bread lines, the locals grumbled that they had nothing to eat because of the refugees; they stayed away from the strange Jews in their long black coats and black hats, with their beards and *payesses.* Didn't they have enough Jews already? At least their Jews looked almost normal, dressed like everyone else, and spoke Czech fluently and German without a Jewish accent. Only their noses and the look in their eyes betrayed them.

Jews and Christians both were prejudiced against Galician Jews. The term "Galician Jew"—or "Polish Jew," for that matter—was filled with innuendo, covering a whole range of undesirable qualities: dishonesty, filth, shrewd dealing, clinging to the dark ages, the reek of garlic and onion. The ten-thousand-odd Brünn Jewish community suddenly came face to face with thousands of poverty-stricken Galician Jews who feared God and spoke Yiddish. The encounter sorely tried their sense of identification. Nevertheless, the refugees were brethren in need of help, and the Jews of Brünn raised money and collected blankets, household articles, and clothing. The newcomers were housed in empty compounds and factories; only the wealthiest among them managed to rent rooms. The women of Brünn took care of children, of the sick, opened nurseries and soup kitchens. But the sharp divisions remained: the refugees were second-class Jews. Though many Bohemian and Moravian Jews lent a helping hand, very few opened their homes, and only a handful—such as, for instance, Franz Kafka and his friend Max Brod—were impressed by the deep-rooted Judaism that filled the Galicians' entire lives; how pale, how meaningless, was the Mosaic Code as practiced by the assimilated Jews of Prague!

The refugee children attended German state schools, as did the majority of local children, though they spoke Czech at home. Czech schools were considered inferior, and Czech was the language of the working class, the maids, the farmers, the craftsmen, reminding Jews of the poverty they tried with all their might to escape. Besides, what did Czech literature have to offer? It had revived only at the start of the nineteenth century, having lain dormant since the Reform Movement's terrible defeat on the White Mountain in 1620. How could one compare Klicpera, Neruda, Jirásek, with Goethe, Schiller, Heine? Who would send their children to Czech schools to learn broken, accented German, when good German was the key to all things—to higher education, careers, government posts, the wide world, and even Zionism?

Brünn's students were among the first to rally to Herzl's call, perhaps because the town itself was seen mainly as a corridor to Vienna. They were led by Berthold Feiwel, editor of the Zionist paper *Die Welt,* who later moved to London, and Robert Stricker, leader of Vienna's national Zionists. Brünn saw the rise of Emunah (Faith), the first organization of Jewish employees of socialist persuasion, and was one of the strongholds of the Maccabi sports association, the Jewish answer to the Slavic Sokol, which combined physical education with fierce nationalism. Jakob Edelstein, however, was not drawn to Zionist youth, which is probably why, sixty years later, not one of the Brünn Jews who settled in Israel could remember him from the nine years he lived there.

When refugee children reached bar-mitzvah age, the community funded the religious ceremony held at the synagogue. On August 31, 1916, Jakob Edelstein reached the age of thirteen, but how or even if his bar mitzvah was celebrated remains unclear. Was his father one of the many refugees mobilized into the emperor's army to serve the rear lines in the quartermaster's corps or the adjutantcy? What did the family live on? These are questions without answers. In later years Edelstein never so much as mentioned the time he spent in Brünn as the son of refugees, even to his closest friends; it was almost as if he wanted to erase the entire period from his life.

At the end of the war, after completing four years of high school, Edelstein entered the Royal Commercial Academy in Brünn, a prestigious intermediate-level institution which trained its students in all aspects of business from essay-writing and shorthand to international finance and banking. Graduating from the commercial academy was no mean achievement in those days, when even a high school education still counted for something.

The commercial academy was housed in a large, impressive building at the foot of the Spielberg, an old fortress of Moravia's rulers. Its dark, damp dungeons had been notorious. Various Moravian freedom fighters had met their death there, leaving their names to live on as a symbol of revolt; and thousands of nameless prisoners had rotted there, and been forgotten. The end of the monarchy in November 1918 seemed to herald the end of the prison as well. Part of it was transformed into a barracks, part preserved as a museum for coming generations who, it was hoped, would be spared all terror of secret police.

For Czechs those were days of grand hopes. After four hundred years of gradual and increasing subjugation under the Hapsburgs, they were intoxicated with their newfound independence. Among other things, their heady aspirations unleashed a wave of hostility against the would-be-German Jews, devotees of the monarchy, black-market dealers growing rich on the profits of war. There were no real Russian-style pogroms, merely broken windows, vandalized property, physical blows in the streets, in parks, and on public transportation, and hostile glances directed at anyone who dared speak German openly. As the terrible weariness from the long-drawn-out war increased, so did the systematic propaganda aimed at the masses. They longed to settle accounts with the Jews as capitalists, Jews as Bolsheviks, Jews as German-lovers, Jews as opportunists suddenly turned Czech. But between the Jews and the masses stood the powerful figure of Thomas Garrigue Masaryk, first president of the new republic. Czechoslovakia, much more than was generally realized, was the true heir of the Hapsburg monarchy—a multinational state with a patriarch at its head: tall, aristocratic, and sporting a white goatee, sixty-eight-year-old Professor Masaryk became the object of Jewish admiration, just as the old emperor had been. In fact, of all the peoples in the republic, it can be said that only the Jews were Czechoslovakians. All the others were either Czechs or Slovaks (suddenly united after a rift of one thousand years, with different religions, languages, and levels of development), along with Ruthenians, Germans, Poles, and Hungarians.

Born at the Versailles conference table, the new republic was no natural entity. It was shaped like a boomerang, with very long borders. Of its thirteen million inhabitants, five million were minorities (3.5 million Germans, 700,000 Hungarians, 400,000 Poles), and its territory consisted of three distinctly separate units: the historical Crown Lands of Good King Wenceslas (Bohemia, Moravia, Silesia); Slovakia; and Carpathian Russia. The German minority made up 22 percent of the population and only now began to refer to itself as Sudeten Germans, after one of the mountain ranges surrounding the western part of the republic where large numbers of Germans lived. They demanded self-determination and sought annexation to the small Austrian republic which was all that remained of the huge Hapsburg empire. But the Czechs, who had fought on the side of the victorious Allies, countered these demands with their own claims to the historical borders of the Crown Lands and the mountain ranges which protected them on three sides; the large German minority was therefore included in the new Slavic republic. The Germans in the border region at first rebelled against the ruling of the Peace Conference. However, calm was gradually restored, and they appeared to have accepted their fate.

The Jewish minority numbered 350,000 and like the new republic itself, consisted of three loosely connected divisions. Their main unifying factor—apart from their Jewishness and, to some extent, their identification with Zionism—was the esteem in which they held Professor Masaryk and the ideals he stood for—his realistic humanism, his faith in justice and the triumph of truth, his belief that man must strive toward self-improvement and assume social responsibility, his concept of democracy as the right to differ—all drawn from the same fountainhead as Jewish ethics. In 1899, Masaryk, then a professor of philosophy at the University of Prague, had spoken out on behalf of the Jews by defending Leo Hilsner, a twenty-two-year-old shoemaker accused of ritual murder and sentenced to death. The blood libel gave rise to a wave of hysterical hatred against the Jews in Bohemia. Masaryk got involved in the affair after the Jewish author Sigismund Mintz, a former student of his, asked him for his opinion on the trial for the newspaper the *Neue Freie Presse*. The Czech nationalist press and the Catholic Church vigorously attacked Masaryk for "selling his soul to the Jews." Students demonstrated against him at the university. Masaryk was not deterred. As he put it, he fought the blood libel not to protect the Jews, but to protect Christianity from prejudice. Hilsner, actually a somewhat shady character, was pardoned in the end, when Karl, the last of the Hapsburg emperors, came to the throne, and he proceeded to wander through Europe, claiming to have made Masaryk famous.

The Jews never forgot Masaryk's part in the Hilsner affair. When in 1917 he came to America to gain the support of the United States government for the establishment of an independent Czechoslovakian republic, he found the Jews eager to listen and help, and it was they, he said, who had the decisive say in the American press. The Zionists, some of whom, such as Nahum Sokolow and Judge Louis Brandeis (whose family was originally Czech), were close friends of Masaryk, welcomed the new republic once the Allies recognized the National Council in exile as its temporary government. They voiced the hope that the minorities in the new republic, including the Jews, would enjoy full freedom, and Masaryk's reply to the Zionists was published in the *New York Herald Tribune* on

October 7, 1918, the day peace negotiations opened. It contained his promise that Jews, like all minorities, would have full rights in the new republic, and expressed support for Zionism, the Jewish national movement, which he saw as a humanistic impulse of inherently moral value. He reiterated this position to the representatives of the Jewish National Committee in Czechoslovakia whom he met shortly after he was elected president. This, then, was the basis of the special status enjoyed by Czechoslovakia's Zionist movement, which was represented by a political party—the Jewish National Party—in both local and parliamentary elections. To be sure, its members and supporters also included non-Zionists; the party leadership, however, was always in the hands of the Zionists and it was they who determined its course.

The Jewish National Committee, which came into being at the same time as the new republic, prepared an extensive program for independent action by the Jewish minority. To no small degree this was influenced by the enthusiastic response of the Zionists to the Balfour Declaration, which spoke of the establishment of a Jewish national home in Palestine. The plan for action they prepared was based on the assumption that Jewish communities would be autonomous in matters of religion, culture, education, welfare, and Hebrew instruction. Most of its points, however, never materialized; the minorities never achieved the independence they had dreamt of, their enthusiasm waned in time, the Jews became caught up in the flow of life. The communists, at one extreme, and the orthodox Jews, at the other, had never regarded the Jews as a nation. Assimilated Czech Jews opposed the very idea of a national committee to represent them. But the main reason for the plan's defeat was the mentality of middle-class, mainstream Jewry (who in this respect were no different from their Czech neighbors). Above all they wanted a comfortable life: to see their children educated and well married, to eat well, make weekend excursions to the woods and annual trips to Carlsbad, Marienbad, or Piešt'any; to sit in cafés with their friends, visit the theater occasionally—and not change the world.

After the war, the Galician refugees began to return home to the devastation the war had wrought. Those who had meanwhile established themselves in their new locations as clerks, artisans, teachers, small merchants, who had recognized the advantages of living in the West (the East at the time meaning Eastern Europe), spared no effort in becoming permanent residents of the new republic. When

Mottel and Mattel Edelstein returned to Horodenka with their daughter, Dora, Jakob remained in Brünn to complete his studies. Most of the foreign Jewish students hailed from Poland, Hungary, Russia, and Rumania, where universities admitted only a small number of Jews. The Jewish students' cafeteria offered them meals free of charge or for a nominal fee, but on the whole they lived in hardship. They gave private lessons, worked in Jewish institutions, took odd jobs, borrowed, received meager support from the community and whatever they could get from their families, and lived on dreams.

Mottel and Mattel again opened a shop, at a different site, in a different Horodenka. On paper the world war ended in November 1918, but in this corner of Eastern Europe, where borders were mobile, it continued long after; perhaps one could say it never really ended but was simply renamed in 1939. The Poles and Ukrainians both sought large independent states, and both looked on eastern Galicia as their rightful heritage. Simon Petlyura and the Ukrainian nationalists who had fought against the Bolsheviks and had seized the same opportunity to viciously attack the Jews, invaded part of Galicia, including Horodenka. And though the Ukrainian authorities had promised the Jews national autonomy in various fields, Petlyura's Cossacks acted in the best tradition of popular Ukrainian anti-Semitism, so that it was with a sense of relief, albeit warily, that Horodenka's Jews greeted the Poles who in 1919 succeeded in ousting the Ukrainians and reuniting their country. Horodenka became a Polish city and in time Marshal Pilsudski's picture replaced that of the emperor.

Jakob Edelstein did not return to Horodenka after graduating from the commercial academy, but remained in Czechoslovakia. He would have liked to pursue a higher education, to study political economy, but it was not within his reach: he could not afford student life, however modest. All he could do was try to attain an education in the only way available to the poor, by reading, and he started with the fathers of socialism: Marx, Engels, Bebel, Kautsky, Otto Bauer, Max Adler. He was no longer the son of refugees, an outsider—he found a framework, a mainstay, friends, when he joined the young people's section of the German Social Democratic Party in Czechoslovakia. Though it had not been a part of the Austrian Social Democratic Party since 1918, the Czechoslovakian SDP still maintained close ideological and organizational links with Vienna, and it sent Jakob Edelstein and other active party members to a seminar in that city. Here Jakob learned the art of public speaking without relying on a written text. Memorize a passage by Marx or Kautsky, the young socialists were told, and when you stand up before an audience, nervous and at a loss, begin with that. Those who know the passage will be impressed; those who don't will listen attentively. Meanwhile you will have had time to collect your thoughts and will be able to continue on your own.

Only two German parties in Czechoslovakia were open to Jews. One was the small Democratic Party, all that remained of the once influential Austrian Liberal Party, led by Bruno Kafka, cousin to Franz Kafka, professor of civil law at Prague's German university, a convert and a sworn Germanophile. The other was the German Social Democratic Party, which attracted Jews because it provided both a home for their dreams of international brotherhood and social justice, and a haven from German nationalism. For close to twenty years it had been led by Ludvik Czech, a Jewish lawyer from Brünn, and this combination—a German party chaired by a Jew called Czech—aptly reflected the national web in which the Jews were caught.

To some Jews, being Czech came naturally. In the small towns and villages of Bohemia, there were sometimes two or three Jewish families who for generations had lived in peace with their neighbors, giving matzot at Passover, receiving sweet braided bread at Christmas. And there was a group of Czech Jews (or Jewish Czechs, as they preferred to call themselves) who had over the years consciously fostered close relations between the two peoples, finding much in common in the routes of oppression each had traveled. But these attempts to draw the two together were frowned on by the Czech intelligentsia. They saw the Jews as the natural allies of the Germans; and the Germans had dealt harshly with the Czechs. They fought the Jews with the slogan *svuj k svemu*—each to his own—and went so far as to organize a boycott of Jewish trade. Karel Havlíček-Borovsky, a journalist with a sharp and militant pen in the cause of Czech liberation, attacked Siegfried Kapper, the first nineteenth-century Jewish author to write in Czech. The Jews are a nation unto themselves, he wrote; their ties to one another and to the ruling nation will always be stronger than to the people among whom they live. They would do far better, therefore, to write in German—or even Hebrew.

In his essay "Hunting in Bohemia," Herzl advised the Jews not to side with either the Czechs or the Germans, who were waging a stubborn battle for linguistic and cultural control of the Crown Lands. His advice was wise perhaps, but hardly practical, especially after the establishment of the Czech state: one could not live in a vacuum. A choice had to be made. Many Jews avoided the dilemma by joining the Jewish-national camp, but here too the German language prevailed until the late thirties. Jewish money financed Prague's German theater, and the prestigious *Prager Tagblatt* was considered almost a Jewish newspaper with respect to its staff and its readership. *Die Selbstwehr,* the central organ of the Czech Zionist movement, appeared in German printed in German Gothic script, and in Prague cafés frequented by Jews German predominated. This rankled with the Czechs, who, after three hundred years of exile in their own country, were trying to eradicate German influence and reestablish their roots. The Jews as yet failed to appreciate the force behind the motives of a nation which had only recently regained its independence, and few remembered the words of Simon Hock, first historiographer of Prague's Jews: no matter how sharp and bitter the struggle between Germans and Czechs, the two nations would come to terms in their lack of sympathy for the wretched Jews. To many Jews, even those who were at home in both languages, turning their backs on German culture simply because Czechs now held the upper hand smacked of cheap opportunism.

2

THE SOCIALIST
SALESMAN

WHILE in the towns and villages of Bohemia and Moravia the Jews may have felt attached to Czech culture, and in the big cities they may have tried to live in both worlds at once, in the German border regions there was no question at all: they continued to identify with German culture. After Jakob Edelstein had buried his dreams of a higher education, he left Brünn and moved to Teplitz-Schönau (Teplice-Šanov), a resort town in northern Bohemia. The town's three thousand Jews constituted nearly 10 percent of the overall population. It was the highest percentage of Jews in Bohemia, due chiefly to the large concentration of Galician Jews, some of whom had settled there at the start of the century and some of whom had come as war refugees.

It is difficult to say what Edelstein's priorities were in choosing Teplitz-Schönau. Party considerations may well have influenced his choice, as the German Social Democratic Party vied with the various streams of German nationalists in the border region. (The latter had bequeathed to German Nazism several ideological fathers, and even the name "Nazional-Socialistische Deutsche Arbeitergruppe" came from a Sudeten movement which had already made contact with Hitler as far back as the early twenties.) Or perhaps he thought he had a better chance of earning a living among his own people. The war had wreaked havoc on the European economy, and even in Czechoslovakia, where industry was highly developed and the labor force skilled and hardworking, jobs were not easy to come by, particularly when one was a foreigner, without family, funds, or vital connections in big business.

Long ago, before the Germans had methodically settled in Bohemia's border regions, Teplitz-Schönau had been a Czech settlement, as its original Slavic name, Teplice, indicated, an allusion to the town's hot springs. This natural endowment made the town one of Europe's most renowned health resorts, frequented by kings and nobility, by Goethe, Schiller, Beethoven, and Wagner. It was superseded by Marienbad and Carlsbad only toward the end of the nineteenth century, when its springs temporarily dried up. Though its livelihood derived chiefly from industry (glass and porcelain) and the nearby coal mines, the town preserved the carefully cultivated aspect of a resort, and was the seat of the Clary-Aldringen aristocracy, whose palace overlooked it from above, separated by an expansive garden from ordinary mortals. Its population was diligent, bourgeois, orderly, and music loving, and did not shrink from Jews more than was proper. Relations between Jews and Christians were on a business footing, confined to business hours. Young people would occasionally mix in cafés and restaurants, but family life took place on two totally separate planes, one Jewish, the other Christian.

The Ostjuden, as the Galician Jews were called in Teplitz, lived apart from the veteran Jewish community with its hundred-year history of increasing assimilation. Like the Jews of Vienna, the Jews of Teplitz-Schönau had already adopted modern ritual at the start of the nineteenth century: their rabbis held doctoral degrees and delivered sermons in German; their temple, designed by a Viennese architect, was one of the finest buildings in town, boasting an organ and mixed choir. But it was full only on the High Holy Days, four days of the year. Some Jews no longer needed religion, and had broken away from the community altogether. Intermarriage was on the rise and the birth rate was declining. Teplitz-Schönau's veteran Jews bore all the symptoms typical of a Judaism that had long ceased to be a living spring but drifted on as a blurred memory, a family relationship, a sense of being different—willingly or otherwise.

The Ostjuden took over the old synagogue, which had served as a warehouse since the construction of the new temple, and turned it into an orthodox house of prayer once more. They set up half a dozen other congregations, kept kosher, and sent their children to Jewish schools. The town's established Jews knew of the Jewish street, with its communal oven for the traditional Sabbath meal, its public bathhouse, and its prohibition against going outdoors on Saturdays, only from literature. They had dispensed with traditional Jewish names for their children, and belonged to all the town's prestigious clubs and organizations—the German sports club, the German hiking club, the German reading circle, the welfare organization for German youth. They held German titles—"Herr Doktor" or "Herr Kommerzialrat"—served on the town council, were middle-class liberals, the backbone of the town's theatrical and musical activity. They frowned on liaisons between their children and the children of the Ostjuden and sometimes accused the latter of inviting anti-Semitism by their aggressive trade practices.

This veteran Jewish community, with its lawyers, doctors, industrialists, its broad European education, had long since forgotten its own origins, those small-time Jewish traders who used to wander from village to village buying up the produce of a bondaged peasantry—flax, feathers, furs, hay. Jewish money was often the only cash ever seen by the peasants, and it passed back into Jewish hands when they used it to pay for household goods, for haberdashery, kerchiefs, fabrics from peddlers who made the rounds of the villages, returning again and again to their customers. The peddlers used to set out on their route on Sunday morning; they did not return home till Friday afternoon. They lived in poverty, scrimped and saved, and penny by penny built up the capital they needed to realize their fondest dream: a store of their own in town.

The Galician Jews started a new cycle in Jewish economic life in Teplitz. They too made the rounds of the towns and villages, selling clothing, linens, fabrics, and household goods on credit. Often they were accused of enslaving their clients to new debts while they still floundered in the old, and the credit merchant occupied the lowest rung of the Teplitz social ladder. By the time Jakob Edelstein arrived, in 1925, most of the Ostjuden already had their own shops in town, though they retained their regional clientele, dispatching agents to collect payments and take new orders.

Jakob Edelstein, now known as "Yekef" in Teplitz, worked as a salesman and credit agent for a large store on Marienstrasse, owned by the two Kletter brothers and their sister, Cila Glassberg, who

23

each supervised a different department: clothing, fabrics, bedding. Unlike the traveling salesmen who worked for larger Jewish firms and factories and spent most of their lives in trains and cheap hotels, returning home only on weekends, Yekef left on his rounds every morning, to nearby Leitmeritz, Trautenau, Aussig, Bodenbach, and returned to Teplitz almost every evening. The company of young Galician traveling salesmen daily boarded the morning train, always taking the same car, the same compartment. Those who observed Jewish law, Yekef included, donned their phylacteries, prayed, then had a bite to eat, and spent the rest of the journey telling jokes and anecdotes until it was time to disembark, each at his station, according to his regional roster.

Every store had a nucleus of between four hundred and six hundred permanent clients, often passed down from father to son. Edelstein had a permanent route, and his best day of business was Friday—payday—before his customers could drink their salaries away in taverns. He dealt mostly with the working class, and after collecting the payments would draw samples out of his suitcase and ask: Well, Mrs. Schmied, what are you ordering today? Traveling salesmen worked for commission, or a small fixed fee augmented by commission, and their earnings depended on their skill and resourcefulness. But Yekef's heart was not in his work, and often enough, when asked about the quality of a specific item, he would reply in all honesty that he didn't know. Unlike that of some of his more adept colleagues, the enthusiastic sales pitch was not his style. He enjoyed meeting people, he said, but it was clear that for him the credit trade was an economic necessity, and his real interest lay elsewhere, in the Social Democratic movement.

Edelstein returned in the evening, settled his affairs at the shop, and had a kosher meal at Mrs. Glassberg's before going to the bare and narrow room he rented. He washed, changed, and was soon off again, to either party headquarters or a lecture at the Red Hawk, the German Social Democratic youth movement. He was home by midnight, and back on his circuit early next morning. On May 1, traveling salesman Jakob Edelstein marched behind red flags in the workers' parade through the streets of the town, run at the time by the German Social Democrats.

Very few people spoke Czech in Teplitz, and those who did were generally civil servants, conscious of their isolation. If you asked a policeman for directions, he couldn't reply in the official state language even if he had understood the question. Yekef spoke a broken

Czech, but a rich and clear German (though his accent still retained traces of his mother tongue, Yiddish). He was a popular speaker in Social Democratic circles, a fact which came to the attention of the local Zionist youth movement. The members of Tekhelet-Lavan (Blue-White) invited him to give a series of lectures on Marxism, a subject sorely lacking in their education, though they called themselves socialists. Yekef's knowledge, his speaking ability, his clear analytical mind, and his persuasiveness left a deep impression on them. Yekef, meanwhile, who had never really felt at home among the Sudeten-born German Social Democrats, accepted Borochov's assumption that Jewish socialism demands a separate solution, and without altering his views in any other way, drew gradually closer to the Zionist camp.

Teplitz-Schönau was one of the strongholds of Czechoslovakia's Zionist movement. The aforementioned Tekhelet-Lavan, Czechoslovakia's first pioneering youth movement; Hehalutz, the general association of pioneering youth movements; and Tarbut, the organization for the dissemination of the Hebrew language, all flourished there. On the whole, however, the Zionist movement in Czechoslovakia had developed slowly after difficult beginnings. Emil Margulies, born in Sosnowiec and armed with a law degree from Austria, arrived in Teplitz in 1903, a new lawyer but a veteran Zionist. With all the fervor of his twenty-six years and a fighting spirit to match, he took on the task of spreading the revolutionary Zionist idea in his new hometown. The local Zionist association was at the time an eccentric and persecuted minority, opposed by the mainstream of German Jewish liberals, who had no qualms about preventing the *Teplitzer Zeitung* (the organ of the local German Progressive Party) from carrying Zionist advertisements. The German Jews feared that Zionism would endanger their status in society and that describing Jews as a nation would call into question their loyalty as Germans. There was a good deal of turmoil, animosity, and social and economic pressure before a truce was finally reached: the Zionists had their sights set on Palestine, but this did not prevent Jews from being loyal to the country they lived in.

Dr. Margulies, who saw to the financing of *Die Selbstwehr,* the official organ of the Czechoslovakian Zionist movement, supported Chaim Weizmann's practical Zionism. In time, however, he diverged from Weizmann, and, together with Robert Stricker of Vienna, formed a more radical faction. His great tragedy was the German language, or rather his lack of talent for other languages. He was one of the founders of Czechoslovakia's Jewish National Party, but never represented the party in Parliament because of his poor command of Czech. He was a representative to the Congress of National Minorities in Geneva, but knew neither French nor English well enough to address that body; he had to content himself with background work and leave the speeches to his colleague, Dr. Leo Motzkin.

Tekhelet-Lavan developed parallel to Germany's Blau-Weiss, a Jewish hiking club, more or less the Jewish answer to the German Wandervogel, with its underlying anti-Semitism. One of the first branches of Blau-Weiss under the Austrian monarchy was set up in Teplitz-Schönau, and its founders all took part in the Great War. When, after four, five, or six years, they returned from the slaughter, older by the count of corpses, they were no longer content with hiking through green meadows and a hazy, romantic Zionism. They sought radical solutions to questions of existence, as Jews and as men. Some of the demobilized soldiers had been deeply affected by the Bolshevik revolution: they had been witness to its beginnings in prison camps throughout Russia, and they joined the communist camp in the belief that a new era of social justice had dawned. Some, after years of suffering, were determined to make the most of the present. And some, at the front and in prison camps, had decided that now, following the Balfour Declaration, was the time for the realization of Zionism, in word and deed.

After the war, Blau-Weiss changed its name to the Hebrew Tekhelet-Lavan; its founders left for farms in Czechoslovakia and Germany to train in agriculture, and in 1920 emigrated to Palestine. Two years later they established Hefzibah, a cooperative settlement, together with former members of the Bar-Kochba students' organization. One of the group, Franz Kahn, a brilliant jurist, who as a young officer had lost his left arm in the Great War, saw no way to join his friends in working the land of Palestine. He chose instead to devote his life to the Zionist idea in Czechoslovakia.

Tekhelet-Lavan did not at the time oblige its members to personally implement its Zionist and pioneering ideals by settling in Palestine and working the land. Nevertheless, the question of pioneering was an endless source of discussion throughout the movement. Again and again it was hammered out, at summer camps, at winter seminars. Was pioneering to be the movement's sole objective, or were there other goals, equally worthy? What about the education of Jewish youth in the Diaspora? Who was to instruct them? Another much debated issue was the composition of the settlements to be established in Palestine: should the Westjuden set up homogeneous collectives, or should they join ranks with immigrant groups from Poland, from Lithuania, from Rumania—in short, with the Ostjuden?

Not all Czech pioneers stayed in Palestine. Some were compelled to return because of poor health, others became disillusioned. Their disappointment stemmed from many sources: poverty, starvation, disease, rivalry with Arabs over the few available jobs, the monotony of physical labor, the life of the collective (to which not all were suited), or, simply, the gap between the dream and the reality. Their description of a land that devoured its settlers nearly destroyed the Hehalutz movement in Czechoslovakia, saved only by the persistence of a handful of faithful followers.

The two Czech settlements in Palestine, Hefzibah and Sarid, were the pride of the Czechoslovakian Zionist movement. From time to time they sent emissaries to Czechoslovakia to participate in educational and propaganda activities, to represent Palestine on various committees, and at the same time to raise funds for their settlements—here a tractor was needed, there a piece of land had to be bought (the World Zionist Organization was on the verge of bankruptcy, and the national funds were penniless). In the spring of 1927, within the framework of his tour of the Mediterranean countries, President Masaryk visited Palestine and met with his countrymen—Samuel Hugo Bergmann at the Mount Scopus National Library, with the group at Hefzibah, with Miriam Singer from Deganyah Aleph, the only Czech pioneer at the mother-kibbutz.

At Deganyah Aleph, Masaryk asked Miriam why there was no synagogue in the settlement. "You can't just send an anonymous prayer into space," she replied, "with no address." Masaryk disagreed: any prayer strengthens the heart. For Masaryk, who was seventy-seven at the time, faith was the ultimate ideal and therefore the only objective criterion of all man's deeds. He defined his own faith as reverence, and he found his visit to Palestine and the Christian holy sites a deeply moving experience. For Czechoslovakia's Jewry, it was only further evidence that Masaryk's republic was their home and their haven. The words of the Czech national anthem, *Kde domov muj* ("Where is my homeland?"), truly captured their sentiments. Bohemia was their homeland.

* * *

Jakob Edelstein was twenty-three when he joined Tekhelet-Lavan, quite an advanced age in Teplitz in youth-movement terms—by then most members had already faced their moment of truth: either emigrating to Palestine—that painful radical step, cutting oneself off from home, from family, from the comfortable middle-class life, the familiar green vistas—or choosing, as their parents had, a platonic love of Zion from afar. Yekef soon acquired a faithful following among Tekhelet-Lavan's instructors, all younger than he. His knowledge of socialism, his eloquence, his love of people all impressed them, as did his deep-rooted Judaism, though not one of them knew at the time that he donned phylacteries every morning—a fact that came to light one summer camp and caused a minor sensation among a generation of youngsters whose ties to formal Judaism were less than close. At best they had received religious instruction two afternoons a week, given by the local rabbi or cantor in an empty schoolhouse, where they had learned a little prayer, a little Torah, and a lot of ways to escape boredom. Their present interest was, in part, a reaction to their parents' attitude toward the Ostjuden, and it was considerably influenced by Martin Buber's circle, which had opened the door to Eastern European Judaism and its spiritual treasures to this second generation of assimilated Jews.

Nor did Yekef's low-status job as a traveling salesman pose any obstacle in the eyes of the youngsters, all of whom had a home to fall back on and no need to worry about making their own way. When they set out on weekend jaunts to the surrounding mountains, to the still pine forests steeped in moist fragrance; when they walked along the edge of the Eger River to the point where it poured into the Elbe; when they sought out the blossoming fruit trees near Theresienstadt's old fortress, Yekef could join them only occasionally. He had a living to earn. Yekef, with his heavy-rimmed spectacles, was the image of the scholarly Jew. He always wore long trousers and a tie, dictated by his work and considered by the youth movements the symbol of the decadent bourgeoisie. It was eminently clear that physical labor was not his forte, even if he were to do agricultural training. Better, therefore, that he apply himself to those spheres where his real talent lay: organizational work, lectures, teaching rhetoric. His skills were much needed in Tekhelet-Lavan, which, unlike the communists and radical Zionists, had few speakers who knew how to stir men's hearts, perhaps because in good German tradition they used to prepare their texts carefully, delve deeply into their subject matter, embellish it with quotations, and read the result to their audience; whereas the speakers who sprang from the grassroots of Eastern European Jewry could address an audience without relying on written notes, create a more direct relationship with their listeners, and direct their words intuitively.

Jakob Edelstein's speaking ability was of especial importance in light of the economic crisis that prevailed in Palestine at the time. The recent wave of Polish immigrants had failed to integrate into the country, and open immigration was stopped by the British, who determined immigration quotas on the basis of the country's economic capacity to absorb newcomers. This policy opposed both the spirit of the Mandate, and the Zionist concept whereby the immigrants themselves were to create the economic infrastructure for their absorption. The ban on immigration had devastating consequences for the pioneering youth movements in the Diaspora: how was one to educate youngsters toward working the land in Palestine when immigration to that country was no longer possible? Numerically, perhaps, the difference between eighty-four Czech immigrants in 1925, and no Czech immigrants from 1926 to 1927, was of little importance to the 350,000 Jews in Czechoslovakia; as far as the atmosphere was concerned, however, the difference was crucial. Zionism was presented as a fallen god, adding weight to what the communists had long claimed: the only solution to the Jewish question lay in an uncompromising socialist revolution.

Next to the great vision of a universal socialist revolution, Zionism appeared provincial, reactionary, separatist. Even Social Democracy, despite its readiness for compromise, was more attractive, particularly now, when it was steadily gaining in strength: in Germany, the Social Democratic Party headed the government coalition; in England, the Labour Party had been elected to power for the second time under Ramsay MacDonald as prime minister; and in Czechoslovakia's general elections in the fall of 1929, the Czech Social Democrats won additional seats and were voted back into power, with Alfred Meissner, a Czech Jew and one of the fathers of the constitution, serving as minister of justice.

The economic crisis in Palestine, the bloody riots of 1929, put the Zionists in an awkward position, a fact that did not go unnoticed by the communists in Teplitz-Schönau. They tried to exploit the situation by calling public meetings on such provocative issues as "Judaism and Palestine" or "Communism and Zionism," while the Zionists, in rebuttal, enlisted their own local "big guns" against the leaders of international communism (who, by the way, were also Jews). They put forward Felix Seidmann, the local chairman of the Zionist organization; Edelstein, their only speaker capable of using Marxist dialectic in debate; and above all, Dr. Mirjam Scheuer, a dentist, one of the founders of the Czechoslovakian arm of WIZO (Women's International Zionist Organization), and the daughter of an old Teplitz family. Compared to Scheuer, traveling salesman Yekef Edelstein, who busied himself with youth movements at an age when Alexander the Great had already embarked on his world conquest, was a novice in the art of Zionist argument. Dr. Scheuer pitted her sharp mind and clear political orientation against Bernard Schiff of the communist *Arbeitshilfe,* and attacked the views of Jakob Wassermann, the renowned German Jewish writer, who held at the time that Jews were not a nation, and had never been one. Should a state one day be established in Palestine, a people would no doubt live there, but there would no longer be a Jewish people, and their mission among the nations would come to an end.

Dr. Scheuer was Dr. Margulies's sister-in-law and, like him, belonged to the Radical Zionists. Margulies lived in Leitmeritz (Litoměřice) now, a small town on the banks of the Elbe which for centuries had barred Jewish settlement: *non tolerandus Judeus.* Every now and again, on a Saturday night, Teplitz's Zionist intelligentsia made up a party and called on the Margulieses in Leitmeritz. To amuse themselves they sometimes played intellectual games by choosing a topic from the German encyclopedia at random. It might have been Mycenaean art or Walter von der Vogelweide's poems. Whatever it was, they spent the evening discussing it. Jakob Edelstein, however, was never part of this Zionist elite, whose members on the whole were university graduates. There was another essential difference between him and most of the friends he had made in Teplitz. Because they had grown up in plenty, they were prepared to forgo university (often breaking their parents' hearts), give up their position, their wealth, for the Zionist idea and the implementation of Zionist ideals. It was no hardship for them to do so because the things they relinquished had always been within reach. Not so with Yekef. His dreams of a higher education had been put aside due to the force of circumstance. With no home, no family to fall back on, it was difficult even to be a pioneer. In 1929, when immigration to Palestine resumed, and more young people again left for training farms and to prepare themselves for a new life, Yekef continued to work for Kletter.

This in fact was the basic problem of all the pioneering youth movements in Central Europe: immigration to Palestine was the ultimate expression of a particular world view, not the result of compelling economic want. And what was to be done about those who did not train for a "productive" life in Palestine? For men, productivity meant agricultural work, or at the very least some form of physical labor; for women it meant teaching kindergarten, cooking, taking care of children (the pioneering youth movements were very far from implementing sexual equality, and all service jobs automatically fell to the girls). Even teaching, which interested some of the members (including Haim Hoffman, one of the movement's promising young intellectuals) was considered an inferior occupation and fell short of the ideal of working the land. It was an outlook that derived from two separate streams of thought (stemming perhaps from a single source): on the one hand, the pioneers believed firmly in the purifying nature of physical labor—being in touch with the soil, returning to one's roots, doing something creative; on the other, whether consciously or not, they wanted to get away from the image the gentiles had of the Jews: parasites who lived off *Luftgeschäfte* and exploited the nations that hosted them.

Even intellectuals felt inadequate when they were not partners in the pioneering experience. The philosopher Samuel Hugo Bergmann, one of the founders of Hapo'el Hatzair in Prague (affiliated with the Palestine Labor Party of the same name), and among the first immigrants to Palestine from the new Czechoslovakia, studied shoemaking at the Schneller Institute in Jerusalem while directing the National Library. He hoped to be accepted to Hefzibah one day, but his application remained unanswered.

Czechoslovakia's Hehalutz—the general federation of pioneering youth movements—also had its beginnings in Teplitz-Schönau, as an offshoot of Tekhelet-Lavan. Its major function was to provide occupational guidance and obtain funds for its members to emigrate. During this period it demanded that its members devote at least one year to instruction in the movement, and four years to thorough agricultural training (in exceptional cases the training could be in either carpentry or metalwork). In addition, candidates had to have a full command of Hebrew and be suited to collective life before the movement "released" them for emigration as *freigesprochen* (entitled to emigrate).

Again and again the pages of *Die Selbstwehr* (especially in summer, when youth activities were most intensive) raised the question of what was to be done about those members who did not emigrate to

Palestine. Inevitably they would be swallowed up by the bourgeoisie and end up dancing tangos and playing cards in cafés. Some argued that the exclusiveness of the pioneering ideals posed an obstacle: only a small percentage (between one and two percent) of the Jewish youth organized in Zionist movements actually trained for emigration. And of these a tiny proportion, perhaps one in ten, eventually emigrated. Perhaps two youth movements were needed, one directed at Palestine, the other at the Diaspora. But platonic Zionism in the Diaspora could not be separated from practical Zionism in Palestine, claimed those opposed to such a division. And those youth-movement graduates who opted for the hapless alternative of life in the Diaspora in the end found an outlet for their Zionist impulses: the Maccabi sports organization, which affirmed Zionism without demanding sacrifices; B'nai B'rith, or other Jewish fraternities; or working for the Zionist Funds or the Zionist Socialist parties. Deep in their hearts, however, they were left with the feeling that they had failed.

3

SWEETS WITH A SWASTIKA

IT required a great deal of talent and a strong, ambitious personality to overcome the disadvantages of Polish origin, a traveling-salesman's career, and no university degree. Within three years Jakob Edelstein was influential in all Teplitz-Schönau's Zionist institutions and a key ideological figure among Czechoslovakia's Socialist Zionists. He never trained as a pioneer, yet he firmly believed that the chief function of the youth movements was to educate youngsters toward productive work and pioneering. At summer camp at Hehalutz training farms in Leitmeritz, where members worked little and talked a lot, he lectured on young people's future political functions and other theoretical matters. In the autumn of 1929, Tekhelet-Lavan appointed Yekef to the Hehalutz central committee to coordinate cultural and educational activities. Yekef's friends hoped that his appointment would raise his spirits. He seemed a bit of an idler in his preoccupation with theory over practice, and had developed a reputation for being uninterested in girls; the lack of interest was apparently mutual, mainly due to his somewhat unattractive physical features: a flat face, a squat nose, small eyes behind thick spectacles. He had in fact formed an attachment to Mali Mauer, the daughter of a Teplitz Galician family, a member of Tekhelet-Lavan, a wan, intelligent girl, serious and reserved. Mali wanted to leave on training, while Yekef wouldn't or couldn't, at least not yet. He asked Mali to wait for him, but she went to Vienna to study domestic science, married an emissary from Palestine, and emigrated as a pioneer. Yekef bared his heart to Uriel Fluss, a member of Tekhelet-Lavan's leadership committee. He told him that above all he had sought a meaningful relationship with Mali, but she had wanted something more physical. It was a somewhat surprising admission by a bachelor in his mid-twenties, especially since Mali was a gentle girl, far removed from any blatant sensualism. True, most young people did see their youth-movement membership as something of a license for sexual freedom, a symbol of rebellion against the restrictions and prohibitions of their bourgeois homes. But not Yekef. He remained true to the traditional upbringing he had received at home. It was a despondent young man who in the fall of 1929 came to work at the Hehalutz central office in Moravská Ostrava, a soot-filled city of steel industries and coal mines, where Czechoslovakia's Zionist Organization had its headquarters.

Moravská Ostrava, or Ostrava for short, had the third largest Jewish community in Czechoslovakia after Prague and Brünn. Because of the new republic's elongated shape, Prague, its capital, was now at the western tip, a day's journey by train from the easternmost regions. In 1921, the Zionist Organization therefore decided to move its head office to a more central location, from Prague to Ostrava, which was in the heart of the country. Ostrava also had a more heterogeneous Jewish community than Prague. Many of its seven thousand Jews were of Polish origin and, as was common in the East, the population included craftsmen and blue-collar workers as well as academics and businessmen. The question of centralism, however, may have been merely a theoretical response to a de facto situation. In 1921, in protest against the Zionist establishment, which was accused of having turned the movement's work in the Diaspora into an end in itself, an Ostravan attorney, Dr. Rufeisen, was elected chairman of Czechoslovakia's Zionist Organization. But before he accepted the position, he laid down two conditions: the head office would move to Ostrava, and Dr. Franz Kahn would continue to direct it, as he had done in Prague.

Ostrava was the center of the steel and coal industry—a forest of smoking chimneys. Most of its industry was controlled by the Viennese Rothschilds and Baron Gutmann's family (immortalized in song by the Czech national poet, Peter Bezruč, as sapping the marrow of Silesian miners, together with other "benevolent" Jewish figures: tavern keepers, informers, and rapists of innocent young girls).

For a while, before Yekef moved to a rented room, he slept in one of the Hehalutz offices, as did Willy Feuerstein, delegate of Hashomer Hatzair, the Marxist youth movement, and the two became friends, despite their theoretical differences, a rare phenomenon in relations between members of the two movements at the time.

Yekef was responsible for Hehalutz's cultural program, which tended to follow the same fluctuating course. Every fresh leadership started full of zeal and boundless energy, organizing courses and seminars and issuing publications. However, enthusiasm would peter out within a year or two, the entire leadership body would change—as did the emissaries from Palestine—and the whole cycle would begin anew.

In March 1930 the Hehalutz central committee convened in Ostrava and devoted most of its deliberations to the question of Carpathian Russia, where thousands of Jewish families lived in dire want and hunger. Like the rest of Carpathian Russia, the Jews too were a story in themselves. The general population consisted chiefly of Ruthenians, mountain Slavs similar to Ukrainians, and Jews—many of whom had come from nearby Rumania, Galicia, and the Ukraine—who on the whole resembled their Ruthenian neighbors: two-thirds of the hundred thousand Jews lived in villages, raised corn and potatoes, and tended sheep. Their agricultural methods were primitive, their harvests paltry. To eke out a living they worked as porters, tailors, shoemakers, petty artisans, and in afforestation. They lived in one-room wooden cabins with seven or eight children, in scattered mountain villages sometimes five miles or more from the nearest railroad station. The winter snows cut them off from the rest of the world, and Jewish life proceeded as if the Enlightenment had never happened. In the West the ratio of Jews to the overall population was 1.4 percent; in sub-Carpathian Russia it was 15 percent, and in Mukachevo (Munkács), the big city, it was 45 percent.

When Ludwig Singer and Max Brod, members of the Jewish National Committee established after the revolution of 1918, first traveled to Carpathian Russia, they discovered a new and unknown Jewish world. Most Western Jews knew of Carpathian Russia's Jews only from *Exile in the Valley,* the wonderful collection of stories by the Czech writer Ivan Olbracht. Ruthenia was promised autonomy when the new Czechoslovakian republic came into being, but it never materialized, the pretext being the familiar one that its citizens were not ready for self-rule; meanwhile the Czech governor continued to rule the province in almost colonial fashion. For the Jews, the annexation of Ruthenia to Czechoslovakia was a mixed blessing: transportation improved, the lumber industry developed, schools were opened, but the cheap commodities produced by large western factories spelled ruin for small-scale local craftsmen.

The Jews became a pawn among the vying nationalities. The Hungarians, the Ruthenians, the Czechs—all tried to draw the Jews into their camp and Jewish children into their schools, where their languages were taught. The village Jews spoke Yiddish and Ruthenian, while the intelligentsia and middle class had long preferred Hungarian, from the days when the region had belonged to the Hungarian part of the twin monarchy. Since the central government built schools and cultural institutions according to the proportion of every nationality within the overall population, the Czech government encouraged the Jews to affirm their own nationality rather than attach themselves to any of the others, who tried to undermine the republic. The Czechs even agreed that the Jews' national affiliation need not be determined by mother tongue, as was the case with the other nationalities. Thus, in the 1930 population census, 88 percent of the Jews of Carpathian Russia and 57 percent of all the Jews in Czechoslovakia declared themselves Jewish nationals, even though many were unclear as to what this meant. In the same census, only 21 percent of the Jews in Czechoslovakia regarded themselves as Slavs (Czech or Slovak) and 12 percent as Germans.

This massive affirmation of Jewish nationalism was an unprecedented phenomenon in Central Europe, undoubtedly influenced by the nationalist struggle between Czechs and Germans, Slovaks and Hungarians, Ruthenians and Poles. It was an arena in which Jewish nationalism became an honorable escape into neutrality; a fact, however, which did not prevent the outbreak of anti-Jewish incidents as the world economic crisis of the 1930s sharpened. In Bohemia and Moravia these incidents were on a small scale, transient and insignificant in the eyes of most local Jews. In Prague, German and even Czech students clashed with Jews mainly because they feared that they were taking over the medical profession; Jews constituted between 25 and 40 percent of all students in institutions of higher education. Jewish shops were stoned following the screening of German films, and on May Day, when members of the Labor

Zionist movement marched in the workers' parade, they were met with cries of "Go to Palestine!"

Another racist incident reared its head in Carpathian Russia, when two Jewish peddlers were accused of murdering two Christian children, reminding Jews in the West that the ghetto era had not yet ended. No damning evidence was presented against Steinberg and Lieberman, but the trial dragged on for over two years and closed only after President Masaryk intervened personally.

On March 7, 1930, Masaryk celebrated his eightieth birthday. The Zionist institutions collected funds, planted a forest in his honor near Kibbutz Sarid, held festive gatherings, and talked of his affinity for Judaism. For Jews, as for Czechs, Masaryk was the *tatíček*, the beloved father. Out of his own pocket came funds for Hebrew schools and the Jewish students' cafeteria. His close friends included author Karl Poláček, who wrote with that particular brand of Czech-Jewish humor which gazes at the world indulgently, shrugs, and does not inspire warriors. It is hardly surprising, therefore, that when in 1929 Count Reventlow suggested to the Prussian parliament that the Jews again don the badge of shame and be addressed as "Jude," *Die Selbstwehr* reacted with a smile and a comical ditty. How else should one react to a suggestion to return to the dark ages?

Moravská Ostrava was not far from the Polish border—the site of a bitter battle between Czechs and Poles when the republic was founded—and one day, Jakob Edelstein asked for, and was given, leave and financial assistance to journey to Horodenka to see his family, for the first time, apparently, since he had left it as a child. He found a new Horodenka, with paved streets and electric lights, modern, postwar buildings, parks and boulevards, cars and buses, and the Polish language commanding all. Mottel and Mattel Edelstein scraped a living out of their small housewares shop, opened after the war, and his sister, Dora, an attractive girl and careful dresser, worked as a clerk in a legal firm. But the rumor among the Jewish community was that Yekef supported his parents to the best of his ability. In his suit and tie, speaking pure German, Yekef personified the westerner, the pride of his family. He returned to Ostrava later than planned and never referred to the reason for his sudden trip.

Edelstein's sojourn in Ostrava brought him closer to the top ranks of the Zionist Organization and forged his ties with Dr. Rufeisen and

Dr. Franz Kahn, who headed it. To the pioneers Rufeisen was always Doctor Rufeisen, but Kahn (who was also a lawyer, though he had never practiced) they called Franz or Franzl. Kahn was born in Pilsen and raised by his grandmother after his father emigrated to America. He was erudite, had a wonderful sense of humor, and a perpetual store of jokes. He was a curious mixture of believer and skeptic, philosopher and man of action, an ever-hopeful pessimist. Perhaps this was the secret of his attraction for young people. He and his wife, Olga, were both employed by the Zionist Organization, he as director of the Zionist office, she as his secretary, and even on Sundays they were busy with Zionist work. In the evenings they went to meetings, and their vacations were spent at congresses and conventions; their two children learned to be alone. In 1921 Kahn was one of the organizers of the twelfth Zionist Congress, and ever since he had played a central role at every congress.

Yekef had hoped that at the end of his year's work for the Hehalutz head office the movement would find him a job in Prague. He spent some time in the capital, devoting himself chiefly to Socialist Zionist affairs. The Zionist institutions in Prague, however, offered few salaried jobs, particularly at the level which interested him; and journalism, which supported many proponents of Zionism, was no place for him. His writing was dry, unembellished, theoretical, devoid of all humor—in stark contrast to his speaking ability, where his fiery eloquence captivated many an audience. His only alternative was to return to Teplitz-Schönau, this time to support a family.

Shortly after his return to Teplitz in 1930, Jakob Edelstein married Miriam Olliner, sister to Max Olliner, one of Edelstein's students and friends from Tekhelet-Lavan and the Socialist Zionists. Yekef's salesmen colleagues considered the match arranged, while Miriam's friends felt she could have done better had it not been for the fear of being passed over at the ripe old age of twenty-three. Miriam, with her high forehead and large brown eyes, was four years his junior; alert and delicate, she loved music and theater, two fields which Yekef scarcely noticed. She had completed the German *Lyceum* and taught English in high school as well as giving private lessons. The Olliners, owners of a textile warehouse, also originally came from Galicia, and their home was both Zionist and traditional; candles were lit on the Sabbath and Jewish holidays observed. Yekef's mother attended the modest wedding, arriving from Horodenka for her one and only brief visit, and the couple started married life. Unlike most of his youth-movement colleagues, who tended to scorn the institution, Yekef regarded marriage as a binding, lifelong relationship, with no room for outside dallying. Miriam kept a kosher home, and Yekef observed Jewish tradition more carefully than in his bachelorhood; or perhaps it was simply more apparent now that he had rented a flat and had a home of his own. His friends noted with some surprise that it was possible to be a socialist and observe religious law at the same time. For Yekef, the blend was natural: true socialism was after all found in the Bible. Karl Marx had merely systematized it, supplied a technical formula to realize its precepts of justice, and adapted the vision of the Prophets to the new era.

The Sudeten Jews felt the surge of German nationalism, and the growing influence of the Nazi Party across the border, more strongly than did the citizens of Prague, which was somewhat of a kingdom to itself. In Prague, Dr. Albert Einstein's reaction to the victory of the National Socialist Party, which won almost six million votes in the 1930 elections, appeared perfectly reasonable: "It is due to the economic crisis, a childhood disease of the German republic. While Jewish unity is always desirable, there is no call for a special Jewish reaction to the election results."

In Teplitz-Schönau, as in other Sudeten towns, one felt the gradual change in mood of the German population. Their chief livelihood derived from light industry, which had been hard hit by the depressed world economy. The then welfare minister, Dr. Ludvik Czech, had introduced the system of "Czech vouchers," which gave some assistance to those out of work who were not yet eligible for unemployment insurance, but nonetheless the feeling that the Czech authorities were indifferent to their fate took hold of the Sudeten Germans and festered.

Perhaps what was at work was not so much a change in mood as a change in the willingness for camouflage. The German border areas had given the world several ideologues of extreme German nationalism: Karl Hermann Wolf, Rudolf Jung, Hans Knirsch, Hans Krebs, all of whom preceded Hitler in despising the Jews as a race. At the turn of the century in the town of Eger, guards were posted to observe which Germans bought their Christmas presents from dirty Jews, and as early as 1900 a notice in a local café read: "Czechs, Jews, and dogs prohibited." In the German institutions of higher education in Prague and Brünn most of the non-Jewish students were Sudeten Germans who brought with them their active hatred of Jews. In 1922 they held violent demonstrations against the appointment of a Jewish professor to the position of rector of Prague's German university.

Still, in Prague the German nationalists were merely a minority tolerated by the Czechs; in the Sudetenland, they were a major factor. The numbers of young men wearing white knitted stockings and leather breeches and women in dirndls, parading their nationalism, increased every day. When young Nazi thugs attacked Jews in the streets of Teplitz, with cries of "Another of those Poles!" the Jews of Teplitz, represented by Margulies and Jakob Edelstein, reacted vigorously: "We will not overlook the audacity of the swastika people, and will do all in our power to prevent further incidents. We are twenty kilometers from the German border and well aware of how great the danger is of imitating what goes on in Germany."

In May 1932 the Edelsteins' only son was born and named simply Arieh, plain and clear, not as a Hebrew adjunct to his "real" name.

In July, at the opening session of the tenth Zionist Convention, Dr. Rufeisen, the chairman of the Zionist Organization of Czechoslovakia, discussed the difficult times that had befallen Jews and the infamous attempts to blame them for the world economic crisis, couched in terms of racial theory and Jewish inferiority. Against this attempt by German nationalists to strip Jews of their legal rights, Rufeisen held up the Czech example: here Jews were free and no legal or administrative restrictions had been imposed on them, while in other parts of Europe anti-Semitic tendencies were spreading like a plague. "But we dare not ignore the fact that, influenced by the German example, attempts have also been made by the Czech public to propagate the same anti-Jewish theories" (an allusion to the aforementioned case of two Jewish peddlers being tried for the murder of two Catholic children in Velka-Bresna). His address was greeted with enthusiastic applause, especially after he voiced his confidence that the Czech authorities would do all in their power to prevent a return to the anti-Jewish hatred of the Middle Ages.

German National Socialism won its great victory on January 30, 1933: Field-Marshal Hindenburg, president of the Weimar republic, asked Adolf Hitler to form a new government, and the party's racial platform suddenly became official policy, accompanied by a spate of anti-Jewish violence. Czechoslovakia's Jews saw photographs of Jews in Goethe's Frankfurt being made to scrub sidewalks, of Munich's Jews carrying posters denouncing themselves, and heard the tales of outrage told by thousands of refugees who began to stream toward Czechoslovakia. First to come were political refugees, Social Democrats, communists, including many Jews, who fled for their lives. Then came those who fled simply because they were Jews.

It had taken hardly a week after the Nazi takeover for Hindenburg's circle to realize the enormity of their political error. They had assumed that Hugenberg of the Stahlhelm would be the decisive figure in the new government; instead, Hitler held the reins and Fascism the upper hand. A revolution was impossible and the present situation could continue for years. Germany had become a Fascist state.

Dr. Kahn, who had been sent by the Prague Zionists to get a clear picture of the situation, sent back a sobering report. "As for the Jews: there's no point in repeating what has appeared in newspapers. The police and S.A. seized the Zionist Organization's building with its courtyard on Meinekestrasse, aimed their weapons at the windows, and ordered the building shut down. Since Tuesday all phones have been tapped. As to what the Jews should do, one of our people in government circles (whose name must not be mentioned) had this to say: 'The situation is tragic and there is no way out.' It's no good relying on the Center parties. The only hope is to find support among the National Socialists themselves, and in fact this is what Dr. Oskar Weissman has done, without the consent of the Zionist Organization: he has signed a declaration expressing support for the National Socialists in the hope that this would help the Jews. As you know, there are several anti-Semitic points in the National Socialist program, but these are not mentioned in the election platform. The Zionist Organization awaits the resumption of activities any day now. Bars have been put on the windows and locks on the doors, to gain time in the event of an attack from the S.A.; they view the situation with pessimism. A pogrom may well take place, with or without bloodshed. Contact with formerly influential persons can no longer be of benefit. Attempts to organize self-defense have been nipped in the bud. The Zionists are almost helpless in face of the new situation. A Fascist state: what does one do? Talk of setting up an underground sounds here like a program for juvenile pranks."

After the initial shock, however, at the dissolution of the Reichstag, Hitler's overwhelming election victory, and the subsequent violence, calm seemed to be restored to the Jews of Germany. Letters abroad denied the terrible reports published in newspapers across the world: the Spree River was not awash with hundreds of bodies; there had indeed been some retaliatory acts on the part of the hotheaded S.A., but the government had now taken steps to stop them; the general feeling was that the worst was over—the physical danger to life was past, and now only economic ruin was feared; there was hope of a revolution within the year, the monarchy would be reinstated, the Nazi government would fall, and the socialists would again take up the reins of state. The Jews were inclined to stay put and defend their rights rather than flee. The boycott of Jewish shops, doctors, and lawyers declared on April 1, 1933, was greeted by the German public with ambivalence. On the whole they agreed with the basic assumption that the economic influence exerted by Jews in the Reich must be curtailed; nevertheless, they were uncomfortable with violence, particularly when it elicited sharp reproof from abroad.

Hitler understood that for the time being he had better move quietly rather than with grand strokes. Most Jews, however, interpreted this tactic as an essential change in Nazi policy, which was beginning to recover from its "childhood disease." Generations of European experience showed that almost every change in government had been accompanied by violence against the Jews which had eventually subsided. Dr. Theodor Lessing, a philosopher and Jewish educator who had in the past converted and later returned to Judaism as a Zionist, had in 1925 earned himself the animosity of German nationalists by sharply opposing the election of Field-Marshal Hindenburg as president of Germany. When the Nazis came to power, he fled to Czechoslovakia, settled in Marienbad, and lectured on the future of Germany and its Jews (in his view, gloomy), according to his personal credo: "I am German and will remain German. I am Jewish and will remain Jewish. I am a socialist and will remain a socialist." After his lecture in Teplitz-Schönau in 1933, the town rabbi, Friedrich Weihs, and other local Zionists escorted him back to his hotel. Dr. Weihs, who taught religion, spoke of the mood of the Sudeten Germans, especially the young. (While he gave his class religious instruction, the class next door sang the Horst Wessel song, children brought home candies embossed with a swastika in the center instead of the traditional flower, and German pupils had stopped greeting him.) He warned Dr. Lessing that his life might be in danger, but even if the latter had heeded his warning, there was little he could do. Thousands of political refugees were seeking asylum in Czechoslovakia, and it was impossible to get police protection for them all. A few weeks later, Dr. Lessing, who had a price on his head, was murdered by Nazi agents who had managed to cross the border undetected. This was the first political murder executed by the Nazis on Czechoslovakian soil, and it caused an enormous uproar.

4

STATELESS CONSULATE

CZECHOSLOVAKIAN Jews reacted to Hitler's rise to power according to their nature and their geographical situation. In the border regions, in the Sudetenland, the sense of danger was more heightened than in Prague. In the capital, where President Masaryk responded to events in Germany by reiterating his unswerving faith in democracy, the Zionist organizations held protest meetings and were confident that "it can't happen here." The Jewish National Party called for public meetings and Margulies, head of the party and always the fighter, resolved to embark on a vigorous counterattack. According to Paragraph 147 of the 1922 German-Polish Convention, Germany undertook to protect all minority rights in the region annexed to her. In a letter to the Zionist Executive in London, Margulies proposed that a protest be lodged with the League of Nations at Germany's violation of the said paragraph vis-à-vis Upper Silesia. "A petition must be organized by Jews throughout the world and the initiative must extend to all Jews everywhere. Geneva expects the initiative to come from the Jews. . . . They must not remain silent and wait for others to act on their behalf. [The petition] must be based on legal evidence—not on 'atrocities'—on the violation of an international agreement in that the Jews of

Upper Silesia who are lawyers, hospital doctors, university professors, and government clerks are not permitted to work."

On behalf of Fritz Bernheim, a minor employee in a government warehouse in Gleiwitz who had been fired by the Nazis and subsequently emigrated to Czechoslovakia, Margulies submitted a petition to the League of Nations, since by the terms of the Upper Silesia Convention any citizen whose national rights had been infringed could apply to the League. Margulies attached a hundred applications from Jewish organizations to the Bernheim petition, much to the consternation of von Keller, the German delegate to the League, who claimed that one Bernheim had no right to speak for all the Jews. To support his contention, von Keller submitted letters from assimilated Jewish organizations in Germany who protested the right of any Jewish minority to speak on their behalf. An ad hoc committee of jurists rejected the German objection, and in May 1933, the Bernheim petition was brought before the Council of the League of Nations. In this way at least the rest of the world learned of the civil rights problem of the Jews of Germany.

At the Geneva Congress of National Minorities, the Germans had, of course, pointed out the astonishing fact that while countries all over the world censured Germany for persecuting Jews, they themselves were reluctant to accept those "surplus Jews who wish to leave Germany." Still, Hitler, fearing reprisals on German minorities in Poland and elsewhere, knew how to adapt his policies to the prevailing mood, at least outwardly. In September of that year, Germany informed the League of Nations that Jewish civil rights in Upper Silesia had been restored. This state of affairs, in which the Jews of Upper Silesia lived as if on a protected island, continued until July 1937, at which time the 1922 agreement between Poland and Germany expired and Hitler could ignore both world opinion and the League of Nations.

In 1933, everything was still fresh; the alarm could still be sounded, diplomacy could still prove effective in dealing with Germany. In Prague, German refugees printed pamphlets describing events in the Reich in order to arouse the world's conscience against the Nazi government. The Jews could still be confident in themselves and their economic strength: there were ways and means to fight. Angelo Goldstein, representing the Jewish National Party, urgently appealed to Minister of Justice Meissner demanding stern action against the anti-Semitic writings that appeared in the *Sudetendeutscher Beobachter,* the official organ of the Nationalist Socialist

Workers Party (NSDAP). The party had been newly organized under Konrad Henlein, a gymnastics teacher from the border town of
Asch, as the Sudeten German Party (SdP), a colorless name chosen
under pressure from the Czech government. In 1933, the SdP was
still a minority factor among the German population in the republic, and the Zionist Organization could still hold its summer school
on Mount Keilberg, right on Germany's doorstep. But above the
homes across the border were flying the red flags with a black
swastika in their center.

As more and more Jewish refugees poured into Czechoslovakia,
interest grew in the possibility of emigrating to Palestine. Dozens of
people came daily to the Palestine office to inquire about obtaining
an immigration certificate. The Palestine office, which opened in
Prague in 1921, was by way of being a consulate for a nonexistent
state. The directorship had changed hands several times, and its
activities were rather limited, as was the flow of traffic between
Czechoslovakia and Palestine: in 1932, only 180 Czechs had traveled to Palestine—eighty-five immigrants, twenty returning tourists, and seventy-five outgoing tourists. Now the Palestine office in
Prague had to be reorganized and its scope of activities widened.
This task fell to Jakob Edelstein, selected by the Palestine committee
of the Zionist Organization.

The Edelsteins moved from Teplitz-Schönau to a rented three-
room flat on Bilkova Street, a few minutes' walk from the Jewish
community center and offices on Dlouhá Street, the heart of all
Zionist activity in Prague. It was still a Jewish neighborhood, though
the small patchwork ghetto houses had been torn down at the end
of the last century, when the quarter was renovated. The Jews,
particularly those who were better off, had scattered throughout
the city but still lived in concentrated groups, near the synagogue or
near their own kind, those they could argue with and those they
could befriend. The old Jewish district, bounded by the Old City
square and the Vltava River, retained its Jewish character and contained a number of fine old synagogues: the Alt-Neu, the Maisl, the
Pinkas, and the Dushna; it also housed the Jewish "municipality"
building, graced by a clock with Hebrew letters and hands that
moved counterclockwise. The stores still bore Jewish names, and
some of the old Jewish families still lived in the neighborhood where
their parents and grandparents had grown up, even after the small
houses gave way to four- and five-story bourgeois apartment build-

ings with floral reliefs and stucco facings that attempted to emulate the marble fronts of aristocratic homes.

The Edelstein flat was modestly furnished, in keeping with the salary of the director of the Palestine office and the tastes of both Yekef and Miriam, neither of whom was accustomed to spending money either on themselves or on luxuries. In this respect Miriam was very different from most Jewish women in Prague, whose basic wardrobe requirements were a black Persian lamb coat and a string of pearls. The only luxury she did permit herself was an occasional visit to the theater with a friend or relative. (For Yekef any gathering, committee, or meeting was far more important than *Carmen* or *William Tell.*) Those who had known Miriam when she was single found that after her marriage to Yekef, she was quieter, more reserved, less inclined to smile.

On Friday evenings, Yekef ushered in the Sabbath and made the benediction over the wine, as was the custom among eastern European Jewry (very rare in Prague). There were always guests to share the Sabbath meal, chiefly Palestinian emissaries. On one such occasion, Yekef told Yehuda Rezniczenko, emissary of the General Workers Union in Palestine and a frequent Sabbath visitor, that he put aside a hundred crowns every month for the journey to Palestine. He did not, however, say whether the trip was to be made as a tourist or as an emigrant.

Edelstein arrived in Prague in the tempestuous year of the murder of Arlosoroff and amid the feverish preparations for the Zionist Congress, which was to be held in Czechoslovakia that year. A rising star in the Zionist movement, and director of the Jewish Agency's political department, Haim Arlosoroff visited Germany in May 1933 to get a close look at what was happening and investigate the possibility of the mass emigration of German Jews. On his way back to Palestine, he stopped in Prague and conferred with local Zionist leaders on the question of aid for Jews in Germany. When, two weeks later, he was murdered on the beach at Tel Aviv, the Czech Zionists, like those all over the world, were profoundly shocked.

Originally, the eighteenth Zionist Congress had been planned for Carlsbad (Karlovy Vary), Czechoslovakia's largest health resort, with its tranquil surroundings, abundant (and kosher) hotels, assembly halls, parks, and the opportunity to take the waters and ease digestive systems saturated with goosefat and cramped from excessive sitting. Now that Hitler was in power, however, Carlsbad was too close to the source of trouble: it would be difficult to ensure the safety of congress participants among the German population. At the last minute, therefore, the congress venue was moved to Prague, sorely testing the organizational staff, led by Dr. F. Kahn.

The Zionist Congress officially opened at the Lucerna auditorium on August 21. The one major innovation was that German was no longer the dominant Congress language. Because of the political situation in Germany, the speakers chose to deliver their greetings in Hebrew (which few understood), English, French, and Czech. It was pointed out that Jews had lived in Bohemia for a thousand years and had much in common with the Czechs. "We live among a people who know the meaning of freedom and will know how to fight for it," Dr. Rufeisen said, and ended with the chief tenet of Dr. Masaryk's faith: "Truth triumphs." Nahum Sokolow, who as president of the Zionist Organization delivered the central address, had agreed, after a good deal of discussion, to modify his criticism of the German government so as not to harm the Jews in Germany: "We are friends, not foes, of Germany, and admirers of her culture. We have no desire to pit one people against another, we look to peace. But when it becomes a question of our survival and honor, we cannot keep silent. Where is culture, where is Europe, where is the League of Nations? Has our people been sentenced to eternal banishment from country to country? The two-thousand-year tragedy is unfolding awesomely before our eyes."

People spoke so much of a "terrible tragedy" and "the destruction of Jewry" that the words became meaningless, and when their hour truly came, they had lost the power to shock. (Dr. Franz Friedmann, an attorney and journalist who represented the Jewish National Party on Prague's City Council, wrote that year of "a war of annihilation against the Jews of Germany"; he meant economic annihilation.) Following heated debates in which the Revisionist faction demanded a firm decision censuring Nazi Germany and cooperation in the efforts toward economic sanctions against her, the Congress formulated a compromise resolution: so long as Jews were deprived of their rights and humiliated, Zionism would neither rest nor remain silent. The Congress issued an appeal to the world countries to help Jewish refugees find shelter; applied to the Mandate government demanding that the gates of Palestine be opened wide for massive immigration from Germany; and called on the League of Nations to take steps against the dangers that threatened German Jews.

Czechoslovakia's Socialist Zionists had sent three delegates to the Congress, one from the working committee, known by its German abbreviation, AGSZ. For the first four days, Dr. Haim Kugel represented the AGSZ and then, as agreed, Jakob Edelstein took his place. Even though he did not address the assembly, Edelstein felt it important to be present. It was an opportunity to meet all the leaders of the world Zionist movement, to clarify positions, to study the practical question of the immigration of German refugees to Palestine. Since January 1933, about six thousand Jews had emigrated to Palestine from Germany, and a similar number was expected to do so before the quota was filled. Jakob Edelstein pointed out that the growing immigration was not without its pitfalls: some of the emigrants were completely unprepared. Whether they emigrated as pioneers, or certified as investors, physical fitness alone was not a sufficient criterion for "releasing" candidates; they must be psychologically prepared as well. The representatives of the Palestine offices all emphasized the importance of selection and insisted that the immigrants had at least a basic knowledge of Hebrew and a year's training before they were sent to Palestine. Nevertheless, it was decided in the present circumstances not to adhere too strictly to this principle, since not all the refugees could undergo training. Some were too old; others, political refugees, were in physical danger and had to emigrate quickly. In general, however, in Prague as in London and Jerusalem, the opinion was that Palestine should not be flooded indiscriminately with immigrants from Germany: candidates should be weeded out on the basis of age, occupation, and Zionist background, so as to prevent a rush of urban immigration at the expense of the agricultural settlements. The goal, after all, was gradual, planned immigration over a period of ten to fifteen years.

Haim Barlas, director of the immigration department of the Jewish Agency, noted at the convention of the Palestine offices that their chief function was to organize "good, comfortable, and inexpensive immigration, with a minimum of bureaucracy and a congenial attitude toward the immigrants." But what good was a congenial attitude when the number of potential immigrants from Germany far outstripped the number of certificates the Mandate government was prepared to grant? Careful winnowing was unavoidable. Immigration certificates for German pioneers were allotted by the Palestine office in Prague, but required authorization by the Hehalutz office in Berlin, which knew the candidates from their training period in Germany. One refugee, Emanuel Büchner, who took shelter in the Sudeten town of Brüx, asked the Prague office if he could earn a living in Palestine as a Hebrew teacher. Edelstein was doubtful: there was no lack of excellent teachers in Palestine, one had to be eminently qualified, and the salary was poor. Comrade Büchner would do better to acquire a productive skill, such as that of electrician, which he claimed to have some experience of. "But you must be prepared for physical labor in Palestine. Anyone who emigrates on a pioneer's certificate must be prepared to work as a menial laborer wherever he is required."

When the certification committee met in Prague, Büchner's application was rejected on the basis of the German Hehalutz's report: he had not performed well during training, and did not appear fit for physical labor. He would have to undergo training before he could expect a certificate. Büchner and his family refused to accept the rejection. There followed a heated exchange of letters in which the Büchners accused the Palestine office and Edelstein of favoritism and accepting bribes for certificates. In January 1935, after a two-year struggle to immigrate, Büchner committed suicide. Edelstein reported the incident to Jerusalem and suggested that the matter be closed. But Büchner's fiancée's father now blamed Edelstein for Büchner's death. The matter was brought before an honorary tribunal of the Czechoslovakian Zionist movement, and later before the Zionist Congress Court. Both bodies found the accusations against Edelstein unfounded.

The circumstances, not the individuals, were at fault: the gates of Palestine opened and shut according to British policy, and they never opened wide enough to accommodate all the refugees who tried to flee the Nazi regime by emigrating. Granting certificates, therefore, of necessity became a matter of close scrutiny and selection. Nor in this case can Büchner's shaky emotional state be disregarded: the first people to leave Germany, after all, were the prophets of doom, those caught in the throes of fear. Normal people could hardly be expected to relate seriously to the words of the popular Nazi song: "When Jewish blood is spilled by the knife, it will be better for all." Their ability to take anti-Semitic Nazi propaganda at face value was hampered by the limits of their healthy human logic.

What could one possibly think of the plan proposed by Julius Streicher, editor of *Der Stürmer*, for the worldwide solution to the Jewish "problem": the confiscation of all Jewish property, merciless economic sanctions imposed on Jews, the systematic deprivation of Jews' rights, and the imposition on them of legally alien status in all "Aryan" countries; the compilation of an index file including each and every Jew in each and every province, city, and local jurisdiction; the establishment of a Jewish state in some sufficiently large territory under Aryan control where Jews would be deported and forced to settle. Since Palestine was too small for the purpose, the island of Madagascar seemed a most suitable place.

German refugees continued to stream into Czechoslovakia, settling mostly in Prague and in the German border areas. To some extent, their situation was better in Czechoslovakia than in other countries. In the first place, Czechoslovakia was prepared to accept them: no sooner had they started coming than President Masaryk decided that his country would grant shelter to them all, and Dr. Beneš declared for all the world to hear that this small republic was proud of the help it was extending them. In addition, German was the country's second language, and even those who preferred not to speak it could nevertheless understand it. As for jobs, despite unemployment, despite the difficulty of obtaining a legal work permit, there were still opportunities to be found in the German press, in German publishing houses, and in small shops and businesses. The authorities granted all German citizens and stateless persons residence visas, and all citizens of other countries were permitted to stay, at least temporarily.

In the first year after Hitler came to power some four thousand refugees came to Czechoslovakia, as did an equal number of returning Czechoslovakians who had been living in Germany. At the start, refugee committees were set up according to political affiliation—Democrats, Social Democrats, Communists. The Jews also set up a refugee aid committee, headed by Dr. Josef Popper, president of B'nai B'rith and the Council of Communities. The living spirit behind it, however, was a truly remarkable woman, Maria Schmolka, director of HICEM. Nobody really knew what the letters in HICEM stood for (it was an acronym for three American Jewish organizations that helped immigrants and had transferred their sphere of activities to Europe once the flow of emigration to America had slackened). But everyone knew what they meant: help in times of trouble.

Once it became clear that it would take more than a few months, or even a year, for the Nazi regime to topple, and that the German refugees were in fact immigrants, the social work center in Prague, headed by Haim Hoffman, took charge of Jewish refugees' welfare. The refugee aid committee continued to deal chiefly with legal questions, the acquisition of documents, and the funding of emigration—which had even then become an exceedingly difficult task. In time, the refugee committees all joined together under a single umbrella organization, with Maria Schmolka as a kind of high commissioner for them all. Maria, or Marshka, as she was commonly called, was at first glance somewhat forbidding: her masculine gait, her short hair drawn back from a too high forehead, the gray suit she always wore, the mannish hat, belied the woman and child who dwelt inside her. On the one hand she was a master organizer; on the other, she was gentle, compassionate, naïve. Her parents, the Meissners, had owned a textile shop in old Prague, and after her father's death, Maria ran both the family business and her own small, private bank (an unheard-of occupation for women at the time). At the age of thirty she married an attorney and widower thirty years her senior. When, after a brief but happy marriage, Dr. Schmolka passed away, Maria, to take her mind off her grief, decided to tour the Near East, including Palestine. Up till then she had been active in Social Democratic circles and had considered herself primarily Czech; she returned with a heightened sense of both her Jewishness and her allegiance to Zionism. She devoted herself energetically to WIZO and the Jewish party until she found her true vocation in helping refugees, and that pushed everything else aside.

She lived in a small house in the Old City with dark corridors and high ceilings, with paintings and objets d'art chosen with care and knowledge, where the telephone never stopped ringing and refugees often waited for her on the doorstep. She had access to all decisive state bodies and for the sake of her refugees was prepared to use whatever connections she could. She and her friend Hannah Steiner, president of WIZO and director of the refugee aid committee, worked a twenty-four-hour day without salary, even paying for the frequent traveling they had to do in the course of their work. (As did Jakob Edelstein: if he was sent to lecture at some remote town— and he was one of the most popular lecturers—he instructed those who sent him to donate his fare to the Socialist Zionists; when he did present an expense account, it never included more than two items—travel and tea.)

All Zionist roads in Prague led to Dlouhá Třida, "the long boulevard," which was actually neither long nor a boulevard. It was an ordinary Prague street, with gray stuccoed houses and cobbled sidewalks; but it was a Jewish street, the connecting artery between the new city and the fifth district, the former Jewish city. On one of the corners of Dlouhá Třída stood the Beit Ha'am, the Jewish community center, which had opened in 1930. It was a modern structure, built of unadorned concrete, iron, and glass along straight and simple lines. Its six floors housed the entire Zionist world: the Jewish National Fund, the Jewish Foundation Fund, *Die Selbstwehr* and *Židovské Zprávy* (the Czech weekly), the Palestine office, the Maccabi and Hagibor main offices, the youth movements, function halls, lecture rooms, as well as a cinema on the ground floor and the most important Zionist institution of all— Café Aschermann (or Aschermannka for short).

The Palestine office at the time occupied only two small rooms in the community center, and people who came to see Jakob Edelstein or Růža Levy, his administrative secretary, generally did so without an appointment. If they found Yekef in, fine; if not, it was no great matter. If he was in but unavailable, they whiled away the time in debate. In Café Aschermann, everyone knew everyone else. As in all self-respecting cafés, habitués had their own table, where they sat every day at the same time with the same friends. There was even a Hebrew table, with Hebrew newspapers for the select few who could speak the language and had not been forever thwarted by the conjugation of simple tenses. "I was forty years old when I began to study my national language," Max Brod wrote, and at seventy he had not yet fully mastered it. Like all cafés, Aschermann's was always crowded, hazy with smoke, and bubbling with sound; not the loud tones of discord, nor the whispers of chessplayers (who had their own meeting places), but the hubbub of voices deep in discussion.

After all, people didn't go to cafés to have coffee—they could do that at home. They went to meet friends and read newspapers. The larger cafés kept not only the local papers but dailies from all the capitals in Europe and women's journals too. On the whole, the middle class (to which most Jews belonged) invited only family and close friends to their homes, and managed the rest of their social life in cafés, under the watchful eye of the headwaiter, whose profession was somewhat of an art, requiring tact, intelligence, memory, wisdom, insight, and common sense. The waiters were regulars and required no prompting. They themselves said "The usual?" and brought the coffee, the strudel, the *Frankfurter Allgemeine Zeitung* to the individual in question. Women had their café *jour,* the day of the week they devoted to meeting friends, exchanging recipes, complaining about maids, discussing children's illnesses, and trading addresses of seamstresses and furriers. Cardplayers, bohemians (with a small *b*), journalists, Czech authors, German nationalists, students, Zionists, all had their own café. Yekef was not one of Aschermann's professional cafégoers. He had neither the time nor the inclination, though he would drop in every now and again to chat with friends. He was never seen at restaurants, never found at parties, and as far as his friends knew, he had only one weakness: from time to time he would slip away from the office and disappear into the darkness of the Koruna or one of the many other cinemas in the neighborhood, to see a thriller or western.

Unlike in Berlin and in Vienna, there were not many enormously wealthy people among Prague's 36,000 Jews, apart from the Pečeks, the Rothschilds of Czechoslovakia. Descended from a Jew blessed with ten children, of the village of Pečky in southern Bohemia, the Pečeks kept their empire a family affair. From real-estate dealings and a coal agency the Peček brothers had built up a mighty kingdom of mines centered in the Sudetenland. But they also owned other concerns in various areas of industry spread across Europe, as well as a bank whose main branch was in a handsome building on Bredovska Street, in the heart of Prague. The Peček Palais, as it was called, was always the first stop for every Jewish fund-raising campaign, and it had a separate department that dealt only with donations. Most Prague Jews, however, were comfortably off middle class; though there were some poor Jews, mostly among the aged, the only Jewish beggars in Prague were to be found among transient Poles.

Observant Jews were relatively few in number; foremost among them was Dr. Salomon Lieben, a true humanitarian. He treated many patients without taking any fee and often gave them money for food, coal, or medicine too. Another noted religious Jew was Mordecai Jiří Langer, son of an assimilated family and brother to the Czechoslovakian national writer František Langer. Jiří Langer vanished one day, spent several years in the court of the Rabbi of Belz, and returned a hasid, garbed in the traditional hasidic long black coat, much to the surprise of all Prague's Jews. He tried to combine his two separate worlds—Prague and *hasidism*—in his book *The Nine Gates.*

Though German-speaking Jews in Czech Prague were a minority

within a minority, and a generation had already grown up who spoke Czech both at home and in school, German was still the dominant language of Zionism. From time to time Czech-speaking Zionists were treated to conventions in their own language, and *Židovské Zprávy* was published for their benefit, but in Prague's small Zionist world they were a minority. Since everyone knew German— even if it was that special brand of Geman with distant echoes of Bohemia's ghetto dialect—that was the language they used when talking to Edelstein.

5

BETWEEN PRAGUE
AND JERUSALEM

CZECHS CALLED PRAGUE *Matička* ("Little Mother"), and though Franz Kafka felt the sharp nails of a mother who clutched her victims unrelentingly, most of her citizens loved her as devoted sons. It was almost impossible to live in Prague and not love her. Again and again one walked along the banks of the Vltava and felt anew that telltale pang at the sight of the arched bridges, the palace, the Gothic cathedral of St. Vitus rising across the river. Prague was beautiful at every hour, in every season: wrapped in snow, like a chestnut vendor; surrounded by blossoms, like a spring bride. A city's beauty is measured by her secrets, and Prague's veil of mystery was everywhere: in the enchanting palaces of the nobility in the third district, in the vaulted passageways between houses, in the forgotten little squares, in the dwellings cleaving to churches, in the alchemists' street, with its toy houses adjoining the palace, in the old Jewish cemetery and the creviced tomb of the *Maharal*, Rabbi Judah Loew. Though the generation of Jews who had grown up in the republic knew of the *Maharal* only from the gentiles and Meyrink's story "The Golem"; though they had never heard of David Ganz or Yehezkiel Landau, or known the splendor that had adhered to Prague's old Jewish community when it was the largest in

Europe, they still took pride in being natives of Prague: the designation still ranked with quality.

Only the very wealthy owned cars. Lesser mortals took taxis only when the route they were traveling demanded it: to the train station, when laden with luggage for summer vacation; to the hospital; to the cemetery. At other times they relied on the two red and white coaches of the streetcar, which rode along rails in the cobbled street with sparks shooting out of the electric wires above and a bell that could be heard in the distance. But for the most part, people walked. A half-hour walk was not unreasonable, especially when there was pleasure to be found all around: the sight of shop windows, the fragrance of coffee, the smell of new fabrics, the pungent odor of beer; maids walking dogs, village women selling pickles out of a barrel or flowers in springtime and fresh vegetables in early summer. Some, like Yekef, actually preferred to travel on foot, as he told Dov Itzkowitz, a teacher at the Munkács Hebrew school, when they walked along the river from the center of town to Podoly: the streetcar made him ill.

Heavy floods and severe unemployment sometimes made the situation of the Jews in Carpathian Russia even worse than that of the German refugees, which was why the Palestine committee applied for a special allotment of two hundred immigration certificates on their behalf. When, in 1934, news finally came from Jerusalem that the certificates would be granted, Edelstein reported great rejoicing, and even non-Zionist organizations were prepared to help. Most of the immigrants were penniless and could not afford the journey to Palestine, and in those days the Jewish Agency did not pay one's fare. In fact, it even extracted a levy of two and a half pounds from newcomers for making arrangements. "Immigration is not just a sacrifice," wrote Werner Senator in response to a request that the tax be canceled for pioneers from Carpathian Russia. "It is also an opportunity for young people to begin a new life." With notable modesty, Edelstein announced that a committee had been established in Prague to help the Jews of Carpathian Russia, comprised of prominent Czechoslovakian Jews—Josef Popper, Hannah Steiner, Maria Schmolka, and Jakob Edelstein, secretary of the Palestine office. Within a year of taking over the office Edelstein held a key position in Prague's (small) Zionist world, primarily the result of his work on behalf of German refugees.

Two hundred and fifty German refugees emigrated to Palestine in one year—so many compared with previous years, so few compared with what was needed. Every Monday evening, when the express train left Prague for Trieste, the same scene was enacted at the Wilson railway station. Hundreds of Jews, mostly young people, gathered on the platform to take leave of the pioneers and tourists bound for Trieste, where they would transfer to a boat for Palestine. The emigrants, in leather coats or rainwear, some with women and children, their faces radiant, words of farewell or Hebrew songs on their lips, horas danced near the waiting train—the Czech travelers gazed in some bewilderment on what appeared to be the sacred rites of some primitive tribe. Yekef escorted every group to the station, and as the train pulled out, those left behind burst into song: "Tehezekna" and "Hatikvah."

Women emigrants were not allocated separate certificates but were tacked on to the men. As a result, Edelstein conceived the brilliant idea of explaining to the British Consul in Prague that in Palestine marriages were performed according to Jewish law, and religious ceremonies were therefore sufficient for immigration purposes. The consul was convinced, which meant that every male with an immigration certificate could take with him a woman he had married by religious ceremony. At first the ceremonies were actually performed, but Haim Hoffman quickly realized that this was superfluous. He ordered several hundred marriage certificates from a Jewish printer, filled them out, signed them, procured the signature of an additional witness, and had a Zionist rabbi from a small Bohemian community, Rabbi Saager, attest on the reverse side that the two parties had entered into a marriage contract according to the law of Moses and Israel.

Prague soon became the wedding center for potential immigrants, but not for long. In the middle of 1934, the Jewish Agency's immigration department in Haifa complained that a nineteen-year-old German refugee, called Sigmund Garfunkel, had brought as his wife a forty-two-year-old Czech woman, Margaret Yaakobson. The couple's only marriage certificate was a religious document issued by a Czech rabbi, and it was with the greatest of difficulty that an investigation by the British authorities had been averted. Edelstein confessed that the match was somewhat surprising, but more surprising still was the outcry raised by the Jewish Agency: since German refugee immigration certificates were issued to men only, women could not emigrate unless they were married. Moreover, most of the refugees had no documents at all, including Polish pioneers who had fled to avoid conscription into the Polish army, and to be officially married by civil law, one had to produce documents from one's previous place of residence. These were unobtainable, and therefore there was no choice but to rely on religious ceremonies. Edelstein hoped that he had clarified the matter to the satisfaction of all, but Jerusalem felt otherwise: "Your reply is irrelevant," they wrote. "The groom is 19, the bride is 42 and from Czechoslovakia."

More care was taken to match the couple's ages, and the system continued to work until Hehalutz in Poland decided to try the same thing. The British Consul in Warsaw was less trusting than his Prague counterpart. He referred the matter to London and from there, through the consul in Prague, Edelstein received the ill tidings: there would be no more weddings without proper registration. But his troubles were not over yet. The honorable rabbis in Jerusalem wanted to know if the couples who had been ostensibly married by Jewish law would require a divorce by Jewish law, and on this point Edelstein could set their minds at rest: there could be no problem as no ceremony had in fact been performed; the couples had merely been issued a certificate, and the Prague marriages were therefore invalid under both civil and religious law.

Alongside the system of "instant certificates" operated the infallible system of bribes and connections. Edelstein put Shimon Ornstein, who was in charge of finance and immigration, in touch with the marriage registrar in Teplitz-Schönau. Without troubling the happy couple to appear before him, and on the basis of written data submitted to him, the clerk issued official documents for a modest "per unit" reward. A similar arrangement operated in Slovakia. Ornstein himself matched the couples and saw no reason to ask for their consent. Before they emigrated, he simply notified the bearer of the immigration certificate that he would meet his wife in Trieste, and gave him her name. Amazingly enough, some of these casual marriages actually endured and became lifelong partnerships. Others, however, were a source of bitter conflict: objections often came from the brides' families, from mothers who had dreamt of an entirely different sort of wedding for their daughters, with bridal gowns, and bouquets of flowers; and sometimes from the bride herself who, upon emigrating, suddenly found that she did not want to be put asunder from her heart's desire.

There was some justice in Haim Barlas's claim that the fake marriages had resulted in the Mandate government's decision to

issue separate immigration certificates for single men, single wom-
en, and family men. "We lay the blame for this harsh decree on those
offices which did not put a stop to such practices," he wrote to
Prague. In order to remove all suspicion, the matchmakers—Edelstein, Hoffman, and Rabbi Saager—stressed that it had all been
done without reward and with the best of intentions. But Jerusalem
was not quick to forgive. It was not a question of accepting money,
wrote Dr. Senator: we vigorously oppose arrangements of this nature, which lead only to undesirable consequences and tragic situations.

The problem had also a moral-ideological aspect, which was what
aroused Ada Maimon, one of the first women to campaign for
sexual equality in Palestine. She felt that the very fact that women
were denied all possibility of entering Palestine unless they were
someone's fiancée, wife, or daughter only exacerbated their sense of
inferiority; it was hardly any wonder that they saw themselves as
second-class citizens. Ada, the daughter of a rabbinical family,
found on a visit to Czechoslovakia that every kind of Jew, including
the orthodox, took part in the fictitious marriages. She considered
these a source of "dishonest dealing and indescribable demoraliza-
tion. As a rule," she wrote, "no young woman doing pioneer training
in Czechoslovakia is without a man at her side. The [immigration]
certificate serves as matchmaker and encourages free love." At a
combined meeting of the Hehalutz leaders and the director of the
Palestine office, Ada raised the question of "sex for certificates."
One of the young men tried to play down the matter, saying that the
girls weren't raped—they agreed willingly. But the joke fell flat with
Ada. She was deeply offended, and all Yekef's efforts to patch things
up proved ineffective. She left Czechoslovakia with a poor impression of the pioneer groups, the education they received while training, and the morality of the girls. "The hunger to emigrate and
increase the number of immigrants should not make us lose our
senses." The solution, she felt, was to issue an equal number of
certificates to male and female pioneers, even if this meant a de-
crease in the overall number of immigrants.

As if there were not enough Zionists contending for certificates,
non-Zionists also came along and demanded investor's certificates.
Yekef disapproved: these people were not interested in immigration, but in transferring their wealth. "In our view, Palestine can't
benefit from the influx of non-Zionists and anti-Zionists, people

who, as is well known, would invest their money in other countries if they were assured of the same interest rates." He brought the matter before the Palestine committee, who, however, felt it too complex for their jurisdiction and referred it to the ultimate authority: the Jewish Agency in Jerusalem. What does one do with a man who comes to the Palestine office in Prague and openly declares that he has never been, and never intends to be, a Zionist, and nonetheless requests an investor's certificate? Edelstein concluded that the candid Mr. Beneš was not a desirable immigrant and rejected his application. Whereupon Mr. Beneš applied directly to the British embassy in Prague. In a highly confidential letter, Edelstein asked the Jewish Agency to act in the interests of the Zionist movement and see that the authority of the Palestine office was not impaired. But Jerusalem was more pragmatic: it was hardly realistic to expect the British consulate to support a rejection on Zionist grounds. Itzhak Greenbaum, of the Agency executive, demanded that more care be taken in future to avert direct appeals to the British.

Jerusalem's word was law, and often it was exceedingly difficult to get her to modify her position, as the question of transportation routes showed. The Jewish Agency worked with the Lloyd Triestino shipping lines, which meant that Czechoslovakian immigrants were first sent by train to Trieste and from there, by boat, to Palestine. Sometimes the Palestine office in Prague neglected to give sufficient notice of a group's arrival, and when the immigrants got to Trieste, they found the pioneer hostel already filled with immigrants from other countries. Nor did the Zionist budget run to putting people up in hotels. For immigrants from the western part of the republic, the journey through Trieste was an added inconvenience. Had they sailed from Rumania or Greece, the trip would have been shorter, and far less costly. Again and again Edelstein returned to this same point: with a group of thirty-five immigrants and their families, a sum of fifty thousand crowns could be saved. Was Jerusalem indifferent?

Jerusalem was firm: the decision about exit ports to Palestine was based on the contracts the Jewish Agency had with shipping companies. Edelstein felt that this was quite wrong: how could the difference between 1,300 and 1,700 crowns per person be a matter of no consequence?

God resides in Jerusalem and all who dwell there partake of His authority. There was no doubt as to the nature of the relationship:

like obedient children, the Palestine office in Prague asked for guidelines and advice, and with the knowledge invested in it, Jerusalem responded accordingly.

Toward the spring general elections of 1935, the Jewish National Party again faced the problem of meeting the necessary quota of popular votes (which had meanwhile been raised) to gain seats in Parliament. Influenced by the German mood, the Polish minority, which had been the Jewish National Party's partner in the last election, had become more demanding, and a new partner had to be found. This time an election alliance was formed with the Social Democratic Party and earned much opposition from the Jewish public. Opponents of socialism were clearly against the alliance, while Jewish nationalists thought it a disgrace that the Social Democratic platform said not a word about Jews. In protest, Dr. Margulies resigned from his position as chairman of the Jewish Party, and Poalei Zion, angered by the fact that Czechoslovakia's Social Democrats had entered into an alliance with the bourgeoisie, called on its members to vote for other socialist lists. Nevertheless, as agreed, the Jewish Party was awarded two seats in parliament, filled this time by Angelo Goldstein, a Czech advocate who represented Jews in the Crown Lands, and Haim Kugel, who represented Jews in eastern Czechoslovakia. The Socialist Zionists now had their own man, and Edelstein a friend, in parliament.

The Jews had their wars and the Germans their victories. In the general elections of April 1935, Konrad Henlein's Sudetendeutschen Party won more seats than any other, and entered parliament with forty-one members, including Karl Hermann Frank, Henlein's deputy. Henlein, a gymnastics teacher who had been raised in the romanticism of the German Wandervogel groups, was intelligent, had polished manners, and knew how to charm the British when, after his victory, he went to London to describe the oppression under which Sudeten Germans lived. Frank, on the other hand, was a primitive, half-educated son of a family that supported Georg von Schönerer, one of Hitler's ideological fathers and the inspiration for his *Volk* cult. He owned a Nazi propaganda shop in a small town in northern Bohemia, and was a raging demagogue. But now there was no longer any need for restraint: the Sudeten Germans were free to rally around the SdP banner of "national self-determination."

Two thirds of the Jewish people now lived under dictatorial regimes, denied all possibility of self-determination and self-defense. What they experienced was reminiscent of the darkest days in Jewish history, the Crusades and the Inquisition—with one essential difference, however: now there was a Zionist movement, as David Ben-Gurion proclaimed at the nineteenth Zionist Congress, which opened in Lucerne in August 1935. Annual immigration figures had reached the fifty-thousand mark, the number of Jews in Palestine was 350,000, or 27 percent of the overall population, and Zionism seemed almost strong enough to counter Jewish suffering. A sense of strength, heightened by the feverish pace of congress activity, made it easy to forget two essential facts: how few Jews actually were Zionists, and how much Jewry as a whole depended on the gentiles.

In December 1935, due to failing health, President Masaryk resigned from his post. "With the help of God I'll continue to watch over you a while longer, and see how you do," he told his people before he left the Hradčany Castle and retired to his country home in Lany. He still carried himself erect, though he was frailer, more transparent. There was no doubt as to his successor: it was Dr. Eduard Beneš, who had held the post of foreign minister since the founding of the republic. Beneš, a short man with a small mustache and a heavy Czech accent whatever language he was speaking, had been Masaryk's right-hand man since the Versailles Peace Conference and held a senior position at the League of Nations. But Beneš was not Masaryk—not in stature, character, or outlook. He was a professional diplomat, sober, dry, pragmatic, analytical, totally lacking in Masaryk's personal charm and ability to inspire unquestioning trust. Nevertheless, it was clear that politically the fifty-four-year-old Beneš would continue along Masaryk's democratic road, and no far-reaching changes would take place.

After a period of relative quiet, the Nuremberg laws in defense of German blood and honor came into effect in September 1935, and brought with them a new wave of Jewish refugees. Up till then, refugees had still traveled in the opposite direction: thousands who had fled to western Europe for nonpolitical reasons had found neither a permanent sanctuary nor a means of livelihood, neither encouragement nor sympathy, and had returned to Germany in the hope that there they could make a living—if not in business and the free professions, as in the past, then at least in productive trades. And they would be in their homeland, where their roots were. After all, Western statesmen also believed Hitler when, in May 1935, in an address to the Reichstag, he said clearly and in several ways that Germany needed and wanted peace; that she recognized Poland as the homeland of a great and nationally conscious people; that she neither wished nor intended to annex Austria; that she had solemnly recognized France's borders, and given her pledge, and relinquished all claims on Alsace-Lorraine. It is little wonder that the *Times* of London found Hitler's speech reasonable, sincere, balanced.

Among the new refugees who came to Prague following the Nuremberg laws (which were aimed primarily at purging the reconstructed German army once Hitler had declared the Versailles Treaty invalid) was a twenty-year-old gymnastics teacher named Fredy Hirsch. Tall, handsome, erect, Fredy had a German air about him. He wore a short leather coat and black boots, always looked presentable, and loved discipline—only his face betrayed his Jewishness. Fredy took charge of physical education in the youth movements, which had been somewhat neglected, and was admired for his athletic prowess. But the leaders of Hehalutz and Maccabi Hatzair (to which he belonged) treated him somewhat patronizingly: he was no intellectual.

Though Czechoslovakia was still a safe haven in a sea of intolerance, there too the question of Jewish survival became more difficult. Gone were the days when businesses were passed down from father to son and continuity seemed certain. Now one had to think carefully about choosing a profession, rather than turn automatically to commerce or clerical jobs. An institute for vocational guidance was set up in Prague, aimed chiefly at stemming the flow of young Jews from Carpathian Russia into western Czechoslovakia by training them for skilled jobs where they lived. This internal westward migration of Carpathian Jews, seeking work in the cities as unskilled laborers, peddlers, or even professional beggars at barmitzvah celebrations and weddings, worried the local Jews; they did not want "foreign Jewish elements in the image and way of life of Bohemian Jewry" descending on them. Czech Jews made no attempt to hide their distaste for the observant Jews, while as far as the Zionists were concerned the problem was economic: Carpathian Jews belonged to the lowest social stratum and only aggravated the problem of aid in Bohemia and Moravia. Therefore, according to the tested Zionist formula, stress was laid first and foremost on productivity and vocational training. In time the "Joint" (the combined American Jewish welfare organization, established by affluent American Jews after the First World War) also entered the picture, and Maria Schmolka, Hannah Steiner, and Jakob Edelstein negotiated with them over the question of occupational training for Czechoslovakian youngsters.

At a meeting of the Palestine committee on July 30, 1936, Edelstein reported on his last tour of the training divisions. In general the situation had improved: there was almost no unemployment (there had been times when 30 percent worked in services, 10 percent in agriculture, and the rest at anything that came to hand, mainly construction). Sanitary conditions were also better, some progress had been made in the cultural sphere, and the chief problem was social life (collective living was something one had to learn the hard way). It had become clear to Edelstein during his tour that all the movements had exaggerated the number of members they had in training in order to gain more certificates, and the small pioneering organizations had no faith in his neutrality, due to his close affiliation with the main Hehalutz organization. Perhaps a salaried clerk should be engaged to supervise the matter.

This suggestion was vigorously rejected by Werner Senator, one of the "non-Zionists" on the Jewish Agency Executive and head of the immigration department, who was in Prague at the time, and who asserted that no one could doubt Mr. Edelstein's impartiality. Like most visitors of German origin, Senator was impressed by Edelstein, as was Kurt Blumenfeld, the former president of the Zionist Federation in Germany, a distinguished intellectual of the German school who had emigrated to Palestine at the start of the Nazi regime and joined the directorate of the Jewish Foundation Fund in Jerusalem. The two men met when Blumenfeld came to Czechoslovakia to raise funds, and formed close ties while traveling through the country together, despite their twenty-year age difference. One of the things they discussed was the possibility of Edelstein's coming to Palestine, where he could do publicity work among the younger generation on behalf of the Jewish Foundation Fund.

March 7, 1936, President Masaryk's birthday, was a national holiday. As always on that day, the republic's red, white, and blue flags swayed in the wind and the president's favorite song was sung at festive gatherings: "My son, my son, have you yet ploughed?" Brass bands played in city squares and public parks, and, as on all Czech holidays, beer flowed freely. The entry of German forces into the Rhineland may have inflamed international observers, but to merry-making Czechs the matter seemed very far away. However, France, with her hundred divisions, was unwilling to act against three German regiments in the Rhineland, a zone demilitarized by the Treaty of Versailles. And Britain was unwilling to help France should she become embroiled in war. It became patently clear to Beneš, a known Francophile, that if France was not prepared to fight German aggression so close to her own borders, she was hardly likely to take up arms for Czechoslovakia, despite the defense pact between them. After all, there were hundreds of miles of German territory between them. From now on Czechoslovakia would have to rely on her own efforts to protect her own borders. The world could not be counted on. Even the League of Nations, which Beneš had helped found and had always supported faithfully, had failed miserably in its handling of Italian aggression in Abyssinia. In a frenzy of activity, Czechoslovakia began fortifying her border with Germany.

In the spring of 1936, the question came up of Jewish participation in Berlin's summer Olympics. Maccabi and Hakoah (which included some of Czechoslovakia's top swimmers) in the end decided not to take part: the Olympics would only strengthen Hitler's position in the world. But the Jewish Czechs favored the inclusion of Jewish athletes in Czechoslovakia's delegation: their religion was irrelevant. Jews in Czechoslovakia had been a legally recognized minority since the establishment of the republic, and as a result, conflicts between Zionists and assimilated Jews had gradually weakened. Nevertheless, from time to time, feeling still ran high, as when a group of Jewish Czechs sued Ostrava's Jewish community for using its own funds toward the maintenance of a Jewish school. Since they felt that Judaism was only a religion, and since the community was responsible only for religious matters, it had no business interfering in education and welfare, which were clearly state affairs.

In light of the world situation, Edelstein called for a united Jewish front, and this was his position also when it came to relations between Jewish Czechs and Zionists. He felt that the arguments put forth by Jewish Czechs—that membership in the Zionist movement detracted from loyalty to the republic—were no longer relevant. Surprisingly enough, to support his position, he quoted Léon Blum, the French socialist leader and then premier, who had spoken out in favor of the World Jewish Congress which was to convene in Geneva that year. Blum had written that though he felt himself completely French and nothing in French culture was alien to him, he was at the same time also Jewish. He had never experienced anti-Semitism, he said, because he had never alienated himself from Judaism. And while in France Jews lived in peace and well-being, in other countries millions of Jews suffered from discrimination, and Zionism must therefore be supported. Just so in Czechoslovakia, said Edelstein. It is because we defend our Jewish interests that we have gained the respect of the Czechs. They too have known protracted struggles for national independence.

Edelstein appealed to Jewish Czechs to take part in the first World Jewish Congress that was to represent all Jewish bodies, organizations, and institutions: even if it should fail to come up with a practical solution to Jewish suffering, the congress was a necessary show of solidarity. Jewish Czechs could not remain indifferent to Jewish suffering. If they only considered how many wretched Jews from eastern Czechoslovakia had found a living in Palestine, and how much money had been sent back to poverty-stricken parents in Carpathian Russia, they would lend a hand to acquiring land in Palestine and not look on as bystanders. Edelstein's appeal gave rise to debate in the pages of the *Rozvoj*, the official organ of the Jewish Czechs. The newspaper rejected Edelstein's arguments and in particular his analogy to Blum: in their view he was totally rooted in French culture and as loyal to his homeland as they were to theirs. The poem by Siegfried Kapper, the first Czech Jewish poet, was still a true reflection of their feelings:

> Only don't call me "non-Czech."
> Like you I belong to this land,
> Just as your hearts beat for the homeland,
> So does mine burn with devotion.

In early summer of 1936, the Jewish Party called on all Jews to buy the defense bonds issued to fortify Czechoslovakia's borders and build up the army in face of rising German aggression. The Jewish public and organizations responded generously, took part in civil-defense courses, learned antiaircraft drill and first aid. They showed that they identified with what the republic stood for and were prepared to defend their democratic country, together with all its citizens, anywhere, anyhow.

6

A TWO-WAY TICKET

BY MID-1936 there was a respite in the violent disturbances in Palestine (in which almost one hundred Jews had been killed), the Arab general strike came to an end, and the Peel Commission, appointed in July 1936 to get at the root of the problem, started its hearings. It seemed a good time for the directors of the Palestine offices to convene in Jerusalem to discuss immigration, since for fear of British censorship and the watchfulness of various European countries, correspondence was hampered. About a dozen European directors participated, and the deliberations lasted a few days; Jakob Edelstein's first visit to Palestine was a brief one. Between sessions he toured Old Jerusalem, met friends and acquaintances, and on the eve of his departure wrote to Arieh Ofir at Kibbutz Afikim: "My impression is that the plan concerning my work will perhaps materialize. God willing, I shall sail back on October 13, on the *Jerusalem*." For some time, Yekef had been wrestling with the decision of whether or not to emigrate to Palestine himself. It was agreed that he would leave in the spring of 1937 and, initially, organize and coordinate the activities of the Foundation Fund among young people. After his return to Prague, however, he took some time to reach a decision. At the beginning of January he was still not sure, but when he finally made up his mind to emigrate in the early spring—for the time being alone, until he could settle affairs in Palestine—there was no longer any holding him back: his excitement exceeded all reason. His decision was not popular with the Zionists at home, since from their point of view, Edelstein was needed in Prague, not in Palestine. Yehuda Rezniczenko was sailing on May 12 as a special emissary to Prague to deal solely with party affairs. It was unthinkable that now, of all times, when the Czechoslovakian members had finally persuaded the united party in Palestine to dispatch such an emissary (after much effort and negotiation), with all the preparations for Congress coming up, Comrade Edelstein would abandon his post. "We urge you to postpone your trip to Palestine for a few months, because it jeopardizes all our efforts to help the party in Czechoslovakia."

Yekef refused. Nobody really knew whether his trip was immigration, preparation for immigration, or a lengthy visit. When Rezniczenko, a member of Kibbutz Givat-Haim who had served twice as an emissary to Czechoslovakia and was well acquainted with affairs there, reached Prague, Edelstein was already in Galicia, taking leave of his parents. In June 1937, he arrived in Palestine, full of enthusiasm and raring for action on behalf of the Foundation Fund.

Edelstein threw himself into his work with drive and energy and soon succeeded in alienating various staff members with what they saw as his aggressive methods. In his fluent Hebrew, he told them that not enough was being done to harness young people's potential. He would coordinate, he would activate, he would mobilize Palestinian youth on behalf of the youth in the Diaspora, for a mammoth rescue operation was necessary. Every day he brought in new plans and innovative suggestions and demanded their implementation. He paid no attention to reality, and reality paid no attention to him. He had no office, but worked in a corner of the boardroom; no secretary, let alone the two he had asked for; and no budget. The £1,000 required to begin had not yet been granted, for Eliezer Kaplan, treasurer of the Jewish Agency, had not yet approved the establishment of the new department.

Edelstein traveled throughout Palestine to meet young people, and the reality he encountered was very different from what he had imagined. The youth of Palestine were busy with defense, with armed struggle; as far as they were concerned, youth in the Diaspora lived beyond the mountains of darkness. Some of the surprise he felt was evident in the article he wrote after meeting representatives of the thirteen youth movements at a convention in Jerusalem in July 1937. "It was interesting to hear what the younger generation has to say about the present political situation. At first it was impossible to escape dissatisfaction with the fact that the convention did not speak of politics at all, or of the question of partition. Is our youth unfamiliar with these problems? Only later did it become clear that in their eyes they did not exist, for they were firmly resolved to continue along their course, ignoring political decisions, and taking up arms against anyone who tried to reduce the living space of the Jewish people."

The convention decided to establish a central information office to represent the youth movements, the Funds, and the propaganda department of the Zionist Executive. With budgets from these three bodies, Edelstein, who saw himself director of the center-to-be, hoped to deepen the educational activities among youth and, through modern propaganda methods, build a newer, fresher, and younger Zionist Organization. "Will the delegates to Congress understand the call of our youth who are the most vital part of the Zionist movement? Will they understand that the work with youth and information is not a deviation from important current political issues but, on the contrary, the proper complement to political decisions and the practical response to political demands?" The answer to this rhetorical question was given neither in deeds nor in words, but in the total absence of interest in his plans. Which of the very important people on the Zionist Executive, at the height of debate on the partition of Palestine following the report of the Peel Commission, even paid attention to a new immigrant or temporary resident from Czechoslovakia who still thought first and foremost of youth in the Diaspora? In believing emigration to mean sure advancement in the Zionist hierarchy, Edelstein had made a common error. He had not realized that as a new immigrant one was helpless, defenseless, vulnerable, dependent on others; one had to start afresh, as though all the commendable Zionist work in the Diaspora had never been.

Because Edelstein himself was not a pioneer, he remained an outsider. He had made a fundamental error in emigrating as an official, a functionary, when the prevailing spirit of the Labor Movement in Palestine ruled otherwise: a man must first prove himself capable of physical labor. Indeed, Itzhak Fenniger, the Hehalutz emissary to Prague from 1935 to 1936, had urged Edelstein to go to kibbutz for at least six months or a year, even if he was not suited to physical labor: it would enhance his personal standing. The members of the collective agricultural settlements, who played a decisive role in the Labor Movement, were disparaging of those "spoiled" few functionaries who came to Palestine and immediately filled official posts. In the eyes of the Labor Movement, physical work was a kind of entrance test. But Edelstein interpreted this coolness toward him as an abandonment in this difficult period of adjustment by the members and emissaries and guests who had been so friendly in Prague when they had come to him at the Palestine office.

The times themselves were difficult. On July 11, 1937, the Peel Commission published its findings and recommended the partition of Palestine between Jews and Arabs. The Jews were to receive one sixth of the territory of Palestine and Jerusalem was to remain under British rule. The Jewish community in Palestine and the entire Zionist movement were in the throes of a raging controversy: partition, yes or no? All eyes focused on the twentieth Zionist Congress with mounting anticipation and anxiety, reminiscent of the crucial days of the Uganda affair, when Zionism had been divided between those who were prepared to accept, and those who rejected, the British offer of a Jewish homeland in British East Africa. Now, too, the camps were split: whether to hold out for more and reject partition outright, or to seize the present opportunity, which would at least enable the immigration of hundreds of thousands of Jews, permit the struggle for the extension of partition borders to continue, and lay the foundations of the future Jewish state. Edelstein, like Chaim Weizmann, president of the World Zionist Federation, David Ben-Gurion, general secretary of the Labor Federation, and most of Central European Jewry, was prepared to accept partition. As far as he was concerned, the report of the Peel Commission allowed for only two alternatives: a tiny Jewish state, or the continuation of the Mandate government and all it presaged: maximum restrictions on immigration, a ban on selling land to Jews, and the establishment of an Arab agency to counter the Jewish Agency, with the entire Arab world, not just the Palestinian Arabs, ranged against the Jewish people. This could only mean an overwhelming victory for the Arab terrorists, who would be spurred on by the decisions of the Mandate government to further rioting. The continuation of restricted immigration meant the end of all possible succor for the world's persecuted Jews. A Zionist movement incapable of providing a practical solution to Jewish suffering could not hope to gain the sustained support of the Jewish people or lead them in the struggle. Feelings of despair, weakness, and helplessness in the face of a future with no exit would take their toll.

Zionism, which in recent years had become the center of Jewish life in the Diaspora and justifiably sought to lead the nation, would be defeated.

The atmosphere at the twentieth Zionist Congress, which opened in Zurich in September 1937, was heavy. Menachem Ussishkin, head of the Jewish National Fund, rejected partition and Weizmann pressed for it. Supporters of the plan were aware of the minute proportions of the proposed Jewish state, but they felt that the fate of the entire Jewish people hung in the air. Weizmann voiced his anxiety over the fate of European Jewry by repeating what he had said in his two-hour address before the Peel Commission: "There are in this part of the world six million people doomed to be pent up in places where they are not wanted and for whom the world is divided into places where they cannot live and places which they cannot enter."

Edelstein left Palestine quietly to participate in the congress, and told Dov Biegun, one of the few people with whom he discussed his stay in Palestine: "It's interesting: immigration is the crowning glory, the realization of all one's dreams and longing, but when you get to Palestine, you're no more than a fifth wheel, and nobody is interested in you."

The Foundation Fund in Jerusalem assumed that Edelstein would return at the end of Congress: three months was hardly long enough to decide that immigration was a mistake. When there was nowhere to return to, one could overcome all difficulties, all the pangs of absorption. But Edelstein did have somewhere to return to—after all, Miriam and six-year-old Arieh were still at home in Bilkova Street—and, indeed, pressure for his return had mounted. He was needed in Prague, in the Palestine office, in the party, in the Zionist Organization, in Hehalutz: he would remain a while, and then set out for Palestine again. Hallelujah! Comrade Edelstein advised that he would return to Prague on approximately October 20, and stay at least until March 1938.

In these last days of 1937, a Fascist and extremely anti-Semitic government was set up in Rumania under Octavian Goga. This development, in a country that had been allied with Czechoslovakia and Yugoslavia in the "Little Entente," caused serious concern among Czechoslovakian Jews who followed current events. They feared that it might influence the mood in Czechoslovakia even more than events in Germany. In Czechoslovakia the persecution of

German Jews had aroused a wave of protest, sympathy, and desire to help, thanks in no small degree to traditional Czech hatred for the Germans. But Rumania was a friendly country, and the republic's younger generation had been raised with the idea of Czech-Rumanian-Yugoslavian fellowship.

Goga, under the slogan "Rumania for Rumanians," immediately restricted Jewish economic and civil rights, and, in a private conversation with a visiting friend from France, even raised the question of a solution to the Jewish problem in Eastern Europe: "Transfer them en masse to some uninhabited territory . . . some island they could not leave—Madagascar, for example." In Czechoslovakia, too, more voices spoke out in favor of emulating Goga's policies, particularly in the economic sphere, and it was feared that the Jews might constitute an obstacle to the traditionally friendly relations between the two countries. True to their convictions, the Jewish Czechs felt that the Rumanian developments should be regarded in light of Czech state interests, and Jewish origin must have no bearing on the matter. The political alliance with Rumania was more important than the Jewish problem.

As soon as Goga's government took over, the short border between Czechoslovakia and Rumania was closed to Jewish refugees who tried to flee the country there. When an outcry arose, chiefly from the Zionists, demanding that the Czech government open its gates to Jewish refugees from Rumania, reaction came from an unexpected quarter. Ferdinand Peroutka, one of Czechoslovakia's most prominent publicists and friend to Masaryk, Beneš, and Karel Čapek, published an article called "Notes on the Czech People and the Jews" in his weekly journal, *Přítomnost*. Peroutka claimed that the lack of anti-Semitism in Czechoslovakia was not to be attributed to enlightened leadership but to the fact that the role played by Jews in public and economic life was not of unreasonable proportions; any attempt to increase their numbers, however, would unleash a storm in this country as well. The Czechs could not save world humanism and must first of all look after themselves. Czechs, even liberals, were clearly beginning to turn their backs on Jews, although many of Peroutka's friends spoke out against him.

The signs increased, but few knew how to read them properly. Toward the beginning of 1938, the largest Czech political party, the Agrarians, published an article in its daily by party chairman Rudolf Beran suggesting that talks be opened between Czechoslovakia and Nazi Germany, hinting at the cancellation of the 1935 mutual defense agreement between Czechoslovakia and the U.S.S.R. and the coopting of Henlein to the government. Karol Sidor, the representative of the Slovakian Agrarian Party in Parliament, proposed to the foreign affairs committee that a body be appointed to deal with the transfer of Jews from Slovakia and Carpathian Russia to Birobidzan; in his view they were all communists anyway. Why were Slovakians compelled by economic circumstances to emigrate across the seas while the number of Jews—people who loved German and named their children after characters in Wagner's operas—rose?

The Jews sent delegations to people in key positions in the eastern part of the republic and were reassured. The governor of Carpathian Russia promised that he himself, on the strength of his authority, would stamp out any signs of hostility toward Jews. Even Jan Ivak, the representative of the Slovakian Fascist Party, had only friendly advice: "No one means to persecute Jews or lead a campaign against them. All one asks is that they adapt to present circumstances," he said during a debate in parliament on the suggestion that the Jewish communities be reorganized. "After all, Jews still believe in the Talmud, and it teaches them to consider only their own."

It was a far cry from Thomas Masaryk's words to Karel Čapek: "He who has Jesus in his heart cannot be an anti-Semite." But Masaryk already lay in the simple rural grave at Lany and many of the republic's citizens, Jews among them, felt orphaned. When, on September 14, 1937, following ten days of his increasing decline, news spread of Masaryk's death, men wept unabashedly in the streets while teachers with tears in their eyes told their pupils that *tatíček* Masaryk was gone. Hundreds of thousands of people waited for hours at the Hradćany Castle, where Masaryk's body lay in state, to pay their respects—not out of obligation, but out of an inner need to express their grief. With Masaryk died the faith in democracy as a moral necessity.

The political situation was tense. In October 1937, the authorities banned political meetings and the Jewish Party had to postpone its national convention, planned for the end of that month. Edelstein's first lecture after returning from Palestine was also canceled because of the general ban, but he returned to work full of energy, much to the relief of all the bodies, committees, organizations, and funds in which he had been active. He again left for a tour of the

74

training camps, again devoted himself to fund-raising. The Zionist funds ran a campaign in November that year and Czechoslovakian Jews were asked to "give, and give generously, for tomorrow might be too late." ("Late," in this case, meant for the purchase of land by Jews in Palestine. In Czechoslovakia, there seemed to be no need for haste.)

Nineteen thirty-seven drew to a close. What a year it had been! The annual survey by Dr. Lichtwitz, editor of *Die Selbstwehr*, was gloomy: violent disturbances had again erupted in Palestine; in Poland, pressure was being exerted for a million Jews to emigrate; in Rumania, in Hungary, in Lithuania, Jews were pressed to leave; and from the other side of the world, from North and South America, from Australia, everywhere the response to the plight of the Jews was the same: what a pity we have no room for them.

A cloud hung over everything. When the Hebrew repertory company Habima negotiated a tour in Czechoslovakia in the fall of 1937, two large theaters in Prague were prepared to stage performances. Habima itself was hesitant, however, since Hebrew theater in Czechoslovakia was unlikely to attract large audiences. But after their trips to Warsaw and Bucharest were both canceled the company renewed its request to come to Czechoslovakia at the beginning of 1938. The Prague theaters had meanwhile backed down for fear that the mob would break their windows; many Jews, too, were apprehensive that Habima's appearance would arouse Czech hostility. Nevertheless the company came to Prague in January and performed *Uriel DaCosta* and *The Dybbuk* at the Free Theater to enthusiastic audiences.

The twelfth National Convention of the Zionist movement in Czechoslovakia was held at the beginning of March 1938 and as always, Edelstein was among the delegates, the speakers, the mediators. In his opening speech, Rufeisen tried to show that the loyalty of the Zionists to the republic in no way fell short of the loyalty of the Jewish Czechs. He argued against assimilation and pointed out its futility: Hitler, after all, was returning the assimilated to the Jewish people, with three generations of interest. There was talk of the terrible eventualities that might be expected, but in general the atmosphere was optimistic: the Jewish people lived on, as evident too from the plan of action. It was noted with satisfaction that Hebrew schools had finally been recognized as state schools, and that a new youth center had been established. All that remained was to prepare textbooks on Jewish history and Hebrew language instruction, to build youth hostels in the big cities, and to set up youth clubs throughout the republic.

On the day the Convention published its cultural plans, Austria was united with Germany in the Anschluss.

7

IT CAN'T HAPPEN HERE

HITLER ENTERED Austria on March 12, 1938. Without firing a single shot, his troops moved forward in a victorious cavalcade and the Austrians welcomed them with open arms. For Czechs it was a nightmare: German forces now surrounded the republic on three sides in an ever tightening noose. All Europe held its breath: it seemed as if a mighty machine had begun to move and there was nobody to stop it. With the annexation of Austria, Czechs felt that Hitler was *ante portas*. Soon the Germans would resume their tour of conquest and war would be imminent—for there could be no doubt that the Czechs would defend their homeland until their dying breath. It was clear that Czechoslovakia would never relinquish the German border regions, whose citizens, out of a sense of strength, now demanded *Heim ins Reich* more vigorously—a return to the German Reich to which they had never belonged.

Austrian Jews suddenly found themselves the target of a storm of violence as Austrians tried in a few days to catch up on all the fun Germans had been having for five years. The laughing, spitting mobs taking cruel pleasure in seeing Jews on bent knees scrubbing sidewalks; the looting of Jewish shops; Jews being dragged out of homes, beaten to death on side streets, and swallowed up by jails and concentration camps; the eruption of consuming hatred which for years had lain hidden beneath hypocrisy; the ashen-faced refugees whose world had suddenly fallen apart—all made it frighteningly clear: this was what was to be expected in a country annexed to the Reich. As to the hundreds of daily Jewish suicides in Austria, the Reich's propaganda minister, Josef Goebbels, offered his own explanation: the general suicide rate had not risen, he said in his first address on Austrian soil; the only difference was that now it was Jews who were taking their own lives, rather than Germans (roaring applause from the huge crowds).

Three days after the annexation, Sturmbannführer Adolf Eichmann called together the leaders of the Zionist movement in its Palestine office, including the elderly Adolf Böhm, author of the book *The Zionist Movement,* and currently president of the Jewish National Fund in Austria. Tall, with an intelligent face and dashing appearance in his SS uniform and shiny black boots, Eichmann impressed the group, who were all, except for the frail Dr. Böhm, compelled to remain standing while he spoke. To their great surprise, he showed much knowledge of all aspects of the Zionist movement, quoted parts of Böhm's book, and sprinkled his talk with Hebrew words (not for nothing had he spent a year teaching himself Hebrew).

The Jewish leadership in Austria, including Dr. Desider Friedmann, chairman of Vienna's Jewish community, his assistant, Robert Stricker, and Dr. Josef Löwenherz, director of the community offices, were arrested on March 18 and taken to the Dachau concentration camp. At the end of March, Eichmann summoned six of the remaining community leaders, including Dr. Alois Ruttenberg, director of the Palestine office, to the Metropol Hotel, where temporary Gestapo headquarters had been installed. Eichmann made it clear that he meant to solve the Jewish question in Austria once and for all and purge Vienna and all Austria of Jews as quickly as possible. Böhm, pleading his age and failing health, turned down Eichmann's suggestion that he represent the community, and the task fell temporarily to Dr. Ruttenberg.

It was suddenly and clearly brought home to Czech Jews what fate awaited those with no land to call their own, and how utterly helpless they were in the face of hostility and indifference. One night, a month after the annexation, the SS rounded up all the Jews of Kittsee (one of the seven well-known Jewish communities of the Burgenland region in eastern Austria) and the neighboring village, and, without permitting them to take anything with them, led them to a tiny island in the Danube, near the shores of Czechoslovakia. The Czech border police found them the next morning, provided them with food, and brought them to Bratislava, capital of Slovakia, from where they were expelled to Hungary, from where they were deported back to Austria. The evacuees spent three days and three nights, exposed to the cold and the wind, in the no-man's-land between Austrian, Hungarian, and Czechoslovakian borders, while police from the three countries, equipped with bayonets, prevented the "invaders" from crossing into their territory.

Shocked by the fate of the Burgenland Jews, the Bratislava Jewish community found a stopgap solution: they hired a tugboat on which the sixty-eight refugees managed to reach the Hungarian banks of the Danube. The Hungarians, however, would not let the refugees set foot on Hungarian soil; permission to stay aboard the tugboat was limited and had to be renewed again and again by Jewish intercession. Direct appeals to the rest of the world to grant asylum to the refugees went unanswered, as did appeals to international refugee organizations. Maria Schmolka decided that Jews themselves must take the fate of their brethren into their own hands: "This terrible tragedy must end. Jewry can't admit to helplessness before the entire world, on top of all the humiliation it is being made to suffer now."

Maria Schmolka visited the tugboat in July and saw the conditions in which the refugees lived. When she returned to Prague, she worked out a detailed rescue plan together with Jakob Edelstein: four old people would be allowed to stay in Czechoslovakia; with the help of relatives, ten would be given entry visas to the United States; and twelve would receive immigration certificates as pioneers (more was impossible, Palestine notified, since it had at its disposal only thirteen until the present quota was filled). Four large families (twenty-seven people in all) would emigrate on investor's certificates if the requisite £4,000 could be raised. The rest—the old and the sick—would ask for asylum in Hungary. Maria Schmolka journeyed to Paris and London to enlist the help of the Joint, Czechoslovakia's Jews held a special campaign, and on August 10, four months after the Burgenland Jews had lost the ground beneath their feet, news came from Jerusalem that the visas were on their way.

"If, despite the heavy restrictions on immigration, despite the fact that the number of people who seek certificates is a thousand times greater than the number granted, despite the fact that the situation of the Jews is growing worse from day to day and in more and more

79

countries Jews find themselves helpless, if in these circumstances only Palestine could offer a home to the Burgenland Jews," then for Edelstein it reaffirmed his faith in Zionism, for it offered the paramount solution to the Jewish question. True, Zionists had never claimed to have the answer to every Jew's individual problem, but they had hoped to attain a level of political and economic independence whereby they themselves would be able to decide who required urgent help and to whom it should be extended. Indeed, the response of the Jewish Agency to the appeals made by Czechoslovakia's Zionists showed the extent to which these hopes had been realized. Edelstein arrived at this encouraging conclusion following the absorption of forty immigrants after efforts spread over more than four months.

Czech Zionists grumbled over the hysterical letters arriving from Palestine to the effect that the conquest of Czechoslovakia was imminent: Czechoslovakia stood strong, and even if she were to last no more than seven days in a war against Hitler, she would at least bring into the war the Western powers to crush the Germans. Perhaps it would be better if Hitler were assassinated outright, reflected one Palestinian, Itzhak Shimkin, an engineer who hailed from Odessa and owned an electric plant in Haifa. He took the matter up with the leaders of the Jewish community in Palestine. Ben-Gurion was opposed on principle to personal terror, and felt that one never knew: a worse Hitler might arise. Moshe Shertok, director of the political department of the Jewish Agency, felt that any attempt on Hitler's life would invite disaster on the Jews of Germany and jeopardize the transfer agreement on Jewish capital in return for German goods to Palestine. Shimkin contacted Erich Moller, a former Czechoslovakian and one of the owners of the Ata factory, who had a large and wealthy family in Czechoslovakia and Austria. The Moller family was prepared to help, but not without approval from the Zionist establishment. Shimkin, who hoped to use the opportunity of Hitler's victory cavalcade through Austria in which the Führer was to ride in an open car among thousands of people, waited in vain for approval and meanwhile the moment was lost. Since, according to all the signs, Czechoslovakia was to be Hitler's next target, Shimkin decided to relocate the assassination plan on Czech soil.

The loss of the Austrian market wreaked havoc on Czechoslovakia's economy. Another wave of refugees arrived, including many Czech citizens who had lived in Vienna and now frantically sought shelter with friends and relatives. They sat with bowed heads, these uninvited guests, and asked: what next?

No political acumen was necessary to know that Nazi sights were now set on Czechoslovakia. In fact, even before the Anschluss, Hitler had spoken of ten million Germans in two neighboring countries who had not yet achieved national freedom. Soon after Austria's annexation, Henlein went to Hitler for further instructions and was told to present his demands as soon as he felt the Czechs were ready to accept them. And though these instructions were not widely known, it was clear that something was brewing from the confident behavior of the members of the SdP.

At the end of April, Henlein's party convened a special meeting at Carlsbad to formulate their demands: recognition of the Sudeten German entity and its citizens' right to self-rule. The Czechs were prepared for considerable concessions, but not territorial ones, which would endanger their line of defense and therefore the very existence of the republic. Negotiations proceeded slowly; various formulations were drawn up and discarded. The Sudeten Germans were sure of themselves: all their dreams would come true within a few months.

In Sudeten towns, Germans already greeted one another openly with "*Heil Hitler!*" Maids in Jewish homes hung pictures of Henlein in their rooms, and the more loyal ones offered their employers friendly advice: "If I were you, I wouldn't stay here." Teplitz-Schönau became a Nazi town: at a meeting of the German Welfare Organization, in which Jews were also active, one of the members rose and said that henceforth only those who fully identified with National Socialism should perform administrative functions. "If so," the German Social Democrat mayor said, "I no longer have anything to do here," and he left the room together with Dr. Weihs, the town rabbi. Dr. Clary-Aldringen, the scion of Teplitz's old patrician family, said not a word in their favor but let the undesirables walk out. The Democratic camp started to disintegrate. The first Jews started to leave town, some, the wealthier ones, emigrated across the ocean, others moved farther inland, and from time to time moving vans could be seen outside Jewish homes being loaded with household possessions. But most of the Jews, especially the older ones, were determined to stay: out of love for their home, an attachment to their property, which was the fruit of so much labor, a sense of common responsibility, and because they were sure that they, who had been born here, would come to no harm, as their good German neighbors had so often promised. Many stayed from a sense of identification with the republic, so as not to weaken Czech resistance by leaving.

Nationalist fervor swept over the Jews, even those who spoke only broken Czech. Now was no time to talk of emigration to Palestine; now, when the Czechs were preparing to fight for their lives, how could the Jews run away? Their place was beside the stalwart Czechs. Following an appeal by the Czech government for a one-time donation to the defense fund, 150 million crowns were raised, and about half this sum came from Jews. The Zionists felt like all the other Jews: "The Czechs stand firm to defend themselves and their democratic government. It is unthinkable that we will be the first to leave. We must show that our destiny and the destiny of Czechoslovakian democracy are one and the same." Angelo Goldstein, the member of Parliament for the Jewish Party, went to see Beneš, who told him: "We are not afraid. We will defend both democracy and you." The Jews would gladly do anything asked of them for the security of the country, and they pledged their unconditional loyalty; they would never forget that the graves of their fathers had rested on Czech soil for over a thousand years, nor were they unmindful of the twenty happy years they had lived in the republic—such was the closing note at the conference of the Jewish Party held in May. Just as Czechs always said in days of oppression: "We were here before Austria and we will be here after Austria," so Goldstein now said on behalf of the Jews: "We were here before Hitler and we will be here after Hitler."

This was no time for internal Zionist politics, and the presidency of the United Socialist Party, members Reiss, Hoffman, and Edelstein, suggested that all forces unite to meet the coming municipal elections, scheduled for the end of May and beginning of June. Goldstein wanted to set up a central Jewish committee comprised of prominent figures, including the writer Max Brod, as well as representatives of the more moderate Czech Jews. But Hoffman and Edelstein refused to authorize any group of people who were not responsible to an electorate. "Today, only the Zionist movement has the right and authority to accept the nation's leadership," they claimed, a position supported by Rufeisen as chairman of the Czechoslovakian Zionist Organization. (Rufeisen had run into financial difficulties, to no small extent due to his Zionist activities; he had lost all his property, sent his wife and three children to Palestine, and was now preparing to join them, taking with him all his books and furniture.)

Hoffman and Edelstein proposed the establishment of a national Jewish organization, which would be authorized to negotiate with the Czechoslovakian government and all other elements on behalf of the Jewish minority, and see to the extension of Jewish schools and welfare institutions if need be. In face of the expected dangers, there was an impulse to unite, just as there had been in Germany six years previously. "This is in no way a retreat from our Zionist position," Hoffman and Edelstein declared. "On the contrary, we must realize that only the Zionists can direct the politics of the Jewish people as a whole, and the Socialist Zionists must lead them." Edelstein again issued his call to Jewish leaders at a meeting of the Zionist National Convention where he talked of the question of immigration to Palestine and the transfer of capital. Maria Schmolka and Margulies agreed with him: the times called for unity.

At the end of May 1938, war again seemed to be around the corner. News reached London and Prague that Hitler was planning to attack Czechoslovakia (which in time was verified, the information being based on the plan code-named Operation Green), that a large force of German troops was concentrated on the Saxon border, and that the Germans were going to strike within days (information which did not match the facts: Hitler had set zero hour for October 1). At the start of May, Henlein advised that negotiations between his party and the Czechoslovakian government on the degree of independence to be accorded the German minority had broken off. He traveled to London to arouse British public opinion against "the discrimination, oppression, and suffering" to which Germans were subject under Czech rule, and on the way back he stopped off to see Hitler at Berchtesgaden. At the beginning of May, an incident occurred at the border crossing near the town of Eger in which a Czech border guard shot and killed two young SdP-ers on motorbikes who had refused to obey the order to stop. Their deaths gave the Sudeten Germans two "tortured saints," and two wreaths were placed on the fresh graves on behalf of the Führer himself. Across the border, a battalion of Sudeten German volunteers began to organize to free their homeland from Czechoslovakian oppression.

On May 20, after an emergency session of the Czech government, general mobilization was ordered, and Britain and France applied heavy diplomatic pressure in Berlin, London, and Paris to warn

Hitler of the danger of Western intervention should he go to war against Czechoslovakia. Hitler was incensed at the Czechs and at Beneš because of the threat of war and his loss of prestige, but for tactical reasons he saw fit to inform the Czechoslovakian delegate in Berlin, on May 23, that Germany had no aggressive intentions toward Czechoslovakia and that all reports about the concentration of German troops on her borders were totally unfounded. The British and French heads of state sighed with relief that war had been averted, and Czech morale soared: not only had they shown their willingness to fight, if necessary, but, in addition, Britain and France had supported them. Maps were hung in Prague shop windows with German territory marked in one color, and Britain, France and the U.S.S.R. in another; the caption below read: THEY'RE BIGGER—THERE'S NOTHING TO FEAR.

Summer came and with it the preparations for Slet, the four-yearly pageant put on by members of the Sokol organization, reinforcing the sense of strength and unity. All Prague was decked out in flags and slogans, youngsters from provincial towns, from Yugoslavia, Bulgaria, France, and Poland paraded through the streets, dancing, singing, and waving gaily colored kerchiefs. At the large Masaryk Stadium in Strahov tens of thousands of people participated in gymnastic shows, men, women, and children—entire fields of color swaying in unison with marvelous accuracy, like poppy fields, or wheat stalks, with red, blue, and white flags, ribbons, and flowers: Long live the republic!

In the wake of the Anschluss, Franklin Delano Roosevelt, president of the United States, called a conference of thirty-three countries—including all South America, the Scandinavian countries, Australia, and New Zealand—to join in a common effort toward aiding the emigration of German and Austrian refugees, a step hailed by the Jewish organizations as one of the great humanitarian acts of the twentieth century. The real motive behind the American initiative was to avert pressure on the United States to change her immigration laws. According to these laws, the number of visas given any one country was based on the proportion of Americans of that particular country of origin in the overall American population of 1910, up to a maximum of 153,774 immigrants per year, of whom more than half came from Britain and Ireland. Furthermore, the American authorities were careful to ensure that people who might constitute a burden on the public did not enter the United States.

The site chosen for the conference was Evian-les-Bains, a pretty resort town on the banks of Lake Geneva, no doubt thought conducive to talks of suffering and persecution. Prior to the conference, which opened on July 5, 1938, Western newspapers were full of descriptions of the long stretching queue which waited outside Vienna's American consulate day and night, and of the afflictions Austrian Jews were made to suffer. Nazi behavior in Austria was totally unrestrained. Thanks to a reign of terror and Eichmann's systematic emigration techniques, they managed to make a fifth of Austria's Jews leave within five months, an emigration rate that Germany reached only after five years.

Following the lofty opening remarks, the delegates to the Evian conference rose one after another and each in turn regretfully informed the assembly that their country had no room for refugees. Some of the countries were prepared to accept people with agricultural skills, some refused to take businessmen or intellectuals. Australia, with its wide open spaces hungry for settlers, was reluctant to import a racial problem to a country where one did not exist, and agreed to accept 5,000 people per year. Denmark and Holland, which had already absorbed thousands of refugees, said that they were willing to continue to grant them asylum, at least temporarily, and to the best of their ability. And the United States agreed henceforth to accept the full quota of immigrants from Germany and Austria, namely 27,000 per year, rather than a third or a half of the quota, as it had done in recent years. The Dominican Republic proposed a vague scheme for settling 100,000 Jews on its land, to be financed by Jews, of course.

The refugees themselves were not permitted to appear before the conference, but their representatives, including Maria Schmolka on behalf of the Jewish organizations in Czechoslovakia, were allowed three minutes each in which to speak their minds before a subcommittee. After a week of deliberations, the Evian Conference adjourned without any tangible results—apart from the establishment of an intergovernmental committee to continue discussions. To the Germans, the message was clear: the West might raise an outcry against Germany's treatment of Jews, but they did not want the Jews either. The results of the Evian Conference only confirmed Germany's policy toward the Jews, as Hitler well understood when he told Goering a few weeks later: "We must say to the world: why do you keep talking about Jews all the time? Take them!"

The refugee organizations in Czechoslovakia now concentrated all their attention on a feverish search for countries prepared to grant entrance visas to Jews without means (wealthy Jews had no problem finding a refuge for their money). And for the first time there were also Czech citizens who sought help, as well as Austrians and Germans. Jewish newspapers started publishing a column "From the World at Large," describing to the Czech Jews places such as Ecuador, San Domingo, Cuba, and various other countries whose location on the map they barely knew. Throughout all the years of the republic, there had been virtually no Jewish emigration from Czechoslovakia: for what more could a man want than the forests and meadows of Bohemia?

After the German entry into Austria, many longtime Zionists, especially from the Sudetenland, arrived at the surprising conclusion that emigration to Palestine was not meant only for others and for later: the time was now. Fifty candidates for investor's certificates were called to the Palestine office and warned against dubious deals and investments. Czechoslovakia had become a paradise for land speculators from Palestine, people looking for an easy profit at the expense of Sudeten Jews who wanted to buy a piece of land of their own while they still could. At Edelstein's initiative, the Palestine office in Prague opened a special section to provide investors with information, to advise them on investments in agriculture, industry, and stocks, to check out prospective partners in Palestine, and to ascertain if the price asked for a particular project was fair. Some profiteers even promised the Sudeten refugees certificates for money, and usually vanished as soon as payment had been effected. Only the Palestine office and the Jewish Agency were authorized to grant certificates, if there were certificates to be granted.

In an article that appeared in the *Jewish Calendar* for the year 5699 (1938 to 1939, according to the Christian calendar), Edelstein summarized the activities of the Palestine office since he had taken over in 1933: in the last five years 3,762 people had immigrated to Palestine, including 714 German refugees and 942 pioneers. Edelstein explained that the certification committee of the Palestine office determined a candidate's priority rating on the basis of a point system. The number of points was decided according to profession—i.e., its suitability for Palestine—family status, age of children, Zionist background, and knowledge of Hebrew. For example: a married candidate with children aged between fourteen and sixteen, whose occupation was agricultural, would be credited with more points than a barber with small children, who would find it difficult to integrate into Palestine (whoever dreamed of hairdressing salons at the time?).

8

MUNICH AS A TEST OF CHARACTER

MAY, JUNE, JULY 1938—negotiations between the Czech government and Henlein's party proceeded at a snail's pace and finally
reached deadlock, while in London and Paris there was growing
concern. Neville Chamberlain, the British prime minister, shared
the common assumption that Czechoslovakia was next on Hitler's
list of acquisitions, but Czechoslovakia's independence did not strike
Chamberlain as vital to British interests, especially since Britain was
neither militarily nor emotionally prepared for a confrontation with
Germany. It was therefore necessary to compel the Czechs (for
whom Chamberlain had no great fondness in any case, mainly
because of their 1935 defense agreement with the Soviet Union) to
accept the demands of the Sudeten Germans before Hitler made
them do so by force—and if that happened, who knew how far the
war would extend then? It was clear that an agreement with Germany meant far-reaching concessions by the Czechs, but there
would also be advantages, as the *Times* pointed out: life would be
more comfortable in a homogeneous country without an alien population tied by origin to a neighboring nation.

The Czechs proposed amending their constitution to grant more
rights to minorities. But Henlein, who had been struck by the
degree of understanding he found in London of the Sudeten Ger-

man demands, now sought full independence. The British decided to send an ostensibly independent mediator to Czechoslovakia rather than a member of the Foreign Office, and they chose Lord Walter Runciman, a seventy-year-old shipowner who was an ardent advocate of the solution of political problems by peaceful means (and was therefore close to the prime minister's conciliatory policies). It hardly mattered that his knowledge of some remote Slavic country called Czechoslovakia was almost nonexistent. And so that no one could accuse Britain of interfering in Czechoslovakia's internal affairs—and have it known that Czechoslovakia had bowed to pressure—President Beneš was told to invite the mediator on his own initiative.

In early August 1938, Lord Runciman's delegation arrived in Prague; the next day, in their frock coats and top hats, they drove to the Hradčany Castle in black Rolls-Royces for their first official meeting with Foreign Minister Krofta, Prime Minister Hodža and President Beneš. The Sudeten Germans now demanded full equality, full freedom to belong to the German nation, and full self-government. The Czechs rejected these demands on the grounds that they would lead to the gradual destruction of the republic. Beneš was willing to make concessions, but not the kind that meant the disintegration of the republic, and in this he was fully supported by loyal citizens, as was evident from a manifesto issued by demobilized military officers, which proclaimed that it was better to die than submit, and not a particle should be relinquished. The British military attaché in Prague had reported high morale among the Czechs, while the British military attaché in Berlin had claimed the opposite. Runciman tended to believe the man in Berlin. Under pressure from Runciman, who from the start treated both Beneš's government and Henlein's party as equal claimants, the Czechs were now prepared to grant self-rule to three regions where German concentration was largest, to replace the Czech civil service with a German civil service, to remove the Czech police, and to review the constitution, submitting a new draft for approval by parliament within three months. The introduction of an international police force was also considered to oversee the execution of the agreement and the separation of borders.

Lord and Lady Runciman spent weekends at the homes of the German nobility in Bohemia. At Prince Hohenlohe's mansion, Runciman met Henlein for the first time and was not overly impressed: he thought him an unintelligent ham. The English found that the best way to soften up the SdP delegates for negotiations was to feed them ham sandwiches and ply them with beer. On one occasion, mellowed by beer, Kunert, one of the German delegates, confided to Robert Stopford, a member of the British delegation, that their true intent was not to attain rights for the Sudeten Germans but to procure the neutralization of Czechoslovakia. At times the negotiations between the Czechs, the Sudeten Germans, and the British seemed at a standstill, but Lord Runciman pushed and pleaded: he sought an agreement that would be acceptable to Hitler, at any cost.

At the end of August, Lord Runciman visited Teplitz-Schönau, accompanied by Henlein, Karl Hermann Frank, Dr. Clary-Aldringen, and the honorable leadership of the SdP. Henlein delivered a rousing address, the mobs shouted "*Sieg Heil!*" and the town's Czech population kept quiet. In their own country they had adopted a policy of restraint, as had the Jews in Palestine. "Under the Austrian monarchy we felt safer than we do today, on the soil of the republic," long-standing Czech civil servants in the Sudetenland declared bitterly.

At the beginning of September, President Beneš summoned the two German delegates to the Hradčany and asked them to submit their demands in writing, promising to accept them in advance. The astounded Germans quickly staged an incident with Czech police in Moravská Ostrava and broke off negotiations: the last thing they wanted at this point was an agreement with Beneš's government. On September 12, at the convention of the National Socialist Party in Nuremberg, Hitler attacked Beneš and Czechoslovakia venomously, and demanded justice for the Sudeten Germans—or he would take matters into his own hands. This inspired uprisings in several Sudeten towns, accompanied by the looting of Jewish shops, but the Czech army managed to quell the unrest within two days. Henlein fled to Germany, and a worried Chamberlain asked for a meeting with Hitler.

Chamberlain flew to Munich and from there to Hitler's eagle's nest in Berchtesgaden, in the Bavarian Alps. He gave the Führer his personal approval for the severance of the Sudeten region from Czechoslovakia, and returned to London to gain the assent of his government. Runciman was summoned from Prague to London to submit his recommendations, and these turned out to be even more extreme than Hitler's own demands: among other things, they asked for a guarantee from the Czech government that she would not attack her neighbors even after she had been stripped of the natural defense of her mountains. Only one detail remained: to get the Czechs to agree to gradual suicide. On September 19, the British and French delegates in Prague made Beneš an offer he could not refuse: all regions where more than half the population was German would be ceded to Germany in the name of peace and Czechoslovakia's vital security interests. The Czech government turned down the generous offer, however, since in their view it spelled utter German domination, sooner or later.

But the Western powers were not prepared to take no for an answer. On September 21, two delegates roused Beneš from his sleep, demanded that he withdraw his rejection, and delivered an ultimatum: he must either relinquish those regions with a German majority or England and France would hold Czechoslovakia responsible in the event of war, and would not honor their obligations toward her. Against Hitler, the Czechs had remained firm. But abandoned by their allies, those pillars of Western democracy in whose image they had built the republic, they broke: the Hodža government decided to comply with the ultimatum, and raging demonstrations took place against capitulation and the Runciman delegation, toppling the government. The job of heading the new government was entrusted to General Sirovy, a hero of the Czech Legions who had lost an eye in the First World War. The following day, Chamberlain flew back to Germany, this time to Godesberg on the Rhine, ready to submit.

August saw a rapid exit of the Jews from Teplitz-Schönau and other Sudeten towns. At this stage the exodus was still orderly; the Jews still took away their furniture, their possessions, their household goods, and with a heavy heart closed up shops where in any case customers had become scarce because of the German boycott. By September, however, departure had become flight. The Teplitz train station resembled a refugee camp as Jews and Czechs waited for trains to take them inland. There were endless crowds at the bus stop to Prague, while the wealthy hired cars to take them to their destination. Till mid-September, members of the Zionist youth movements still notified the local leadership of their departure. Later, they no longer bothered.

Mulo Schmied, one of the last Tekhelet-Lavan instructors to remain in Teplitz-Schönau, organized contact with Prague through bicycle messengers; in the end he too decided to travel to the capital to consult with Edelstein. The Edelstein flat on Bilkova Street looked like a displaced persons' camp: apart from Jetti Olliner,

Miriam's mother, and her younger brother, who had fled from
Teplitz, dozens of refugees were bedded down on the floor on
mattresses. Mulo Schmied spent one night there; Yekef told him to
return to Teplitz and destroy any papers that might harm the
movement by falling into the wrong hands, and then to leave with
everyone else. In a Teplitz almost empty of Jews, Mulo packed up
some household items (his mother had fled to safety, to her brother
in Poland), marked the crate FRAGILE, GLASS, and was not surprised
to find that his German neighbors—with whom his family had lived
in the same building for fifteen years, always maintaining friendly
relations—refused to help him drag the crates. On the eve of Rosh
Hashanah, the Jewish New Year, Mulo Schmied left Teplitz for
good. He spent another two nights with Yekef, and then continued
his journey to friends in Brünn.

Hitler did not appreciate the sacrifice Chamberlain was prepared to
make at Czechoslovakia's expense: an agreement in principle to the
annexation of Sudeten no longer satisfied him. Germany must
conquer Sudeten immediately. The problem must be finally solved
by October 1, at the latest. On the day that Chamberlain met with
Hitler, Czechoslovakia ordered a general call-up. Despite the harrowing tension, morale was high and Czechs were willing to make
the supreme sacrifice. Within two days, and in an orderly fashion,
one million men were mobilized. "The Czechs are ready to fight to
their last drop of blood, even if only the Russians will support
them," Dr. Rufeisen wrote to his wife in Palestine. The Jewish
National Party published a manifesto of its loyalty to the republic:
the Jews of Czechoslovakia must follow the example of both the
Jewish community in Palestine and the Czech people—they must
not hide, not flee, but fight.
    Czechoslovakia rejected the Godesberg memorandum because it
denied her all possibility of national existence. Those were the last
days of summer, golden, balmy, sun-streaked days. The city streets
were empty of men; Prague was still, calm, and very beautiful, a
painful contrast to the general sense that war was unavoidable.
Hitler ordered his five armies, which had been on the alert for zero
hour on October 1, to advance toward the striking point near the
Czech border. France instituted partial conscription. Hungary, encouraged by Hitler, now demanded the annexation of Slovakian
border regions with a Hungarian majority, and was informed by
Yugoslavia and Rumania that they would go to war against her

should she attack Czechoslovakia, their ally. After all, what had united Rumania, Yugoslavia, and Czechoslovakia in the Little Entente was the fear of Hungarian revisionism, which refused to accept the loss of large areas of the Hungarian state, torn from it by order of the Trianon treaty at the end of the Great War and by the establishment of new national entities.

On September 25, three days after the Godesberg meeting, Jews celebrated their New Year and Prague's synagogues, always packed during the High Holy Days (and only then), were filled to overflowing. The congregation of regular templegoers had been augmented by thousands of Sudeten refugees and Prague Jews who in normal times had never set foot inside a synagogue, not even on the Day of Atonement, the holiest day in the Jewish year. Now however, they felt a need to seek God's charity against the coming trials, and to be among brethren in their hour of trouble. Dr. Weihs, the rabbi of Teplitz-Schönau who with a heavy heart had followed his flock out of town, now prayed in the beautiful synagogue on Dushna Street.

Hitler understood that for a small gesture he could get almost anything he wanted. All he had to do was allay British fears of another world war. In a letter to Chamberlain, he promised to guarantee Czechoslovakia's borders formally once they were rearranged. Now everything depended on the Czechs—would they act wisely? Chamberlain made it clear in his letter to Beneš that in the event of war, Czechoslovakia would be conquered and the powers would be helpless to save it or its people from the consequences. The British suggested that by October 1, the critical date, Hitler be given at least a symbolic enclave containing the towns of Asch (Aš) and Eger, two SdP strongholds. The French went further: they suggested that by that date the Czechs evacuate three entire provinces. Mussolini was willing to mediate, and Chamberlain could inform an applauding British parliament that Herr Hitler had invited the heads of state of Italy, Britain, and France to solve the Sudeten problem peacefully at a consultation in Munich. The threat of war had been averted, God be praised.

True, the Czechs were not permitted to participate in the deliberations on their fate, but it hardly mattered. Chamberlain had promised Beneš that he would not forget Czech interests for a moment. The discussions at party headquarters in Munich began in an atmosphere of good will—and two Czech representatives waited in one of the adjoining rooms to hear what the outcome of all this goodwill was to be for their people. After five hours they learned that the terms had become even harsher than the latest English proposals which they had rejected. They were presented with a map and shown the regions they must evacuate immediately, in the first of four evacuation stages to be completed by October 10, with military installations to remain intact. And once the question of the Hungarian and Polish minorities had been solved, Czechoslovakia would receive guarantees from the powers with respect to her new borders. No answer was required from the Czechs, since these were not proposals. It was a finished agreement, made without them and at their expense.

Chamberlain returned home victorious, having brought his people peace with honor, "peace in our time," and on September 30, the Munich Pact was formally presented to Kamil Krofta, the Czechoslovakian foreign minister, together with a request that he send two representatives to the international committee that was to supervise the implementation of the agreement. Now that the French and English had not only abandoned Czechoslovakia, but had also threatened to side with Hitler should Czechoslovakia reject the Munich terms, Beneš saw no choice but to agree. "We were prepared for reasonable concessions, the kind our country could live with. We wanted to show the world that Czechoslovakia, a real, sane, successful, and progressive democracy, did not want to add to the difficulties of other countries and was prepared to contribute to the general peace in Europe," he wrote a few months later. "But we never expected the kind of agreement achieved at Munich, whereby, in the name of self-determination, 1,200,000 Czechs, more than one tenth of our people, were annexed to other countries. We never expected an agreement that would destroy our country's economic foundations, leave the republic with indefensible borders, and economically and strategically transform it into a pawn in Hitler's hands. . . . When we saw that our nation of ten million was surrounded by eighty million foes, equipped with a sophisticated military machine, and that we could not stand alone against the overwhelming advantage of the enemy forces intent on invasion, we had to submit to the Munich dictates which were supposed to bring us temporary peace. . . . One of the reasons we submitted was that the four world powers had ceremoniously signed a document, guaranteeing the independence of the Czech people and the new borders of the Czech state."

The Western powers had betrayed Czechoslovakia, but she was still free to decide to fight on her own (the U.S.S.R. had been prepared to come to her aid, but in order to do so, her forces had to pass through either Poland or Rumania, and it was highly doubtful that they would have been allowed to do so). The assumption had been that Czechoslovakia, with her sophisticated fortifications, would be able to hold out against the Germans for between two weeks and a month, and by that time perhaps, despite everything, the world powers would come to her aid. But the cost in human life was bound to be frightful, and beautiful Prague, with her thousand towers and all the treasures of her glorious past, was likely to be wiped off the face of the earth. Beneš assumed that war between Hitler and the Western powers was in any case inevitable, and that when it ended Czechoslovakia could resume her independence, having been spared the slaughter and devastation. On October 5, the Jewish Day of Atonement, Beneš resigned as the Germans had demanded; because his life appeared to be in danger, he went into exile in France. In November, Emil Hacha was elected in his place, a sixty-six-year-old judge of the supreme administrative court who had worked for the government since the time of the monarchy, a man of poor health, conservative, a devout Catholic, and thoroughly respectable.

In a choked voice, General Sirovy went on the radio to tell the Czechs what they had been sentenced to: "We have been betrayed; we stood alone, and decided that we must choose between limited territory and the death of our entire nation, and we saw it as our sacred duty to save the nation." The Czechs' initial reaction to this announcement was paralyzing shock, an unwillingness to believe that all the talk of fighting to the last drop of blood had been nothing but rhetoric. It couldn't be true, it was a nightmare, it would pass. Karel Čapek wrote a poem called "Prayer"; the radio announcer broke down and wept while he read it. Čapek, who had given the world a view of the future in *The White Plague,* in *R.U.R.,* and *The Makropoulos Affair,* who had foreseen a dominant Fascism, the mechanization of man, and the nuclear bomb, was unable to bear the pain, the despair, the anguish of the coming times: a few months after the Munich Pact, he died of what was diagnosed as flu, but was in fact a broken heart and the loss of his will to live.

On the eve of Yom Kippur, just before the implementation of the last stages of the Munich Pact, the rabbi of Teplitz-Schönau felt he must return to the remnants of his flock. In Teplitz's elegant temple, which in former times had been crowded with congregants, the chandeliers still burned as an act of faith, lighting up the marble walls, the golden ornaments, the silver-belled Torah scrolls still in their place; but in the great hall there was only a handful of old, of sick, of welfare cases, the lost, the abandoned, the forgotten. "Behold me before thee like a vessel filled with shame and confusion. O may it be thy will, O Lord my God and the God of my fathers, that I may sin no more, and as to the sins I have sinned before thee, purge them away in thine abundant mercy and not by means of affliction and sore diseases." Thus ended the concluding prayer of the Day of Atonement. Teplitz-Schönau's ancient Jewish community ceased to exist. Rabbi Weihs took away with him the community records in case his people might need them (and, indeed, he received hundreds of requests for documents required by immigration authorities).

The German entry into the Sudeten region inspired the local Germans with the same hysterical fervor that had seized the Austrians six months before. Women wept with happiness and flung themselves onto the necks of their liberators, young girls showered flowers on the soldiers in gray uniform, and, whooping joyfully, men removed Czech signposts and dismantled the border barricades with Germany. All along the roads, fair-haired children in pretty clothes waved swastika-decorated flags, prepared long in advance. Hitler drove in his open Mercedes through Eger, Asch, Carlsbad, and Reichenberg, and the crowds went mad: "*Sieg Heil! Sieg Heil!*" Henlein's party voluntarily dissolved and the SdP joined the mother-party. The slogan *Heim ins Reich* was perhaps historically inaccurate, but the slogan "home to the NSDAP" certainly fitted the facts. In the end Hitler received more than he had initially demanded: an area of 17,000 square kilometers containing 2,800,000 Germans and 800,000 Czechs, and all fortifications intact. Czechoslovakia lost most of her coal deposits, and the heart of her steel and cement industries; all railway and telephone lines were broken—and still the Führer's triumph was incomplete: the Munich Pact had ruined the pleasure he had anticipated in conquering Czechoslovakia in a war of vengeance.

The Czech people, army, and parliament accepted the dictates of the Munich Pact without violent opposition; the Sudeten was evacuated almost without a shot being fired, the army obeyed orders, the soldiers simply wept or cursed those who had brought them to this juncture: the Western powers, democracy, Beneš, and the Jews. Different peoples react to identical situations in different ways: a spirit of submission swept through the nation. Most of them were bourgeois or petty bourgeois by nature, people who had over the centuries grown accustomed to foreign rule and learned the wisdom of servile revenge—accepting orders from above and mocking those who gave them on the quiet—a wisdom that Schweik developed to an art.

Just as the prospect of defending their life and honor had buoyed them up, so the pain of submission now let them down. The Czech spirit was broken. Some consoled themselves as they had under the monarchy: we were here before Austria, and we will be here after Austria; the main thing is that our young people are not going to their deaths in a losing war. Masaryk's humanistic realism became opportunistic realism: if you can't sing with the angels, then howl with the wolves—and obey German orders.

The new republic still contained 300,000 Germans, and, much to everybody's surprise, they were not permitted to cross over into Reich territory and join their brethren. Students who wanted to study in Germany were told to continue their studies at German universities in Prague and Brünn. There were other strange phenomena, to which few people paid any attention: the Czechs started erecting new police and custom stations on their side of the border, while no such signs were evident on the German side. Why build border stations, after all, if the plan was still to conquer what remained of Czechoslovakia, as Hitler secretly told his generals a few days after the Munich Pact? Openly, however, he declared that he had no further territorial ambitions in Europe and he did not want Czechs in the German Reich (this last perhaps was true: he did not want Czechs at all, anywhere).

The Czechoslovakian republic grew increasingly smaller. The Slovaks, for the most part an agricultural people with a thin stratum of intellectuals, had resented the Czechs since the start of the republic. Instead of the equality they had anticipated, the Slovaks found themselves in an inferior position to the enlightened, "Western" Czechs, who were industrialized and held the reins of power, even in Slovakia, and sometimes with a flagrant air of superiority. The Catholic People's Party, led by the priest Andrej Hlinka, had for years sought German support for its separatist aspirations, and it now found a sympathetic ear, just as did Hungary and Poland, who demanded that the provinces with Hungarian and Polish majorities be annexed to their respective countries. During the Sudeten evacuation, Slovakia declared independence and Czechoslovakia earned a hyphen to her name and the constitution of a federate state. At the end of November, within the framework of the Munich Pact and according to the Vienna Agreement, the powers gave Poland the industrial and mining region of Teschen. Its population was mixed, and its Poles had never resigned themselves to being a part of Czechoslovakia. The Jews of Teschen fled to Czecho-Slovakia, mainly to nearby Ostrava.

By the Vienna Agreement, large areas of southern Slovakia with a Hungarian majority were annexed to Hungary. Slovakia shrank but gained an independent government headed by priest Josef Tiso, the successor to Hlinka, who died shortly before his dream was realized, bequeathing his name to the Hlinka Guard, a military body modeled after the German striking force, and equally liberal. Privately, Tiso spoke of a Slovakian solution to the Jewish problem: their separation and the destruction of their economic influence, without the Germans' cruelty. But when a Jewish delegation called on the priest, they were received with friendliness, and the priest several times said that racial anti-Semitism would gain no entry into Slovakia (in the final analysis, religious anti-Semitism can also work wonders). Tiso in fact remained true to his promise, after his own fashion. The anti-Jewish laws adopted in Slovakia were similar to the Nuremberg laws, but they were built on a religious base: anyone who had converted before 1918 was considered Slovakian regardless of his parentage. Immediately after the Munich Pact, Ferdinand Durčansky, the deputy prime minister of the new Slovakian government, went to Goering to convey Slovakia's wish for full independence with close political, military, and economic ties to Germany. The Field-Marshal tended to approve: a Czech state without Slovakia would be even easier to destroy.

Even Carpathian Russia finally achieved autonomy, after Hungary had taken a succulent bite out of her that included Munkács and Uzhgorod, her two largest cities. There was, however, no mass Jewish exodus to Czecho-Slovakia from the regions of Slovakia and Carpathian Russia which passed to the Hungarians, as had been the case in the Sudetenland. The life of a refugee in Fascist Slovakia or Carpathian Russia appeared no more attractive than the life of a citizen in Fascist Hungary, and perhaps even less so. The republic's east-west railroad lines now passed through Hungarian territory, but the Czech army was still stationed in Carpathian Russia, and the head of the new autonomous government assured the Jewish mediators that no extreme solution was being sought for the 75,000 Jews who remained there. The paths of the Jews in the three parts of the republic, which had converged only twenty years before, began to separate, little by little.

Ostrava was now truly on the German border, and its sizable and aggressive German minority, like all the Germans in Czechoslovakia, was entirely confident that redemption would come. In this atmosphere, Ostrava was no longer a suitable center for the functions of the Zionist Organization, especially since the journey to Prague, which in ordinary times had taken less than six hours, now took almost a whole day because of the choppy rail route. Prague was now the Jewish center, for all intents and purposes. Here the refugees concentrated, the Palestine offices and consular legations had their premises, and here was the bulk of all Zionist activity. Immediately after the Munich Pact, a Zionist action committee had been set up in Prague that included Arthur Bergmann, chairman of the Foundation Fund, Oskar Aschermann, chairman of the Jewish National Fund, Jakob Edelstein, director of the Palestine office, and Otto Zucker, deputy chairman of the Jewish National Party, which under the new "National Unity" government had ceased to exist. A handsome and sought-after bachelor who loved music and art, Zucker, aged forty-six, was appointed director of the economic department of the expanding Palestine office, mainly because of his wonderful talent for organization. A construction engineer by profession, he had at one time won a tender for the construction of a pedestrian tunnel at one of Berlin's major intersections. The conditions of the tender had asked that the work not disrupt city traffic, and he managed to complete most of the job in a single night. He was the architect of the Ullstein building in Berlin, and in Prague, too, he had erected several modern edifices using impressive technical innovations.

The action committee asked permission to manage affairs for and on behalf of the Zionist Organization until it moved from Ostrava to Prague. It was not simply a question of changing sites. The focus of power also changed. After Dr. Kahn left Ostrava and moved to Prague, he was only one in a group of several active leaders, though he still carried considerable authority—and a growing anxiety about things to come. Adding to the general apprehension at what might happen in Czechoslovakia was concern over affairs in Palestine. Hope lay in immigration, but what if the British prevented immigration? Where was one to find the strength to bear the present? Dr. Paul März, the new chairman of the Zionist Organization, also planned to move from Ostrava to Prague, as soon as he had liquidated his legal practice. In an attempt to comply with German wishes, the Czechs had started limiting the activities of Jewish lawyers, and the bar association decided not to accept any new Jewish members. Jewish doctors in welfare clinics and government hospitals were fired. Jewish civil servants (the few there were) were retired on pension, and Jewish professors were removed from German institutions of higher learning. All citizenship documents, issued since the start of the republic in 1918, were to be reviewed, and all foreign subjects who were neither Czech nor Slovak nor Ruthenian (namely, the Jews) were to be expelled. And all this was to be done in the name of the Czecho-Slovakian republic, which had now become an "authoritarian democracy" that had dispensed with the need for a parliament.

Czecho-Slovakia was still an independent state, and the four powers had promised to guarantee its existence. Britain and France had quickly accepted the fact that Czecho-Slovakia, or what remained of it, was now part of the German sphere of influence, while the Germans, despite the feelers put out by the Czecho-Slovakian foreign minister, František Chvalkovsky (who had formerly represented his country in Rome and was a known admirer of Fascism), were in no hurry to grant the promised guarantees. What surprised Chvalkovsky in particular, as he told the French delegate in Prague after his meeting with Hitler on January 21, 1939, was the degree of importance that the Führer and his foreign minister, Ribbentrop, attached to the Jewish question; it was out of all proportion to any other issue. Both had told Chvalkovsky that Germany could not give guarantees to a country that did not rid itself of Jews. Chvalkovsky promised the Führer that Czecho-Slovakia would lend its shoulder to the solution of the Jewish problem, though the task could not be completed in three months, mainly because the Jews did not want to leave of their own free will. "Into which country should the Jews be cast, and on which border should it be done?" Chvalkovsky wanted to know. The German border, the Polish border, the Hungarian border were all closed to Jews.

In his conversation with Chvalkovsky, Hitler called the Jews vermin, held them responsible for the difficulties between Berlin, Paris, London, and Washington, and spoke of their annihilation: the disease must be stamped out. It was merely a variation of what Hitler had said in his speech at the Reichstag to mark the anniversary of the Nazis' accession to power on January 30: "Europe cannot rest so long as it has not found a solution to the Jewish question. I would like today again to be a prophet: if international Jewish financiers in and out of Europe will again succeed in dragging the world into war, the result will not be the Bolshevization of the world and a victory for the Jews but, on the contrary, the destruction of the Jewish race in Europe."

Of all the demands the Germans made on Czechs—integration into the German economy, quitting the League of Nations, a neutral foreign policy, and joining the treaty against the Comintern—the demand to limit Jewish influence and push Jews out of economic life was the most attractive. The right-wing Czech parties had also dreamt of this. However, Britain exerted counterpressure by attaching a condition to the relief loan she granted Czecho-Slovakia, namely, to refrain from persecuting Jews. Still, "moderate steps toward normalization in the distribution of national wealth" was not exactly persecution. Immediately after the Munich Pact, Britain, with pangs of conscience, had authorized a £10 million loan for the rehabilitation of Sudeten refugees, one third of the amount Czechoslovakia had negotiated for with the Western powers (the lengthy conscription had been an enormous financial burden, the republic's economy was ruined, exports had shrunk, Czecho-Slovakia had lost not only her pride and secure borders but her economic independence as well). Robert Stopford, a member of the Runciman delegation and an expert on international financial aid, was appointed to supervise the use of the loan, and to ensure that there was no discrimination among the various categories of refugees, with particular attention to German-speaking refugees whose rehabilitation within the republic had become impossible.

The Jewish leadership feared that the utter dejection felt by the Czechs, as a result of the blow they had been dealt at Munich, would spread to the Jewish population, whose morale would sink too. In fact, more people left the Jewish community than had in previous years, though the number was still in the hundreds. There were Jews, those who felt themselves bound heart and soul to the Czech people and their culture, who tried to take the final step and convert: why go on dragging the terrible yoke of Judaism, why burden our children with it? Worried parents, particularly those who had intermarried, sent their children for religious instruction to a priest or had them quietly baptized. Others sought only the baptism certificate that opened the way for emigration to South America and ranged in price from 800 to (should Christian parents also be required) 1,500 crowns.

9

ZIONISM'S FINEST HOUR

THE MUNICH PACT contained no direct reference to the Jews, but almost every paragraph affected them in one way or another. The clause on population exchange promised non-German residents the right to choose between remaining where they were and being annexed to the Reich, or moving to the Czechoslovakian republic. This right, however, like many others, applied to the Jews only on paper; in actual fact, those few Jews who had not yet fled were deported by the Germans across the new border immediately after annexation. The Czechs refused to absorb the Jewish refugees, who roamed from town to town, and everywhere the local population tried to get rid of them as quickly as possible; eventually they concentrated in the big cities—Prague, Brünn, Ostrava—where it was easier to disappear. Sometimes they walked through the streets as if they were deaf, not knowing Czech and afraid to speak German: the Czechs must be given no cause to return them across the border. Because it was dangerous to speak German openly, the German-language *Selbstwehr* was shut down, and the chief organ of the Zionist movement was henceforth *Židovské Zprávy*, the parallel Czech-language weekly.

Prague's hotels were full of refugees, with not a vacant bed to be had. Edelstein's flat became an overnight shelter for every refugee from Teplitz-Schönau who needed a roof over his head, and his office, on the second floor of the community center on Dlouhá Street, was an address of salvation. They came by the thousands: acquaintances, friends, former associates, the Ostjuden from Teplitz who had helped Edelstein when he started out there, loyal veteran Zionists who now came to ask for visas to Palestine. They all asked, begged, wept, pointed out their eligibility by virtue of their past, and there was nothing to give them but hope, in the next allotment of certificates.

Jewish refugees feared they would be turned over to the Germans by Czech police. "Don't write to Czecho-Slovakia on political issues, don't curse Germany or Hitler. Everywhere there is censorship, everywhere there are Fascist agents, Hitler is virtually in control," wrote Leo Hermann, general secretary of the Jewish National Fund, who, having come from Jerusalem to his native Prague, was shocked to the depths of his soul by the "unalleviated hell" he found there following the Munich Pact. For the first time newspapers began to appear with blank spaces where items had been censored. "Don't write in Hebrew," requested Franz Kahn. "Every letter is censored and a Hebrew letter may be held up for weeks." Hermann came to Prague to console and encourage. He spoke to Zionist forums, despite the ban on public assembly, and sought to establish contact with the various British institutions represented in Prague. He feared that the Czechs might return the Sudeten Jews to German territory against their will, and he returned to London to sound the alarm and arouse British public opinion. His chief purpose was to fight for the rights of Jewish refugees to remain within Czecho-Slovakia's borders even if they had declared themselves German nationals in the 1930 census. And he also wanted to ensure that the monies of the British loan would not find their way to the German National Bank (which demanded part of Czecho-Slovakia's gold reserves in proportion to the number of people annexed to the Reich), but would be used for the relief of Jewish refugees.

What was to be done with the Jewish refugees? There were 92,000 refugees registered in Czecho-Slovakia, mostly Czechs, whom the government was prepared to help rehabilitate. The only solution for Jewish refugees, and German refugees who had fled for political reasons, was emigration. Jews could also look to their brothers for help. The legal status of the 30,000 Jewish refugees was vague, their economic situation trying. Even though most of them had managed to come away with some money, their real wealth—

their homes, shops, and industries—had remained across the border. Their money was running out and winter was around the corner. Their children found it difficult to integrate into Czech schools (and the atmosphere in German schools did not tolerate Jewish children). The Jewish institutions faced their greatest challenge, Edelstein wrote to the Zionist public after the Munich Pact. The Jewish people have always found a way out in times of trouble. The greater the danger and hardships, the more intricate the problems, the more swiftly Jews have joined together in a common effort. While in the near future, he wrote, emphasis will be put on finding countries of immigration, emigration alone would not solve the Jewish problem. Jews should take part in the rehabilitation of the republic in the knowledge that Czech and Jewish interests are identical. Together with HICEM, the Palestine office—aided by the Joint and the committee for German Jews—would spare no effort in helping the Jews integrate economically and training them for a fresh start in productive fields and manual occupations. Preparations were under way for counseling offices, and courses would be given in child care, cooking, shoemaking, and other trades; language courses would include Czech, English, and Spanish—all according to the tried and tested pioneering formula of salvation through productivity.

In the increasingly anti-Jewish atmosphere, the Jewish Czechs at first tried to save their own skins. The Sokol sports organization, which had until then professed Masaryk's humanism, came out with its own solution to the Jewish problem: all those who had immigrated to Czechoslovakia since 1914 would be returned to their countries of origin, as would those who had declared themselves German or Hungarian nationals in the 1930 census, while those who had declared themselves Czech or Slovakian (about one quarter of the Jews in the republic) would integrate into Czecho-Slovakia's various social strata according to their proportion in the overall population. If people must be cast off a sinking ship, better that they be foreigners than our own people. The Jewish Czechs adopted a similar line: a clear distinction should be made between those Jews who have always regarded themselves as an inseparable part of the Czech people, and all others, though some of the more moderate assimilated Jews withdrew from this position.

There were Jews whose confidence was undermined by the anti-Semitic atmosphere. Perhaps the Czechs were right, and Jews really did stick out and provoke the gentiles. Their fur coats teased and irritated. They spoke mostly German, and when they did speak Czech it was often too loud. There had to be something to the claims of Jewish loudness, Jewish haste, Jewish greed, Jewish inferiority; such hatred does not spring from nowhere.

It was natural that the Zionists, who had felt something of the loneliness of a people apart even before it was forced upon them, should be the ones to take the initiative and organize Jewish life. More and more they assumed official responsibility as society at large rejected the Jews. The Zionists had not been affected by their rejection as deeply as those Jews who had always considered themselves an integral part of the Czech people and were now suddenly dubbed "foreigners." How could they be foreign in a country to which their ancestors had come a thousand years ago? It was the Zionists who led the welfare work in Prague, Brünn, and Ostrava. Thousands of Jews, lost in a turbulence whose origins they could not fathom, now flocked to Hehalutz and the Zionist youth movements. Youth-Aliyah, the organization that sent children to Palestine, and until very recently a monopoly of German youth—and which Czech Jews had long regarded as a rescue operation for the offspring of those unfortunates who lived in danger—had originally been given a poor reception when Kurt Baumgarten and Balu Spitz of Tekhelet-Lavan had visited Teplitz-Schönau to promote it. Now Youth-Aliyah became a formal institution with an office, a secretary, a telephone, and medical examinations for immigration candidates to Palestine. Most of its activities were financed with the help of money generously donated by parents who hoped at least to get their children out. Aliyah-Bet (what the British defined as illegal immigration) came out from underground, and the Palestine office took charge of transferring capital, both officially and not entirely so. Zionism had hit on ambitious times.

Kahn asked the Zionist Executive in London to send someone to Prague to see what was happening, but London refused: the imminent publication of the White Paper, which would drastically curtail immigration to Palestine, required that all hands now remain in London for political action. Prague therefore decided to send a delegation there to describe the situation of the Sudeten refugees and ask for as many certificates as possible. In early November, Edelstein, Rufeisen, Goldstein, and Zucker set out for London. But the day they arrived was Kristallnacht in Germany, and that same week Britain announced her intention of dropping the partition plan.

The Zionist Executive convened under a cloud of burning synagogues, the destruction of tens of thousands of Jewish institutions, shops, and homes, planned and "spontaneous" outbreaks of murder and robbery in a campaign of vengeance for the murder of Ernst vom Rath. Vom Rath, the first attaché at the German embassy in Paris, had been shot by Herschel Grynszpan, whose family had been expelled by the Germans into Poland. All eyes were now on Germany and Austria, and in light of the outburst of violence there the problems of the Jews of Czecho-Slovakia did not seem urgent. World sympathy was with the Jews of Germany; it was on their behalf that protest meetings were held in European capitals and cables and memorandums sent to international organizations in an effort to save them. After Kristallnacht there was no escape for the Jews of Germany either, wrote George Rublee, a New York lawyer who had been appointed that year to direct the intergovernmental committee set up at the Evian Conference to deal with refugees. "I checked absorption possibilities with representatives of the South American republics, the British Dominion commissioners, and spokesmen of the Imperial colonies. All gave me negative answers." Rublee noted that week by week various countries adopted new laws and regulations to make it more difficult for immigrants to enter, and there were no more countries open to refugees. After negotiations with Rublee, for example, the British minister for the colonies declared that the Empire could absorb twenty-five settlers in Kenya.

The incidents of Kristallnacht had perhaps not yet managed to alter Chamberlain's conciliatory policy, but they had a decisive influence on British and American public opinion and in this way contributed to the changing policy adopted by these countries toward Hitler. Edelstein understood that the German Jews had priority when it came to rescue, since they were now threatened with deportation to concentration camps; in Czecho-Slovakia, it was simply a question of bearing trying times and economic hardship. He held lengthy debates on the subject with Dr. Erich Munk, the Youth-Aliyah doctor, and others who were convinced that the same fate awaited all the Jews of central Europe.

Nevertheless, the delegation did not return empty-handed after ten days in London: they brought back a pledge that the committee for the Jews of Germany, led by Weizmann, would extend its activities to the Sudeten refugees, and that four hundred pioneers would be accepted to training divisions abroad in Denmark, England, and Holland, from where they would, in time, emigrate to Palestine.

Youth-Aliyah was promised between one hundred and two hundred places, which meant that one day, after these youngsters had become independent, they could bring over any parents above the age of fifty—an important consideration for immigration in the distant future. And, after much deliberation, the Jewish Agency representatives undertook to grant almost five hundred certificates to Czecho-Slovakia, mostly for investors, for the half-year ending March 30, 1939. All in all, however, only a tiny proportion of all those who sought to emigrate would be able to do so. Who had first claim on the certificates? Veteran Zionists? People whose lives were in danger because of their political views? Older people whose world had suddenly been shattered? Young people with their lives still before them? Families with small children? Investors? The selection was harrowing. Pressure was exerted on Edelstein from all sides: from Palestine, from London, from people in key positions, from former emissaries, from friends trying to get either themselves or their families out. For years afterward many people harbored resentment against him for not responding to their pleas.

About a hundred written applications arrived at the Palestine office every day, and a similar number of hopefuls came in person. The line at times stretched down the stairwell. Somewhat bitterly, Edelstein pointed out that together with veteran Zionists longing to reach the land of their dreams, there were now unfamiliar faces— people who only a few months ago would have laughed at the suggestion that they settle in Palestine, who could have helped build up Palestine and lay the foundations for mass immigration but had left the work to others. Even those who for years had put obstacles in the way of Zionist work now came.

Leo Hermann tried to secure at least a small part of the British loan to Czechoslovakia for the rehabilitation of Jewish refugees. He went from office to office in the British government, and searched for a contact with the new Czecho-Slovakian government, where there were few Jewish sympathizers. The first person he turned to was Jan Masaryk, Czecho-Slovakia's ambassador in London, a personal friend of Weizmann's and of the Sieff family, who co-owned the Marks and Spencer department-store chain, particularly Mrs. Rebecca Sieff, the president of WIZO. Hermann had been President Masaryk's guide in Palestine when the latter had toured the country in 1927, and he found his son sympathetic and understanding. Jan Masaryk viewed anti-Semitism as barbaric, and as the first stage in the process of Germanization. He was full of bitterness against

France, and especially England, and told Hermann that Czecho-Slovakia as a German satellite held no interest for him; he did not even want to set foot on its soil. What concerned him now was the fate of the Jewish people and the future of Palestine. Czechoslovakia's fate had been decided, but the Jewish people and Palestine could perhaps still be saved. The new Czecho-Slovakian government had asked Masaryk to continue as ambassador in London, at least for the next six months when the British loan was being negotiated; and Masaryk used all his contacts in Britain and Czecho-Slovakia to ensure that at least half a million of the total ten million pounds sterling would be devoted to the rehabilitation of Jewish refugees in Palestine.

The Czech government was generally in agreement with the complex financial arrangement: Czech Jews immigrating to Palestine would pay the Czecho-Slovakian treasury the half million pounds sterling in crowns (at 30 percent above the official exchange rate, an increment defined as "financial help for refugees"), and, in return, the Jewish Agency in London would receive the equivalent in English pounds. But the Czecho-Slovakian government wanted the maximum number of Jewish emigrants as reward for her generosity. After exhausting negotiations, it was agreed that 2,500 would leave in the first half of 1939; even this was a fanciful figure in view of the restrictions on legal immigration to Palestine. When Eliezer Kaplan, treasurer of the Jewish Agency, and Leo Hermann came to Prague in November, they brought with them a commitment for four hundred "capitalist's" certificates. Seen in the light of the number of applicants, the figure was paltry; but it was enough on which to base negotiations with the Czech authorities over the transfer of the expected half-million pounds.

During Kaplan's stay in Prague, Dr. März approached him openly about the question of illegal immigration. Prior to Munich, most Czech Zionist leaders had had their reservations about illegal immigration, and when Tzevi Yehieli, one of the people active in Aliyah-Bet, arrived in Ostrava and tried to raise the necessary 120,000 crowns (approximately £600) for illegal immigrant ships, he was unsuccessful. Now the relationship was reversed. The Revisionist faction was active in this field and paid little attention to whether an immigrant had the appropriate Zionist or pioneering background. And the Jews of Brünn contributed generously to the Revisionist operation on condition that at least some of the Sudeten refugees would be evacuated, thereby perhaps alleviating some-what the anti-Semitic atmosphere in the city.

With an eye to an easy profit, private travel agencies sprang up, of which the most famous was Black Rose, named after the building in which it was located. The company was started by a Jew called Robert Mandler and two slick Greeks who in normal times were involved in smuggling merchandise—gold, hashish, arms. Now they added a more remunerative cargo to their interests: Jews trying to get to Palestine, no matter how, though they were well aware that the immigration papers supplied by the travel people were of a highly dubious nature.

Kaplan told März to do as he thought best, though privately he expressed reservations; and after the visitors left Prague, the top ranks of the Zionist Organization in Czechoslovakia decided to include organized illegal immigration in its activities. Of the 2,500 immigrants who were meant to leave as part of the transfer agree-ment of the half-million pounds, 1,000 were slated for illegal immi-gration. After all, the Czech authorities (refugee affairs now came under a special department at the welfare office) did not care how the Jews left for Palestine, or whether or not they had valid entrance visas, so long as they left, and the more the better.

By now the watchword was departure—but organized departure, not at any price, on any condition. A considerable group of Jews started to organize for agricultural settlement in the Dominican Republic, the only country to suggest a scheme for mass Jewish immigration at the Evian Conference, to be effected on government land with Jewish money. Despite the feverish attempts to find immi-gration sites for the Sudeten refugees—the U.S.S.R. was prepared to take a small group of communists; Canada wanted only agri-cultural laborers; Australia was willing to accept people whose lives were in danger, but not many; and everyone had in mind non-Jews—Robert Stopford had serious reservations about the grandi-ose Dominican scheme. There was no guarantee that the refugees would get the land promised, and if they did, that they would be able to glean a living from it; perhaps they would die of starvation, having lined the pockets of various despots.

Almost every day, Hermann phoned Prague about the transfer agreement, still waiting for approval by the Czech authorities. True to his promise, Jan Masaryk phoned Prague at the end of December 1938, on his last day as ambassador in London, to try to speed up the authorization of the agreement from the Czech side. At the last moment, on the verge of approval, an absurd obstacle presented itself: the Czechs demanded that ten thousand Jews leave within one year in exchange for the half-million pounds. The Zionist institutions insisted on the agreed 2,500, knowing they had not even this amount of certificates. Stopford, whose attitude toward Jews was more sympathetic than was common in British institutions, was required to intercede before the Czechs would settle on the minimum figure. In the middle of January 1939 the agreement was finally signed by Kalfus, the Czecho-Slovakian foreign minister, and František Friedmann on behalf of the Jewish Agency.

What the Czechs did not know at this time was that the Palestine office had at its disposal only a hundred and fifty of the promised four hundred capitalist's certificates. The remaining 250 had gone to immigrants from Germany in the wake of Kristallnacht. The Jewish Agency tried to secure a commitment from the Mandate government for the other 250 certificates in the coming quota, but the answer was that the Palestine government could not mortgage the future. In despairing letters to Kaplan, Prague's Zionist leaders threatened to resign fearing the collapse of the Zionist movement should the complex negotiations with the Czechs now fail because it was impossible to emigrate. Kaplan admitted that an error had been made: the Mandate government should have been asked to set aside some certificates for Czecho-Slovakian immigrants when negotiations first began in November. But now it was December, and too late—all the certificates had been distributed. There was nothing to be done but wait for the next allotment in April 1939—a matter of a few months, no more.

Leo Hermann and Dr. Ullman, who had already been to London several times in connection with the transfer, tried to arrange temporary residence visas in England for refugee children and au pair girls in order to arrive somehow at the figure of 2,500 who had to leave Czecho-Slovakia by the terms of the agreement. Immigration procedures were incredibly involved. Documents had to be produced showing that all taxes had been paid (including a dog tax even for those who had never owned a dog), a demand almost impossible to fulfill for Sudetenland refugees. Finally, the treasury agreed to a lump sum to be paid to the tax authorities. Lists had to be submitted, with copies, of all household articles the immigrants meant to take. Passports, medical certificates, visas had to be arranged, and money matters settled with the Palestine office. It was all time-consuming: here a stamp was missing, there a seal or signature. In February 1939, Edelstein reported to London that all obstacles had finally been removed and the agreement could be implemented. The first immigrants under the transfer agreement set out.

After a good deal of persuasion, the Czechs and British agreed to include ten Czech citizens in the agreement, and ten privileged veteran Zionists, among them Max Brod, Felix Weltsch, Angelo Goldstein, Emil Margulies, and Dr. Kugel, started preparing for immigration with no sense of urgency. One hundred and fifty holders of capitalist's certificates, with their families, were to leave in mid March, as well as one hundred and fifty Youth-Aliyah youngsters; immediately thereafter four hundred Hehalutz and Maccabi people were to set out for Yugoslavia, from where they would sail on Aliyah-Bet boats to Palestine. At the beginning of the month, the illegal immigrants started gathering in Prague and Brünn to prepare for departure.

When Eliahu Dobkin, the head of the Jewish Agency's immigration department, visited Prague and saw the dimensions of the immigration planned and the difficulties involved, he demanded that Hoffman and Edelstein stay in Czecho-Slovakia at least another year. Both men agreed to remain at their posts and shoulder the responsibility; but a Fascist dictatorship might take over any day, and Hoffman and Edelstein were known to be closely connected with socialist circles. To ensure their safety, therefore, Hehalutz headquarters in Prague decided to give them two of the forty certificates set aside for pioneers. At the beginning of March 1939, Edelstein wrote in confidence to the Jewish Agency in Jerusalem: "The presidency of the Zionist Federation in Czecho-Slovakia has decided that Dr. Hoffman and I must leave on immigration this year. We will travel on pioneer certificates, without wives or children, and we plan to return to Czecho-Slovakia eight days later." The presence of the two men in Prague was now essential, and permanent immigration was impossible for the moment. They intended to obtain a multiple entry visa during their brief stay in Palestine, so that they could return whenever necessary, free of quota restrictions.

10

THE GERMANS CAME PREPARED

JUST AS HE HAD used the German minority to annex the Sudeten region to the Reich, so Hitler now exploited Slovakian aspirations of independence to vanquish what remained of Czecho-Slovakia. The invasion order had been given in December 1938 and, on the assumption that no active resistance was to be expected from the Czechs, was to be executed by the regular forces without any additional conscription. In early February 1939, Vojtech Tuka, the Slovakian prime minister, visited Hitler and requested that Slovakia be granted full independence and be freed finally from Czech domination. By the beginning of March 1939, encouraged by the Germans, the activities of the Slovakian and Carpathian Russian separatist movements had reached such proportions that the government in Prague deemed it necessary to intervene. On March 6, President Hacha dissolved the government in Carpathian Russia and, three days later, that of autonomous Slovakia. He ordered Tiso and his colleagues to be placed under house arrest, declared a state of emergency, and gave Hitler the excuse he sought for immediate action. On March 11, Seyss-Inquart, the governor of Austria, and several German generals burst in on the Slovakian government while it was in session and ordered them to declare their severance from Czecho-Slovakia at once. Tiso escaped his house arrest, was flown to Berlin, and was presented with the formulation of the declaration of independence; and on March 14, the independent state of Slovakia was born, a development that released Britain from her promise given in Munich to guarantee the security of the republic of Czecho-Slovakia, on the grounds that one could not guarantee what no longer existed.

Suffering from a weak heart and deeply concerned, the president of Czecho-Slovakia requested an interview with Hitler in an attempt to prevent bloodshed. Dr. Hacha arrived in Berlin on the night of March 14, and was ushered in to Hitler after midnight. Hacha expressed his belief that Czecho-Slovakia was in good hands under the Führer, and sought to procure Hitler's assurance that the Czech people had the right to an independent national existence. But Hitler, who was not inclined to be charitable toward the aging Hacha, informed him that the German army had already been ordered to invade Bohemia and Moravia: the German divisions would start to move at 6 A.M. The Czechs had two alternatives: they could either receive the Germans quietly, or they could resist—and all opposition would be mercilessly quelled (after all, for every Czech battalion, the Germans had an entire division). In other words, the choice was either peaceful relations between the Czech and German peoples or the destruction of the Czechs. Hacha and Foreign Minister Chvalkovsky at first refused to sign the surrender which had been prepared on their behalf. The frail president fainted in agitation and had to be revived by Hitler's personal physician. In the end, however, a broken Hacha signed the document: to preserve quiet, order, and peace, he placed the security of the Czech people and Czech country in the hands of the leader of the Reich.

On March 14, business proceeded as usual at the HICEM office in Prague. A list was drawn up of refugees who required urgent immigration to Bolivia, just as a day earlier such a list had been prepared for England. There was little practical import to these lists, but they served to bolster the morale of potential immigrants. The radio announced Tiso's visit to Hitler; in the office was a veteran German refugee who had fled from Berlin to Vienna, from Vienna to Carlsbad, from Carlsbad to Prague. With the smile of experience, he asked: "How does it feel to have the Nazis approaching for the first time?"

It was clear that drastic changes were imminent. Youth-Aliyah decided to round up the youngsters who were supposed to leave on March 20, and quickly rented a house for them in one of Prague's northern suburbs. On the evening of March 14, the Youth-Aliyah people met with the leaders of the pioneering youth movements at Hehalutz headquarters to plan a course of action. Hoffman had asked Milena Jesenská—Franz Kafka's Milena—what, in the opinion of Beneš's circle, was likely to happen in the next few days. Jesenská felt that Prime Minister Rudolf Beran, the former chairman of the Agrarian Party, would join the government of General Gajda, leader of the Czech Fascists, or, at worst, rule would pass into Gajda's hands and a Fascist dictatorship would take over. Armed with this information, those present at the meeting tried to set down guidelines for work should the movements have to go underground. In the event of an emergency it was decided to work in triads, each triad being responsible for a specific task. The sacred movement-party key was relinquished, and all those present were given a code name.

Before the meeting adjourned—so that the participants could get to the train station to take leave of the immigrants traveling through Ostrava to Poland, Constantia, and Haifa—Hoffman phoned the head of the Ostrava Jewish community to clear up some technical details. Receiving no reply, he tried the Ostrava community offices, where a panic-stricken caretaker hastily hung up after informing Hoffman: "What, don't you know? The Germans have entered Ostrava!" Irma Polak, one of Prague's leading women Zionists, received a similar message while preparing to leave for the train station. She took Dr. Kahn aside at the train station, and said that the train must be postponed: they could not send people straight into the arms of the Germans. Dr. Kahn put a finger to his lips and said that not a word must be said to the immigrants; they would have to hope that all would pass peacefully. Those in the know assumed that the Germans were simply passing through Ostrava on the way to independent Slovakia, or that borders were again being rearranged on the basis of the Munich Pact, or that the Germans were trying to establish a corridor between Silesia and Austria to give them a territorial continuum.

True, German newspapers had published hair-raising descriptions of the acts of terror perpetrated by Czechs on helpless Germans, and in German circles rumor was rife that German forces were to invade Czecho-Slovakia, but to most Jews, these rumors appeared totally illogical: even without invasion, the Czechs were doing all they could to satisfy Hitler. Why, that very week, on Sunday, German citizens had celebrated the twentieth anniversary of the Sudeten German uprising against their inclusion in the Czechoslovakian republic. They had hung flags outside their windows, all brand new, all of equal size, all with a swastika. And, as instructed by the authorities, the Czech population had not even reacted: they were to do nothing to provoke the Germans. Two days later, members of the Hitler Youth had paraded through the streets of Prague, shouting "*Sieg Heil!*" with Czech police at their sides to protect them. Surely the Germans could find nothing reprehensible in Czech behavior, and was not Hacha even now with Hitler in Berlin? There could be no invasion while negotiations were under way.

At the Wilson station, near the train to Constantia, stood another train, destined for Stockholm. On it were five hundred wives and children of German socialists who had recently been moved to Britain and France by Stopford and his colleagues, following rumors of an expected German invasion. That very day, a member of the British delegation had managed, after feverish attempts, to obtain a collective Polish visa for the wives and children, and now everyone—the British, the refugees, the Jews, the immigrants— were all at the train station together, counting the minutes as they waited for the trains to pull out. Stopford, Kahn, Edelstein, Ullman, and Hannah Steiner walked up and down the trains from compartment to compartment, bidding farewell to friends and acquaintances. The travelers bound for Constantia asked Stopford about the rumor that the Germans had invaded Ostrava. "There's not a shred of truth in it," he replied, just as Kahn and Edelstein had said. At 11 P.M. the train pulled out on schedule, and wound its way eastward. Those who, like Max Brod, had ordered sleeping compartments, slept, weary from the excitement. At 4 A.M. the train pulled into the Ostrava station, where silent German soldiers were posted. The Czech border police and customs officials worked at incredible speed. They stamped passports without checking, did not rummage through suitcases, took no interest in the lists of articles. With evident impatience, they hustled the passengers forward, calling "Next, next," and in no time at all the train had left the station and crossed into Poland. Kahn had been right, the risk had been justified. The Germans who had entered Ostrava early, so as to prevent the possibility of Polish forces entering Czecho-Slovakia during the general invasion, had not yet managed to organize. The army had not yet received its orders. The last train from the Czecho-Slovakian republic got away with close to one hundred and sixty certificate holders and their families who reached Palestine safely.

Early in the morning of March 15, his Jewish landlady woke Avraham Reich with cries of "The Germans have come!" Reich sped to Yekef and found him wrapped in a prayer shawl, reciting his morning prayers. Edelstein decided that the first thing to do was to remove incriminating information about the transfer of capital from the files of immigration candidates.

In Jewish homes, the first to learn that German forces had entered Czecho-Slovakia were the maids, who rose early to light the stoves that cool, dark winter morning, and, as usual, switched on the radio to have some music while they worked. The Polak family in their home in Podoly were awoken by the cries of their loyal maid, and Irma Polak's first thought was concern for Maria Schmolka: her struggles on behalf of German refugees had undoubtedly implicated her. "You must leave at once," Irma told her friend on the phone. "You're the seventh person this morning to demand that I leave," Maria replied, "but I have no such intention." Irma rushed to the HICEM office, but Maria wasn't there. She had gone to the American embassy to try to save a political refugee at the last minute. When she finally returned, she and Irma went home together to burn the papers she had in her house: the testimony of witnesses to what was happening under the Nazi regime, letters from people who had helped smuggle out political refugees, addresses. The maid lit a fire in the laundry room and there they burned the papers until 2 P.M.

When Haim Hoffman heard the announcement early morning, he hurried first to Hans Lichtwitz, code-named Uri as of the day before. He and Lichtwitz took two revolvers for which Hoffman had no permit and threw them under a pile of leaves in a deserted public park. A light snow fell, and few people were in the streets. It would be another few hours before the Germans got to Prague and managed to organize themselves, Hoffman assumed, and he went to the community center on Dlouhá Street. He found Dr. Kahn in his room, his face drawn, but quiet and controlled. The two men decided to leave only a handful of people to man the offices and to work out a communication system with the rest.

Edelstein went to the British consulate to find out how the

occupation would affect the immigration candidates and to collect, among other things, the two certificates Hehalutz had allocated him and Hoffman—just in case. But he remembered that Miriam did not even have a passport and he asked Hoffman to use his connections with the Prague police in order to get her one. When Hoffman reached police headquarters, however, the SS were already there, and he retraced his steps. Edelstein, on the other hand, was successful in his mission, and he returned from the consulate with an envelope containing twelve permits—entrance visas to England for the members of the Zionist leadership, including März, Kahn, Zucker, Reiss, Hoffman, and Edelstein, which had been prepared in advance at the initiative of the Zionist Executive in London. The permits stated that they had been issued "in recognition for devoted work on behalf of German refugees," in itself sufficient cause to incriminate them with the Gestapo. In addition, Edelstein had also the two pioneer certificates, dated the previous day, which the British consul had given him and Hoffman, together with a warm letter which might have proved equally dangerous.

A cold wind blew from the Vltava River; the streets were still, as pale-faced refugees sought political asylum at the British and American embassies: refugees from the Reich, anti-Nazis, socialists. The British took in British subjects, particularly journalists, for whose safety they feared, and half a dozen political refugees, including Rudolf Katz, an Austrian communist (who was executed twenty years later during the Slansky trials). Wenzel Jaksch, the leader of the German Social Democrats, found asylum with the Americans, but the hundreds of others, mostly Jews, who had come to beg for a visa, for temporary shelter, were very politely turned away: nothing could be done for them.

German students gathered near the Deutsches Haus, opposite the old Prashna Brana. Windows of German homes were decked out with swastika flags and flowers. Anxious mothers escorted their children to school, which had opened as usual. The first German forces reached the outskirts of Prague after 9 A.M., and by ten they were in the heart of the city. The winter weather had not impeded their progress: thousands of open cars and convoys moved through the city streets carrying soldiers in gray uniforms, as silent as those who watched them from the sidewalks. Here and there some people cried, some raised fists, some whistled in contempt. The Germans did not respond. Even the German citizens who had taken to the streets, waving flags and calling "*Sieg Heil!*" could not turn the entry of German forces into Prague into a victory parade, after the manner of the Austrian and Sudeten invasions. For the first time in the history of their tour of conquest, the Germans had entered a hostile country.

The staff of the Palestine office—Leo Janowitz, the secretaries, Peppi Steif and Mrs. Marikov, and Harry Tressler, a clever, curly-haired young man who had been sent by Hehalutz to help with the workload at the office—stood on Narodni Street, one of Prague's main roads, and watched the passing convoy of the German invasion force. What now? They, too, thought first of the potentially incriminating documents and, following a phone call between Leo Janowitz and Yekef, rented a room in a hotel that charged by the hour (not usually for paperwork), and brought suitcases full of files from the community center. At first they burned only bank orders in the coal stove in the room, but because the selection of isolated papers was slow work, after a while they started to burn entire portions of files.

Toward noon, the Zionist leadership met at Kahn's flat on Lodecka Street. Emil Margulies, who had initiated the Bernheim petition, had meant to leave on the train the night before, but some unfinished business got in the way and he had postponed his departure to the following week, when the next boat left for Palestine. Hoffman urged him to leave immediately: he was in greater danger than anybody else. The regular train to Budapest left in two hours; perhaps he could still get through. Margulies allowed himself to be persuaded, rose, left, and managed to get away, as did hundreds of others who took the initiative, simply purchased train tickets, and went. Those who tried their luck the next day found the borders already closed.

Dr. Kahn opened the meeting with the question of who was to leave and who to stay. He was staying himself, as were März and Edelstein. Key positions were reallocated, with März and Kahn on the leadership, František Friedmann as liaison with the Czech authorities, Otto Zucker head of the transfer department, and Edelstein head of immigration. Everyone felt that Hoffman, with his close ties to the German socialists and other political refugees in Czecho-Slovakia, was in great danger and should leave as soon as possible.

Some of those present felt that until this moment the Zionist Organization had not encouraged its leaders and instructors to emigrate; now they were trapped in a Nazi regime and must be rescued. Edelstein disagreed: for years the Zionists had claimed to be the true and responsible leaders of the Jewish people, and yet they had never really succeeded in reaching the Jewish masses. This was a historical moment: the Jewish population felt lost and were looking for someone to lead them. They could not be abandoned now. Mass emigration might have to be organized, or, if this too proved impossible, the Zionist leaders would have to face the problem of protecting the multitude until the storm had passed, and, whatever happened, their place was now at the head of Jewry.

The Germans came prepared with lists and addresses. In the late afternoon, a group of security police, led by Polizeikommisar Fuchs of Berlin, arrived at the community center on Dlouhá Street. They found Dr. Kahn in the Zionist Organization's offices, as well as Shimon Enoch, an emissary from Kibbutz Na'an who had insisted on keeping the Hehalutz office open. They were questioned about the activities of their offices and about immigration, and were asked the whereabouts of certain people. Felix Weltsch? Gone. Max Brod? Also gone. Hans Lichtwitz? Dr. Hoffman? Kahn answered valiantly that he did not know where they were at that moment, but even if he did, he would not say. The security police locked up all the empty offices, leaving only the Hehalutz and Zionist Organization rooms open. Nobody was arrested.

Lichtwitz was still in Prague, hiding with friends while the Gestapo searched for him. As a favor to his father, a senior official in the railway administration, Czech railway employees were to smuggle him out in a locomotive to Ostrava. From there he crossed the border into Poland through underground passageways in abandoned mines. When he reached Warsaw he phoned Edelstein to say that he had arrived safely. "Thank God," Edelstein replied, "one worry less." A golden era had dawned for smugglers on both sides of the border: people fleeing Czecho-Slovakia were prepared to pay thousands of crowns for passage along clandestine routes to Poland in order to escape the Germans, and almost five thousand Jews fled after the Germans invaded Czecho-Slovakia. Many of them hoped to reach the West; a few, for ideological reasons, intended to join the struggle against the Germans. And most, temporarily, settled around Lemberg.

Youth-Aliyah also called a meeting on invasion day, attended by several emissaries from Palestine. They spoke in hushed tones and sat in the dark so as not to alert the neighbors as to how many people were present. It was agreed that the temporary emissaries should leave that very night, no more large forums were to be convened, and ongoing work was to be run by the triads. It turned out that the staff of the invasion army had set up headquarters only a few hundred yards from where the youngsters waiting to emigrate were housed. Two members of the Youth-Aliyah secretariat went to inform German headquarters of the children's presence, hoping thereby to ensure that the children would not be harmed. And indeed the matter passed peacefully. The Germans had not yet achieved their proverbial efficiency, and, more important, Prague was not Vienna. Soldiers acted with restraint; instead of the tormented Germans they had expected to find, from the depictions in the Reich press, they found only calm. Jews were not attacked and the only assault launched by the German army was on Prague's well-stocked food and clothing shops, and German bookstores, which carried titles long banned in the Reich.

In the evening, the Führer arrived in Prague, and there were no hysterical mobs to greet him. Present among the silent crowds who watched the black cars speeding by was engineer Shimkin from Haifa. He had come on his own initiative, after failing to receive approval from the Zionist institutions to assassinate Hitler in Austria. In his pocket he carried a grenade, but the cars were closed and it was impossible to guess which was the Führer's. Shimkin had managed to enter Czecho-Slovakia legally, but that same night he stole across the border and returned to Palestine, having accomplished nothing. Hitler went inside the Hradčany Castle, seat of Bohemian glory, where rooms had been hastily prepared for him. He appeared at the window for a moment, for the sake of the Germans waiting below, and quickly retreated. It was his first and last visit to Prague, and he never improved his relationship with the Czech people. In a photograph that immortalizes the arrival of the German High Command, Hacha looks short, and General Sirovy thickset, next to the tall Germans in their long coats, who appeared almost noble in the spotlights. A curfew was imposed, Prague's streets were deserted, and all footsteps echoed in the distance.

Already, on invasion day, Hitler had declared Bohemia and Moravia to be a protectorate, and few people understood the meaning of the strange word, inspired by the legal connection between France and Tunisia. Reich citizenship was bestowed on all Germans, while the rest of the population became subjects of the Protectorate. At the head of the independent administration stood a Reichsprotektor, but foreign affairs, military matters, and transportation were handled directly by the Reich. Appointed to the new position was Konstantin von Neurath, foreign minister of the Reich regime until he was replaced by von Ribbentrop in 1938. Von Neurath, an old-fashioned aristocrat, a moderate bureaucrat, seemed to suit the Czech character. The transfer of authority was orderly, and Czech civil servants hardly even bothered to destroy any documents before the Germans took over. Employees kept a low profile and continued in their jobs, just as they had been asked to do on the radio: to overcome their pain with level-headedness, and not exacerbate the situation with emotional outbursts; to accept what fate had dealt them and adapt to the new conditions as quickly as possible. Hacha continued as president and Alois Elias, formerly the transportation minister in Beran's government, was appointed prime minister. Henlein, who had drawn up a detailed memorandum for the solution of the "Czech problem" right after Munich, was appointed head of the civil administration, a position that effectively put an end to his days of glory, while Karl Hermann Frank, his deputy in the SdP, received the decisive appointment of secretary of state.

Only Reich followers in Carpathian Russia were to be bitterly disappointed that fateful March 15. Their ambitious dream of a large Fascist Ukraine, incorporating eastern Galicia, where Ukrainians had never accepted Polish rule, was not to be. The independence they had so longed for, which was to be only the first step toward realizing this dream, lasted only one day. For on the same day that German forces entered Czecho-Slovakia, the Hungarian army invaded Carpathian Russia and effortlessly subdued the local national guard, with mute approval from the Germans. Carpathian Russia returned to Hungary, to which it had belonged under the dual monarchy; and it was safe to assume from this arrangement, that, contrary to what commentators had long claimed, the Ukraine's grain stores did not head Hitler's list of priorities. His sights were set on Poland, and Stalin was well aware of the implications this held for the Soviet Union.

On the day Hitler invaded Czecho-Slovakia, Weizmann learned the contents of a British government document which was the basis of the White Paper. Roughly summarized, its provisions were: a Palestinian state within ten years, Jewish immigration restricted to 10,000 people annually, the immigration of 25,000 refugees, total immigration not to exceed 75,000, and subsequent immigration only with Arab approval. That evening, Jan Masaryk, an old family friend, dined with the Weizmanns. He was a changed man, his spark of life extinguished. After a lengthy silence, he pointed to his puppy and said, "He's all I have left, and believe me, I'm ashamed to look him in the eyes." Masaryk told Weizmann of the talk he'd had with Chamberlain following Munich. He had accused Chamberlain of having betrayed Czechoslovakia, to which the prime minister had replied: "Mr. Masaryk, you believe in Dr. Beneš, and I trust in Herr Hitler." When, after the German invasion of Prague, Weizmann heard Chamberlain ask the House of Commons why the English should endanger themselves for some remote country about which they knew little and whose language they did not understand, his natural reaction was: "If that's how they speak of the Czechs, what can the Jews expect from such a government?" It was clear that they could not hope for much active aid or sympathy from the Western democracies. Just as the British had tried to appease Hitler, so would they try to appease the Arabs.

Only after protests from an enraged public in both France and Britain did the two governments lodge a formal protest with the Reich against the invasion of Prague. The Reich, of course, produced the document signed by the unfortunate Hacha as confirmation of the will of the Czech people. (Hacha defined the republic that had died after only twenty years as a "fleeting episode in the history of the Czech people" who had again returned to the German sphere of influence.) The Germans left the Czechs with an illusion of independence consisting of the authority to handle commercial negotiations and the appointment of Chvalkovsky as the Protectorate's envoy in Berlin. It was only prudent, therefore, to do the Germans' bidding, rather than arouse their ire: there was still something to lose.

The security police arrived along with the army. Equipped with lists and aided by the local population, they systematically arrested communists, socialists, and known anti-Nazis, particularly from among refugees. It is estimated that between two thousand and twenty-five hundred people were arrested on the day of conquest. Nevertheless, Jews were not assaulted, nor ordered to scrub sidewalks, as in Vienna, nor beaten up by the mob; although in several towns the local authorities showed commendable diligence and took the initiative into their own hands. In Moravská Ostrava, which had a large German minority, Jewish businessmen were led to Gestapo headquarters on the day after invasion and forced to transfer their businesses to Aryans. Synagogues were burned, the Jewish community was ordered to clean up the rubble, and their addresses were removed from property records.

Gestapo envoys, three members of the Czech secret police, came to the welfare institute and HICEM offices, which were in the same building. They were still somewhat embarrassed by their new functions and apologized for having received an order to close down the offices and take the employees away with them. At HICEM Hannah Steiner held in her hand a list, prepared the day before, of people who were likely to be in great danger in the event of a German invasion. She shoved the list into the hands of Michael Jakobi, HICEM's legal adviser, who succeeded in getting away while the police were busy sealing up the main door. At the welfare office, a clerk took matters into his own hands and managed to burn the file on German refugees before the police arrived, but all of HICEM's files fell into German hands.

Hannah Steiner was arrested. When Maria Schmolka heard, she immediately went to the Gestapo, said that she was in charge of HICEM, and was arrested on the spot. At first the two women— Maria, aged forty-nine, and Hannah, forty-five—shared a cell with thirty other women in the police jail, and the Czech guards helped wherever they could: smuggling in food, "losing" cigarettes in the cell. After three weeks, Steiner was released, but Schmolka was transferred to the central prison in Pankrac. Her diabetes and ischiatic condition, from which she had long suffered, grew considerably worse in prison, and she was only permitted insulin after the intervention of Robert Stopford, who threatened an international scandal if a woman known all over the world was denied medical care. She was interrogated several times at Gestapo headquarters in the Peček Bank building on Brodecka Street, now known to Czechs as Pečkarna, and the very name instilled terror. (The two branches of the Peček family had left Czechoslovakia before the Munich Pact, and had even sold some of their considerable property to the Reich for foreign currency; their assets in Czechoslovakia and Germany were at the time estimated at $100 million.)

The communists, who were better informed as to what was happening in the international political arena, had long since been instructed on escape routes in times of emergency. Officers in the Czech army determined to continue the struggle against the Germans, people who understood the full significance of occupation, went underground or stole across the Polish or Slovakian borders (the only routes still open). But the overwhelming majority of Jews in the Protectorate were too concerned with immediate family worries to think about the distant future. What now? What was to become of the business, the shop, the job at the bank? What about studies, and savings? Their chief worry was for livelihood, not life. The first thing to do was adopt austerity measures, give up luxuries, and above all, come what may, keep the family together.

Most Jews in the provinces, the towns, the villages, salaried employees who after years of struggle had finally managed to build a life for themselves in one form or another, never even considered emigration during the early days of occupation. What could they do to such small fry, after all? What could happen to a pensioner? To a clerk? At worst he would be fired and have to take whatever work he could find, even menial jobs; the main thing was to see it through. A store of food should be set aside, housewives reflected, shoes, wool; prices might go up. We're in this together, the Czech neighbors said; Hitler hates us too. Why emigrate? Where to? Under the republic there had been virtually no Jewish emigration from the western section now called a Protectorate. If Jews had relatives abroad, they were mostly in neighboring countries—Austria or Germany—and many had returned to Czechoslovakia as refugees. Very few had relatives across the sea who could help them emigrate. They had no assets outside, no idea what one could do in some South American country whose language they did not speak. This was their home, come what may; here they would always have a roof over their heads, bread to eat, and family and friends to fall back on in times of need. "You don't abandon your country when it is in trouble," wrote Karl Poláček, expressing the view of many. Those whose families had emigrated to Czechoslovakia from Eastern Europe remembered the stories of their parents and grandparents about pogroms in their old homeland: the rioting all stops in time, and even if some people are killed, the majority nevertheless survives. In the first few weeks of occupation, the Germans did nothing to encourage the mass emigration of the Protectorate's Jews across the sea, knowing full well that such an exodus would have to come at the expense of Jewish emigration from the Reich and Austria; and those countries had to be purged first. On the day after the invasion, Goering wrote an urgent letter to the Reich representatives in Bohemia and Moravia, demanding that they refrain from unrestrained Aryanization of Jewish property; he himself would decide the appropriate moment, dimensions, and speed of the measures to be taken.

Most Jews did not feel as if a gaping abyss had suddenly opened before them, between yesterday and today; they did not consider the situation as unprecedented or unparalleled. They saw it as a continuum, albeit a frightening one, a worrying one, fraught with danger; but not the end of their familiar world. In the first few weeks of the Protectorate, life continued almost as usual, without any drastic changes, except for the overnight change in road traffic from left to right. Here an old German friend suddenly broke off relations; there an acquaintance quickly passed to the other side of the street. All Jewish law offices were transferred to Czechs according to a decision that had been taken by the Bar Association even prior to invasion. Here and there signs appeared, marked "Aryan Shop." But the pace of life had not changed. The Czech population even felt some improvement in economic conditions. Unemployment gradually went down. Many laborers went to work in Germany, where salaries were higher. The German authorities, in those first weeks, left the question of the Jews to the Czechs, and the latter hoped that all the Jewish wealth, especially that of future emigrants, would fall into their hands. But first the Czechs needed time to learn to live in a Protectorate.

Everyone had to learn: how the government worked, what the complex relations were between the Protektor's office and Karl Hermann Frank, who had direct authority over the police but was subordinate to Himmler, the commander of the SS and security police. They had to learn the difference between regular police, who dealt with arrests and dispersed demonstrations; police who dealt with criminals; and the security police and Gestapo, who dealt with political matters. They had to try to sort out the duplication in functions, and the tension between the army and the Gestapo. To their great surprise, the Czechs discovered that even those in German uniform could be bribed, especially the lower ranks, with whom they had daily contact; and bribery became almost a national duty.

The Czech people showed their opposition to conquest in their own way. On April 21, the Führer's birthday, a national holiday was declared in the Protectorate. A huge fete was held at the Masaryk Stadium in Prague, but three sides of the stadium remained empty. To mark Hitler's birthday, Czechs placed wreaths at the foot of the statue of Jan Hus, the symbol of Czech liberation from the Catholic Church; at the grave of the unknown soldier; and at the foot of the statue of President Wilson. When, on one occasion, the Philharmonic orchestra played Smetana's "My Homeland," the audience burst into enthusiastic applause which lasted fifteen minutes, and the conductor kissed the notes. The heroes of the Hussite wars would still wake from their sleep and come to the aid of their people. Schweik's spirit was revived: when the Germans sought to base their rule on one of the key "National Unity" organizations, 97.4 percent of the Czech population voted for it, transforming the affair into a demonstration of national identification. In movie houses, the audience laughed in the dark at snatches of newsreel from Germany, and waiters in cafés presented the *Völkischer Beobachter* and other Nazi newspapers upside down. In the evening, Czechs sat in the capital's beer gardens, drank, traded rumors, and waited for a miracle.

The German security services were not overly impressed by the sporadic anti-Jewish incidents initiated by Czechs: "It is not to be concluded that the entire Czech population has adopted an anti-Semitic stance. The ordinary Czech on the street—as opposed to the government—no longer views the Jewish question as a problem. His only emotion, and it predominates over all others, is hatred for the Germans (hidden because of external circumstances). True, there are groups who take an aggressive anti-Jewish line, but they are the minority and have little influence," the report to Berlin read.

During the early days of conquest hundreds of Jewish refugees— particularly those for whom Prague or Brünn was already the third or fourth station of their flight from Hitler—tried to take their own lives. Local Jews did not share their despair: they would wait and see what happened.

The major concern was continued emigration. Several hundred people with certificates were waiting with their families, ready to leave, as were four hundred pioneers slated for illegal immigration. Two days after the invasion, the Youth-Aliyah head office in London phoned Prague to reassure its members: should the Youth-Aliyah group arrive too late for the ship leaving on March 21, they would be given berths on a different ship. But the illegal immigration people in Warsaw sent word that the boat docked at the Yugoslavian port could not wait much longer; should the pioneers and Maccabi emigrants from Czechoslovakia be delayed, Polish emigrants would be sent in their place. Taking his life in his hands, Hoffman ordered a phone call to Youth-Aliyah in Warsaw. Such a course of action might well endanger all future immigration from the Protectorate within the framework of the transfer agreement; the places on the boat must be kept for the four hundred pioneers waiting for exit permits.

Kahn, as the representative of the Zionist Federation, and Shimon Enoch of Hehalutz, who had been at the Zionist center when the Germans came, were summoned to Gestapo headquarters for interrogation. They were questioned separately and politely—no violence was used against them—and informed that the Germans were interested in continued immigration. The chief of the Gestapo in Prague, Polizeikommisar Fuchs, asked Kahn about the nature of Zionism and the means of immigration, and at the end wanted to know: are we as terrible as we are made out to be? Kahn's courageous reply was: you inspire fear. Fuchs, a Berliner and moderately even-tempered man, appointed Kahn sole representative in all matters connected with immigration to Palestine. (Kahn wanted no part of German sympathy or mercy, and when asked where he had lost his arm he would reply that it had been in a car accident; his pride would not let him tell the Germans that it had happened when he was an officer in the Austrian army during the Great War.) Kahn returned from his encounter with the Gestapo in shock: immigration would continue, but for the sake of immigration and rescue they would become lackeys of the Nazi regime. They would call "immigration" what in effect would be deportation, and they would help the Germans plunder and call it "donations to the Foundation Fund." Jews will want to spit in our faces and we will have to do shameful things to save them, he told Hoffman and Edelstein. Kahn was the only one who grasped immediately the terrible contradiction that confronted the Jews: rescue was impossible without collaborating with the Germans. But he was a pessimist, older than his forty-four years. Edelstein, eight years younger, with his faith in the God of Israel, was more optimistic. United, the Jews would manage, thousands of young people could be sent to Palestine, and if the price was contact with the Germans, then it had to be paid. "Edelstein thinks that God guides his hand," Kahn used to tell März.

Edelstein too was asked to report to Fuchs, to explain the exact nature of the Palestine office. A week after the invasion, Edelstein wrote to London, saying that there was hope that the transports to Palestine would shortly resume, and he asked for special consideration for the Jews of the Protectorate in the next allocation of certificates.

While the Palestine office remained closed, its staff usually got together at Peppi Steif's flat. Peppi was Edelstein's secretary, a young, hefty woman who protected Yekef against the onslaught of refugees and guarded his door like a lioness. While waiting for the office to reopen, the staff members sometimes played bridge, or listened to records, usually classical music—two activities in which Edelstein took no part: to him, symphonies were "long music." Yekef used to ask for cantorial pieces by Yossele Rosenblatt and listen to them again and again, sometimes humming along, while the others were absorbed in bridge.

On the whole the atmosphere was optimistic: after all, in Germany the Nazis had been in control for six years already and Hehalutz still functioned; pioneers still went to training divisions outside Germany, and immigration still continued. Even under the Nazis, 45,000 Jews had already managed to leave Germany for Palestine and take with them millions of marks, usually with German approval. On March 29, Moshe Shertok received a cable informing him that the Palestine office had reopened. The Gestapo had given Edelstein the keys and work could resume—under German supervision, of course.

Word came from the Gestapo that the Youth-Aliyah and pioneer immigrant groups could proceed with their plans: the German authorities required a list of names so that they could issue exit permits. Accompanying the first group of seventy youngsters were to be six bearers of certificates—including Hoffman and his wife. Kahn hesitated. How could he put Hoffman's name down on the list? He hadn't even slept at home since the invasion. Hoffman thought that it was worth a try now (with a slight modification in the name), while the Germans were not yet fully organized. And the Germans did in fact return the list, together with a collective exit permit. Kahn and Edelstein came to see the youngsters off, spoke with emotion, and asked Hoffman, the first member of the leadership to leave since the invasion, to report fully to the central Zionist bodies, to Weizmann and Kahn, the chairman of the Joint. The first illegal transport of Hehalutz and Maccabi to leave after the invasion was also fortunate: they left on April 4, and two weeks later arrived safely at the shores of Palestine. The speedy journey enhanced the general optimism about continued immigration, both legal and illegal.

11

IMMIGRATION MUST CONTINUE

LENGTHY DISCUSSIONS took place among the Zionist leaders who remained behind—Kahn, Zucker, März, Edelstein—on the question of relations with the Germans. One such meeting was attended by Moshe Baumgarten, who heard Kahn say that in future, if possible, he would take no part in dealing with the Germans; he did not elaborate. Edelstein, on the other hand, argued that they had to deal with the Germans, if only to accelerate emigration—and he was prepared to do the job. Moshe and the other young people from Youth-Aliyah supported him: they wanted a proud, firm Jew to face the Germans, not someone who would submit readily, nor a fawning or assimilated Jew. In any case, there were no volunteers for the job. Edelstein was the youngest of the Zionist leaders, filled with energy and a sense of mission. He developed good relations with Fuchs, chief of the Prague Gestapo, and could telephone him whenever necessary. When speaking to the Germans on the phone, he would respond in German fashion with "*Jawohl*," and Kahn, hearing him, would cringe: "Don't stand to attention when you speak to them," he said. To Edelstein, it was unimportant: the main thing was that emigration should continue. Was it not common practice to negotiate with the enemy for the release of hostages? Did not Moses go to Pharaoh to discuss the exodus of the children of Israel from Egypt?

A gradual shift took place in the positions of Kahn and Edelstein, almost as if a general and colonel had exchanged ranks. But Kahn remained the decisive figure in the background, and Edelstein conferred with him on all matters. After Zionist work was allowed to resume, Edelstein called together the entire staff of the Zionist movement at the suggestion of Dr. Tauber, one of his close friends from Teplitz-Schönau. The meeting took place in Moravia, at the community center in Olmütz, rather than in Prague, and Edelstein gave a sober analysis of the situation. He did not despair: they would manage. Dr. Tauber, who now worked for the Foundation Fund instead of in the legal profession, followed guidelines laid down by Edelstein. The Gestapo demanded that all fund-raisers report to the local office of the security police both when they arrived in a specific town and before they left, so as to submit a list of the donors. Edelstein feared German retaliation, not against those who contributed, but against those who did not—a fact the Germans were apt to construe as an attempt to sabotage emigration. He therefore told Tauber not to submit the lists to the Gestapo, and advised him to adopt various evasive tactics. Once the pretext was that he had not managed to prepare the list, once that there had not been any donations, merely pledges.

When Edelstein felt that he had an overall picture of the situation and could give a more or less objective report of the functions of the Zionist movement and the possibilities available in the new state of affairs, he sent a detailed letter in early May to Eliahu Dobkin, a member of the Jewish Agency Executive and one of the founders of the Ha'Ihud Party. "First of all it seems to me important to decide that our friends who hold formal functions in the Zionist movement should remain where they are. Dr. Kahn and I are considered the official representatives of the movement vis-à-vis the authorities, and we are both trying to achieve practical results with the necessary diligence."

The letter, which was written in German and sent through the regular mails, was formulated with care. It was primarily a call for Ha'Ihud to send emissaries to Czechoslovakia ("I am the only member of the circle in a responsible position"); extensive educational work was required and could succeed only if instructors came from Palestine and assumed its management.

One of the problems that the Zionist movement faced under occupation was regular and orderly contact with the Jewish population now that the Zionist newspapers had been banned: "The Palestine office is at this time putting out a newsletter which is rich in content and seems to me to fill the necessary condition for close contact. Other possibilities are visiting different places and consulting with colleagues. Everything depends on there being enough reliable people. Without any connection to the events: our Zionist life will continue, we'll see to that, and I believe that we'll also be able to keep our promise."

When Eichmann, the specialist on expediting Jewish emigration, came to Prague from Vienna, Edelstein was summoned to the Peček Palais. As Edelstein later reported to the Palestine office, Eichmann demanded that sixty thousand Jews emigrate within one year. Edelstein replied that it was impossible, particularly since emigration was impeded by systematic arrests, chiefly of Polish citizens. Since only thirdhand evidence has remained of the conversation between Edelstein and Eichmann, it is not clear how Eichmann reacted, nor whether, as a direct result of this meeting, Edelstein was permitted to leave for Palestine to try to attain the maximum number of certificates and promote illegal immigration.

Edelstein arrived in Palestine at the end of May, for one week, and he did not hide the fact that his wife, Miriam, and son, Arieh, had remained in Prague as hostages, especially when he was urged by various people from Horodenka, Teplitz-Schönau, and the Hehalutz leadership, to stay in Palestine and work from there to get his family out of Czechoslovakia. "I no longer have a say in the matter," he replied. He spent one night with Willy Feuerstein at Kibbutz Merchavia and spoke of his disappointing meeting with Ben-Gurion. Willy's impression was that Edelstein might perhaps have stayed in Palestine, but according to all other reports of conversations he had during his brief visit, Yekef never even thought of endangering his family and abandoning the Jews of the Protectorate so long as he had not achieved his goal. To the extent that there was mention of a job in Palestine, it referred to a later time, after mass immigration to Palestine had been completed, when he would come with the rearguard.

In practical terms, Edelstein's visit changed nothing with respect to expanding immigration. Apart from some words of comfort, the leaders of the Jewish Agency and various party members had nothing to give him. The Czech community in Palestine was small, numbering about six thousand, and though it included several well-known and distinguished people (Samuel Hugo Bergmann; Dr. Ticho, an ophthalmologist; Hans and Erich Moller, owners of the

Ata textile concern; engineer Richard Pacovsky; Dr. Aschermann, a gynecologist), they exerted little influence on the political foci of power in the Jewish community in Palestine. Sometimes in the company of his friend, Reich, or brother-in-law, Max (Miriam's elder brother, who had emigrated to Palestine), Edelstein met with Teplitz-Schönau Jews (at Egon Popper's two-room flat, a veritable mansion in those days) and with people from the Jewish Agency's political department, and on all occasions he demanded immediate action: the Jews must be gotten out en masse as quickly as possible.

In his talks with Haim Hoffman (who later Hebraicized his name to Yehiel) in Palestine, Edelstein revealed what he really thought of Eichmann (as he did to Ella Markus, his Czech correspondence secretary in Prague): with one leg resting on a chair, Eichmann spoke pleasantly while trying to extract information from him. He asked hundreds of questions about Judaism and Zionism, and Yekef's problem was how to reply without giving anything away, how to gain Eichmann's trust while being evasive.

After he returned from Palestine, Edelstein seemed truly despondent for the first time since the occupation. He gave vent to his depression in talks with Harry Tressler, his regular escort—a sort of mascot, messenger boy, and conversation partner, all in one: the people in Palestine can't help us. There's no one to talk to. The Jewish community in Palestine has enough worries of its own and won't make time for the worries of others. As for world Jewry—which includes many fine and wealthy Jews—it is not organized. We must create what the Germans claim has long existed: a world Jewish international. At present, Jewish world power is nothing but a myth.

Indeed, those were dark days for the Jewish community in Palestine now that the White Paper's recommendations had been instituted, limiting immigration to 75,000 certificates over the next five years. At the end of that period, the Jewish population in Palestine would constitute one third of the overall population, and any further growth of the Jewish national home would depend on Arab approval. The British grew harsher in their war against illegal immigration, and Weizmann wrote bitterly to his friend Leopold Amery, a member of the British parliament who had sharply attacked the policies of the colonial office.

> You will no doubt have learned about the ghastly scenes enacted here during the last few days in connection with the capture and expulsion of shiploads of what are called illegal immigrants, and of

the deep resentment that these scenes have aroused among the Jews here [in Palestine] . . . Untold tragedies are being enacted along these coasts. Boats, overloaded with refugees from German concentration camps, are floating about for weeks on end in the Mediterranean, their passengers starved and afflicted with the diseases of hunger and exhaustion, among them women, and children of tender age. Some of these boats were recently seized by British patrol vessels, dragged to Haifa and then pushed again to the open sea with their human cargo, although it was known that they were not seaworthy and that their provisions would not enable them to hold out for more than a few days. I wonder whom an enlightened judge would charge with illegal behaviour—the unfortunate Jews who are fleeing from hell which is Central Europe to the country where a National Home was promised to them or the Government which, despite its solemn pledges and international obligations, is imposing arbitrary restrictions on Jewish immigration and is driving the wretched victims of its policy into the open seas?

The report on his tour to Palestine which Edelstein submitted to the Prague Gestapo and which was transferred to the special department for Bohemia and Moravia at the Reich Security Head Office (RSHA) in Berlin gave no hint of doubt or disappointment, and its matter-of-fact tone shows only a desire to gain time.

According to the mission imposed on me, I was to make contact with all the relevant institutions in Palestine and, on the basis of confidential discussions, obtain a suitable number of certificates for the Protectorate. Moreover, I was to see that the pertinent economic and welfare organizations direct their attention to immigrants from the Protectorate in order to ease their absorption into Palestine. I was received by the immigration department of the Palestine government and submitted a detailed report on the activities of the Palestine office, with particular stress on the capability of our candidates. I was able to point to the fact that immigrants from the Protectorate had fully proved themselves both with respect to work and social acclimatization. The fact that a large percentage of our immigrants successfully underwent occupational retraining and that these people have stayed in agriculture understandably impressed the government favorably. Senior officials promised me that they would accord the Protectorate their due consideration when the time came to allocate certificates.

I had a series of talks with the Jewish Agency Executive in which I formulated our demands. I did not confine myself to a request for all the available types of certificates, but also demanded maxi-

mum consideration for our young people with regard to job place-
ment in various European countries where they could stay temporarily until they emigrate to Palestine. I told the Jewish Agency of
our work in occupational training and our handling of Jewish
youngsters, and I hope that I managed to find understanding for,
and appreciation of, our demands.

Edelstein briefly reviewed his meetings with representatives of
the Jewish National Committee, which had promised economic and
social aid; his visits to kibbutzim and other agricultural settlements
to clarify absorption possibilities; and his talks with businessmen
who hailed from the Protectorate and had promised to give special
consideration to hiring their fellow countrymen. The list of distinguished people with whom he had met consisted only of various
Jewish Agency functionaries, except for Sir Edwin Samuel, the
representative of the Mandate government.

It was a brave attempt to show activity. Edelstein pointed out that
he had been in contact with all the institutions that take students
and youth—the Hebrew University, the Technion, Mikve-Israel,
Ben-Shemen, WIZO. The sum total of all his efforts was: 220 immigration certificates for students, 164 for youngsters, 195 for children aged thirteen to fifteen, 255 for investors and their families, in
the coming allocation for April to September 1939. Together with
all the other types of permits, Edelstein was promised that 1,393
people would immigrate from the Protectorate.

"To this should be added the assurances [we received] with respect to indirect immigration through occupational training in various countries; that is, the Palestine office will be able to allow over
three thousand people to emigrate by the end of September. Obviously this operation will be successfully executed only if the suitable
necessary conditions will technically prevail in the Protectorate." So
that the Protectorate's relatively large share in the certificates to be
allotted could be properly appreciated, Edelstein noted that they
constitute 20 percent of all the certificates issued to immigrants
across the world. He did the best he could.

"During my visit, the association of immigrants from Bohemia
and Moravia was founded in Palestine; it works closely with immigrants from the Reich and from Ostmark, and these two bodies are
recognized by the German consulate in Palestine. The German
consul in Haifa was good enough to receive me and I reported to
him on my activities in Palestine."

12

EICHMANN PRESSES
FOR EMIGRATION

ALIYAH (immigration to Palestine), *kvutza* (group), *sicha* (discussion), *madrich* (instructor, counselor) were new, esoteric words filled with magic for thousands of Jewish students and high school pupils who had grown up in a Czech environment. Often brought up by their parents to stay away from insulating Jewish society, they had sometimes absorbed a critical "Christian" attitude toward Judaism—only to find themselves suddenly merely tolerated, or even ostracized, in Czech society. Their natural reaction to this blow to their pride was to seek a new source of pride: the pioneering Zionist youth movements.

Sometimes these young people felt as if all their lives they had in fact been striving for the impossible: to be accepted by Czech society as equals, as Czechs in every respect apart from a few minor, old-fashioned family customs. For many it was a revelation. They realized how comfortable it was to live among fellow Jews with whom there was no need to be on guard; how effortless, how unnecessary to make an impression. How many wonderful experiences derived from life in the youth movement: how good it was to hike through the woods (sometimes with restricted access to water, as training for the land of the desert), to camp out in tents, sit in parks, engage in stormy ideological debate or exercise drills, and to sing Hebrew songs with all one's heart.

Agricultural training was an adventure: sleeping on hard mattresses, sprouting blisters on one's hands, milking cows, drying hay, gathering potatoes on a cold and rainy autumn day, soaking up warmth around an open fire, experiencing first love in body and soul, far from parental supervision, waiting eagerly for cake parcels from home, telling Czech laborers of faraway Palestine and arousing their envy: there they would work, not as slaves on large estates, but as free men in a collective where all men are equal.

Meanwhile, at home, Mother prepared a trunk lined with wax paper. Carefully, almost as if she were laying away a trousseau, she put in the requisite articles for a pioneer in Palestine: sheets, towels, blue work clothes specially sewn by the home seamstress, heavy work boots. The young intellectuals—intended to be lawyers, poets, musicians, scientists, doctors—loaded straw onto wagons, took out oxen to plough the beet fields, and found the life they lived on training farms full and meaningful. They wrote poems and read them to their companions around a kerosene lamp. They found an answer to their search, and a goal for their longing: one day they would leave for a sun-soaked land, about which they knew very little, despite the Zionist literature they had read and the lectures their instructors delivered.

At the Youth-Aliyah office, where only a few weeks previously the first list of emigrating children had been prepared under protest from their parents, the latter now almost came to blows in their attempts to get their children registered. JU-AL, Prague's Youth-Aliyah school, was a one-year course for youngsters aged between fourteen and sixteen which offered Hebrew, history, mathematics, physics, chemistry, biology, gymnastics, and singing, in preparation for emigration to Palestine, which—the advertisements promised—would take place at the end of the year. Some of the instructors put aside their own agricultural training and came to teach at the school: here lay the real promise and future of Jewry. The teachers, now addressed only by their first names, served as an example for the youngsters and became the figures of authority in their lives, rather than the children's worried and bewildered parents.

During the first few weeks of the Protectorate, Jews were only gradually pushed out of their jobs and cut off from their livelihood. Thus far, such action was generally the result of private initiative or local diligence, and a realistic approach to life on the part of non-Jewish employers, who for years had kept their social or economic envy of Jews in check. But as of June 21, three months after the

Germans came, Jews were now officially defined as a separate race in the Protectorate, a definition conforming to the Nuremberg racial laws "in defense of German blood and honor." Here, too, 1935 (the year in which the Nuremberg laws became effective in Germany) was chosen as the cutoff date for membership in the Jewish community.

The definition was not simply theoretical: on its heels came instructions from the Reichsprotektor for registering Jewish property, as had been done in the Reich. Jews were no longer masters of their businesses, whether real estate, farms, bonds, art objects, or jewelry. Nor did the Protektor bother to notify the government of the Protectorate in advance about the implementation of the Nuremberg laws; the fictitiousness of the government's powers became increasingly obvious. For a brief moment its members considered resigning in protest. They were particularly annoyed by the fact that the considerable Jewish wealth, estimated at half a billion dollars, was to slip out of their hands. In the end, however, it was decided to postpone the gesture for a more appropriate occasion. Two weeks later, the government issued instructions about the removal of Jews from public life: Jews were no longer permitted to hold jobs in courts of law, belong to public organizations, participate in politics, or perform before audiences. They were not allowed to teach school (except in Jewish schools), or to serve as attorneys, doctors, pharmacists, or construction engineers.

Every detail in the long list of regulations dealt a blow to life, income, and spirit. German "trustees" were appointed over large Jewish firms and businesses, often sending the Jewish owners home, empty-handed, as soon as they took over. People who had devoted their lives to local voluntary organizations—the volunteer fire squad, the amateur choir—saw their membership annulled with the wave of a hand. What had been built up over years of toil vanished overnight. Kurt Tieberger, chairman of the Hehalutz committee and owner of a varnish factory, wrote a despondent letter to Willy Feuerstein at Kibbutz Merchavia: "I am at the moment transferring my property—an incessant assault on nerves and mind. Not merely because of the property lost, the ejection from work, the forced unemployment, the worry about family, but because of the mental agony. All human feeling, all idealism, is lost."

Over one hundred and forty anti-Jewish laws and regulations had been issued in Germany by 1939, a gradual process that stretched over six years. For the Jews of the Protectorate, however, they came as a sudden flood. During the first few years of the Nazi regime, the Jews of the Reich, convinced that they must fight for their civil rights, had still lived with the delusion that laws could be changed by public protest, by appeals to the world. The Jews of the Protectorate had learned from experience: the Jewish leadership could do no more than try to ease the suffering and promote emigration. Before the Germans came, the Jewish community organizations in Bohemia and Moravia had played only a marginal role in public life; usually people turned to them no more than twice during their lifetime, at birth, and at death, and sometimes when they married, if they chose a religious ceremony rather than a civil one. Most Prague Jews regarded the old Jewish municipality building as a curiosity, not an institution of central importance in their lives; most paid their community fees out of inertia, sometimes reluctantly. And for its part, the community administration devoted most of its energy to fostering religious life in accordance with the interest shown, and to small-scale charity works. A supreme council of communities had at one time been elected, but it was an exceedingly flimsy organization. As for the Zionist Federation, only a small minority of Jews were members. Czechoslovakian Jewry had in fact no central Jewish leadership.

Following the nineteenth-century emancipation, Jewish isolation from the general public waned, and so did the influence of the Jewish community on Jewish life. Now a reverse process took place: as Jews became more and more cut off, their relationship to the community perforce grew stronger. The community organizations, together with the Zionist movement, became the only hope for welfare, studies, emigration, and help in finding work or a place to live. The functions of the Palestine office and the Prague Jewish community administration converged, adjusted, and united, and cooperation increased. Longtime differences between Zionists and Jewish Czechs (including Dr. Emil Kafka, chairman of the Prague Jewish community and František Weidmann, community secretary) diminished, though they did not disappear; the key people of both organizations met for a few hours every day to work together.

The exodus from commerce and the free professions forced on Jews by the new laws caused people to seek new directions in craftsmanship and physical labor, whether for purposes of emigration or to start afresh here, in Bohemia and Moravia. To meet this need, the community ran dozens of courses: on building stoves and sewing bed linen, on metalwork and infant care, on typewriter repairs and baking, on shoemaking and poultry-raising, on women's hairdressing and jazz (for a better future in the United States), as well as language courses in English and Spanish at beginners' and more advanced levels. Most of the courses took three to four months and were given three to four hours daily. By that time, perhaps, emigration would be possible or a way would be found to earn a living.

Former conventions were no longer valid. In normal times, no son of a Jewish bourgeois family would have considered marriage without knowing how he was to support a wife; most Jewish women, after they married, ran their homes with the aid of a maid, at most helping out in the family business. After all, it was the husband's duty, as perceived by both society and himself, to support the family. Now, devoted fathers who had never known idleness suddenly found themselves helpless and humiliated: they, who had always given to charity—and usually generously—were suddenly on the receiving end. The real value of the courses was perhaps more as occupational therapy than as occupational retraining. People discovered hidden talents, remembered long-forgotten crafts, mentally prepared themselves for a new chapter in their lives.

The first group of immigrants to San Domingo, which was supposed to have left in March, was for the time being stuck in the Protectorate, but meanwhile other plans sprang up for collective emigration. Many Czech Jews feared setting out in the world on their own; they felt that in the company of people close to them, their severance from the homeland would be less painful and they could maintain a bond with what had once been their republic. In Kolin, as in other provincial towns, a group was formed for overseas emigration which hoped to set up a communal village to raise bees, cattle, and fruit, and develop home industries. The group included experts in agriculture, tanning, canning, and textiles. They asked the British government to sell them land in one of their sparsely populated colonies, they wrote to members of Parliament, to well-known scientists, to the Colonial Office; at best they received a polite reply to the effect that every colony was sovereign and should be approached directly.

There was a project for settling in the South American colony of French Guiana. A representative was sent to Paris, and the French government promised to send a commission to Guiana to assess the receptiveness of the local population and the possibilities of Jewish settlement. In the meantime, the Kolin group was offered a place in

New Caledonia, a French prison colony on an isolated island a thousand miles east of Australia; this too they were prepared to accept. They were asked to submit a list of candidates in triplicate and wait for an answer. So as not to overlook any opportunity, the Kolin people also appealed to the Rhodesian government. The first question of the Rhodesian delegate in London was how much money future settlers had. About twenty million crowns, came the reply. But how much would they be bringing with them in hard currency? Only their fare, to be paid by the Jewish welfare organizations. And so Rhodesia fell through. The correspondence, the appeals, the fact-finding trips made by representatives—all took time. Weeks passed, months, and meanwhile it was the summer of 1939.

The situation of candidates for immigration to Palestine was no different. After the occupation, everything started all over again as if the transfer agreement did not exist. The British froze the "transfer" funds and would release them only with the approval of the national bank in Prague. Friedmann, Kahn, Zucker, Edelstein, and März (who remained in constant telephone contact with Leo Hermann in London) patiently began renegotiations, and, after a great deal of effort, finally gained the necessary approval from the Czech national bank. But the Protectorate's financial affairs were now controlled by the German Reichsbank, and the Germans refused to have the money released in London. Again there was nothing to be done but to ask Robert Stopford to intervene. On Stopford's own initiative, and thanks to his personal contacts (John Simon, the British foreign minister, was his brother-in-law), the British parliament in three days approved a special law for the establishment of a trust fund for Czech refugees, which could pay the remaining £425,000 of the £500,000 grant given to the Jewish Agency, on condition that the latter would confirm the number of immigrants agreed on in January 1939. Accordingly, as a first payment, the fund transferred £133,000 to the Jewish Agency in Jerusalem, making it clear that the balance would be paid only if and when additional emigration from the Protectorate was approved.

The British were skeptical: what if the Protectorate Jews transferred the money and then decided to remain where they were? To which Leo Hermann replied that a man who gets a ticket to heaven does not choose to stay in hell. But what if the Gestapo prevents them from leaving? This was a more difficult problem. Hermann asked friends in Prague to explain to the Gestapo that the British required a guarantee to the effect that 1,200 bearers of certificates, and their families, would be allowed to emigrate to Palestine, pointing out that the British were not prepared to rely on the signature of the Zionists alone. In the middle of August, the necessary confirmation, signed by Eichmann himself, was finally received.

Significant changes had meanwhile taken place in Prague. In the middle of July, Fuchs, the SS officer with the Berlin accent, suddenly vanished. The next day, the Gestapo summoned Edelstein to the Peček Palais. When he returned, he told the usual crowd which had gathered around him at the Palestine office that a center for Jewish emigration would be set up in Prague as well; Eichmann, who until then had been based in Vienna and made only guest appearances in Prague, had moved here with his staff. The establishment of a *Zentralstelle* for Jewish emigration in Prague was part of overall German policy: in January 1939, Interior Minister Goering instructed Reinhard Heydrich, head of the Reich Security Head Office, to solve the Jewish question as efficiently as possible through emigration or expulsion, given present circumstances. On July 15, the Reichsprotektor published his orders: all Jews wishing to emigrate must in future request permission from the central authority in Prague; it alone could organize emigration, issue the necessary permits, and supervise the collection of taxes from emigrants.

The weekly report put out by the Jewish community office shed light on the practical measures involved: up to now the community had not been organized to handle emigration. However, that week the community had been instructed to open an emigration department, which would employ ninety people. On July 28, the community secretary traveled to Vienna to learn from the Austrian experience of an emigration department so that a similar one could be instituted in Prague.

At the same time, Richard Israel Friedmann, a twenty-eight-year-old bachelor who worked for the Viennese Jewish community, was transferred to Prague. After the Anschluss Friedmann had concluded that there was no point in fighting for Jewish civil rights within the Reich. The only hope, he felt, lay in emigration, and he had organized the Viennese community to accelerate the process, deal with visas, and attain the necessary foreign currency for travel fare. Friedmann, who out of a perverse sense of Jewish pride insisted on being called "Israel," a name that all male Jews in the Reich had been required to take since August 1939 (women had to add

"Sarah" to their names), tried to impress on the Jews of the Protectorate the urgency of the situation. He pressed them to emigrate quickly and to disregard their property and real estate at all costs, and to forget about income and possessions. Very few understood his anxiety; some even wondered if there was any point in emigrating at all—Hitler was bound to fall soon.

Prague was not Vienna, as Eichmann pointed out twenty years later. In his view, Prague lacked a capable Jewish activist such as Dr. Löwenherz, the chairman of the Viennese Jewish community. In Prague, things moved slower and less successfully. The reason for the slow trickle of emigration from Prague lay perhaps in the fact that the mass exodus from Austria had swallowed up most of the resources, energy, and initiative of the world's Jewish welfare organizations, and decreased the available absorption sites. Two hundred emigration candidates were supposed to report every day to the Zentralstelle, which had taken over a handsome villa in Prague's quiet suburb of Strešovice. But the number of applicants who came was in fact much less—about half this figure. Perhaps the reasons were more personal: Eichmann never found a common language with the Prague functionaries, whose German was different, harder, foreign.

Eichmann left Vienna's Zentralstelle in the hands of Rolf Günther and Alois Brunner, and devoted most of his time to managing the emigration center in Prague along with his assistant, Hans Günther, twenty-nine years old, tall, and slim, an indisputably Aryan figure in keeping with the prevailing ideal. Günther was one of the few people in Eichmann's operation who was not Austrian by birth (he and his brother, Rolf, were sons of a distinguished family: their father, Dr. Hans Günther, was one of the major ideologues of the race theory on which National Socialism was based). Eichmann brought with him to Prague four SS officers and half a dozen lower-ranking officials whose basic job was to guard everybody. During the first few days that emigration files were submitted, the guards began to amuse themselves, as they had in Vienna, by beating up the Jews who had been waiting on line since the early hours of the morning. Jewish representatives intervened with Eichmann, and the people queueing up were no longer molested. Henceforth, Jews were subjected to blows only behind walls, and the violence was used for specific purposes of persuasion rather than indiscriminately.

Everything was more complicated in Prague than in Vienna. Eichmann had to contend not only with the Reich's institutions but also with the government of the Protectorate. Struggles took place behind the scenes with on one side the Protectorate administration and the military, who generally exerted a more moderate influence, and on the other the security services and National Socialist Party activists, who sought to adopt a more radical line. The zealots included the Sudetenites, led by Karl Hermann Frank, who hated the Czechs as much as he hated the Jews, and wanted them both evacuated. The regulations issued by the general staff of the security police at the Peček Palais contradicted the orders of the Zentralstelle, and the various arms of the German regime were divided by conflict and latent competition. Edelstein was quick to discern all this, but most Jews understood nothing about the hierarchy of power in the German mechanism of darkness; even the name Eichmann meant nothing to them.

Eichmann also brought to Prague the erstwhile business consultant Bertold Storfer, a Viennese Jew who had formerly supplied the Austrian army. A businessman with international contacts, Storfer had a great deal of self-confidence, and he had placed his talents at the disposal of the German authorities, organizing rapid mass emigration from Austria. On the whole, Storfer did justice to his position. He made connections with shipowners and competed with the Mossad (the Jewish organization dealing with illegal immigration to Palestine), without worrying too much about whether or not the passengers could actually reach the shores of Palestine. His job was simply to ensure that they left Austria. Now he had come to organize illegal immigration from the Protectorate officially, and the local Jews regarded him with a great deal of suspicion. He immediately called a meeting with the representatives of the Brünn Jewish community to discuss the transport organized by the Revisionists which was about to leave: in future the composition of the transports would be decided according to German interests, with no reference to Palestinian or local Jewish purposes. The old and sick would also be included, and payments would be raised substantially.

Edelstein first met Storfer at Eichmann's office. Storfer, who knew Eichmann well from Vienna, went straight up to his desk, to be greeted with the shout of: "Three paces away from me!" Describing this incident to the staff of the Palestine office, Edelstein remarked, "If Eichmann had treated me like that, he would not have extracted another word from me." The most important quality in dealing with the Germans, he said, was to preserve one's dignity.

During one conversation Eichmann told Edelstein that he (Eichmann) had informed the Viennese Jewish community that he was willing to let them have Herzl's remains in return for a greater number of immigration certificates; let it be known, therefore, that the deal applied also to Prague. Eichmann insisted that between sixty and seventy thousand emigrants had to leave within one year; he did not care how. When Emil Kafka, chairman of the Prague Jewish community, pointed out the difficulties and expense of carrying out such a plan, Eichmann threatened to arrest three hundred Jews every day and send them to Dachau, where they would soon "show a keen interest in emigration."

Technically, speedy emigration was easier in Austria because most Austrian Jews lived in Vienna, whereas in the Protectorate, less than half of the Jewish population lived in Prague; the rest were scattered all over the country in Brünn and Ostrava, in dozens of provincial towns and hundreds of villages and hamlets.

On August 13, 128 representatives of Jewish communities from all over the Protectorate gathered at the old Jewish municipality building on Maisl Street to hear the ill tidings from Kafka: the Jews of the provinces must move to Prague without delay, and from there they must emigrate as soon as possible. It was only natural for Dr. Kafka to recall an historical analogy—the expulsion of the Jews by Empress Maria Theresa, when twenty thousand men, women, and children had been banished from Prague in the depths of the winter of 1744. Then, however, they had been allowed to disperse in neighboring countries; while now, during the darkest period in the thousand-year history of the Jews of Bohemia, they must leave for distant lands. "Much to our sorrow, our turn has come somewhat belatedly. The available immigration possibilities have all been exhausted by the Jews of Germany, Austria, and Poland, and the gates to the outside world are already closed to the Jews of Czechoslovakia." Still, the situation must not halt the search for places of refuge. Jewish strength had always lain in its ability to adapt to new conditions, and it was therefore incumbent on Jews to disregard sentiment and their devotion to Czech soil, and to implement orderly emigration.

František Weidmann, secretary of the Prague Jewish community, took the floor after Dr. Kafka to announce that Jews from the provinces would be transferred to Prague in stages. First to move would be families with emigration opportunities who would settle their affairs in Prague. Emigration would have to commence immediately, since the Jewish community had been ordered to supply the Central Emigration Authority with a daily quota of two hundred emigration applicants. Jews must not allow events to overwhelm them, Weidmann concluded: for two thousand years Jews had been banished from place to place, but the verse of Scripture still held true: "Do not fear before them, for I am with you to deliver you, so saith the Lord." His words were written down carefully by the police clerk in attendance, who noted at the bottom of his report that the meeting had adjourned in total silence and there had been no public disorder.

Public leaders of small communities met to consider the future: what was to become of the sick and the old, of property and apartments? Where would they live in Prague? What about the vast majority who had no means of financing emigration? There were some towns in which the local authorities displayed amazing energy, demanding that the Jews decamp within two weeks. Appeals were made to Eichmann through intermediaries from the Czech government, asking if family heads alone could go to Prague to arrange emigration, while their families waited at home. In the name of efficiency, communities were asked to furnish the Gestapo with statistics on their members (according to age, sex, and occupation) and on local Jewish organizations. The swelling Prague community administration added a statistics department and a housing department to its operation.

Preparing the emigration file was an exhausting experience, fraught with obstacles. First, every Jew had to have a destination and the assurance of an entry visa. He had to type out sixteen forms in sextuplicate, answering every question in full (answers such as "not applicable" were to be avoided), attach three photographs, a birth certificate, a marriage certificate, a local-citizenship certificate, a character reference issued in the last six weeks, an affidavit from the municipality attesting to place of residence, receipts showing that all taxes had been paid, a certificate from the Treasury to the same effect, separate lists with documentation of all property, even that in the Reich or the Sudetenland, a list of all jewelry, a list of all the goods he meant to take with him, with separate evaluations of their worth made by official assessors for all types of assets—furniture, household goods, furs, carpets, books. The property and jewelry lists were transferred by irrevocable power of attorney. Effects leaving the country were taxed at 100 percent of their value. They were exporting Jews, not money, and official policy was to strip the Jews of as much of their possessions as possible, so that they would constitute a greater burden on their host countries after emigrating; in this way they would invite more opposition from the local population, thereby serving the propaganda interests of Nazi Germany.

Only after all the documents were ready and the candidate was assured of an immigration certificate, an American affidavit, or an immigration visa from an overseas country, could he take his file to the Zentralstelle. He went first to the basement, where Jewish community employees checked his file to make sure that everything was in order, wanting to give the Germans no excuse to vent their anger; they tried to reassure the applicants, who were often nervous and frightened. Next the candidate went to the central hall, where representatives of the various government offices sat in separate booths, and finally he reported to the first floor, where one of the SS people determined the rate of tax he would have to pay to the "Emigration Fund"; the official rate was 25 percent of his property's value, and it too remained in German hands. About three weeks later, the applicant was recalled to the Zentralstelle to receive his exit permit—and sometimes, at the very last minute, when he was already penniless and living out of a suitcase, Anton Burger, Günther's assistant and extortion expert, demanded an additional payment to cap it all, sometimes twenty, sometimes thirty, sometimes fifty thousand crowns, depending on his mood and the sum he thought he could extract.

Burger was the only one at the Zentralstelle who raised his voice against Edelstein; on one occasion, when Burger started shouting, Yekef put a hand to his ear and said, "Excuse me, what did you say? I didn't hear." When Burger, who was vain and half-educated, was to give a talk to the SS on the German orders of knighthood, he brought Edelstein the background material and Jakob wrote the speech for him in pure Aryan German. Harry Tressler and the staff of the Palestine office, to whom Yekef read his work of art, nearly burst their sides laughing, but Burger told Edelstein a few days later that the talk had gone very well.

It was a war of nerves, a race against time: even people who had immigration opportunities could not possibly prepare all the paperwork in time. In the interim, their entry visas expired and local consuls would not renew them. The situation of certificate holders for Palestine changed from day to day: those who had owned property only yesterday were suddenly penniless and could not pay the

30,000 crowns for the £1,000 demanded from immigrants on investor's certificates, and the additional 350,000 crown tax. The Jewish Agency in Jerusalem started to put pressure on Prague. The people with certificates might not manage to leave before the quota expired—why waste certificates? Perhaps it would be better to give them to immigration candidates from other countries. And what about the "transfer" monies, which Palestine awaited even more eagerly than it did immigrants?

It was not clear if the Germans would allow a delegation from the Protectorate to attend the twenty-first Zionist Congress, which was to take place in Geneva from August 16 to 26. The Prague people asked Eichmann to permit a large delegation to participate so that, in their own words, they could make more vigorous demands for a greater number of immigration certificates and insist on expediting illegal immigration. For the moment the Germans were still quite generous in issuing exit permits if the purpose of the journey was to increase emigration. Kafka and Maria Schmolka were allowed to attend the Joint convention in Paris in order to raise money for the purchase of travel tickets in foreign currency, and to fund the community's activities. (Schmolka had been released from the Pankrac prison in late May, after the intervention of influential Czechs and pressure from foreign legations.)

The Germans also gave Balu Spitz an exit permit, after Yekef, through his good relations with the British, managed to get him a visa to enter Britain as a businessman. Balu's job in London was to try to obtain work sites for pioneers on training outside Czechoslovakia. At the time there were 750 pioneers in training divisions, which were supposed to close down by the fall, when the potato and beet harvests ended. In October the pioneers would be left without housing or income, and Eichmann would be pushing for emigration.

On one of his daily trips to the Peček Palais, Edelstein asked for an exit permit for Moshe Baumgarten so that he could deal with Youth-Aliyah affairs. Eichmann demanded to see Baumgarten in person; when the latter came, he pointed to diagrams on the wall, a scheme of the various office stages Jews had to pass through to emigrate, and then asked him to which youth movement he belonged. When Moshe told him Maccabi Hatzair, Eichmann wanted to know to which kibbutz movement they were affiliated. When Baumgarten replied, "Ihud Hakvutzot," Eichmann said knowledgeably, "I'm well acquainted with them. They're connected with

Hapo'el Hatzair." He told Moshe to inform the London people that at least two hundred Jews must emigrate every day, or there would be terrible consequences to pay. He also told him to emphasize just how serious the situation was, and he warned him to accord no interview to the German refugees' newspaper, published in Paris. On the way back to the Palestine office—about a fifteen-minute walk—Yekef spoke to Moshe of the burden it was to be in daily contact with the Germans, stressing that he did it out of a sense of obligation. Somewhat ironically, he spoke of those "delicate souls" who knew that the job had to be done for the general good but were not prepared to contaminate themselves through contact with the Germans. For him, the constant contact with the SS was an incessant battle with fear. Edelstein was no dauntless, heroic figure; it was enough to look at him: a bespectacled Jewish clerk, who shrank from violence and had never in his life raised his hand against anyone. Sometimes, when he was unexpectedly called to the Gestapo, he would feel a weakness overcome him, turn pale, and have to go to the toilet—and yet he went, his stomach in turmoil, but never betraying his fears.

On August 14, regulations were issued regarding contact between the general population and Jews: Jews were barred from public parks, hotels, beaches, restaurants, and cafés, unless they were Jewish businesses or had separate facilities for Jews; hospitals, old-age homes, and welfare shelters were all to practice segregation. On the face of it, the punishment for breaking these rules was not very serious—fines from 10,000 to 50,000 crowns, or imprisonment ranging from twenty-one hours to fourteen days. But beyond the punishment hovered the threat of concentration camps—Dachau, Mauthausen, Buchenwald—and there, it was said, terrible things went on.

The Jews' reaction to their forced isolation was the same as always: they would manage, they would not break. Salomon Lieben, physician and humanitarian, converted the Jewish orphanage into a Jewish hospital, rented a flat in the old part of the city, and installed in it the elderly who had been cast out of public institutions. The community newspaper noted that the restrictions on Jews' appearing in public places made the seriousness of the situation eminently clear, and that week more people than ever sought information on emigration possibilities.

13

A JEWISH COLONY
UNDER SS PATRONAGE

THE SECURITY police approved the exit of ten delegates to the Zionist Congress, but the passports of the delegates' families had to be deposited with the Germans as a guarantee against their return. Irma Polak, who was permitted to participate in the WIZO world convention, to be held before the congress, left first, and by means of a prearranged code notified Prague that the trip and border check had passed safely. The delegation, headed by Kahn, traveled to Geneva as a group, though Edelstein and Baumgarten did not manage to leave on time and they followed later. Their luggage was carefully checked at the Swiss border and the German customs official, to make sure that nothing had been concealed, even opened Yekef's phylacteries case with a knife. Moshe could not contain himself and muttered, "*Aziss-punim,*" a term the Jews of Central Europe reserved for wickedness or insolence. The remark angered the German official, though he did not understand what it meant, and only after Yekef calmly explained that the reference had been to the train station they were coming to did Moshe avoid arrest.

It had been decided in Prague that the delegation from the Protectorate would not participate in the deliberations of the general assembly. Only Kahn was to deliver an address, prepared in advance. This was the first time since 1921 that Kahn had taken no part in either the preparation for, or the management of, the congress. Coming from Prague to green and tranquil Geneva was like landing from another planet, or returning from hell to earth. On August 24, at 9 P.M., at the ninth session of Congress, Dr. Kahn delivered his address in German, on behalf of the Jews of Bohemia and Moravia:

> Esteemed Congress, on behalf of the Zionists of the Protectorate of Bohemia and Moravia, represented at this Congress by eight delegates, we ask you to accept this expression of our devotion and loyalty to the Zionist movement and Federation. Let not my words be interpreted as lacking in humility should I remind you that in days past, when the burden of Jewish suffering did not affect each of us directly, we had a strong Zionist Federation whose concrete activities toward developing the land of Israel stood out by virtue of their steadfastness and growth.
>
> Nor did we contribute to the Jewish community in Palestine the least worthy of its settlers. Our pioneering youth has established settlements in Palestine which we are proud of, and today too we have large reserves of young people besieging the gates of Palestine and demanding the right to enter, not because of their present distressing situation, but because of their past Zionist education.
>
> Behind the united ranks of the youth stands the multitudinous Zionist middle class, academics, businessmen, clerks, and even many craftsmen and farmers who are dismayed that they did not fulfill their Zionist ideals when young.
>
> Their objective situation is harsh and demands that they emigrate at once, but their subjective needs demand that they emigrate to Palestine. They no longer stand before you as publicists, donors, or fund-raisers, but as people converging on the doors of the Jewish community in Palestine.
>
> In their name, we, the delegates of the Protectorate, ask the Zionist movement to help them emigrate and put down roots in Palestine.
>
> We are not fleeing in panic, nor do we lack a program. We do not come totally empty-handed. We do not come without Zionist education, but with a disciplined Zionist foundation which hopes to enhance the constructive and creative forces of the Jewish community in Palestine. We intend to establish control mechanisms and institutions of self-help so that our immigration will not end in defeat.
>
> We hope that the Zionist Federation will not deny us its encour-

agement, just as the Zionist idea bolsters us in this, the most difficult hour of our lives.

Kahn's words were greeted with prolonged and vehement applause, and Shlomo Kaplansky, the chairman of the session, remarked that "in its acclamation, the congress had truly expressed what it could not say in words, in response to the declaration of our brothers and friends from the Protectorate with whom we stand together in sorrow and hope." However, in view of the White Paper policy, the congress participants had little else to give the Czech Zionist who had come to ask for help. As Menachem Ussishkin put it during the closing address: "Central European Jewry, a million suffering people—how difficult it is to offer them encouragement. Heaven alone can have mercy on them. Palestine too is powerless. Perhaps the coming catastrophe will bring them salvation."

On August 23, the news of the so-called Molotov-Ribbentrop Pact between Germany and the Soviet Union hit the congress like a bolt from the blue. The Soviet Union had agreed to remain neutral should the Germans resort to war, thereby removing the threat of a second front and leaving Hitler free to concentrate his forces on Poland (nobody yet knew of the confidential clause relating to the future partition of Poland). Now war seemed unavoidable. Only in March, after the Germans invaded Czechoslovakia, had Chamberlain understood that Hitler's sights were set on conquering Europe, and in the same month Poland received guarantees of British aid in the event of an attack. The guarantee was issued chiefly as a deterrent, however; in practical terms, the British forces really had no way to come to the aid of the Polish army. Hitler demanded an immediate solution to the "Polish problem" (just as in the spring he had demanded a solution to the "Czechoslovakian problem"), by which was meant the questions of the Polish corridor in Prussia, the free city of Danzig (Gdansk), Upper Silesia, and self-rule for the German minority. And he too assumed that Britain and France would not allow themselves to be dragged into war because of Poland. The Poles asked Britain for arms and money, but by the end of the summer they had received nothing.

After the blow dealt by the Nazi-Soviet Pact (Molotov and Ribbentrop were the foreign ministers who signed the agreement), the Zionist Congress accelerated its deliberations. Debate was cut short and resolutions were adopted in haste: the moral and legal validity of the White Paper policy was rejected (as it had been by the Mandate Committee of the League of Nations). It was felt that Europe was on the eve of war. Some of the Polish delegates were anxious to return home: it was their duty to fight with the Polish army. Friends urged the delegates from the Protectorate not to return to Czechoslovakia, but how could they not return if their families were being held hostage? Only Ullman, Kahn's assistant, remained in Geneva to act as the liaison with the free world, with everyone's approval. Baumgarten hesitated, and went to hear Ben-Gurion speak before the emissaries from Palestine. Ben-Gurion asked them to return to their missions, for they were needed now more than ever, and Moshe decided to return to Prague.

Chaim Weizmann delivered a moving and emotional parting speech, filled with anxiety over the future: "I have no hope but this, that we'll all meet again alive." Friends who had been through a lot together in the Zionist movement parted in tears and consoled one another: perhaps the war would bring redemption. As Moshe Kleinbaum had said during the deliberations: "We entered the First World War with the Basel Plan and came out of it with the Balfour Declaration; a paper for a paper. Perhaps for a Jewish colony in Palestine numbering close to half a million people, we'll come out of the world crisis with a Jewish state."

Irma Polak and Edelstein took the same train from Geneva to Prague. Their compartment was filled with German soldiers on their way to the eastern front, and the two remained silent most of the journey. Edelstein was depressed and worried when he returned: hard times lay ahead.

On the morning of September 1, German airplanes bombed Warsaw and German forces started advancing eastward. The Poles turned to their allies, but the British and French still hoped for a settlement if Hitler would only agree to halt his army, even in Poland. The British parliament and public demanded intervention and on September 3, very hesitantly, the Germans were issued an ultimatum. When this too was rejected, Chamberlain declared a state of war. France was dragged in reluctantly after Britain, and the Commonwealth countries joined in solidarity; once again, the world was at war. This time there was none of the enthusiasm there had been in the summer of 1914, when war had come after decades of peace.

Now, only twenty-one years after the end of the First World War, many people still remembered its horrors and were filled with foreboding, though nothing had yet happened in the West. The Poles fought alone, the British air force did not bomb German troops, the French army had not moved. The Poles defended themselves valiantly, but their army and equipment dated from another era. They held out for three weeks and were overwhelmed. A hundred thousand Poles retreated to Rumania to mobilize for the continued battle against Hitler. The Poles were romantics—not realists, like the Czechs.

Many Poles, including their foreign minister, Beck, passed through Horodenka on their flight, less than a mile from the Rumanian border. And swift on their heels, on the Day of Atonement, followed the Soviet army. Edelstein's parents, his sister and her family had remained in Horodenka, which—like all of eastern Galicia—was now annexed to Russian territory according to the partition agreement between Hitler and Stalin.

Stalin had waited in the background until the Germans had done their work. Only then, in the second half of September, did he take his share of Poland, which was now cut up for the fourth time in its history. About two million Polish Jews now lived under German rule, and over one million under the Soviets. "Half of Europe's Jews now live under Hitler and Stalin's despotic regimes," Weizmann noted in a letter to Moshe Shertok, "and it is difficult to choose between them."

As soon as war broke out, the SS in Ostrava seized dozens of local Jews, piled them onto a truck, and drove them straight to the battle area, where they were forced to get down and were never seen again. The Germans demanded that community leaders submit the names and addresses of all Polish citizens. Even before the war the Germans had singled out the Polish Jews in the Protectorate and the Reich for special measures. Some had been deported, some arrested, some sent to concentration camps; some had been imprisoned in the Spielberg fortress, the site of scenes of torture for freedom fighters who had opposed the Hapsburg monarchy. Some had managed to remain hidden in the Protectorate, moving stealthily from place to place. Youth-Aliyah had in its care about two hundred children of Polish refugees who had no idea of their parents' whereabouts.

Since Kafka, head of the Prague Jewish community, was in Paris when war broke out, the order to submit lists of Polish nationals and stateless former Poles known to the Prague community was transmitted through Edelstein. Community affairs were now managed by Dr. František Weidmann, who until then had served as secretary. Twenty-seven-years-old, corpulent, round-faced, and pug-nosed, Weidmann was honest and clever, but softhearted and indecisive (what ambitious attorney would choose in normal times the unimportant job of community secretary when he could open his own practice or work for a large concern?); and from the moment that Kafka was away, Weidmann leaned on Dr. Kahn. The Prague community leaders met to decide whether or not to hand in the names. The Germans claimed that they had their own lists and needed only to complete them; should the community fail to furnish them with lists, they themselves would "fill in" the names—indiscriminately. Here Edelstein—who, whether one saw it as weakness or not, was consistent in his fear that confrontation with the Germans would only bring worse consequences—saw no choice but to turn over the names. Kahn was opposed; März hesitated. Finally, it was unanimously agreed that the community would submit the list of names, but wherever possible warn the people concerned in advance to give them a chance to go into hiding. The weekly report of the Prague Jewish community for September 9 to 15 openly announced that the names had been given to the Germans. It noted that the arrest of the Polish subjects (whose number was estimated at one thousand) had caused "a great deal of disquiet among the Jews in Prague and in the provinces, and the entire community staff had had to be mobilized to reassure the relatives of those arrested."

At the height of the war with Poland, close to the Jewish New Year, Eichmann, on one of his many whims, gave the Prague community one week in which to write and turn in a history of the Jews in Bohemia and Moravia. The Viennese Jewish community received similar instructions. Kahn, Friedmann, März, and Edelstein each agreed to write one chapter, the secretaries worked day and night, and the job was completed on time. Ten days later, on Yom Kippur, the Jewish population learned that they had to turn in their radios; in contrast to their procedure with other regulations, the Reich authorities decided to confiscate the radios without any official announcement, and the staffs of the community office and Palestine office enlisted the aid of the youth movements and informed the Jewish public by word of mouth. In the same way, without written instructions, Jews learned that they were confined to their homes after 8 P.M. every evening. When they tried to ascertain from the Czech police whether such an order had in fact been given, they were told that the Czech authorities knew nothing about it. Representatives of the Czech police and Prague municipality turned to the Jewish community for information and were redirected to the Zentralstelle.

That same week, as ordered by the Germans, the community completed a statistics report on Jews in the Protectorate broken down according to age and place of residence. The count was 90,147, of whom 90 percent were Jews by religion and 10 percent as defined by the racial laws. Twenty-one percent of the Jews in the Protectorate were over sixty; 10 percent under fifteen. The overall figure showed that about 35,000, mainly refugees from the Reich and the Sudetenland, had managed to leave the Protectorate in the short space of time between the Munich Pact and the invasion, and between the invasion and the war.

After the two million Polish Jews who had ended up on the German side of partitioned Poland were handed over to the Germans (having been subjected to acts of murder and horror during the brief war), it became clear to its leaders that the Reich could no longer be purged of Jews by means of gradual emigration. A confidential council met in Berlin on September 21, near the end of the war with Poland; as a result Reinhard Heydrich dispatched to all relevant bodies in the civil and military administrations general guidelines relating to the Jews in the conquered regions. In his letter he distinguished between the "final target," which remained undefined and would take a long time to implement, and the various stages leading up to "it"; these were to be put into effect at fixed time periods, since the methods by which "it" was to be executed required thorough preparation from both the technical and economic points of view.

The first measure to be adopted toward this target was the concentration of the Jews from the Polish provinces in the large cities, to facilitate greater control and future evacuation. Only cities with railroad junctions or nearby rail lines were to be chosen. Every Jewish community was to form a council, comprised of distinguished persons and rabbis who had remained at their posts, and the council was to bear full responsibility for carrying out all instructions from the Reich, including taking a census of all Jews in its region and providing for their housing and livelihood.

Heydrich's memo carried a warning cautioning utter secrecy.

Because the exact nature of the final target was not spelled out, it was also possible to assume that the intention was the mass deportation of the Jews from the Reich territory across the demarcation line with Russia. As a first step, orders were given to expel the Jews of western and northern Poland, of western Prussia, and of eastern Upper Silesia (parts of whose areas had formerly belonged to Germany and had been annexed to Poland in 1918) to the territory of the General-Gouvernement, as conquered Poland was now called.

Adolf Eichmann, who participated in Heydrich's confidential council as the representative of the Center for Jewish Emigration, was well aware of the enormous opportunities offered by the conquest of Poland. As early as 1938 he had made clear in a report he had been asked to prepare that the Jewish "problem" could not possibly be solved by emigration (for financial and other reasons). Twenty years later, during the preparations for his trial in Jerusalem, Eichmann confessed that the problem had absorbed him even outside working hours: he used to discuss the possible solutions at Sunday-morning meetings with Stahlecker, the head of the security police and SD (Sicherheitsdienst) in the Protectorate, who was also formally in charge of the Zentralstelle. On the one hand, Palestine was not available and emigration sites were growing increasingly scarcer; on the other hand, pressure was mounting from on high to get rid of the Jews. But with the conquest of Poland, an opportunity had suddenly presented itself to solve the Jewish problem to the satisfaction of all concerned, in Eichmann's eyes an almost "Zionist" solution, in fact: the Jews could be given a large territory and establish an autonomous government, a sort of "Jewish state" under German patronage, at least temporarily.

The idea of a territorial solution to the Jewish question cropped up again and again. In November 1938, Hitler spoke of it to Goering, and in his talk with the Czechoslovakian foreign minister in January 1939, he mentioned the extensive regions belonging to England and the United States where all the Jews could fit in and then "the Anglo-Saxon countries so abounding in philanthropy could be told: Here, you have them! They'll either die of starvation, or you'll make good all your talk and practice what you preach." Alfred Rosenberg, the chief ideologue of the Nazi Party, expounded the idea in a meeting with foreign diplomats and representatives of the world press. Rosenberg pointed out that Palestine was too small to absorb millions—even now Jewish settlement was causing the Arabs to revolt. Moreover, the Zionist state to which the

Jews aspired was in fact not designed to offer shelter to the Jewish multitudes but to create a Jewish power base in the Mediterranean and a refuge for scoundrels from the world over. Jewish emigration dispersed throughout the world was fraught with danger, both racially and politically, for Europe and other parts of the globe. The only solution therefore was to concentrate the Jews on a reservation in some sparsely populated territory across the seas. The democracies themselves could decide which of the three countries they had suggested—Alaska, Guiana, or Madagascar—was most suitable, though it was obviously a shame to waste Alaska, with its northern climate and geographical proximity to Canada and the United States, on the Jews.

With the conquest of Poland, however, the Germans no longer needed the rest of the world's approval for a territorial solution. Everything was still in flux, Eichmann felt, and Jewish settlement could be combined with the evacuation of the Poles. Since Eichmann was only a lieutenant colonel (Obersturmbannführer) and therefore, at least according to him, did not have direct access to Heydrich, it was Oberführer (brigadier-general) Stahlecker who laid the plan before the head of the security services and received his approval. The idea was to deport the Jews of Polish Katowice and Teschen, now included in the Reich, together with the Jews of Ostrava—a city that had always been a pioneer in taking anti-Jewish measures—and at the same time expel the Polish refugees who had fled to the Protectorate when war broke out, just as, six months previously they had fled in the opposite direction. It was to be a trial run, and if successful would be followed by large-scale evacuation.

The proponents of the idea lost no time. In early October, Stahlecker and Eichmann flew to Moravská Ostrava, and from there via Cracow to Warsaw. The entourage set out eastward in two cars, toward the new border with the Soviet Union, to the district of Radom, to choose a suitable site from the point of view of both rail connections and absorption capacity. When Eichmann returned to Prague, he summoned Edelstein and Richard Israel Friedmann; the two men understood from his talk of a Jewish settlement that the area in question lay between the San and Bug rivers, where the raging war had left a dwindling population. Because of its proximity to the Soviet Union, the Jewish colony was to serve as a buffer state.

Speaking to Gauleiter Wagner, the regional commander in Katowice, Eichmann made it clear that the transports were only experimental. After four transports from Katowice and Ostrava, an interim report was to be submitted to the Reich Security Head Office and would in all likelihood be passed on to the Führer, during which time the Germans were to wait for further instructions regarding the mass expulsion of the Jews. Eichmann told the regional commander that Hitler had meanwhile ordered the "relocation" of 300,000 Jews from the Reich and Ostmark and asked Wagner to assist toward this end.

In his instructions to the security police in Ostrava, which were based on orders from Müller, the chief of the Gestapo, Eichmann noted that a Jewish advance unit was to be sent ahead to prepare a transit camp for the coming transports. Unlike future transports, which were to be chosen without any regard for age or sex, the advance unit was to be composed of only able-bodied men and was to include builders, engineers, various craftsmen, and at least ten doctors. The men would be permitted to take along their personal effects and 300 Reichsmarks each. The community was to pay fifty crowns for every member of the transport, and supply building materials, tools, food, and medicine. The train was to comprise both passenger and cargo cars, like the Wehrmacht trains carrying soldiers to the eastern front, so as not to arouse attention. The Viennese Jewish community received similar instructions regarding the transport of 1,000 to 2,000 men, and the transportees were even promised that their wives and children over ten years old would follow shortly. When the first transport left Vienna, Rolf Günther, head of the local Zentralstelle, assured Löwenherz that the transportees would be grateful to him for having been sent to a place where they could expect good working conditions and a regular food supply. Dr. Löwenherz could rest easy over the fate of the people who had left.

The Gestapo asked Salo Krämer, head of the Ostrava Jewish community, to draw up a list of physically fit men between the ages of seventeen and thirty-five, who were prepared to volunteer for occupational training at the camp. The words "training" and "Jewish state" were specifically mentioned during this conversation, and Krämer was told that an autonomous Jewish colony was to be established. When it appeared that there were few volunteers for the prospect, all Jewish men under sixty from Ostrava and the environs were obliged to report to the riding school where German doctors, without examining them, found that they were all fit, apart from a few invalids whose disability rating was over 70 percent. Pneumonia or angina pectoris posed no obstacle.

Jakob Edelstein received a missive signed by Anton Burger: by order of the Zentralstelle in Prague, he was to report to the chief of the border police in Ostrava on October 16, 1939, at 8 A.M. Similar instructions were delivered to Richard Friedmann in Prague, and to Messrs. Storfer, Grün, Boschan, and Murmelstein of the Viennese Jewish community. Löwenherz asked that Murmelstein be released since, as ordered by the emigration authorities, he was busy writing the history of the Jewish people, a task that no one but he could undertake; the request was rejected. The community representatives were told to bring enough food and clothing for three to four weeks. And Storfer used the brief stay in Ostrava to submit a report to his superiors at the Central Emigration Authority on the state of the transports slated for illegal immigration, to point out how vital his presence was in Vienna and in Prague, and to offer his candidacy, on the basis of his vast experience, for the position of financial director of the Jewish colony, should it be established.

On the morning of October 18, as the train pulled out from Ostrava along a side route and headed eastward, hundreds of wives and relatives stood on either side of the road, waving handkerchiefs and weeping. The Germans explained to the local press that the journey signified neither expulsion nor extirpation, but was a voluntary project organized by the local Jewish community for purposes of occupational training and preparation for emigration in a region under Reich sovereignty, free of all restrictions from the authorities. The guard personnel—fourteen SS, with one officer, and eleven border police for 901 passengers—occupied the first car, and the Jewish leaders sat in the second. En route "several of the leaders suffered exceedingly unpleasant surprises," as Edelstein wrote in his report when he returned, without saying that Richard Friedmann had been beaten up by the commander of the escort unit, who had had a personal account to settle with him from his Vienna days. In the other compartments, too—after the first day of the journey, which passed almost in high spirits—the atmosphere was gloomy: from Cracow onward, the windows remained shut, and at the station stops, they were not permitted to get water.

At the last station, Nisko, on the San river, a group of SS officers awaited the newcomers, and the engineers and builders were ordered to erect a barracks camp across the river. A large convoy set out on foot with horse-drawn wagons belonging to the local farmers to cart the building materials. They crossed the San on a makeshift bridge, got stuck in the mud, and reached the windswept area near the village of Zarzece only in the evening. And there, on a desolate hill, one of the officers—who those in the know whispered was Eichmann himself—delivered a curt address: here, at this site, the Führer promised the Jews a new homeland. There were neither flats nor houses; if they built, they would have a roof over their heads. There was no water. The wells were polluted with cholera, dysentery, and typhus. If they drilled and found water, they would be able to quench their thirst. The first nights, so Edelstein wrote, everyone slept in the rain, under the open sky, until the first barracks were built.

A group of 450 older men was brought from Nisko to Pisczina, where a few hundred Jews lived, and was housed in the local synagogue. During the night, the Polish villagers attacked them, killed one, seriously wounded another, and beat up and robbed dozens of others. The funeral of the first victim, a resident of Ostrava called Mendel, which took place in the cold and in the rain, added to the general dejection. Some of the men fled at night to the woods, took shelter with Jews in the adjoining villages, or strayed into bogs. Some were escorted the next day to the Russian border. They plodded through the mud for miles, little by little casting off most of the cargo they had brought with them. They were led to a deserted region where the SS fired several shots into the air and ordered them to continue east toward Russian territory. Anyone who turned back would be killed.

The Ostrava transport was followed two days later by two others, one from Vienna and one from Katowice (including twelve small children). A few dozen skilled personnel were left in the barracks camp, and everyone else was ordered to disperse in the neighboring villages. Within two weeks about six thousand deportees had arrived in Nisko. It became apparent that the local residents lived in dire poverty and ignorance, communicable diseases were rampant, and the dispersion of the Jews throughout the villages, as the Germans demanded, put them in danger of infection and death. There was not a single local doctor or pharmacy in the entire region, and the Jewish leaders therefore approached the priests and village elders and offered to finance and establish Jewish hospitals to treat the sick free of charge. In return, the villages would supply salaried escorts to lead the Jews, in groups, to the Russian border. However, when it turned out that the Polish guides led the Jews straight into the bogs, robbed them, beat them up, and left them to their fate, the Jews decided to organize their own self-defense. The young and strong among them armed themselves with sticks and some hung empty leather shaving cases on their belts to resemble holsters. Groups of doctors began calling on the villagers, and through their contacts were able to purchase food which was shared by all, to augment the provisions the Jews had brought from home. The Germans provided nothing.

Edelstein and Friedmann found that Eichmann had deceived them: the war had not emptied the district of its residents and the local population viewed Jewish settlement as a threat to their existence. In the evening, in the barracks, some of the young men discussed the possibility of killing the few SS guards and making their escape. They decided that it would not be difficult to do so, but nobody really meant it seriously. They were too conscious of the possible consequences for their families back home. Nevertheless, the scheme reached Edelstein's ears; while taking the night watch near the warehouse he made Goldshi, one of the Hehalutz members from Ostrava, swear to abandon the idea: it could spell disaster for thousands of people.

The German command ordered the community representatives to tour the local settlements with a view to finding additional living quarters, without, however, alerting the local authorities to their activities. "But," as Edelstein wrote, "the gentlemen proved inefficient." German soldiers arrested them a few days after they left the barracks and brought them to the regional administration. When asked what they had been doing, they replied that the security police had enjoined them to prepare living quarters for Jews in the area bounded by the San, Bug, and Wisla rivers—a district slated to be a Jewish colony. The regional commander did not know what they were talking about and released them, though he instructed them to report to the chief of the security police in Lublin.

While in Lublin Edelstein visited the Jews from Ostrava who, having been tortured by German soldiers on their journey east, were now receiving treatment in the Jewish hospital. Edelstein and Murmelstein obtained the agreement of the leaders of the Lublin Jewish community to house some of the sick and wounded from the Nisko transport in the town, despite the terribly crowded living conditions and the fact that the Lubliners at first regarded the representatives of central European Jewry with a great deal of suspicion: they too had heard nothing of a Jewish reservation to be established in the neighborhood, and they thought Edelstein and his companions were either German agents or provocateurs.

The Lublin Jewish community, that venerable spiritual and rabbinical center, had learned in the few weeks of German occupation exactly what German rule meant. In the first few days the Germans evicted several hundred families from the wealthier suburbs overnight and pressed the town's 45,000 Jews, as well as 6,000 refugees from western Poland, into the old Jewish district, where the density was so great that people had to bed down in cellars, pens, and storerooms. The Germans pilfered from Jewish shops and homes systematically, demanding anything they fancied—fabrics, leather, silver; and they amused themselves by tormenting the alarmed residents, making them sit on burning stoves, beating them, taking men away as hostages, forcing them into hard labor. The situation in Lublin was more depressing by far than in the barracks camp; Edelstein felt that in the Protectorate—perhaps because of its proximity to such centers of "civilization" as Vienna, and, indeed, the heart of the Reich itself—the Germans would never permit themselves the liberties that they took undisturbed with the Jews in Poland.

"There was a meeting of the regional commanders in Lublin and it appeared that nobody had the slightest inkling of any settlement plan," Edelstein recorded. "The chief of the Lublin security police traveled to the brigade commander in Lodz, returned a few days later, and instructed the Nisko Jews to return to camp and stop all work since further transports of Jews to Poland had been prohibited. The community gentlemen returned to Zarzece, where they were told that the transfer of Jews from the Reich to Poland had been temporarily halted until February 1940."

It is still not clear exactly why the transports to Nisko were stopped. During his trial in Jerusalem, Eichmann said that it was due to the intervention in Berlin of Hans Frank, who, as governor of the General-Gouvernement, was opposed to all further concentration of Jews in his territory: he would solve his Jewish problem in his own way. What is known is that the military was against Jewish transports to Poland before they transferred authority to the civilian administration.

Most of the Nisko Jews were led, group by group, to the Russian border, where Russians sometimes shot at them to turn them back and Germans shot at them to prevent their return. Hundreds died wandering, from disease and exhaustion; they sank into swamps, drowned in the river, or were killed by Poles, Ukrainians, Germans, or Russians. According to Edelstein's estimate, in one month between 3,500 and 4,000 of the 6,000 people brought to Nisko crossed into Russian territory. Many of them later met their deaths in Soviet labor camps; many fell into German hands during the war with the Soviet Union; many died of cold and starvation; 123 returned to Czechoslovakia at the end of the war as soldiers in the Red Army.

When, a week after the first transport left for Nisko, Eichmann announced from Berlin that "the transports of Jews for occupational training must cease until further notice," without elaboration, the commander of Ostrava's security police was bitterly disappointed: the groundwork for a fresh transport was progressing nicely and many of Ostrava's Jews, who had fled town, had meanwhile been apprehended. Eichmann was therefore asked to permit the departure of the transport that was ready, even if only for the sake of the prestige of the local security police. Eichmann was sympathetic; the diligent Gestapo commander was rewarded, and four hundred Ostrava Jews joined the Katowice transport. Heydrich and the Reich Security Head Office learned from the Nisko experience that the solution to the Jewish problem demanded full coordination of all parties involved and could not be implemented without the most thorough preparations.

Reports of the Nisko transports and the fate of the transportees soon reached the West, and Dr. Lichtheim, director of the political office of the Jewish Agency in Geneva, notified the Jewish Agency in Jerusalem of the entire affair. His information included the fact that the scheme had been close to Eichmann's heart, and had been abandoned perhaps because the central authorities had never favored it. The Prague Jews did not know the exact purpose of Edelstein's sudden journey. Rumor had it that a large labor camp was to be established and Yekef was meant to lead it. In his absence, Erich Munk, a radiologist by profession, a sober man and talented organizer, the Youth-Aliyah doctor, represented the Jews in dealings with the Gestapo, and Kahn managed the community's internal affairs, together with Weidmann, appointed by the Germans to head the community after Emil Kafka decided to remain in the West with his sons.

Edelstein returned to Prague, looking well. The account he gave of the expedition to the staff of the Palestine office consisted mostly of anecdotes, such as the time when the corpulent Dr. Murmelstein had been made to ride a horse. At a meeting at Dr. Kahn's apartment he gave an optimistic impression and said that there was a good deal of conflict between the German military and the SS. The Nisko plan had failed because the army did not agree to Jewish concentration in the area, he said, and the Jews should exploit this tension and perhaps even try to find a direct avenue to the Wehrmacht's senior ranks in the Protectorate. From the way in which Dr. Kahn pursed his lips, it was clear to those who knew him that he was not comfortable with Yekef's words. Edelstein had several meetings with key functionaries at the Czernin Palace, the seat of the Protectorate offices, and Harry Tressler, who waited for him on the street, could tell by his face, even from afar, how the meetings had gone. After one such conference, Yekef said to him, "You think only the Jews are afraid of the Gestapo? The Germans themselves are afraid of them."

Edelstein returned from Lublin determined to prevent additional transports of the Protectorate's Jews to Poland, knowing full well that the law-abiding and somewhat naïve Jews of Bohemia and Moravia would find it difficult to cope with the trials of life in the East; they would soon fall prey to disease, and a protracted stay in Poland as refugees would mean death for many. Furthermore, Edelstein believed that the Germans regarded Poland as a no-man's-land, while in the Protectorate they had to consider the Czech populace and the country's proximity to the West. Three months later Edelstein met with Moshe Shertok, who recorded the following in his diary: "Upon [Edelstein's] return from the Lublin region, the Zionist leaders resolved to inform the authorities that, come what may, they would not abet such emigration. The Zionist Federation could be dissolved, the leaders could be sent to Dachau, but they would not lend their hand to atrocities. Edelstein believes that it is the courage of Prague's Zionists which has stood between them and various evils."

In October 1939 Eichmann was promoted to Hauptsturmführer (captain), and transferred from Prague to Berlin. He was to head the Central Emigration Authority, while Hans Günther took over Prague's Zentralstelle. The unification of the security police and the security services of the National Socialist Party was completed during this period, and at Himmler's orders, the Reich Security Head Office, consisting of six offices headed by Reinhard Heydrich, came into being. The Gestapo took its place in the system as the fourth office, run by Heinrich Müller, and it included a separate department for "the implementation of evacuation in the eastern sector," for which Eichmann was the special referee. Eichmann's presence in Prague was now confined to visits and generally boded ill. In the middle of November, he summoned Weidmann and Edelstein and asked if the daily quota of applicants to the Central Emigration Authority could be increased. Because of the war, the number of candidates had dropped to a few dozen a day, and unless it was raised, emigration would be stopped altogether. Both men replied that in all likelihood they could see that the daily figure was raised to 120 until the end of November, but thereafter it would depend on the availability of foreign currency for emigrants. Following this conversation with Eichmann, Weidmann and Edelstein went to Vienna to confer with their counterparts on the remaining emigration possibilities. Löwenherz had also been threatened: if all the Jews in Austria had not emigrated by the end of November, transports to the East would be renewed. However, if they had left by then, the employees of the Palestine office and the community staff members would be permitted to emigrate to the country of their choice.

14

IF ONLY THERE WERE DOLLARS

As a result of the war, emigration possibilities were considerably reduced: shipping lines raised their fares to double and more, and demanded that passage be paid in hard currency in a neutral country, a fact that made the emigrants more dependent on Jewish welfare associations and relatives abroad. The Germans, despite all their pressure to expedite emigration, were not prepared to give up Jewish money. They could emigrate, yes, but as paupers; and who in the world wanted paupers? Several consulates canceled the validity of visas already issued; many countries stopped issuing visas altogether. Switzerland closed her borders, while the Scandinavian countries accorded transit visas only on the basis of a Scandinavian guarantor. In a gloomy report, Hannah Steiner noted that as far as emigration sites were concerned, only the Philippines and some South American countries remained.

Steiner now managed emigration affairs alone. Maria Schmolka had been surprised by the war in Paris, and because she risked rearrest if she returned, she responded to her friends' pleas and decided to remain outside, where she could perhaps accomplish more for Protectorate Jews. Her chief concern was for her friend Hannah Steiner, and she tried unflaggingly to get her and her husband, Ludwig, out of Czechoslovakia. Schmolka moved to London, renewed her contacts with the Czechoslovakian exiles, especially with Jan Masaryk, and there helped found the National Committee of Czechoslovakian Jewry.

Hitler's conquest of Poland had changed very little in the West. Contrary to general predictions, the Germans had not bombed England, and despite the accelerated pace of arms production and the expectation of renewed war, the British went about their business as usual. At times one even got the impression that the real enemy was the Jews who were trying to emigrate to Palestine. There were 2,900 certificate holders and their families trapped in Germany, Austria, and the Protectorate because the British now regarded them as enemy subjects and barred their entry into Palestine. In response to appeals from Weizmann, the colonial office replied that for political reasons it had been decided to take no measures to facilitate the emigration of refugees from Germany to Palestine unless they had managed to reach a neutral country before the war broke out. The British Foreign Office admitted openly that they did not want to concern themselves with enemy subjects. It was feared that Nazi agents might infiltrate immigrant ranks and that the Germans would use immigration for this very purpose. Weizmann exerted all his influence, and Masaryk also intervened on behalf of the 1,200 certificate holders in the Protectorate: he suggested that the Foreign Office consider them potential citizens— when the time came, he and Dr. Beneš were willing to declare that the Jews in question had relinquished all previous citizenship as soon as they stepped outside the borders of the Protectorate. The Colonial Office ignored the Jewish Agency's guarantee that there was not a single Nazi spy among the hand-picked certificate holders, but in the end a settlement was reached: two delegates, one from the immigration department of the Palestine government and the other from the Jewish Agency, would carefully check all emigrants arriving in Trieste from the Reich and only after their identity had been ascertained would they be issued visas to Palestine.

However, this was only one side of the problem. The war had caused a serious shortage of ships in Italy, since most vessels had been turned over to the army. Only after a great deal of effort (and a high price in dollars) was agreement reached with the Adriatica company for the *Galila* to make five special trips between Trieste and Haifa from October through December 1939. Then the obstacle of Italian transit visas cropped up. If the emigrants left the Reich without British visas, how could they be issued Italian transit visas? It was eventually decided that the Palestine office in Prague (as in Vienna and Berlin) was to submit a list of passengers to the Italian consul which would be sent to Rome for approval by the Palestine government's inspector, and the transit visas would be granted on the basis of this approval. But this was still not the end of it: the Italians were reluctant to grant the visas because the Jewish passports stated that the bearers could not return to the Protectorate. What if the British withheld entry visas to Palestine? The emigrants would remain in Italy. The Germans must cancel the passport restriction. Edelstein went to Eichmann and assured him that none of the Jews would return to the Protectorate even if they were refused visas to Palestine. So, to effect the final departure of the Jews, which had been held up for months, Eichmann agreed to issue exit permits that ostensibly included the right to return.

Haim Barlas, head of the Jewish Agency's immigration department in Geneva, which had been set up when the war broke out, bore the lion's share of the work involved in processing the emigration of the certificate holders and the contacts with the Italian and German foreign offices. In one of their frequent telephone conversations on the matter, Edelstein said, "If I could only speak to you in person!" and Barlas promised to try to arrange it. He obtained an exit permit for Edelstein for a three-day stay in Trieste through the Central Emigration Authority in Vienna, and meant in that time to take Edelstein to London and Paris. But Edelstein was nervous that he would not return on time, and instead he appealed to Weizmann in writing.

Edelstein's letter to Weizmann was a cry for help. The only hope of saving the Jews of the Protectorate from the horrors of transport to Poland was to implement an emigration program. Attached to the letter was a report on the situation of the Jews of the Protectorate: 20 percent were of a suitable age and fit for physical work, and 20 percent could be trained for productive jobs. Edelstein depicted the tension between the Czechs and the Germans and its detrimental consequences for Jews: recent events had shown that the danger to life was greater than even the worst pessimists had imagined. His description of the Nisko affair was dry and to the point, "because a factual report cannot convey the anguish, pain, and despair of thousands. And all this is still not the end. A catastrophe of unprecedented dimensions threatens the Jews of the Protectorate, unless the scheme can be thwarted through increased emigration.

"Primary attention should be given to the tens of thousands of children, including those whose fathers have been deported to Poland, the children of Polish citizens in concentration camps or prisons who for all intents and purposes are orphans, and children of people with American affidavits who must wait their turn. Every Jewish family in a neutral country should take a child as a guest into its home.

"It is only natural, in light of their love for Palestine, that thousands of Jews in the Protectorate await with longing a chance to emigrate. We have no wish to lodge complaints against any quarter, but we must demand that authorized bodies respond to appeals from the Protectorate much more positively than they have done thus far. It is still not too late, it is still possible to help, and help must come.

"The situation has forced us to consider emigration possibilities which until now have for various reasons been ignored," Edelstein went on, referring to the then current settlement scheme for Bolivia. He asked that it also include Jews from the Protectorate: there were after all a thousand strong young people on agricultural or occupational training at the time, as well as three hundred farmers from the Sudetenland, all ideally suited to such a plan. "We learned from the American consulate in Prague that people aged between eighteen and twenty-seven may be able to emigrate to the Philippines," he wrote, and asked that this be verified immediately. He also urged that steps be taken to renew the visas for the British colonies which had been issued to citizens of the Protectorate and revoked when war erupted. "The fate of the Protectorate's Jews now lies in the hands of world Jewry. If the Jewish relief organizations abandon us, if contrary to our expectations our call for help remains unanswered, a calamity will befall the 90,000 Jews of the Protectorate. We have the utmost faith that you will help, and we await your answer and your measures. Arrange for visas, for certificates, try and obtain foreign currency, think of the Jewish children in the Protectorate!"

Edelstein's stay in Trieste was a series of meetings, consultations, and written appeals, and a nerve-racking wait for replies and for German permission to extend his sojourn by a few days. In a conversation with Barlas and Ullman (who acted as the liaison between the Protectorate and the free world), Edelstein set forth his various plans for augmenting emigration, expounded the idea of "guest-children," and asked Barlas to try to get the Zionist institutions to agree in principle to deal with emigration to countries other than Palestine. At the end of the talks, Barlas left for Geneva, London, and Paris to enlist all the help he could, promising to inform Edelstein of the results while he was still in Italy. He traveled to London and personally delivered Edelstein's letter to Weizmann, who had already tried to interest the minister for the colonies in a plan to bring 20,000 children from Poland and Rumania to Palestine, even if it had to be within the framework of the White Paper.

Edelstein's appeal to Morris Troper, director of the Joint in Paris, was also a plea for help: until now the Protectorate Jews had not overly burdened the welfare funds, and if they called on them now, they did so because of their terrible plight. Only the quick and vigorous intervention of the welfare organizations could alleviate the situation and perhaps avert disaster altogether. Barlas was to present Edelstein's plan for preventing further transports to Troper, and in his letter Edelstein asked Troper to let him have his reply by December 5, the day on which he was meant to return to Prague. He wanted to know to what extent the Joint would be prepared to allocate foreign currency and find emigration sites. Troper was particularly interested in the "guest-child" scheme, but his answer left no room for doubt: the Joint would like to help but could do so only according to its special functions and financial capacity, and it could not commit itself to specific dates. "We hope to continue to extend aid to your country also in future, but only within the framework of the present agreement." (No untoward rigidity toward Prague was intended; the fact was that since 1938, the Joint had been inundated by appeals from all corners of Europe, and though its budget had doubled in the space of one year, its resources were still limited.)

Edelstein sent Ully (as Ullman was generally called) to Nahum Goldmann, president of the Jewish Congress. He was to give him a clear picture of the situation of the Jews in Bohemia and Moravia, and enlist his aid. ("Our predicament is so grave that there is no time for superfluous words.") He appealed to Sally Mayer, an industrialist and philanthropist who now represented the Joint in Switzerland, and to Leo Hermann, and every appeal echoed the same refrain: the resumption of transports to Poland could be avoided if at least ten thousand Jews left Czechoslovakia in the next six months. The problem was financial—visas could still be bought with dollars to finance illegal immigration to Palestine. "According to our calculations, £80,000 can be raised from our friends throughout the world," Edelstein wrote Leo Hermann, of which

£43,000 could be allocated for "special training," a term that cam-
ouflaged illegal immigration. The illegal-immigration people,
whom Edelstein met in Trieste, were prepared to take out a shipment at the beginning of January, if money could be found, and
Ullman was to be ready with an answer no later than December 20
so that the German quotas for December and January could be met.

From Trieste, Yekef also wrote to Max Olliner, Miriam's brother in
Palestine, and asked him to arrange for his and Miriam's mother,
Mrs. Jetti Olliner, to immigrate. He also asked him to get permits
for Miriam and Arieh to emigrate without him, for it was unlikely
that he would be permitted to leave in the near future. Max Olliner
replied that he would take care of it and Yekef had nothing to worry
about: he, Max, could support the whole family. Edelstein asked the
Jewish Agency to grant certificates and permits to the thirty people
necessary in Prague for current work; if they could not be assured of
immigration at a later date they were liable to leave soon with the
illegal immigrants, thereby endangering all the work being done.
When they parted at the Trieste train station, Barlas said to Edelstein: "Could you stay, perhaps?" Yekef replied in agitation that he
could not, his family was in Prague. His certificate remained at the
Palestine office in Trieste. Maybe, despite everything, he would be
able to leave someday.

Before he left for Trieste, the Germans had instructed Edelstein
to assess the Italian mood, their attitude toward the Germans, and
their reaction to the war. After he returned, he closeted himself in
his room, wrote a report, and had the staff of the Palestine office
destroy all his notes, his rough copies, even the carbon paper he had
used. The report was thirty pages long, and Harry Tressler, who
read it, saw how carefully thought out it was: it had gone into great
detail to say nothing. The Italians were loyal to Mussolini and will
follow him; however, there were groups that did not wish to become
embroiled in war; and other such general conclusions. When Yekef
left to submit the report to the Germans, he told Harry: "If I don't
return, it means they understood that the report says nothing." But
he did return, and he was even able to say that Burger had been very
pleased.

The economic situation of the Jews in the Protectorate had followed
a steep downward turn since the outset of the war. In the autumn,
thousands of Jewish employees were fired from public institutions,
factories, and banks, by order of the Reichsprotektor, many with no

advance notice. While some could still depend on family support, the number of people who now relied on the community rose sharply (the welfare kitchen distributed 5,000 lunches daily). Many Jews had assumed that the German purpose really was "Aryaniza- tion" and hastened to transfer their businesses to Czechs (sometimes to friends), only to discover that the Germans did not consider Czechs to be "Aryans"—their purpose, in fact, was to lay their own hands on Jewish wealth. On the other hand, when Jews transferred their businesses to Germans, they provoked the ire of the Czechs, particularly in the provinces and small towns. As in the past, the Jews were caught between two millstones of hate and hate. There were Czechs who informed against the Jews if the latter tried to remove any of their goods or merchandise before the property was transferred to Aryans. And there were towns, especially in Moravia, where the Jews were ordered to shut down their shops even before the date set by the Germans.

The Czechs saw in the war with Poland confirmation that a small country stood no chance against the Germans, and to some extent, they even rejoiced at the defeat of the Poles who had treated them so disgracefully during the Munich Pact. It seemed to them that despite everything, they had chosen the wiser course: they had spared themselves a disastrous war, the destruction of their cities, and hundreds of thousands of casualties. The German police and military forces in the Protectorate were relatively small, workers had not been harmed, conditions of farmers had improved, and even when food rationing was imposed in October, Czechs still enjoyed better rations than residents in the Reich proper. Nevertheless, anti- German hatred grew, the result of German inflexibility and the gradual loss of Czechoslovakia's remaining independence. Septem- ber 30, the anniversary of the Munich Pact, was marked by a boycott of public transport, and on October 28, the republic's national holiday, Czechs donned festive garb, took to the streets, and ob- served a two-minute silence. Here and there people called "Long live Beneš!" And Karl Hermann Frank, who was interested in fan- ning the flames and sought an opportunity to adopt strong-arm measures against the Czechs, ordered his police to intervene. Two people were killed and many others wounded. The funeral of Jan Oplatka, who died of his wounds two weeks later, turned into a public demonstration and led to further clashes between Czech students and the police. Twelve hundred students were arrested, nineteen were executed without trial, and hundreds were imprisoned in concentration camps. Frank ruled with an iron hand and was rewarded for his efforts by promotion to SS Obergruppen-führer.

The brutality with which the demonstrations had been quelled shocked the Czechs, and their hatred for the Germans knew no bounds. Rumors spread that the Germans meant to prohibit weddings for three years, that German doctors were to inject a chemical that induced mental retardation into all Czech children. Panic-stricken mothers who took their children out of school by force were arrested by the police, which aroused the workers. Despite the state of emergency, Czechs had the feeling that the hour of reckoning was drawing nigh. When Ella Schultz, Edelstein's Czech-language secretary, left for Palestine with her husband, the Czech customs official at the border said, "Is it worth it? It'll all be over in a few weeks."

The first edition of the *Jüdisches Nachrichtenblatt–Židovské Listy,* the new German-Czech newspaper put out under German supervision by the Prague Jewish community and the Zionist Federation, appeared on November 24, 1939, and opened with a warning: all Jews must be conscious of their responsibility to the Jewish public as a whole. The act of a single individual could have disastrous consequences for all. All steps that might endanger the Jewish public must therefore be avoided altogether, particularly political or pseudo political activities, and any contacts that could be construed as such. Jews were to keep away from rumor-mongers and agitators.

Though the newspaper was published with German approval and its express purpose was chiefly to promote emigration, it contained between the lines a wealth of information on the Jewish world and on Palestine. It spoke openly of the German desire to be rid of the Jews, but almost every article rang with some note of encouragement and consolation, with the familiar refrain being: we must ensure the continuation of the Jewish people. Censorship was imposed on the newspaper twofold: first the Germans had to approve the proofs, then the Czechs, who sometimes proved even more severe critics than their German counterparts. Toward Hanukkah, Dr. Tauber, the editor, decided to use the story of the Maccabees to hearten its readers with a bit of national pride. The German censor told Kahn that he was well aware of what the story said between the lines, though he erased nothing. Tauber, like other key functionaries, was not allowed to emigrate, but Kahn decided that the time was ripe to get him out: he brought the article as proof that Tauber was unsuitable for his responsible position and that it would be better to be free of him. Tauber got away: he left the Protectorate in December and sailed on the *Galila*'s last run.

The farewell notices that appeared in the *Židovské Listy* during October and December—"We emigrated to Switzerland and greet all our friends, Dr. Otto Kurz and his wife"; or "Greetings to all friends and acquaintances on the occasion of my immigration to Palestine. Gideon Polak"—left the readers heavy-hearted: those who could were getting off a sinking ship. Following an incident with the Gestapo, because it was he who had recommended that Maria Schmolka travel to Paris, Dr. März gave in to Kahn's repeated pleas and left. Rufeisen was out of Czechoslovakia during the invasion and never returned. Shimon Enoch fled after Edelstein received information that the Gestapo was following him. When Moshe Baumgarten left to escort a Youth-Aliyah transport, the scene at the train station was almost a demonstration: everybody came to bid the children farewell. Among those leaving was Raphael, Kahn's son, called Titus by his parents (their daughter Susie had left beforehand and traveled with a youth transport to England to await immigration there). Kahn was upset, and with tears in his eyes, asked Moshe Baumgarten to keep an eye on his boy. "I am sure that he will be well looked after in Palestine," he said, "but I'll never see him again." Titus was too young to understand the gravity of his father's words, and Moshe too preoccupied with travel arrangements to give them much thought.

It required a great deal of love and a dose of despair to tear oneself away from one's children and forgo the consolation of their presence for who knew how long—months, perhaps years, perhaps forever.

> Eva Beermann from Olmütz is on training in Denmark and seeks her father, whereabouts unknown. She is well and looks forward to their reunion.

So read an announcement in the Jewish newspaper. At the start of the new academic year, thousands of Jewish pupils were discharged from school. Some were absorbed by Jewish schools; most, however, continued to study in small groups with Jewish teachers who had been left without work, with students who were not allowed to pursue their studies, or with unemployed relatives.

It was sometimes difficult to decide what was preferable: the emigration of at least one or some members of the family, or the moral support of the united family. Prof. Voskin-Nahartabi, director of Prague's rabbinical seminary, who had many friends in Palestine, did not use the immigration permit placed at his disposal because his daughter Tamara was ill at the time. Otto Brod, Max's brother, refused to leave without his in-laws. The pioneers who emigrated illegally often did so with great misgivings: they were abandoning their parents in their most difficult hour, and emigration was in fact an act of selfishness.

With the start of the war, instructions were issued to mobilize Jews for public works, and the community consequently set up an employment office, headed by twenty-three-year-old Heinz Schuster of Hehalutz, because it was assumed that the functions of the two bodies overlapped. The main task, after all, was to place young people in agriculture, industry, and road construction, so that they could support themselves and train for productive jobs until they finally departed. The pages of the controlled newspaper sometimes resembled a Zionist paper of yore, carrying appeals such as: "Return to the land of your forefathers: Prepare for a new life! The country needs strong people." The accompanying pictures of kibbutz children and fruit-pickers only enhanced this impression. In the fifteen years since its inception Hehalutz had been a lone cry in the wilderness, on the whole ignored by most comfortably off Jews. Now, however, it had become a mass movement, with all the advantages and disadvantages that this entailed. Most of the new members had joined without any ideological background. But their gradual isolation from non-Jewish acquaintances and childhood Czech friends often acted as a more effective spur than a dozen ideological seminars. As the possibility of immediate emigration to Palestine diminished, so Zionist education became more intensive, because it answered a need for young Jews: it made them feel that they had found a haven, and made them aware of a shared responsibility, as Fredy Hirsch wrote in his call to the youth. To Fredy, as a physical-education instructor, education began with strengthening the body and learning discipline and self-control through sports and games. "Cafés and amusement sites have no place in our education. We would rather draw closer to nature in hikes and camps. This is our way of building Palestine." Under the slogan "A healthy youth is a healthy homeland," Fredy preached physical education. "Which do you prefer?" he asked. "A proud and tall suntanned lad, or a flabby, nervous youngster with drooping shoulders? Probably the first. But what are you doing about emulating him? Nothing!" Fredy gave voice to the Zionist ideal of the new strong Jew, to the ideals of the German youth movements, and also to his own personal love for handsome youth.

Winter was around the corner; the community's budget grew from week to week, swelling to tens of millions of crowns. Under Otto Zucker the Foundation Fund, the Jewish National Fund, and the Prague Jewish community held a combined fund-raising drive (60 percent for the community, 40 percent for the funds), under the banner slogan: SACRIFICE—BUILD—LIVE. "A people that cannot meet days of trial wisely and reasonably, is doomed to extinction. But a people that can prove itself in times of hardship is worthy of continuity. Take part in the building of your future and the promise of well-being for the coming generations!" they called; the emblem of the drive was a hollow tree with a new sprig sprouting from its middle. The response, considering the economic situation of the Jews, was handsome. More money was raised than in previous years. The funds were controlled by the Gestapo, but the transfer to Palestine continued through the Joint, and through intricate financial transactions whereby crowns were paid in the Protectorate for dollar help abroad.

Illegal immigration also continued despite the state of war, despite the pressure Britain exerted on the Balkan countries to prevent illegal immigrants from sailing from their shores, and despite the heavier punishments (up to fines of £100,000 or five years' imprisonment) meted out by the Mandate government to shipowners and individuals who abetted the operation. The only opening still available to illegal immigrants from the Protectorate was the Slovakian border, and with the help of the Slovakian consul in Prague, whose love of money exceeded even his loyalty to Fascism, collective transit visas were obtained on the basis of invalid travel documents, marked for Peru or Paraguay, which had also been procured through bribes. Because of the lack of ships, the immigrants were sometimes stuck in Bratislava for weeks and even months, as was the second transport from Hehalutz and Maccabi with its 381 passengers, who were not as fortunate as the first group had been. They were kept in the most primitive conditions, housed in a hostel for single workers under the eye of the Hlinka Guard, and since their transit visas were good for only a few days at a time, they had to be continuously renewed through more palm-greasing and with the help of the local Jewish community, which, despite the ever worsening situation of the Slovakian Jews, did its best to make things easier for the immigrants waiting impatiently to leave.

The main problem was ships and money. Shipowners involved in illegal immigration now demanded £60 per person, three times the price of a first-class ticket on regular passenger lines, and it had to be paid in hard currency and mostly in advance. Ships got caught by the winter on the frozen Danube, captains extorted money, the crews were generally drunk (only sailors who had been expelled from the merchant fleet for breaches of discipline were prepared to work on the illegal immigrant ships). Owing to the ghastly sanitary conditions epidemics broke out aboard the stranded ships, people succumbed to dysentery and meningitis, and dozens of immigrants, particularly the older ones who had not undergone any training and had no friends to lean on, despaired and were even prepared to return to the Protectorate simply to put an end to their suffering. On the shores of Palestine itself, the swift-moving boats of the coastguard intercepted and attacked the ships, refugees were killed, and those who were apprehended by the British were—if not returned to the open seas—at best imprisoned in the detention camp at Athlit. There was little encouragement in the letters sent back to Prague, and nevertheless there were thousands of people who were still prepared to leave as illegal immigrants, as Edelstein told the Jewish Agency in Switzerland: "A British detention camp does not frighten them. Compared to German concentration camps, it's paradise."

In the middle of December, the heads of the Jewish provincial communities met in Prague; representatives of the Palestine office and the Prague community reported on the emigration possibilities still available. The guests were then taken on a tour of the community offices and the Zentralstelle in the hope that the visit would elicit more cooperation from them in the matter of emigration. Over and over the same words were hammered out, both in writing and orally: emigrate, leave, set out; not temporarily, but to start a new home; there was no road back, no stopping halfway. The crux of the Jewish problem, just as Herzl had written forty years ago, was still "Can we stay, and for how long, or must we leave and where to?" The answer was: we must leave, and now.

If only there were dollars! A six-month transit visa for Haiti could still be bought for $550, a visa to Ecuador could still be had for $400. There was still talk of settling those 25,000 acres in San Domingo which Señor Trujillo had kindly offered free of charge, and 200 people had already left from Central Europe for a trial period, to see if they could endure the subtropical climate at all. If their answer was positive, thousands could follow. There was a plan to settle 4,800 people in Bolivia for $300 per person, in an area where the Rio Grande met the Rio Parai, free of malaria and suitable for raising sugar, rice, and corn. For the time being there was no point in making personal applications. The matter was being dealt with. And the generous United States of America had in 1939 granted shelter to 1,650 Czechoslovakian Jews—a figure that actually fell below the official quota.

New hopes again sprang up: after a three-and-a-half-month lull due to the war, the first shipload of refugees reached Shanghai. People with $400, or who could obtain this sum from relatives abroad, could still emigrate to Shanghai without any special visa, and all Shanghai citizens could bring their families over if they could support them. The price of passage to Shanghai was $290 per person. The main thing was for people who had managed to reach other countries to help those still waiting to emigrate. Only if there was a sense of common responsibility would the Jewish people continue to exist.

The newspaper now ran personal ads of a different nature: "Bearer of American affidavit seeks wealthy woman for marriage"; or "Interested in girl from a good Czech Jewish home to emigrate together"; and also: "Who is prepared to take a ten-month-old baby to America to be reunited with his parents? The escort will receive $50 upon arrival." The newspaper carried a list of cheap hotels in Genoa, informed its readers that the best remedy for seasickness was sucking a lemon, and drew their attention to the fact that butter was an unknown commodity in China.

The Jewish newspaper did not mince words: the Jews were threatened by the sword of Damocles unless they emigrated as ordered. When the dominant ideology considered itself exclusive, no ethnic groups could exist, rejected and abased by the regime. While "liberal anti-Semitism" might at one time have been prepared to compromise, this was no longer possible.

Those with a humorous bent defined the newspaper as one colossal poster, bearing the message HERAUS MIT UNS! (Out with Us!). And black humor reared its head, even now, and poked fun at the situation and the absurd: "Two flies fell into a cup of milk. One despaired and drowned. But the other continued to shift about with its legs and was saved on the mound of butter thus generated below.

The more ponderous your attitude to life, the more ponderous life becomes. Never say die."

Edelstein added his own contribution to the emigration literature. He wrote an embracing review of Jewish wandering over the generations, starting with the migration of individuals motivated by economic considerations, touching on organized emigration with the assistance of philanthropic associations, and leading up to the present-day immigration to Palestine. True to his faith in Zionism, he spoke of the blooming of the desert, of the forces that had initially spurred on immigration and that had taken root in the Promised Land. Palestine's capacity to absorb was not dependent on the opinion of one expert or another, but on Jewish will, and it would determine the fate of Jewry.

15

FROM HELL AND BACK

EDELSTEIN TOLD Nahum Goldmann, president of the World Jewish Congress, that he had once asked a senior official in the German administration why the Germans were so bent on Jewish emigration, now, during the war, when the younger emigrants might very well join the British army. To which the man had replied that thousands of young Jews were apt to constitute a danger to the Protectorate in times of internal unrest, whereas a few thousand more or less British soldiers would not change the course of the war. Goldmann noted down these words after meeting Edelstein in Geneva on February 8, 1940. Edelstein had reported to Eichmann in Vienna, and the official purpose of his visit to Switzerland was to investigate further emigration possibilities. He told Goldmann that the transports to the Lublin region had stopped, but they might start up again in the spring if the Jews did not emigrate by then on their own strength.

As soon as he arrived in Geneva, Edelstein went to the Jewish Agency offices and met with Moshe Shertok, director of the political department, whose trip from Palestine to London had taken him through Cairo, Rome, and Geneva. Edelstein had with him several editions of the community paper, and Shertok was amazed at what could be said in a German-censored newspaper: even the sports page carried a speech by Ben-Gurion delivered at the Maccabi convention. On their walk through the city, Edelstein told Shertok that "those in charge of the Jews had recently demanded that the Zionists dispatch a delegation to America to speak to Jewish leaders there, and influence them to send emissaries to Germany in order to negotiate with the Germans on settling Jewish affairs in the Reich." Shertok's reaction was: "The Nazis, apparently, are prepared to spin a web of lies around such a delegation and promise all sorts of help and consolation, when all they really want is to use the delegation for their own propaganda purposes and drive in another wedge against America's entry into the war."

Roosevelt's sympathy was with the British, but for the time being his hands were tied by isolationist elements in the United States. The latter carried a good deal of weight and, of course, were opposed to American intervention in Europe, for reasons too complex and deeply rooted to go into here. There were those who openly favored Hitler's rise to power; even those who did not were still not anxious to become embroiled in war.

Shertok and Edelstein rode together to the Wilson Palace, where they were to address the Zionist functionaries in Geneva, twenty-five people in all. Edelstein's detailed account of the Nisko affair shocked his listeners; in his diary, Shertok crowned Edelstein an anonymous hero who had three times escaped hell only to return to it again. But he refrained from recording the details Edelstein gave of how the Germans tormented the Jewish functionaries, "of the humiliating wiles, the physical torture, the blows and injuries," for "I shrink from arousing pity, even our own." Together with the friendliness, respect, and admiration one felt in talks with people like Edelstein, there was also a feeling of distance, as if the latter already belonged to the world of shadows and his sojourn on earth would terminate when the clock struck midnight.

Edelstein spoke of the miracle of the 3,500 legal immigrants to Palestine and the half a million pounds sterling they had brought with them. He told his handful of listeners that the problems inherent in illegal immigration were not to be solved by abandoning the operation, "but by bringing the worthiest to Palestine, and turning the contemptible away from its shores." This led Shertok to reflect gloomily: "Is anyone worrying about those who stay behind? Will there be permits available for them when troubles overtake them? When the time comes, will the director of the Palestine office have any other choice but to come to Palestine as an illegal immigrant?"

In Shertok's view, "the struggle in recent months had shifted from the White Paper to holding and consolidating positions in Palestine during this emergency period which could continue indefinitely," and he therefore pinned no great hopes even on continued immigration: "Should all hope be lost, and there will be no way to save the Jews in enemy countries, we will demand that the government give us a limited number of permits for colleagues who have disregarded their own safety so that others could be rescued."

While in Geneva, Edelstein made sure of certificates and obtained entry visas to Switzerland for himself, Kahn, Zucker, Franta Friedmann, and their families. Edelstein said that Kahn, on whose behalf März had gone to a great deal of trouble in Jerusalem, was not prepared to leave without the other three. The four felt that they should remain in Prague so long as there was a spark of hope that their toils were not entirely in vain, and they were determined to stay together because there was too much work for one person to cope with. But an opportunity might arise in the coming months for all four to leave together, and it was just as well to be prepared for such a contingency. Edelstein asked that Weidmann also be taken into account, for although he was not a Zionist, his conduct was always irreproachable; if fate had forced them all together, it would be unfriendly and unfair to forget him. As for Hannah Steiner, it was much more difficult to help her and her husband—the authorities blamed her for the fact that Maria Schmolka had failed to return (Schmolka, meanwhile, feeling responsible for the plight of her beloved friend, was moving mountains to try to get her out of Prague; but on March 29, 1940, on the eve of her meeting with Weizmann and the Queen of England, whose intervention she sought on behalf of Hannah Steiner, Maria Schmolka died of a heart attack).

Edelstein was speaking to Kahn in Prague (since the state of emergency had been declared, phone calls from the Protectorate had to be approved in advance and the Gestapo listened to every conversation) when the attentive agent suddenly cut in, and said: "Edelstein, see that you get visas for yourself and ten or fifteen of your friends, so that if need be, you can leave immediately." Yekef was most disturbed by this incident: did it mean that emigration to Palestine was to be stopped altogether? He wrote Leo Hermann in London about it, and Hermann appealed to Weizmann to help save the Prague people.

Privately, Edelstein told Shertok that there were people in the

Berlin Jewish community who in specific instances knew how to stand up to the Germans. "Whereas in Vienna [so Shertok quoted Edelstein in his diary] the people are spineless, and as a result ill treatment there has reached insufferable proportions. The Zionists do not have control over all community affairs in Prague either, so there are some functionaries there who also submit to everything and for all practical purposes serve as the Gestapo's lackeys. The Zionists' rise in power and prestige has put them in a position to assume the leadership of the community, and the Zionist officials have become the focus of recovery, of efforts at mutual assistance and self-help, of finding a way out and a shield against despair. The fact that several responsible people have remained at their posts and did not immediately run for their lives has undoubtedly helped the Zionist Federation strengthen its position and been of incalculable value for morale. In Poland, where all the leaders fled, this left a terrible impression. It was bad for morale and for the reputation of Zionism; the flock has remained without a shepherd."

However, Edelstein was disappointed by Shertok's fundamental attitude, as was Wilfried Israel, formerly an owner of one of Berlin's large department stores. British by birth, Israel had managed to leave Germany and now sought to stir the American public into helping the Jews of the Reich who faced extermination via the eastern transports. For this reason he asked to meet Weizmann, but Shertok told him that he doubted whether Weizmann could help. According to Shertok, any American attempt to make Germany curtail her brutality toward the Jews would, if successful, put the United States in the position of being obligated to Germany, and such obligation would reduce genuine American identification with England, a development that Weizmann could not encourage. Israel disagreed. Edelstein also demanded vigorous action, but to him Shertok also claimed that only quiet diplomacy could be beneficial, pointing out that the position of American Jewry was that direct confrontation of the Germans must be avoided. "They did not speak of saving the Jews, but of alleviating our plight," Edelstein said when he returned to Prague, and he repeated it often: "*Sie wollen nur unser Schicksal erleichtern*"—they only want to ease our fate. He made it clear that in his opinion quiet diplomacy would not work. A cry had to be raised throughout the world.

Weizmann traveled to the United States in January 1940 and took with him Edelstein's report, parts of which had been widely publicized, particularly the idea of "guest-children." On the day that

Edelstein met with Shertok in Geneva, President Roosevelt received Weizmann in Washington to discuss the White Paper and the situation of the Jews in Eastern and Central Europe. He pointed out that even if one ignored the Jews who would be swallowed up by the Soviet Union, or who would disappear and be stamped out under the Germans if the present rate of destruction continued, there were still two and a half million Jews to consider, of which at least one million young and able-bodied Jews could be transferred to Palestine in the coming years.

Roosevelt wanted to know if the matter could not somehow be settled with the Arabs with the help of some form of bribery. Weizmann replied that it was not so simple. "When the war ends," Roosevelt said with a smile, "you'll settle with the Arabs! But first we must win." Weizmann agreed, but added that when the nations of the world met at the peace table, they would again face the problem of the Jews in all its severity.

In his two days in Geneva, Edelstein wrote dozens of letters: to Miriam's relatives, to friends in Palestine, to relatives of people from the Protectorate, and to Dr. Even-Zahav of the Hebrew University, who had arranged students' certificates for the Protectorate: "You may rest assured that the number of certificates you put at our disposal equals the number of lives you saved." As for the many requests for certificates which continued to pour in, sometimes accompanied by recommendations from the nation's leaders: at the moment the Prague Palestine office did not have a single immigration permit, and it was doubtful that it would receive any. The British government had not only rejected the Jewish Agency's appeal to cancel the White Paper for the duration of the war but at the end of December 1939 had actually stopped issuing certificates altogether until the spring "because of the war, the unemployment in Palestine, and the difficulty of transferring capital." As far as the availability of certificates after March 1940 was concerned, "assuming that the state of war will continue, the policy of the Foreign Office will be to accord certificates only to residents of neutral or friendly countries who managed to leave Germany before the war broke out."

Dr. Ullman in Geneva endeavored diligently to implement the "guest-child" plan, but because it was children they were dealing with—flesh and blood people who eat and cost money—the thousands of which Edelstein had spoken became reduced to hundreds, dozens, individuals. Ullman formed a public committee to absorb fifty teenagers from the Protectorate at a training farm in Switzerland for one year, and after much effort obtained the necessary $10,000, but he still required a guarantee from worldwide Youth-Aliyah that the children would leave Switzerland at the end of the year and emigrate to Palestine. The Palestine office in Zagreb and WIZO in Yugoslavia sought permission for another fifty children to stay there, and again a $10,000 guarantee was required. During the same feverish two days in Geneva, Edelstein met with Hans Winter, the Youth-Aliyah representative in Switzerland, and learned that international Youth-Aliyah planned to move from Reich territory, 1,200 children, including three hundred from the Protectorate, to neutral countries (Bulgaria, Greece, Yugoslavia, Italy, and Switzerland), and for this purpose it had to ensure their support and guarantee that the children would stay no more than a year in their host countries before leaving for Palestine. The cost of achieving this for the three hundred children from the Protectorate was £36,000, a sum that the Prague leaders would have to raise. Edelstein and Ullman, the official representatives of the Zionist Federation in Bohemia and Moravia, promised to do all in their power to procure the money and asked only for their share of the funds should a special drive be held. The entire scheme, however, was still in the preliminary stages: meanwhile Winter promised four certificates for children under twelve and mentioned the immediate possibility of *one* child being adopted—on condition that he was orphaned from both parents.

Eva Stern-Michaelis, who served Youth-Aliyah in London, was skeptical of Ullman's plan for even a hundred children: where was the money to come from? Efforts to transfer teenagers from the Protectorate to Denmark had been under way for a long time, but the Czechoslovakian refugee fund in London opposed the allocation of funds for this purpose, and as a result an embarrassing situation had arisen whereby available sites in Denmark were left unused.

Money was the key, and the discussions between Edelstein and Mossad, the illegal-immigration organization, focused largely on financial matters. The Prague leaders had long had cause for complaint against Mossad: they demanded more money from people leaving the Protectorate than from those leaving Germany; they had not honored their previous commitments (an agreement signed between Protectorate representatives and Mossad during Congress

spoke of moving 2,200 immigrants by December, within the framework of the "transfer"); and immigrants had been stranded halfway.
The report prepared by the illegal-immigration people in Prague,
in anticipation of Edelstein's trip to Switzerland, was explicit:
"Should the situation in Palestine and the shipping market not
permit further illegal immigration, Mossad must say so openly, so
that we can disband Hehalutz and not mislead people in vain." For
their part, the Mossad representatives claimed that the Prague Palestine office cooperated with other elements organizing illegal immigration to Palestine.

Following exhausting discussions, a legal agreement was signed,
as though it were an ordinary business transaction in normal times:
Mossad undertook to get 2,400 people out of the Protectorate in the
next three months (if it were not thwarted by circumstances beyond
its control). The first to be taken care of were the three hundred
people stranded in Slovakia and the thousand waiting to emigrate
who had German exit permits; the remaining eleven hundred
could apply for emigration immediately so that they would be ready
to leave by April. Against this, the Protectorate representatives
pledged a sum of £23 per person, and Mossad was to arrange for
transit visas, shipping, and orderly disembarkation on the shores of
Palestine. The Protectorate people promised not to negotiate with
any other transport body, to inform Mossad of all other proposals
for illegal immigration, and not to sign any agreement without
Mossad's approval (since it was known that commercial adviser
Storfer, whom the Germans had just appointed to direct the center
for coordinating Jewish transports overseas, was sitting back at the
Prague Jewish community building, and no contract was to be entered into with shipping lines without his authorization). However,
the Protectorate leaders were to be released from their commitment
should Mossad fail in the task. The protocol and all its amendments
were signed, sealed, and stored, as if yesterday's world were still
viable, as if Mossad were really an institution and not a handful of
enterprising young men dedicated to their cause, operating without
an orderly budget, and contending with conditions that changed
from day to day, sometimes risking their lives against opposition
from the mighty administration of the United Kingdom.

As it turned out, a letter signed by Edelstein and Kahn reached
Geneva several weeks after Edelstein's return to Prague, stating that
since the Mossad people had proved disappointing, they saw no
option but to turn to Storfer to arrange matters, especially concern-

ing the group stranded in Bratislava. Ullman disagreed: it was not true that Mossad did not deliver what it promised. Prague simply did not appreciate the difficulties involved.

Eichmann meanwhile laid down guidelines for illegal immigration from Vienna, Berlin, and Prague: every transport was to be reported to Storfer, who was to ascertain whether or not it could be carried out; he in turn was to report in detail to Eichmann, and only with the latter's approval could a contract be signed with a travel agency.

In March 1940, Edelstein traveled to Berlin for a meeting with Eichmann, since the Gestapo's reorganization now head of department IV/B/4 (emigration and evacuation). Representatives were there from Berlin, Vienna, and Prague, including Löwenherz, Epstein, and Storfer. The purpose of the meeting, which took place at Kurfürstenallee 116, which housed Berlin's Zentralstelle, was to expedite emigration. Ephraim Frank of Hehalutz, who represented Berlin's Palestine office, noticed the remarkable change in Eichmann since his rise in authority. A year before, Jews were still permitted to sit in his presence, but not now. Eichmann told the Jewish representatives that if they failed to fill the emigration quotas, the Germans would implement transports, and Frank took note of the behavior of the Jewish leaders: the Viennese Jews struck him as submissive, the Berlin Jews closely guarded their dignity, and the Prague Jews were somewhere in between.

The jurisdiction of the Center for Jewish Emigration in Prague had meanwhile been extended by order of the Reichsprotektor to include all of Bohemia and Moravia. An emigration fund was soon set up which, in the name of the Zentralstelle, appropriated all Jewish emigrant possessions (thereby achieving a total victory for the Reich Security Head Office over the government of the Protectorate, which had also hoped to share in the Jewish booty).

Opportunities for earning a living continued to vanish: Jews were no longer allowed to work in the retail trade of textiles, shoes, or leather (the chief Jewish fields of trade). The Czech public was informed that since the Jews had failed to draw the necessary conclusions when they had first been ordered to hand over businesses voluntarily, an ordinance had been issued to remove all Jewish economic influence in the Protectorate. Those who had hoped, after handing over their shops, to eke out a livelihood from the door-to-door trade, found that peddling was also prohibited.

Their economic situation worsened from month to month. In December they were barred from owning real estate, in January all payments owed Jews, including salaries, had to be deposited in a blocked bank account from which the owners could draw only 1,500 crowns per week. There followed orders to turn over all bonds, jewelry, and valuable metal articles, apart from wedding rings, silver watches, cutlery, and false teeth (in use).

As a sign of the times, the statues of Moses and Rabbi Loew were removed from the entrance to Prague's old Jewish quarter, and in April, the rules about going out after 8 P.M. were tightened, culminating in a total ban on Jews' attendance at the theater or movies.

The more their external world receded, the more functions the Jewish community institutions assumed: since the inception of the republic, their activities had multiplied twenty-five-fold, and the clerical staff twelve, said Weidmann in an interview with the Jewish newspaper. Parallel with the authority of the Zentralstelle, which extended over the Protectorate as a whole, the authority of Jewish community organization in Prague extended over all the Jews in the Protectorate, and on March 18, 1940, the Germans appointed Weidmann official head of the community with Jakob Edelstein as his deputy. As the Jewish newspaper wrote, with surprising candor, this meant that there was now only one legal body for Jewish affairs—the Zentralstelle, operating through the Prague Jewish community office, whose jurisdiction also included the provincial Jewish communities. In other words, the Prague community office derived its authority from the Center for Jewish Emigration: a new era in the history of Diaspora Jewry. The new administration, which worked in conjunction with a five-member advisory board that included Dr. Kahn, promised to do all it could to strengthen the bond between the Jewish populace and the community administration, and expressed the hope that the public would support the two people who bore the responsibility for all Jews in the Protectorate (Edelstein appointed Dr. Adolf Beneš, known as Dolfa, who until then had handled certificates, assistant secretary of the community).

The head of the community and his deputy announced that experienced people from all sectors of the population would be coopted into the community's administrative framework, which, translated into the language of the Jews, meant that the jobs were to be divided, as arranged, among Czech Jews and Zionists. A special department was added for Jews who did not adhere to the Law of

Moses; like all other Jews, they were to register with the community and the letter *J* was to be stamped in their identity booklets.

By order of Hans Günther of the Zentralstelle, a billboard was prepared that displayed photos of the various departmental directors and leading figures in the community, giving their year of birth and family status. Thirty-seven people appeared on it, including the entire Zionist leadership: Dr. Kahn, responsible to the Zionist Federation; Leo Janowitz (secretary of the Palestine office), director of the certificates department; Dr. Munk, director for the emigration of children and teenagers; Hannah Steiner, director of the department for the encouragement of emigration; Josef Lichtenstein, responsible for workers' transports (meaning illegal immigration); and Heinz Schuster, director of the employment department (i.e., Hehalutz). The community liaison with the Zentralstelle was Avraham Fixler.

Fixler, then twenty-six, had been a member of the first graduating class of the Hebrew high school in Munkács. He was a clever, adroit, ambitious young man, who spoke half a dozen languages and had made his own way from the poverty of his hometown in Carpathian Russia to law school in Prague. To support himself he had worked for HICEM until the Germans closed it down, and then for the Palestine office, from where he reached the Zentralstelle. Round-faced, with a skeptical smile, Fixler had been the target of an early German outburst. At a meeting in Günther's office at the Zentralstelle attended by Weidmann, Kahn, Edelstein, Fixler, and Tressler, Günther vented his anger at Fixler for having failed to prepare some material as ordered. Fixler promised to submit it within twenty-four hours. Then Edelstein—who stood, glasses in hand and blinking his eyes at Günther, sitting behind a desk with sunlight streaming in behind him straight into the eyes of his audience—said quietly, "And if he fails to submit it in twenty-four hours, it won't make any difference; it's on my head." Kahn froze. When they left the Zentralstelle, he remarked, "I couldn't have said that."

From time to time Günther visited the community office to acquaint himself with its workings. Like obedient children, all senior officials, including Aladar Deutsch, Prague's venerable, white-bearded chief rabbi, had to assemble in the auditorium of the Jewish municipality and explain to Günther exactly what their function was. On one such occasion, Günther asked Kahn where he had lost his right arm; contrary to his usual response, Kahn replied, "As an officer in the Great War," but the exchange itself unsettled him. He wanted no more contact with the Germans, he told Yekef. Nevertheless he continued at his post, sighing from time to time, "Why did I get involved in this?" He was torn between a sense of common responsibility for the Jews, his personal pride, and the feeling that he had embarked on the road of no return. Both Edelstein's friends and opponents (of which there was no shortage) often attacked him for his contact with the Germans, to which he always had the same retort: "We are racing against time."

Edelstein, Weidmann, and Richard Friedmann, through whom the Germans transmitted all their instructions, consciously served as a buffer between the Germans and the community staff, and knew very well that they would be held responsible should anything be amiss. In the two and a half years of its functioning, not a single employee of the community administration was arrested or physically harmed. In Geneva, Edelstein had spoken in general of the torture of Jewish representatives, but he never related his own experiences with Eichmann, Günther, Burger, and so on, even to those closest to him. Once, after being summoned suddenly to the Peček Palais, he returned pale, his face blotched, and did not speak for hours. When, as usual, Janowitz, Beneš, and Kahn gathered around him, he said, "Don't ask me what happened," leaving no doubt in their minds that he had been subjected to German brutality.

One day a letter was brought to Edelstein with instructions from the Gestapo to translate it immediately. The letter, written in Yiddish, was from a shoemaker called Alois Hitler. It informed his sister that everybody was well and he was making a living, thank God. Harry Tressler took the letter and the translation back to the Peček Palais and was told to wait. There was a cup of hot coffee on the table and some fresh rolls; when the SS officer entered, he invited Harry to help himself. Harry nearly choked—this was hardly the place to enjoy a cup of coffee. He had never been molested on his frequent missions to the Peček Palais, but he had often been asked to turn his face to the wall so that he could not see who was being led through the corridors. When Harry described the incident to Yekef, the latter commented, "They're harassing this poor Hitler simply because of his name."

Whether because of pressure from Frank, head of the Polish General-Gouvernement, or because of the knowledge that war with

France was imminent and in its wake would come new possibilities of solving the Jewish question, at the end of March 1940 Goering ordered that Jewish transports to the East be stopped. Though the Jews themselves knew nothing of this order, there was still ample cause for optimism: in April, 460 of the Nisko evacuees returned to the Protectorate, and while this figure was one quarter of the number that had left a year ago, the very fact of their return—despite the tales of suffering they brought back—was reassuring: the trains still traveled in both directions, to the East and back. Compared with the situation of the Polish Jews, where the first closed ghettos were now being established, the life of the Jews in the Protectorate seemed almost idyllic. Perhaps, the Prague people mused, the Germans also distinguish between Eastern and Western Jews. This is not Poland.

Among those who returned from Nisko was Dr. Hugo Kratky, a doctor Edelstein had met in Lublin. Kratky began working at the only Jewish hospital still open, in Moravská Ostrava, and soon after, Edelstein appeared, ostensibly to have a growth removed from his vocal cords. Actually, he was to meet secretly with an emissary or emissaries from the Soviet Union, and the hospital had been chosen for the rendezvous site because of its relative isolation from Gestapo eyes. Even Dr. Kratky did not know the nature of the meetings.

Near exhaustion, after months of unrelenting tension, Edelstein stopped off on his way to Ostrava at Tajnicek, near Olmütz. He stayed with Trude and Emo Groag, who had formerly owned a malt factory and now lived at the factory's rural hostel for clerks, on the charity of the supervisor appointed over their property. The Groags promised not to reveal his presence to the Jews of Olmütz and its vicinity so that he could finally have a few days of uninterrupted rest, away from phone calls, office work, the public—and away from the Germans. Here, in green and tranquil surroundings, Edelstein permitted himself the luxury of letting go. He ate, slept, told stories, and even analyzed Emo Groag's handwriting (graphology was a current craze in the pioneering youth movements).

16

WHO WOULD REMEMBER ALL THE PROHIBITIONS?

AFTER THE CONQUEST of Poland, it became a war without a front. The Germans inflicted heavy losses on the British merchant fleet in the Atlantic, but contrary to initial forecasts, which had led to the evacuation of a million and a half children, mothers, and teachers from areas in Britain considered to be at risk, Hitler had not bombed the British Isles. It was thought in the West that Germany could not last more than three years before her economy collapsed and her basic raw materials ran out.

During these months of waiting—"the Phony War"—the French and English decided to aid the Finns, who fought on alone against the Soviet Union, and on the way to destroy the port of Narvik, through which German ships brought iron ore from Sweden, and the Swedish mines themselves, and to mine the access routes in Norwegian waters. Before the Allies could agree on the details of the campaign, however, Finland capitulated and signed a cease-fire with the Russians. Nor had Hitler been sitting idly by. In April 1940, before the British could mine Norway's territorial waters, he invaded Denmark, meeting no opposition, and took possession of all ports between Oslo and Narvik. The British tried to help Norway and were shamefully defeated because of lack of planning, no aerial backup, and too few ground forces. The failure of the subsequent British campaign in Norway, badly planned from the start, brought about the final collapse of Chamberlain's government and led to the appointment of Winston Churchill as prime minister, despite his part in planning the campaign.

On May 10, the day after Churchill came to power, the Germans invaded Holland and Belgium with no advance warning and no pretext of an oppressed minority. With the war virtually at their gates, the British, and especially the French, could no longer ignore military events, as they had done in the case of Czechoslovakia and Poland, and they finally counterattacked. Holland fell within a week, however, and within two weeks the Germans had bypassed the much vaunted Maginot Line, encircled Belgium, and penetrated deep into France. The French fighting spirit—not overly strong to begin with—broke, and the British were forced to retreat from Europe. At the end of May, more than 350,000 Allied soldiers were evacuated from the shores of Dunkirk to England in a wonderfully organized operation which, despite the defeat and loss of heavy arms, was a boost to British morale.

Under Marshal Pétain, the new French government, named for Vichy, its headquarters after the fall of Paris, signed a cease-fire with Hitler on June 22. Hitler was quite generous and left the French two thirds of their country. On the same day that Hitler entered Paris, Russia invaded and annexed the three Baltic states of Estonia, Lithuania, and Latvia, as well as Bessarabia, which had been in Rumanian hands since the Versailles Treaty. Nevertheless, when Churchill declared that England would fight on even alone until victory was attained, his countrymen were in complete agreement. In London there now sat the exiled governments of Poland, Luxembourg, Norway, Holland, and Belgium; in July 1940, Dr. Beneš was recognized as head of the Czechoslovakian government in exile, though the Munich Pact had not been officially revoked.

After the French defeat, Hitler expected the British to negotiate a peace treaty, since he had acted in the best tradition of British fair play and allowed their troops to retreat from Dunkirk. But when Churchill showed no signs of giving him a free hand in Europe, the Führer started preparing the ground for the invasion of England. The Battle of Britain began with the systematic bombing of industrial sites and at the end of August, in response to British bombing over Germany, London also became a target. The Blitz lasted almost continuously for seventy-six nights, during which 30,000 people were killed, hundreds of buildings were destroyed, and the population suffered considerable mental and physical agony in loss of sleep, separation from families, and arduous working conditions. But the British remained undeterred. They had lost nine hundred planes, but German losses were twice that, and in October Hitler was compelled to postpone his plans for the invasion until the following spring, while massing his forces for his most ambitious gamble of all, the attack on the Soviet Union (actually launched on June 22, 1941).

Britain's valiant stand, and the growing anti-German feelings among many ethnic groups in the United States, undermined the isolationists there and allowed President Roosevelt to win the approval of the two legislative houses for the Lend-Lease Bill, designed to furnish Britain with arms and materials on credit. However, despite the increasing influence of pro-war opinion in America, the defeat of Western Europe, Italy's entry into the war on Germany's side, and the formation of the Axis with Japan had a deep, sometimes almost paralyzing psychological effect on every country involved in the war in Europe, occupied or not.

The Jews in the Protectorate felt the vise tightening around them: the ports of Trieste and Genoa were closed for emigration to Palestine, and it appeared that most of those who had fled to Western Europe to escape Nazi rule—to Denmark, Holland, Belgium, and France—had done so in vain. There was no escape in Europe.

The cease-fire with France gave new impetus to the old Madagascar plan, since it seemed likely that Germany would be able to wrest the island from the French in future peace negotiations with the Western powers. Himmler mentioned the possibility again as soon as Paris fell, and Hitler brought up the subject of a Jewish state in Madagascar in his talk with Mussolini on June 18, when the Italians entered the war. The Germans were not accustomed to wasting time, and two days after the signing of the cease-fire, Heydrich wrote to the German foreign minister, Joachim von Ribbentrop, pointing out that Goering (as the head of the four-year plan) had in January 1939 charged him with implementing Jewish emigration from all parts of the Reich. Despite the difficulties involved, he had managed to get about two hundred thousand Jews out of the Reich since taking up his position. But the problem in its entirety—and now it was a matter of about 3.5 million Jews—could not be completely solved by emigration, so that a territorial solution was necessary. The German foreign minister discussed the Madagascar question with his Italian counterpart, Count Ciano, and delegated a young attorney in his office, Franz Rademacher, to work out a detailed report.

To all minds, the only office capable of executing such a mammoth scheme, transferring and supervising millions of people, was the Reich Security Head Office, where the revival of the Madagascar plan was hailed with enthusiasm. A detailed report was required here too, and Eichmann and his assistant, Theodor Danecker, were to prepare it. Eichmann's plan was based on his experience since 1938 and on the material amassed on Madagascar by the French colonial office. The job was completed within a few weeks. Again, the twenty-page report stated that even in the territory of the Reich alone, the solution of the Jewish problem through emigration would be exceedingly slow and difficult, and now, with masses of Eastern European Jews swelling their numbers, emigration was impossible and a territorial solution therefore mandatory. To avoid mixing Jews and other peoples, an island was the best possible solution.

The statistical data on Madagascar's climate, economy, and size included the information that the island was as large as France, Belgium, and Holland put together, with a local population numbering only 3.8 million people. The total number of Jews being considered was now 4 million, including the Jews of France, Denmark, Norway, Holland, and Belgium. From a political and legal point of view, the most desirable framework would be a Jewish colony under German sovereignty, which would in fact be a police state run with a Council of Jewish Elders. The emigration and supervision of the Jews would be controlled by the Reich Security Head Office, with help from the emigration centers in various European capitals and local Jewish communities. The chief function of the Jewish administration would be to see that instructions were implemented without delay. "This method has proved very effective in the work of the Center for Jewish Emigration and it places most of the work on the Jews themselves."

In the first stage, farmers, construction workers, and skilled laborers under forty-five would leave with the necessary tools. The emigrants would be permitted to take a cargo weighing 200 kilograms, and all other Jewish possessions would be transferred to a special custodian; they would be sold and the proceeds handed over to the central emigration fund. According to Eichmann's calculations, the operation would require 120 ships and would take four years to complete. Since, after the signing of the peace treaty, German ships would no doubt be occupied elsewhere, England and France, according to the terms of the treaty, would be made to supply the requisite number of ships. The entire scheme would be financed by Jewish wealth from the Reich zones (attention should be given to the question of whether it would be preferable to expropriate this wealth outright, or to acquire it through voluntary legal transactions with the help of the Jewish communities in Prague and Vienna, the Jewish Federation in the Reich, and the Councils of Elders in the Eastern sector). The peace treaty should also ensure the participation of Jewish capital in Western countries as compensation for the harm caused by Jews, economically and otherwise, as a result of the Versailles Treaty.

The question of a territorial solution (though Madagascar was not mentioned) was also raised at a meeting between the Reich Security Head Office and the Jewish representatives who were summoned to Berlin at the beginning of July 1940 to report on emigration, organization, and finance. Present at the meeting were: Eichmann; his assistant, Danecker; Edelstein and Weidmann from Prague; Löwenherz from Vienna; and Epstein from Berlin. Eichmann heard them out, and then said that emigration efforts must for the moment continue through the Far East and Lisbon, but after the war it appeared that an overall solution would be necessary for those Jews in Europe whose departure could not be solved by individual emigration.

Eichmann wanted to know if the subject had been brought up at all, and if any plans had been made in this direction. When he received a negative reply, he instructed the five men to prepare a brief report touching on the salient features that such a program would need to consider. One of the five (since the protocol was written in the third person, it is difficult to know who) said that the program could be worked out only in relation to a specific territory, since it had to take into account the financial and political considerations that would affect immigration and settlement. Eichmann replied that at the moment they were talking of general guidelines for a scheme that could be efficiently executed in three or four years. Somebody else pointed out the centrality of Palestine: the fact that it already had half a million Jews and was the most important absorption center for the Jewish multitudes would readily elicit the cooperation of the Jewish welfare organizations in establishing a sizable Jewish community there. Eichmann made it clear that the region and form of settlement had not yet been determined, and the report, which was to confine itself to basic ideas only, was to be submitted the following afternoon.

When difficulties were raised about completing the report on such short notice, Danecker explained that all that was wanted was a preliminary outline, and for the sake of illustration, a specific country could certainly be used. Danecker's opinion was that Palestine lacked the appropriate absorption capacity, and that the Arabs were likely to pose obstacles. To this the Jewish representatives replied that in its present form, Palestine could absorb three million Jews, and if Trans-Jordan were added to it, the problem of European Jewry could be solved entirely.

Though Madagascar itself was not mentioned in the protocol of the July 3 meeting, the Jewish representatives knew that that was what the Germans had in mind. In the summer of 1940, when Rafi Friedl, a member of Hashomer Hatzair's leadership and the youth-movement representative on Prague's Zionist executive committee, came to bid Edelstein farewell before setting out for Slovakia, the latter told him that the Germans planned to transfer all the Jews to Madagascar, a scheme that he, Edelstein, saw as the lesser of two evils. Yekef said that he had been asked to prepare a detailed report on the subject and he had crammed it full of Borochov's ideas on the importance of productivity and physical labor. Edelstein sounded quite reasonable, and only after he reached Slovakia did it occur to Friedl how naïve Yekef was to believe that Madagascar could actually serve as shelter until better times. The Slovakian Jews struck him as much more sober, and more anchored in reality, and when Friedl reported to Bratislava's Zionist leaders on this obscure plan for mass Jewish settlement on the island of Madagascar, they dismissed it with a smile.

In July 1940, Netzach, the scouting and pioneering youth movement in the Protectorate, held a general convention attended by delegates from the training divisions, guests from the other youth movements, representatives of the Zionist institutions, and the entire Prague contingent. Since the convention was being held without German consent (perhaps relying on the fact that thus far work had been allowed to continue more or less undisturbed), the participants were asked to assemble at the Maccabi auditorium, in the community center on Dlouhá Street, without arousing any attention; but it is difficult to see how hundreds of youngsters clad in white shirts were meant to go unnoticed in the heart of Prague. After the joy of reunion with old friends, and the customary singing of "Hatikvah" and the "Internationale," Camillo Klein, a tall and handsome youth with heavy black eyebrows, one of the promising young men, summarized the movement's work in the course of this first year of war.

There was reason for pride: groups had been established in various parts of Prague; a new level of *Solelim* ("pavers"), the youngest members of the youth movement, had been started; the scouts had held study competitions; and the oldest level was on the whole busy with educational work in the movement at the JU-AL school or the Youth-Aliyah training camp, or were themselves undergoing training in agriculture, road construction, and forestry, while waiting to emigrate to Palestine. To ease the wait, pioneer hostels, one for men and one for women, had been set up in Prague, and even a small hospital. The future functions of the movement were being discussed when a disturbance was suddenly heard in the auditorium. The speech broke off and SS men appeared on the balcony in the ensuing silence. All those present were registered and orders were given to remove the blue, white, and red flags and to disperse. Those responsible for the convention, including Dr. Kahn, were led away to Gestapo headquarters, but in the end they were released. It had been merely a small reminder that nothing was to be done without German consent.

After Czech and German schools closed their doors to Jews, starting with the 1940 to 41 school year, all Jewish teachers and educators from all over the Protectorate were called together at the Prague community's education department, headed by Josef Pollak, a Hebrew-speaking attorney and author. It was decided that every teacher, regardless of rank or title, would take one or two classes, and education would continue underground. Studies were to proceed in an orderly fashion, either at the teacher's house or at the home of one of the pupils, and parents would contribute toward them to the best of their ability. Bedriška Hostovská (named Bracha by Yekef to save him breaking his teeth over her pure Czech name), one of the clerks at the education department, was sent to the Education Ministry for a curriculum and the necessary textbooks. Fortunately, the doorman was Czech; he directed her to Czech clerks, who helped her wholeheartedly. There was not a Jewish child who remained outside some form of educational framework.

The Hagibor sports field in the suburb of Strasnice, which had for some time been used for training exercises by the Hitler Youth, was returned to the Jews after the intervention of the Prague Jewish community, and that summer it buzzed with children and teenagers. Led by Fredy Hirsch, they participated in numerous games and sports, including soccer competitions, gymnastics, camping, and study groups. The 21st of Tammuz was as usual marked with a program on Bialik and Herzl, and teenagers camped out in tents despite the ban on leaving their homes after eight in the evening. Public parks had long been barred to Jews, and the only grassy stretches at their disposal were in the two old cemeteries in the Jewish quarter and Zizkov, which in normal times were hardly ever frequented. Now children played hide-and-seek among tombstones, mothers wheeled baby carriages along the walks, old people sat on graves and reminisced, and young couples sought out secluded corners to be alone. The Jewish graveyards were revived.

When George F. Kennan, who had worked at the American embassy in Czechoslovakia until the autumn of 1939, returned a year later on a visit, he found Prague still beautiful, as always, but the shop windows had become bare, while the streets were full of German signs and the kiosks of German newspapers. Half a million Germans had been added to the Protectorate, and of these more than a hundred thousand to Prague, and they ruled all large concerns. The capital that the Germans had taken out of the Protectorate since its inception was estimated to be somewhere between half a billion and a billion dollars, apart from the annual taxes, paid by Czechs directly to the German treasury, which totaled a hundred million dollars. The crown fell in value, and there was a serious shortage of commodities: a kilo of butter, which had sold for eighteen crowns before the advent of the Germans, was now rationed out in small portions and cost forty crowns; on the black market it fetched a hundred crowns. Very few Jews, however, could afford black-market prices, and most resorted to them only for the most basic necessities. Jews were permitted a maximum income of 3,000 crowns per couple, and new regulations increasingly stifled all possibility of earning a living. In October, Karl Hermann Frank, secretary of state, signed an order barring Jews from yet more occupations—insurance agencies, travel agencies, transportation firms, pawn shops, real-estate agencies, owning restaurants—which effectively put a stop to all Jewish businesses. In November 1940, they were instructed to hand over the savings account passbooks that every Jewish family had kept against a rainy day.

Nobody could remember all the prohibitions: Jews were forbidden to keep pigeons, fly the Reich flag (their fondest dream, no doubt), go to hairdressers, stay in hotels, use taxis. Shopping hours were gradually restricted until Jews were left with only one hour in the late afternoon—when all the goods in short supply had long since disappeared from the grocery stores and vegetable stalls. Jews were not allowed to move to a new address without permission from the Gestapo, and in Prague they began to crowd together: the Germans began by running them out of the neighborhoods of large detached houses and posh modern apartment buildings. People with two- and three-room flats (which had been the norm) tried to earn some money by renting out a room or two. More and more people could no longer afford the rent for a whole flat, or were evicted, and as of October 1940 the Zentralstelle had to sanction the renewal of all rental leases with Jews. Every edition of the Jewish newspaper carried a long list of flats for rent and flats wanted, still formulated in the old familiar style:

> Central location, elegant studio—sun, bath, hot water, for cultured tenant. Write to: "Cultivated Household."

There were shopkeepers who put food aside for their Jewish customers or stealthily dropped it into their shopping baskets when they came to make their purchases at the late hour permitted them. On the other hand, there were those who wiped out years of friendly relations as though they had never been, and this was true of Czechs in general: every case was individual; each person acted according to the dictates of his nature. Once the racial laws became effective, Czech maids vanished from Jewish homes and Jewish wives learned to manage without them, though they might never have believed it possible. In normal times, many Jewish homes kept a live-in maid who slept in the kitchen or some small dark alcove nearby, worked from morning to night without counting hours, and was free Tuesday evenings and Sunday afternoons. Some maids remained loyal to their employers, brought them food from the country, ran errands for them, and commiserated with them. Jewish women learned to run their homes alone, fetch coal from the cellar, light stoves in the morning, scrub laundry on washboards. Those who knew how to sew could support the family, for the times necessitated mending and making do with old garments, while unemployed husbands, who as a rule had never even rinsed a cup, now looked after the home. Families drew closer; the main concern was to spare the children suffering, to enable them to continue their education, and to hope that the situation would not get any worse.

Little by little, Jews descended lower on the social scale and looked back in yearning. Hannah Steiner complained that Jewish women were not prepared to do menial work in Jewish institutions, old-age homes, and hospitals. Out of twenty-five women referred by the Prague community employment department in early July, only nine returned the following day, and only two persevered.

The Nisko "occupational retraining" scheme was followed by the "Linden retraining camp." In this case, too, the Jews and Germans had similar ideas, but the Jews thought one thing and the Germans practiced another. As Jews were thrown out of private jobs and training sites decreased, interest grew at Hehalutz in establishing a teaching farm, such as had existed in Germany throughout the years of the Nazi regime. The Center for Jewish Emigration expropriated a large Jewish agricultural farm in Lipa (called Linden by the Germans), in southern Bohemia, and asked the communities to supply three hundred laborers on a regular basis, to be supervised by two SS men. Hehalutz itself was to provide a quota of people for Linden, at first for three-month stints, later for six. There was little enthusiasm for the scheme, despite the relatively reasonable conditions—the young men were permitted to write home and receive a large parcel once a month. Their evenings were free for reading, sports, or chess, in which Schmeiler, one of the SS, a simple man from Iglau whom the Jews called Franta, also took part. The Linden program gave rise to ideological debate in the youth movements: should the best instructors be sent to Lipa to set an example to the Czech Jews there? Should they give the job their utmost, remain true to the purifying values of physical labor, and model the new Jew for others to follow? Or should it be regarded as a chore forced on them by the Germans, to be borne as best as possible? The situation decided in favor of the realists.

People who had had American affidavits since the fall of 1938, the days of the Munich Pact, finally received entry visas to the United States, but it was no longer possible to leave through Italian ports, and even those with boat tickets in hand had to look for different modes of travel. The only available route was a train journey east via Warsaw, Moscow, Siberia, Vladivostok, Manchuria, and Shanghai, to the ports of Kobe or Yokohama, and from there to San Francisco or South America. Since the Russian consul in Prague promised Hannah Steiner transit visas, the main problem was a visa for Manchukuo, as Manchuria was known under Japanese occupation. Japan, however, had no legation in Prague, and the Japanese demanded a personal appearance at the consulate in Hamburg before they issued visas. The train journey to the East took sixteen days, but it had one advantage: since Russia and Germany were allies, it could be paid for in marks.

Nobody despaired. Hannah Steiner continued to look for countries that would accept Jews, even if only a handful; the Jewish welfare institutions, especially the HICEM office in Shanghai, acted as a liaison between the multiple threads in the complex web all somehow involved in getting out a single family, a single person; Hehalutz in Hungary negotiated for a greater number of Hungarian passports to be obtained through bribes. The pioneers continued their training and Hebrew studies, consolidated settlement groups, and discussed various ideological forms of settlement in Palestine. Come what might, the future was not to be accepted and suffered as the fate of an individual, but faced actively, with a sense of Jewish awareness and common responsibility.

Envious of Hitler's victories and thirsting for some military glory of his own, in October Mussolini embarked on a war against Greece. Emigration routes to Palestine were blocked and impeded through the Balkans. Dr. Ullman tried to ascertain whether the Vichy government would grant transit visas so that immigrants could sail from Lisbon. Rumor spread in Prague that the Rumanian shipping line had resumed its route from Constantia to Haifa, but Ullman's response, after he had put out feelers in Bratislava, Budapest, and Zagreb, was negative: at the moment it was impossible to sail from the Balkan states. The only open route was overland, through Hungary (where bribery was still all-powerful), Turkey, and Syria; but the Turkish government refused transit to certificate holders, since several hundred European Jews had been barred from entering Palestine and had, as a result, remained in Turkish ports. There was still a possibility for twenty young women to emigrate to the women's agricultural training farms in Palestine, and the candidates were carefully chosen from among hundreds of girls in training. The selection committee included Miriam Edelstein, Olga Kahn, and Truda Janowitz; the girls packed their trunks, completed all formalities, and waited at the pioneer hostel. Meanwhile the more advanced among them studied Hebrew with Prof. Voskin-Nahartabi in lessons regularly attended by Dr. Kahn.

November in Central Europe was always dreary, even in peace-time. It was a cold, gray, and rainy transition period, mitigated by the pleasant anticipation of the coming snows, the winter sports, the infectious warmth of the holiday season. Jews, however, could no longer share in this expectancy. They had little to look forward to. Into this autumn gloom came news of the sinking of the *Patria* in Haifa Bay, and the deaths of sons, brothers, and friends who had been aboard. It was not Mossad, but commercial adviser Storfer who finally succeeded in extricating the Bratislava group, stranded for nine months, as well as several hundred refugees from the Protectorate. In keeping with their ambitious policy of separating nations, the Germans were at the time busy transferring Germans from Bessarabia (now annexed to the Soviet Union) "home to the Reich." Storfer took advantage of the ships that set out on the Danube carrying Germans back to the homeland, and put fleeing Jews on them in the opposite direction, after making sure that Jewish money paid for the German passage as well.

Adviser Storfer's refugees were transferred at Black Sea ports onto old and rickety ships filled to overflowing with their human cargo. In mid-November, two of these ships—the *Milos* and the *Pacific*—approached the shores of Palestine. And on November 19—despite the many appeals for compassion—the British announced that while they were sympathetic to the plight of the refugees, they could not allow such a flagrant breach of the law; the government of Palestine viewed illegal immigration as detrimental to British interests in the Mediterranean. It was decided to transfer the passengers on both ships to one of the British colonies, where they would be detained until the end of the war and then barred from entering Palestine. Weizmann's intercession was to no avail. He asked for special consideration for the very young and the elderly, most of whom had relatives in Palestine, and for the immigrants whose certificates had become invalid as a result of the war. But the British were adamant. The passengers of the *Milos* and *Pacific* were transferred to the *Patria,* formerly a French ship which the British had confiscated.

Meanwhile, the *Atlantic,* or rather its remains (for lack of coal the long journey had been fueled by the ship's wooden parts), also reached Haifa port. Its passengers included the Maccabi and Hehalutz group from Bohemia and Moravia which had been stranded in Slovakia. The British were in the process of forcing them aboard the *Patria* when suddenly a deafening explosion was heard and the ship went under. To prevent the *Patria* from sailing, the Hagganah had meant to blow up its engine room, but the explosives they used were excessive: two hundred and sixty refugees from Hitler's regime lost their lives on the very threshold of their new home, and hundreds of others were wounded. A cry was raised throughout the world, and the British agreed to leave the survivors of the *Milos* and *Pacific* at the Athlit detention camp. But the passengers of the *Atlantic* were dragged by force onto two Dutch ships and taken to Mauritius in the Indian Ocean—not so far from Madagascar, which the Germans had reserved for Jews.

The first news of the *Patria* that reached Prague was vague and did not give the number killed, and for Edelstein it only confirmed the necessity for highly organized disembarkation arrangements on the shores of Palestine in order for immigration to continue. However, when the dimensions of the disaster became known, hundreds of people converged on the Palestine office to try to get some news of their families. Leo Janowitz waited impatiently for the lists of people who had died, fled, or been arrested (they did not arrive until the beginning of 1941). Anxious relatives asked: "What about Georg Morgenstern?" "What happened to Franz Fantl?" "Miriam Lederer's name does not appear anywhere." There were no answers for them, and Janowitz tried to obtain the information from Palestine.

In December 1940, Edelstein traveled to Bratislava to confer with the Jewish institutions on the departure of the last certificate holders (about 160 people, mostly children and young people). The official weekly record of the community reported that "following negotiations, he had managed to finalize the promise of transit visas for Bulgaria, to be granted as soon as news was received that the immigrant ship was ready." Now negotiations for a ship started and looked promising, and efforts were initiated to obtain additional certificates, especially for young people. The question of the next transport of laborers from Hehalutz and Maccabi was taken up with commercial adviser Storfer. As usual, the community reports tended toward optimism with respect to both Jews and Germans. When Yekef returned from Bratislava, he found news from Ullman saying that the group of those exiled to Mauritius had also included members of the Bratislava group. "It's a pity that nobody listened to me," Ullman wrote, "and that the emigrants weren't left in Slovakia for another year." However, the first reports from Mauritius were reassuring: there was ample food, the Jewish community in Rhodesia was very helpful, and people were able to work in their professions. Not too terrible compared to the situation in Eastern Europe.

It gradually became clear that the decision of Prague's Zionist leaders to remain together until they could leave together had not been overly wise, and was no longer realistic. In the spring, certificates still waited in Trieste for Edelstein and Hannah Steiner, but now the Germans would no longer allow them to leave. The certificates meanwhile expired, and Barlas promised to procure a six-month transit visa to Italy for the entire group—Kahn, Zucker, Steiner, Friedmann, Edelstein—on the basis of a Shanghai visa, if Leo Hermann could arrange for financing, and all this until new certificates could be issued. But then Italy entered the war and this possibility also fell through. Leo Hermann appealed to Weizmann, Weizmann turned to Shertok, and Shertok was angry that matters had gone over his head to the chief; still, there were no certificates and no way to get them even through a neutral country. The only solution, after dozens of phone calls between Prague, Geneva, Bratislava, and Budapest, was to transfer certificates to Slovakia or Hungary, and this the British refused to do. In October 1940, when the Prague leaders could finally inform Ullman that Kahn and his wife, Hannah Steiner and her husband, and Otto Zucker had received exit permits from the Germans on condition that they use them immediately, there was again nowhere for them to go and no visas to go with.

Dr. Ullman faithfully pursued efforts to get these five out, and the correspondence on the subject—between Prague, London, Jerusalem, Zagreb, and Istanbul—was a tragedy of errors. In December, März could finally report from Jerusalem that certificates for Kahn and Zucker were on their way. But they could not reach Istanbul to collect them. The women's organizations handled Hannah Steiner's departure, and once again Yekef had no hope of being allowed to leave by the Gestapo.

Zucker, a sworn bachelor all his life, finally married at the age of forty-eight a lovely girl, Fritzi Ziegler, and he laconically informed Hermann, "I've relinquished my bachelorhood. There's very little difference." There was a sense of some reservations in Zucker's private letters about Yekef, whether because of thwarted ambition ("Yekef's exhibitionism has in fact made my work in Prague superfluous"), or because of their different work habits ("you know how hard it is to get Yekef to work in an orderly and organized fashion"). Zucker loved music and art, and had exquisite taste. Yekef had neither the time for, nor an appreciation of, aesthetics. In the summer of 1940, Zucker still had high hopes of being able to play his violin at Hermann's flat in Jerusalem. But in the winter he had to notify Geneva that much to his regret he had to assume the management of the Brünn community, since Elbert, the community secretary, had been called to Prague. "I only hope this will not harm my chance of immigration."

Nineteen forty was drawing to a close, and despite all the obstacles, six thousand Jews had still managed to leave the Protectorate. Even after there was no longer anywhere to emigrate to, and no way of getting there, the Jews were still ordered, every time Eichmann was supposed to visit, to submit emigration applications to the Zentralstelle, giving Shanghai as their destination. It was clear that the whole thing was concocted, since Günther feared reproof from Berlin, but everyone—the applicants, the community staff, the SS—played the game.

The general opinion among the Czechs was that the war could not last much longer, and the Czech exiles in London already held bitter debates on the form of government to be instituted after the war. When Dr. Beneš was asked to grant the Jews as a whole representation on Czechoslovakia's National Committee, he refused, saying that after the war there would no longer be a Jewish minority in Czechoslovakia. The Jews would have to decide whether they were Czechs or nationalist Zionists, and their citizenship would be determined accordingly. He no longer wanted any national minorities in his country. As for the Czech committee, Beneš pointed out to the historian Lewis Namier, who represented the Zionist Federation, that membership would be on a personal, not group, basis. The trouble with the Jews, he said, was that they were divided among religious, nationalists, and assimilated, and the latter vigorously objected to Zionist representation on the committee. Beneš considered some of the Zionists to be too lukewarm, Zionists in word only. A people could not gain or regain its independence unless it concentrated all its energies on it.

When Namier mentioned former Czech tolerance, Beneš replied with a sigh that during the First World War, the situation had been different: then there had been only three men who led the nation, Masaryk, Stepanek (the Slovakian representative), and himself, and the last two had shouldered the daily work. Now he was dealing with ten generals, twenty ministers, and a large number of former members of parliament. When talk turned to anti-Semitism, and Namier raised the question of anti-Jewish hostility in Czech army units, Beneš replied that one of the reasons for it was the fact that the Jews still spoke German among themselves, even as soldiers in the Czech army. Namier reported on the negotiations toward setting up Jewish units within the framework of the British army, and asked Beneš if the Jews conscripted into Czech units would be allowed to join them. Beneš replied that he would have to consult his generals.

In a conversation between Weizmann and John Martin, Churchill's private secretary, on the matter of the Jewish fighting force, Martin said that, speaking as a friend, he advised the Jews to set the wheels in motion now for a Jewish state. The time was ripe. The war was in a difficult stage, although, apart from bombings and shipping losses the economic situation was stable. The first half of 1941 would still be difficult, but a turning point could be expected around the summer, and the Jews should be ready to formulate their peace objectives. Weizmann voiced the fear that even with an Allied victory, the situation of the Jews would still be tragic. An overwhelming victory, after all, could not be achieved without stamping out Fascism completely, and it was not difficult to imagine what would be found in Europe once the curtains rose after such a deadly war. Reporting this talk to the Zionist Executive in December 1940, Weizmann spoke of three million Jews in occupied Europe who would have to be transferred to Palestine after the war, for the days of Jewish exile in Europe were over.

17

ON TWO SEPARATE PLANETS

IN MARCH 1941, Eichmann sent Jakob Edelstein, and Richard Israel Friedmann of the Prague community's legal department, to Amsterdam. A center for Jewish emigration was being opened, and they were to advise Amsterdam's Jewish council how to manage affairs. To some extent, Holland's Jews were similar to the Jews in Bohemia and Moravia: they too were law abiding, mostly middle class, and inclined to optimism. Unlike the Jews of Prague, however, their optimism had a foothold in reality: following clashes between Holland's Nazis and the residents of Amsterdam's old Jewish quarter, a hunt took place through the city streets and four hundred young Jews were arrested and sent to the Mauthausen concentration camp. On February 17 the workers of Amsterdam walked out spontaneously on a general strike to protest this, and they were joined by workers from several surrounding towns. The strike was brutally suppressed by the Germans within three days, but it left the local Jews believing that the Dutch, despite the considerable number who collaborated with the Germans (a partnership which to no small degree was based on the brotherhood of the northern peoples), would not give the Germans a free hand with the Jews: Holland was not Eastern Europe.

Edelstein and Friedmann were not restricted in their movements in Amsterdam, and no Germans were present at their meetings with the local Jewish leaders. Friedmann even sent back long letters to Prague, giving his impressions of his visits to art museums. It is unlikely that Edelstein accompanied him on these jaunts, though the two men had been good friends since their common experience in Nisko. Edelstein had many meetings with the two leaders of the Jewish council in Holland, the diamond dealer Avraham Ascher and David Cohen, one of the local Zionists. Their present function was a direct extension of their activities on the committee for special Jewish affairs, which since 1933 had handled thousands of Jewish refugees from Germany who had either passed through Holland or taken shelter there. Edelstein tried to impress on Ascher and Cohen just how serious matters were and what they could expect in the event of Eastern transports, but they did not heed his warnings, a fact that caused Edelstein to complain to the Zionists when he met them at the home of Marius Kahn, chairman of the Zionist Federation in Holland.

Kahn's house was so crowded that some of those at the meeting had to sit on the floor. Edelstein spoke gravely and made a strong impression: the Germans meant to destroy the Jews and the only solution was not to succumb—which was going to be extremely difficult. He told them that in the Protectorate Jews had been conscripted to lay railway lines and do other forced labor, and similar developments could be expected in Holland: all the regulations that had been instituted in the Protectorate would come into effect here too.

In Holland, too, the first instinct of the Jews was to unite and present the Germans with a solid front. As in Czechoslovakia, the question of contact with the Germans was a controversial issue: should they cooperate with the Germans in order to help all Jews, or should they spurn any contact, as demanded by Ernst Wieser, formerly the president of the supreme court at the Hague, who regarded all dealing with the Germans as de facto recognition of their anti-Semitic policies? In Holland, as in Czechoslovakia, Hehalutz and the Zionist youth movements worked to awaken the younger generation's Jewish pride and prepare them for a new life in Palestine.

Yekef visited the Youth-Aliyah institution in Losdracht, which housed youths from Germany brought to Holland after Kristallnacht. They were waiting to emigrate to Palestine but were stranded without certificates. In a meeting with the Hehalutz people who ran the institution, Edelstein was unequivocally pessimistic as to the fate of European Jewry should the war not end soon—and it was beginning to seem that there was almost no hope that it would.

The Jews of Holland thought otherwise: in that spring of 1941 rumors had multiplied of an Allied invasion in Western Europe, and the faith of the Dutch Jews was infectious. Friedmann returned to Prague optimistic, in sharp contrast to all his previous views; perhaps the turning point was drawing closer after all. Only toward the end of his stay in Holland did Edelstein send his first postcard to Switzerland (stamped by the Wehrmacht before it reached its destination): "You can imagine that my business here is work, not pleasure. I would like to help our friends bear the onus of their work as best I can." Yekef asked Nathan Schwalb, the Hehalutz representative in Geneva, to do something for Youth-Aliyah in Holland, if at all possible.

In mid-May Edelstein returned to Prague, also somewhat encouraged. He told his friends that he had tried to advise the Jewish leaders in Holland about how to resist SS demands in specific instances, but they had thought he was trying to trip them up, even suspecting that he was a tool in German hands. He felt that young Jews were better off in Holland than in the Protectorate, because there was more chance of going underground in Holland and the local population was more willing to help. He said that he had advised the Hehalutz youngsters to organize escape with the help of the Dutch and not to shrink from using arms.

The sixty certificate holders, mostly children and youths, who were finally supposed to set out for Palestine (via Budapest) during Edelstein's absence from Prague, were prevented from doing so. The Germans suddenly withheld exit permits "on principle," as Leo Janowitz informed Ullman in Geneva, "and who knows if it will still be possible to get around this ban." Ullman hoped that Yekef would be able to persuade the Germans when he returned from Amsterdam, but on May 10 Prague's Palestine office was closed down altogether by order of the Gestapo, dashing all remaining hopes of emigration to Palestine. Janowitz, who had directed the office ever since Yekef assumed the management of community affairs, was appointed Weidmann's deputy, replacing Zucker, the head of the community's combined fund-raising, which still continued. And Erich Munk, the Youth-Aliyah doctor, now began organizing medical examinations for the employment department, which meant that obligatory conscription was to take on large-scale proportions. "A few Jews more, a few Jews less, it's all the same," the Germans told Edelstein when he tried to press for continued emigration. "You are all staying here."

Until that point emigration plans were still being made; Kahn and Zucker, for example, finally received two certificates and needed only a transit visa from Yugoslavia. Emigration candidates still waited, their suitcases packed, when in April, the Balkan war erupted and blocked the last route to Palestine.

Before Hitler could proceed with the Barbarossa campaign as planned, he had to make sure of his right flank in the Balkans, where his colleague Mussolini had entangled himself in a war beyond his military capabilities. The German army was in Rumania, one of the allied countries in the Axis, and to reach Greece, agreement was required from Bulgaria and Yugoslavia. After a suitable softening-up process, Bulgaria capitulated, and, following lengthy talks, Prince Paul, the Yugoslavian regent, was also amenable to German troops passing through his country. However, before Paul and his ministers managed to return from the summit meeting in Vienna, a popular revolt took place in Yugoslavia, the regent was deposed, and young Peter, the crown prince, installed on the throne. Hitler viewed the Yugoslavian rebellion as a threat to the entire Barbarossa scheme, and, in great anger, he resolved to make an example of Yugoslavia by punishing her mercilessly. On April 6, German bombers swooped over Belgrade and almost wiped the Serbian capital off the face of the earth. The army advanced with lightning speed, and within a week the last holdouts of the Yugoslavian army were quelled. In a situation somewhat similar to that of Czechoslovakia, the Catholic Croats, like the Slovaks, were rewarded for their loyalty to Fascism by getting their own country.

The Czechoslovakian refugees who had found temporary asylum in Yugoslavia did not manage to elude Hitler. After some time the Germans killed most of the residents of the Kladova camp where refugees from Central Europe were waiting, stranded for lack of ships to Palestine. Two weeks after Yugoslavia's surrender, German tanks were stationed in Athens and the swastika flew over the Acropolis. The British forces that had come to the aid of the Greeks retreated by sea in defeat. The road to Russia was open.

*   *   *

On his return from Holland, the Hehalutz leaders asked Edelstein what he thought lay in store. They were isolated from the outside world, but he had traveled and met people—what did the future hold? Edelstein replied that they must play for time and not antagonize the Germans. "It won't last forever," he said, a phrase he used to repeat at the blackest moments.

Train journeys were forbidden, public parks had long been banned for Jews, but in the suburbs of Prague there were still small woods with patches of green where it was possible to walk and hold youth-movement meetings. As the first of May, generally celebrated in the best socialist tradition, drew near, members of the Netzach pioneering and scouting youth decided not to let the day pass unmarked even now. Festivities were held in a rock cave over the Vltava; the youngsters crawled in along winding approach routes and behind soundproof stone walls sang the "Internationale," "Avanti Popolo," and the other customary songs from the international socialist repertoire.

The Zionist leaders met privately from time to time, usually at Hannah Steiner's flat, to exchange views, coordinate positions, or make small talk. On the eve of the Sabbath, guests—those who were permitted to leave their homes after curfew, unlike the rest of the Jews—were still invited to the Edelsteins' for the traditional Sabbath meal. On these occasions, ten-year-old Arieh sat next to Yekef, his father's hand resting proudly on his shoulder, and in the presence of Miriam and Mrs. Olliner the company reminisced, told jokes, listened to Yekef's stories, and discussed neither politics nor the situation.

Edelstein, like all the Zionist leaders, attached primary importance to the conscription of manpower: the more the Jews were absorbed in the war economy, in industry and vital public works such as the construction of airports, paving roads, laying railway lines, the more hope there was of allaying the threat of transports. Jewish deportation from the Reich had not ceased with the cancellation of the Nisko colony: mass expulsions had been carried out in Posen (Poznán) and other Polish areas directly attached to the Reich. The Jews of Stettin had been cruelly exiled in the depths of winter. In the fall of 1940, after a period of relative calm due to the prospect of a peace treaty with the Western powers, the Jews of Baden and the Saar region had been banished to Vichy France without being allowed to prepare for the journey. In February 1941, transports resumed from Vienna, and five thousand Austrian Jews were sent to the Lodz ghetto. Optimistic as ever, the commentators concluded that if the Jews in the Protectorate, where there was a higher percentage of young Jews than in Austria, were still at home and in their homeland, it obviously meant that the Germans needed them as a labor force.

The Jews in Poland now lived in closed ghettos, dying off by the thousands from hunger and disease. But Protectorate Jews had only a vague knowledge of this, from rumors of heartrending letters written by Viennese Jews. Apparently the only one who had ever actually seen a closed ghetto was Jakob Edelstein, who in the summer of 1941 visited the Lodz ghetto, where 160,000 Jews were struggling to survive. Lodz, or Litzmannstadt as the Germans named it after the German general who had conquered it in World War I, had prior to the occupation been the second largest Jewish community in Europe, and its quarter of a million Jews had controlled the textile trade.

In the spring of 1941, the Germans concentrated the Jews in Lodz's old city and in poverty-stricken districts devoid of sanitary facilities. Mordechai Chaim Rumkovsky, whom the Germans had appointed Elder of the Jews in the fall of 1939, tried to ensure the survival of the ghetto by establishing industrial concerns for the German economy. He found willing partners among Germans with an eye for an easy profit from a ghetto labor force that worked for paltry remuneration. Rumkovsky was an industrialist and devoted Zionist. Before the war he had dedicated himself to helping the community's orphans, and he ruled the ghetto autocratically. He was determined to save "his Jews" through hard work and the sweat of their brows. Though typhus, dysentery, and especially consumption took their toll, work still ensured a minimal food supply, permitted the upkeep of a communal soup kitchen, orphanages, old-age homes, and an educational network, and preserved the spark of life.

What Edelstein thought of Rumkovsky and his firm belief in order, discipline, and iron rule remains unknown. But the lesson he learned at the Lodz ghetto was reflected in his efforts to make sure that the Jews of the Protectorate were occupied in vital works in their protective home ground. Between May and June 1941, all Jewish men in Bohemia and Moravia aged between eighteen and fifty were obliged to undergo medical examinations by community doctors. They were divided into five categories, and if found fit for hard physical labor, they soon received a conscription notice to report for work at the Ruzyn airport or building roads. Jewish labor was in great demand at the factories working at top speed to supply the Wehrmacht, and on the whole the Czechs treated their Jewish co-workers fairly. For their part the Jews tried to prove the gentiles wrong in their common assumption that Jews did not know the meaning of physical work. When, in the winter months, they cleared the snow from Prague's city streets, the municipal inspector expressed his complete satisfaction with the job they had done, as noted proudly in the community report.

In keeping with chronological order, the time has come to speak of the final solution, the annihilation of the Jews as it was planned and executed, though a gigantic gap exists that is more than chronological between the German schedule and the Jewish one. Many, many Jews never knew of such a plan, not even during their last moments, when they stood in the gas chambers. Even there, the Jews continued to believe that they still lived in the familiar world of yesterday—of riots, hunger, anguish, persecution, and hope of a better tomorrow. The idea that people could be gassed to death like insects never crossed their minds. And while this book speaks of Germans and Jews side by side, the two peoples lived in totally different time spheres. Jewish conduct may be viewed as a direct continuation of the pre–death camp world, while German conduct already belonged to a new era, unparalleled in the history of mankind. A gaping abyss separated the two, and those who know that Auschwitz, Treblinka, and Sobibor did in fact exist, and that death factories are conceivable, can no longer comprehend the naïveté of the Jews before the deluge. Post-Auschwitz man can only try to understand, telling himself over and over again that they never knew that mechanized murder was possible.

Once the war with the Soviet Union started in June 1941, emigration was stopped almost completely and the Madagascar program was shelved. The Germans now expected to have at their disposal vast eastern expanses in which to solve the Jewish problem far from Western eyes. On July 31, 1941, Goering instructed SD Gruppenführer Heydrich to complete the task he had been given in January 1939 and to make all the necessary organizational, practical, and material arrangements for an overall solution to the Jewish question on German-controlled territory in Europe; to involve all major institutions whose authority pertained to the plan; and to prepare a comprehensive proposal on the preliminary steps required for the desirable final solution of the Jewish question.

On a summer day in 1941, Heydrich summoned Eichmann and informed him that the Führer had ordered the extermination of the Jews. There is no doubt that from the start Hitler connected the conquest of the Soviet Union with the possibility of an overall solution to the Jewish question through extermination, though no explicit order to that effect has been found with his signature. In March 1941, amid the preparations for the Barbarossa campaign, Hitler had already instructed his military commanders on the special functions of the SS Einsatzgruppen units, functions that derived from "the need to once and for all settle the perennial contest between the two opposing political regimes." For this purpose, special SS action squads had been authorized to liquidate all undesirable elements who for political or racial reasons were liable to pose a security danger.

When war broke out with Russia, Heydrich summarized the functions of the action squads in writing: those to be executed included Comintern members, all commissars, all top- and middle-ranking functionaries in the Communist Party, all Jews in the service of the Communist Party, and all subversive elements. The commanders of the special action squads were instructed orally to remove all the Jews; "remove" meant "put to death," as Heydrich stressed when he briefed the commanders in Berlin before they left for the front: "Jews are the source of Bolshevism and by order of the Führer should be exterminated." And so, hot on the heels of the advancing German army, in Lithuania, Latvia, Estonia, Galicia, and the Ukraine, came the Einsatzgruppen, who busied themselves with the systematic liquidation of Jews. Jews were slaughtered by the thousands, shot, burned in synagogues, and beaten to death on the streets, sometimes with active help from the local population. Heydrich's instructions had been explicit: "No measures should be taken to impede local anticommunist and anti-Jewish elements from purging the conquered areas; on the contrary, these should be secretly encouraged." During the early months of the war with the Soviet Union about half a million Jews were murdered with the help of Russians, Ukrainians, Lithuanians, Latvians, Rumanians, and Hungarians.

There were local variations in the way the plan was carried out, but, to take one example, in Horodenka, Jakob Edelstein's hometown, the method was basically the same as everywhere else. Very few of Horodenka's Jews joined the retreating Russian army; since the partition of Poland in the fall of 1939 there had been precious little in the Communist regime that endeared it to the local Jews. The majority decided to stay where they were and wait and see. In the first half of July, the Hungarian army, fighting on the side of the Wehrmacht, entered Horodenka. The following day a gallows was erected in the square opposite Menahem Mendel Koch's house and a warning was issued that anyone who disobeyed emergency regulations would be killed. The Ukrainian nationalists, true to their anti-Semitic tradition, waited impatiently for a signal to riot, but the Hungarians had their own account to settle with the Ukrainians (for opposing the annexation of Carpathian Russia to Hungary), and they were not amenable. At the end of the summer the Germans replaced the Hungarian army and immediately imposed order. A regional governor was appointed from SS ranks, and the Jews were ordered to set up a council to deal with all Jewish affairs and to hand over all the gold in their possession. Men between the ages of fourteen and sixty-five were mobilized for forced labor. The more fortunate among them served under an anti-Nazi officer named Fiedler who treated them very fairly.

When rumor spread of an imminent liquidation action such as had occurred in neighboring towns, Horodenka's Jews appealed to Hans Hack, the regional governor. He lived up to his reputation for greed and promised to try to get the sentence revoked in exchange for three kilos of gold. Shortly thereafter, the Jews were ordered to report to the local synagogue for inoculations against typhus, and despite Fiedler's warning that it was a trap, about 2,500 of the town's Jews assembled there the next day (the Ukrainians ferreted out anyone who tried to hide). The Jews were herded into the synagogue by SS men and the Ukrainian militia, raring for action, and the following day driven in trucks to the edge of the Dniester, some distance from the town. From time to time the Polish drivers slowed down to allow the more resourceful among them to leap off the moving vehicles. Two deep ditches had been dug near the river a few days back, and when rumor had spread that they were to serve as graves, the Jews turned to the regional governor for information; he had reassured them that they were meant for slaking lime and nothing more.

A festive scene greeted the Jews when they arrived at the site: a band played music, SS officers sat around decked-out tables laden with food and drink—and soldiers waited nearby with machine guns and automatic weapons. The Jews were ordered to remove their outer garments, and were positioned in groups of five on a board across the ditch. A volley of shots rang out and each group fell into the ditch, leaving the board free for the next. Some of the Jews, mainly women who had not suffered mortal wounds, managed to climb out of the ditch during the night and return to life to tell their tale. The following day, the ditches were covered with earth, which continued to tremble for an entire day. The stunned survivors who remained in Horodenka were informed by the regional governor that the action had been carried out under pressure from the Ukrainians; henceforth, however, peace would be restored and there would be no more such incidents. The firing squad presented the Jews with a bill for 10,000 marks—the cost of the bullets they had used.

One after another, reports reached Berlin from the Einsatzgruppen telling of the mass extermination of Jews. The general tone suggested that the first stage had been completed, as in the report on Kovno: 7,800 Jews had been liquidated through pogroms and firing squads, and the bodies had been removed, but it was impossible to carry this form of killing much further. A quieter and more efficient method was needed.

Heinrich Müller, chief of the Gestapo and Eichmann's immediate superior, sent the latter to Minsk to see what was happening. He saw young German sharpshooters firing at Jewish women and infants and was shocked, not by the death of the Jews but by the potential effect of such killings on the German soul: how was one casually to shoot women and children? The young soldiers would either turn into sadists or go mad. In Lemberg, the old capital of Galicia, Eichmann, who reserved an affectionate place in his heart for the Austro-Hungarian monarchy, was particularly struck by the railway building that had been built on the sixtieth anniversary of Emperor Franz Josef's reign, and by the covered canal near the town from which Jewish blood spewed upward like a geyser. There was no doubt left in his mind: a more aesthetic method of mass murder had to be found.

On his travels through the East in the early fall, Eichmann came across various improvements in this field: at Treblinka, the realm of Odilo Globotznik, head of the SS and security police in the Lublin region, Jews were gassed to death in small chambers fitted with diesel engines from obsolete Russian submarines. At Litzmannstadt,

naked Jews were herded into sealed trucks and gassed while traveling. When they reached their destination, the Chelmno (Kulm)
camp, the still warm bodies were flung out, the gold teeth were
removed, and the dead were thrown into open ditches.

This was not the first time that the Germans had resorted to gas
for killing people. In an extension of the policy of exaltation of the
Aryan race (in the course of which thousands of retarded and
disabled German children had been put to death by injection), the
Führer had in the autumn of 1939 instructed the director of his
office, Philipp Bouhler, and his personal physician, Karl Brandt, to
accord doctors more authority so that they could make humanitarian "mercy killings" available to the "sick"—in this case meaning
the mentally ill and retarded. The practical execution of these
"mercy killings" or "euthanasia" fell to Wirt, the Stuttgart police
commander, who subsequently developed a small gas chamber that
used carbon monoxide. Himmler also proved enterprising in this
field, delegating the chief doctor of the SS to find an efficient
method of mass extermination; the latter also recommended the
use of gas. In the fall of 1941 the efforts of the two bodies united in
a large-scale field experiment, and the mercy-killing experts supplied the nucleus of workers for the final solution. Eichmann, as a
specialist on the Jewish question, saw no objection to gassing Jews
unfit for work, if only to avoid further unpleasant incidents such as
occurred with the method of mass shootings.

During this same period, Rudolf Höss, commandant of the concentration camp established in the spring of 1940 near the city of
Auschwitz in western Galicia, close to the German border, was
summoned by Himmler and told that the Führer had ordered the
final solution of the Jewish question: it had to be done now or the
Jews would at some future time destroy the German people. Auschwitz was chosen as the site of the main extermination camp because
of its convenient location: it was a central railroad junction and had
vast open expanses suitable for erecting a sealed-off area.
Eichmann called on Höss in Auschwitz to work out the details, and
together they selected the site of the extermination camp, a farming
region in the nearby village of Birkenau, whose citizens had all been
evacuated. Höss's deputy had on his own initiative experimented
with killing Russian prisoners with gas, and among other things, he
had used Zyklon-B, a well-known trade name for a gas originally
intended for fumigating houses. Its great advantage was that it was
readily available and did not require complicated installations. Af-

ter Eichmann's second visit to Auschwitz it was chosen as the gas for mass extermination. It was decided that transports to Auschwitz would start with those living nearest: first to come would be the inmates of the ghettos in Upper Silesia, then the Jews from the Reich and the Protectorate, and finally those from France and the other Western European countries.

All this was resolved and determined on another planet, beyond the reach of the Jews in the Protectorate. They still lived among the population at large and thought life difficult.

Toward the end of summer the Prague community opened a new department known simply as "G" and headed by Otto Zucker. Very few people were in on the secret. Its function was to prepare the groundwork for the establishment of ghettos in the Protectorate, or, as was thought at the time, labor camps near large industrial concerns such as the Škoda automobile plant and the steelworks in Kladno. Those in the know assumed that the idea had come from Edelstein, who hoped in this way to be able to keep the Jews in the Protectorate. No matter how difficult the working conditions might be, they could not possibly be worse than those in Poland. Labor camps, Edelstein claimed, meant connections with the military, fitting into the war effort, and a reasonable chance that the young and middle-aged would hold out until the end of the war, and he was fully supported by Zucker despite their differences on other matters. Kahn and Munk, who tended to be pessimistic by nature, had more reservations, but they too became convinced that there was no better solution. Edelstein had heard rumors that transports to the East could be expected if Russia fell quickly; as a result he sought support for his plan to set up Jewish centers in the Protectorate among the Germans as well. He met several times with Freiherr von Gregory, a former Wehrmacht officer who had been transferred to the SS and held a senior post in the Protektor's office. Edelstein even tried to convince Günther that neither he nor any of his colleagues at the Zentralstelle stood to reap much benefit from Jewish transports to the East: it meant that the Center for Emigration would no longer be necessary. Indeed, if the Jews remained in the Protectorate and worked for the war economy, Günther and his aides would also remain at their jobs—far from the front.

The community still ran close to a hundred occupational courses ranging from toy making to infant care, house painting, commercial photography, fountain pen repairs, dry cleaning, quilting, vegetable canning, tire renewal, pattern cutting. They continued out of inertia, perhaps, and to keep up morale, rather than for any practical purpose. Emigration, after all, had stopped almost entirely.

The Jewish newspaper continued to publish letters from Czechoslovakian emigrants throughout the world, describing how they had fitted into their new countries: a doctor of philosophy now raised poultry in New York State; Hanka Spitzer now called herself Juana and played in the Trio Classico in Quito, the capital of Ecuador; a former owner of a café in Prague raised coffee in Brazil; a former owner of a cellophane factory in the Sudetenland was involved in cheese production in Chile; a Czech family in Mexico specialized in curing Prague-style ham; a textile merchant sorted wool in Patagonia. "The beginning was hard because we didn't know the language and were not familiar with local conditions," a couple wrote from Argentina. "But the worst is behind us; now we have our own farm and calluses on our hands."

Entry visas to Brazil were now granted only by the personal consent of the Brazilian president. A six-month visa to Cuba cost two thousand dollars. An American affidavit was valid for one year only and had to be replaced by a new one if it expired. The nearest American consulate was in Vienna (that in Prague had closed in the fall of 1940), and anyone who did manage to get German permission to go there had to face a committee composed of three Americans and submit to questions he could not answer candidly on Reich territory. People with affidavits whose turn finally came after a three-year wait could receive an American visa only if they were assured of passage on a ship; the visas were good for only four months and were not extended. But the only possibility of sea travel was through the ports of Spain or Portugal, and the ships that sailed from there were fully booked months in advance.

"Never say emigration is impossible, everyone must patiently wait his turn. There are other ways to cross the seas." Hannah Steiner and her department continued their obstinate struggle from the pages of the *Jüdisches Nachrichtenblatt*: it was not the first time that technical difficulties had stood in an emigrant's way, and until now the department for the encouragement of emigration had always managed to overcome them and find a solution. Franta Friedmann journeyed to HICEM's main office in Lisbon to try to find space on the ships; Steiner continued to dispatch cables (through the Zentralstelle) and write urgent letters so that an individual, a family, a group of six might leave. Another five hundred people managed to emigrate before the gates were finally closed by Himmler in the fall of 1941, a testament to the iron will of Hannah Steiner and her department, and to the concern of relatives across the sea, who spared no effort to remove the obstacles posed by bureaucracy, the absence of good will, and the mobile war arena.

Kahn's moment of truth also arrived, as did Zucker's and that of the other certificate holders, about one hundred and sixty people who were still hoping and waiting to emigrate to Palestine, while in Slovakia and Hungary potential candidates also waited—to see if the Protectorate's certificate holders would fail in their efforts to leave, and their certificates fall instead into their own laps. Zucker rebelled. "Tell all those lying in wait for my certificate," he wrote Ullman, "that I have no intention whatsoever of relinquishing it." He complained that Edelstein was encouraging the aspirants in Prague and Bratislava who were trying to lay their hands on the immigration permit set aside for him, and Ullman agreed with him: nobody, not even Yekef, had the right to transfer Zucker and Kahn's certificates—obtained with so much effort—to other hands. However, at the start of the summer of 1941, everyone capitulated: the precious certificates were transferred to Bratislava and Budapest so that they would not be wasted. All anyone in the Protectorate could do now was hold out and prepare the young people for emigration to Palestine as pioneers once the war was over. "Why the outcry? Why the noise that it is no longer possible to leave?" Yekef said to Trude Groag. "I too am here, we're all here. We'll stay together and leave together for Palestine later."

When food rationing was first introduced, the Jews were allotted the same share as everyone else, but little by little announcements of special distributions began to appear—of onions, fish, garlic, tobacco—with the added stricture that they were not for Jews. In August Jews were forbidden to buy fresh or dried fruit, jam, cheese, fish, sweets, fowl, even wild mushrooms. Regulation followed regulation: bicycles, sewing machines, and typewriters (which had meant some means of support for a family) must be turned in; phonographs and musical instruments (the last bond with the world of music, since Jews had not had radios for two years now) were confiscated. When the order came to hand in woolen clothing and furs (with pockets emptied and no markings), the optimists interpreted this as a hopeful sign: the German army must be in dire straits.

As was customary, people did not keep fur coats at home during the summer months but stored them with furriers to protect them against moths. When furriers were instructed not to return the coats to their Jewish owners—and fur or fur-lined coats were no luxury in the Czech winter—many Jews were left without a winter coat. The community's legal department, through Richard Israel Friedmann, tried to get the Germans to make exceptions, and sometimes the Jews themselves decided the fate of their coats. Sixty-year-old Rosa Hermann refused to accept the verdict ("They're not going to take the coat I've been wearing for twenty years"), went to Gestapo headquarters, and returned triumphant: taken by surprise by an old woman demanding to see the director urgently, the Germans had allowed her to redeem the black Persian lamb she was so fond of. But her luck did not hold out when sometime later the Germans ordered pets turned in, and Rosa and Josef Hermann had to part with Bobby, their miniature pinscher. This was often one of the hardest regulations to endure: a pet was not just property, but a well-loved friend, a source of comfort.

Over and over again the Jews were asked to obey all instructions to the letter: every misdemeanor, even if unwitting, was liable to cost the individual dear and make things more difficult for the Jews as a whole. Every man, every woman, had to be conscious of his or her heavy responsibility toward all.

The prohibitions were formulated in the best German legal language, but each was accompanied by a series of open questions which the community's legal department had to sort out with the relevant German institutions. Following the instruction that Jews were not allowed to walk along the Vltava, which cut across Prague and revealed all the city's beauty, the question arose whether it was still permitted to use the streetcar (albeit the rear car, reserved for Jews) along the river. Was it fair to levy a betterment tax on Jewish real estate that had been "sold" to the emigration fund? How could Jews be fined for lacking the letter *J* on their I.D. cards if stateless refugees had no I.D. card to begin with?

More than seven thousand people now ate lunch at the Prague community soup kitchen, in a city that formerly had very few Jewish paupers, and some took their evening meal there as well. Most Jews ate at Café Aschermann, from which the waiters, the coffee, the cigarette smoke, and the self-confidence had all disappeared. In the daytime, children could spend time in the "heating rooms," playing, reading, and studying, thereby being spared the pain of loneliness and the danger of the streets, which knew how to be cruel. The community administration, the only large enterprise still remaining to the Jews, now embraced the whole of life. It ran five old-age homes, two orphanages, ten children's and youth hostels; it took care of parents whose children had emigrated, of children whose parents had escaped, and it employed six hundred clerks, workers, and auxiliary staff.

Older people who had not been placed in jobs tried to while away the long idle days by playing cards, learning languages, reading all the heavy books they'd never had time for before, knitting with wool from unraveled garments, and guarding the last shreds of their former dignity until their dying day.

> Gustaf Bondy, formerly a theatrical director, died at the age of 81 in Brünn.

> Senior financial consultant Ernst Fisher mourns his daughter, who died in the prime of life.

> Interested in a used winter coat in good condition, for a woman of medium frame; write to "Jewish Doctor."

The adults tried to follow each and every regulation, just as they had been accustomed to obey the law in yesterday's world; the sense of discipline ran in their blood, and they did not want to run the risk of being sent to concentration camps or endangering their families. But young people, particularly if their appearance did not betray them and broadcast their origins, still stole into movies, took walks in the park, and ate pastries at the bakery, with the lightheadedness of youth, its boldness in playing with fire, its anger at its own helplessness. As early as the fall of 1939, Poland's general governor, Frank, had in his wisdom introduced an insignia to be worn by all Jews throughout the territory of the General-Gouvernement—a blue and white band with a Star of David—but in other parts of the Reich the Jews were outwardly in no way distinguishable from the rest of the population, much to the regret of the many radicals of the same caliber as Karl Hermann Frank, who took the matter up with the Reich's Ministry of the Interior in the summer of 1941.

> The hour calls for a Jewish badge and is becoming more and more urgent as food supplies shrink and Czech morale grows feebler. Jews disseminate anti-German propaganda and a label will effectively separate them from the general population and make

rumor-mongering more difficult; it will also satisfy the not inconsiderable part of the Czech population with anti-Semitic tendencies.

The question of a Jewish patch had come up several times among the top Nazi echelons since the war with Poland, but it had not been instituted because of the Führer's opposition, based on foreign-policy considerations. But by the summer of 1941, the international situation had changed radically; world public opinion no longer had to be taken into account, as the Ministry of the Interior pointed out in its reply to Frank. There was therefore no objection to labeling the Jews, on condition that it would not reduce the numbers of Jewish workers in economic enterprises in the Protectorate who, in view of the labor shortage, could not at present be replaced.

The initiators of the scheme soon received satisfaction: on September 19, a Jewish badge was introduced throughout the Reich. All Jews as defined by the Nuremberg laws (except for couples of mixed marriages), from the age of six, had to wear the Star of David, or "the star" (der Stern) as it was called in Czech and German. It had to be the size of the palm of a hand, marked JUDE in black letters, and worn on the left side above the heart. The same instruction, signed by Heydrich, prohibited Jews from wearing badges of honor or changing their place of residence without permission from the police. The Jewish community offices distributed three stars to each of the Protectorate's 88,000 Jews, and good Jewish housewives sat and padded them with black cloth to make them sturdier, and then carefully sewed them onto coats and jackets using a meticulous blindstitch.

When the Jews first took to the streets with the mark of the star, it was a test of courage: how would the general population react? Some passersby averted their eyes, some mocked and smiled, some showed pity in their eyes. Some kept away from the label as though it were a plague. Young Jews went out into the streets with their heads held high: do they mean us to be ashamed? They made sure to smile when they met another Jew: we won't give them the satisfaction. Fredy Hirsch, who attributed such importance to dignity, even organized a meeting of youth-movement counselors and members as a show of pride: the Star of David was not a badge of shame. Black humor sprang up in the best Jewish tradition: the immediate vicinity of the community offices was named "Place de l'Etoile" (after the "square of stars" in Paris), and the road leading to it, "the

Milky Way." In a few days everyone grew accustomed to wearing the patch and it no longer aroused any notice. Only the isolation grew worse.

The Jews of Prague were now crowded into the few districts permitted them, and there was no longer any talk of finding a nice room in a well-cared-for home: the main thing was a roof over one's head, and permission to cook and use the bathroom. Two and three families shared a flat and tried to squeeze into one room the best of the furniture from the homes they had left. They brought all the souvenirs of their past and learned to thread a narrow pathway between sofas and cupboards.

At the end of September 1941, the Jews were obliged to register at the Zentralstelle. First to be registered were the Jews of Prague and Brünn, then the Jews from the outlying regions. They had to fill out most of the questionnaires in the notorious emigration file and submit a detailed list of all their possessions. A thousand people daily reported to the Zentralstelle in Strešovice as ordered, and rumor had it that a labor camp was planned in the Protectorate. In keeping with their proven philosophy of "this too was for the good," the Jews rejoiced that registration was according to families: the main thing was to stay together. Members of the Hehalutz training divisions hoped to set out for the camp as a collective and registered together, sometimes in the face of vigorous opposition from their parents, who wanted their sons and daughters to remain with them.

18

A SELF-SUSTAINING JEWISH CITY

THE GRADUAL rapprochement between the Soviet Union and Britain in the spring of 1941 created a mood of great enthusiasm among the Czech émigrés in London, and when war broke out between Russia and Germany on June 22, Beneš was in seventh heaven. "Hold on to him so he does not fly away," quipped Jan Masaryk, his own forecast being far more skeptical: "The Russians will suffer healthy blows and we'll be stuck with them." President Hacha hastened to assure the Germans that the Czech people identified with them in their struggle with Bolshevism, but asked the Reichsprotektor not to mobilize Czech soldiers for the front—not that there had been any intention of doing so: the Germans regarded the Czechs as too inferior to be admitted into the ranks of the Wehrmacht.

The poor wheat yield of the previous harvest had left its mark. Food rations grew smaller, and unrest was widespread as evinced in several acts of sabotage and a newspaper boycott, organized on orders from London. Karl Hermann Frank complained to Hitler that Reichsprotektor von Neurath was not firm enough; he was allowed to resign because of failing health, but Frank, contrary to his own hopes, was not appointed in his place. Instead, Reinhard Heydrich took over the functions of Reichsprotektor in addition to his job as head of the Reich Security Head Office. The appointment obviously heralded iron rule.

In early autumn, Russia seemed to be finished. German forces advanced from the Baltic to the Black Sea according to plan. Moscow and Leningrad were, in the German view, on the verge of collapse. The Führer's instructions, however, had been not to accept the surrender of Leningrad but to wipe it off the face of the earth. On October 3, Hitler declared that the Eastern foe had been routed and would never rise again: already behind the advancing German army lay a territory twice the size of the entire Reich in 1933.

Heydrich delivered his first speech as Reichsprotektor on October 2 at the Czernin Palace before senior officials of the Protectorate. It was considerably influenced by the Germans' sense of impending victory. Europe lay at their feet. Broadly theorizing on the peoples of Europe, Heydrich classified them according to their racial proximity to the Germans. Unlike the northern, Teutonic peoples—the Norwegians, Swedes, Danes, and Dutch—who in a new European configuration would be permitted to assimilate gradually with the Germans, the Czechs—and all the Slavic nations—were of inferior status and could not hope to be treated as equals. It was unthinkable for the Czechs to regard Bohemia and Moravia, the very heart of the German Reich, as their heritage, and they must be taught who was master. The Czech worker must be assured of filling his belly so that he would continue to work, but the idea was to introduce a reign of terror (albeit controlled, so as to avoid outright rebellion). There was to be no sign of weakness and no individual exceptions, just as no individual Jew would be considered in the final solution to the Jewish question. Indeed, as soon as Heydrich took over, Alois Elias, prime minister of the Protectorate, was arrested for his connections with the exiled government in London, accused of treason, and sentenced to death. A state of emergency was declared, and martial courts were set up that considered only three types of verdict: death, release, or transfer to the Gestapo. In the first wave of terror, 342 death sentences were handed down, shaking the Czech population to its marrow.

Rumors took root in the Viennese Jewish community to the effect that transports were shortly to be resumed, but when Dr. Löwenherz was summoned to Gestapo headquarters in Berlin at the beginning of September, he asked Eichmann about it and Eichmann vigorously denied them. Nevertheless, on October 2, the day of Heydrich's first speech and the Jewish New Year, Brunner, head of

Vienna's Zentralstelle, informed Löwenherz that due to aerial bombings by the British and the necessity of evacuating the Aryan population, some Jews would be expelled to Litzmannstadt from the Reich, from the Ostmark, and from the Protectorate. Families would travel together and the entire operation would be completed by the start of November. The official orders to the regular police force in Vienna, which was to supply the escort troops, spoke of the transfer of twenty thousand Jews from Vienna, Prague, Luxembourg, and various German cities, as well as five thousand Gypsies from Burgenland. Every thousand Jews would require an escort of twelve men and one officer, while the Gypsies would need a somewhat larger contingent. The Jews in the Protectorate were told nothing, though rumors about the operation spread from Vienna to the Prague Jewish community. However, when the community leaders turned to the Zentralstelle for confirmation they were told that there was absolutely no intention of resuming transports.

According to Eichmann, Heydrich, dizzy with his rising power, had declared at a press conference in Prague that the Protectorate would be purged of Jews within eight weeks. After the conference, Heydrich called in Eichmann, the chief of security police in the Protectorate, and admitted that he had made an error. How could the evacuation be completed so quickly if the civil administration of the Litzmannstadt district was vigorously opposed to having more Jews concentrated in its territory, in a ghetto already filled to total capacity, and had even appealed to the Führer about it? In Eichmann's view, the only way to get out of the mess and execute the announcement as stated was to temporarily concentrate the Protectorate's Jews at a single location—before eventually transporting them to the East. Karl Hermann Frank, also present at the conversation, suggested the names of various cities that might serve their purpose, and finally the name Theresienstadt (Terezin) was mentioned: a military fortress dating from the eighteenth century, less than forty miles from Prague. Eichmann was not familiar with the site, and he went to take a look at it. He found it unsuitable, he said, because it was too small (the fortress walls permitted the construction of an inner city of only 500 to 700 meters square). However, Terezin did have other advantages: the barracks were suitable for mass residences, the city walls and fortress easily ensured isolation from the outside world, and no great guard force would be necessary.

Department G of the Jewish community now started work at full speed (without being told anything about Terezin), and its first conclusion was that it was impossible to settle all the Jews of the Protectorate in a single city. Should the order be given nonetheless, the problem could be solved by erecting either one large camp of shacks or several smaller ones. For this purpose, 1,300 shacks would be required, and their construction, together with vital sanitary facilities, would cost 195 million crowns and necessitate a considerable quantity of building materials.

From the wording of the report, dated October 9, it was clear that Department G did not view the idea of a shack camp with equanimity: a relatively large number of Jews had been placed in jobs geared to the German economy, especially recently, and would now have to be taken out of the production line. In addition, non-Jewish labor would have to be used for work for which there was not enough skilled Jewish labor available. Furthermore, hastily erected shack camps tended to fall short of even the most primitive housing sites within existing settlements, and increased the danger of epidemics.

The following day, the Day of Atonement on the Jewish calendar, Heydrich called together a group of senior SS officers, including Frank, Eichmann, and Günther, to discuss the Jewish question and decide what line to adopt regarding the press reports (since the German occupation, the Days of Awe had always been accompanied by disturbances and the Jews generally awaited them in trepidation; and now, for the first time, there was not even the consolation of public prayer, for the synagogues had all been shut down). Heydrich began by noting that according to the plan, transports were to resume in mid-October and would include five thousand Jews from Prague, but the Litzmannstadt side of the operation had posed difficulties that, for the time being, could not be ignored. The possibility was raised of sending Jews to the communist camps under Stahlecker, who had meanwhile graduated to commander of the Einsatzgruppen in Division A, and a plan to deport fifty thousand Jews to Minsk and Riga was also mentioned. The evacuation of the Prague Jews would be carried out in the coming weeks, and the first transports were to include those Jews who constituted the greatest nuisance.

As to the possibility of ghettoizing the Protectorate Jews, it was noted that on the basis of past experience they could consider only an outlying suburb of Prague (rather than a city neighborhood), or a small town without industry. The possibility was proposed of establishing two ghettos, one in Bohemia, the other in Moravia, each to be divided into two subcamps, one for workers and one for service staff. The Jews could quite easily be occupied in work requiring little mechanization, such as the production of wooden soles, or straw covers for military equipment on the eastern front. In return, the Council of Elders would receive the necessary minimum of food and vitamins. The optimum arrangement would be for the Zentralstelle to take Terezin into its own hands, and after the number of Jews had been considerably reduced by virtue of deportations to the East, the entire area could be transformed into an exemplary German settlement, Heydrich said. There were means available to acquire the land, and it should be a good investment, for it was known to be fertile and eminently suitable for vegetable crops.

The small military units stationed at Terezin could be transferred to other locations in conjunction with the Protectorate's military command, and the Czech population, which lived almost entirely off the army, would be compelled to find sources of income elsewhere. Perhaps, Heydrich reflected out loud, in view of the Czech mentality (and as opposed to the policy in the area of the General-Gouvernement in Poland), the Czechs should be placated with the offer of vacant Jewish homes elsewhere, and compensated for the cost of moving with money obtained from the sale of Jewish property.

Every transport was to be subjected to surprise searches, and all garments and textile articles were to be systematically collected: the Jews of Prague, after all, were always handsomely dressed. The Czech population must be warned neither to accept gifts from Jews in the form of clothing, money, or real estate nor to purchase goods from them. The move to the ghetto should not take long, the Protektor decided. Two or three trains, carrying a thousand passengers each, could make the trip every day. The Jews would be permitted to take with them an allowance of 50 kilos, including a small store of food—a system that had worked well in the past. The larger flats in Theresienstadt would be reserved for members of the external branch of the Zentralstelle, the police, the Council of Elders, and for supply warehouses. The Jews would have to prepare their living quarters "underground." In the empty flats, the floors would be covered with straw, as beds would take up too much room.

Primary attention should be devoted to the problem of epidemics; measures would have to be adopted to ensure that they did not spread through the ghetto and its vicinity, and sewage water must not flow into the Eger. Under no circumstances were Jews to be buried. Their bodies were to be burned in the small crematorium, to which the general public would have no access. Guarding the ghetto could be left in the hands of the Czech police, supervised by German security police, and no more than six hundred men would be required for this purpose, working in three shifts. The Führer had demanded that the Jews be evacuated from German territory by the end of the year, Heydrich concluded, and therefore all the problems, including the question of transportation, must be solved without delay.

The next day Günther summoned the representatives of Prague's Jewish community, who knew nothing of this conversation, and charged them with finding sites in Bohemia and Moravia that had less than six thousand residents and might be suitable for a ghetto, and determining how many Jews lived there and how many could be housed at maximum capacity. Since, under instructions from above, the Germans never gave the Jews any orders in writing, Edelstein and other representatives used to keep a record of every meeting, an *Aktenvermerk,* drawn up in the best business language. According to a memo dated October 11, the Jews were to prepare a written report dealing with the major points of ghettoization, including the separation of the labor ghetto from the service ghetto, and covering all the organizational, economic, and legal questions involved. The Jewish leaders (Edelstein and Zucker, or Edelstein and Weidmann) were also asked to prepare an alternative plan for concentrating Jews in the environs of Prague and Brünn, but obviously not in any of the attractive suburbs where the standard of living was high.

The staff of Department G set out through Bohemia and Moravia in search of a city for the Jews. Since they were forbidden to come in contact with the local institutions, their survey had to rely on secondary information sources, such as textbooks, tourist maps, and telephone books. The Germans had instructed them to take various factors into account. The site was not to contain any large factories, particularly in textiles, leather, or sugar; residences were not to be of a high standard, nor in especially scenic locations; the local population should number between 5,000 and 6,000 people and must not include any Germans. These guidelines narrowed down the possibilities considerably: practically all the larger towns in northern Bohemia had textile factories, and the center and south of Bohemia had sugar refineries. Most of the cities on Department G's list were struck off by the Jews themselves, who tried to judge the sites through German eyes: too pretty, used as a vacation resort, located on the main rail line.

Meanwhile, the Jews themselves sought other features for their Jewish city: the possibility of work in industrial concerns, to justify their existence; living quarters nearby, so that workers could leave in the morning and return in the evening to their families in the ghetto; proximity to large cities, which ensured at least a minimal degree of contact with the outside world; and the maintenance of vital sanitary facilities to avoid epidemics, if only for the sake of the non-Jewish population. Their report therefore noted that the best possible solution, economically speaking, would be to concentrate the Jews in the suburbs of large cities, and they even proposed two working-class districts in Prague and two in Brünn.

Concentrating all the Jews of Bohemia and Moravia in a single location was impossible, said the Jews. If only sites with between 5,000 and 6,000 people were being considered, then four or five such places would be needed, and they would have to be in areas with abundant job opportunities for the Jewish labor force, which consisted chiefly of unskilled laborers. To iron out all the legal, administrative, and technical problems involved (and also to gain time), the Jews suggested appointing an action committee comprised of fourteen experts, including engineers, a doctor, a legal adviser, and an industrialist.

The choice was narrowed down to two sites: Guaya (also known as Kyjov), in southern Moravia near the Slovakian border, forty miles from Brünn, a city with no waterworks or industry; and Terezin, which first cropped up in Department G's documents in November. It was clear from the description that the Jews had delicately tried to put the Germans off this possibility: the city has only 219 buildings and there are already 7,818 residents. The reason for the relatively high population density (three times that of neighboring Leitmeritz) was that a large part of the local residents were soldiers housed in large buildings; there was very little living space available even now, and it would be impossible to extend it substantially in the future. If the idea was to settle fifty thousand people in the city, this meant 250 inhabitants per building, a rate that was beyond the buildings' capacity. It was also pointed out that there were no extensive labor possibilities in the environs of Theresienstadt.

Amid all these plans for concentrating the Jews in the Protectorate, the news of the resumption of transports struck like a blow. The first public instruction on transports to the East was signed by chief of police Kurt Dalüge on October 14: five thousand Jews must leave the Protectorate between October 16 and November 3. The staff at the community offices in Prague tried to stall for time. Dr. Hanuš Bonn, director of registration, and his assistant, Erich Kafka, argued that it was impossible to move so quickly. Indeed, only five hundred people turned up the first day, half the number ordered. Karl Rahm, a machinist by profession, who was filling in for Günther at the time, called in Avraham Fixler, the liaison between the Zentralstelle and the community, and asked him who was in charge of registration. Fixler replied, "Bonn and Kafka," at which Rahm went over to the board where the snapshots of all the community officials hung and ripped off the pictures of the two men. Bonn, a promising young poet, and Kafka were arrested and brought to the Gestapo for questioning. They never returned. Some two weeks later news was received that they had "drowned while trying to escape from Mauthausen." Lack of time could not be considered a valid excuse any longer. People had no idea what they might expect in Poland. When a Czech friend told Kurt Immergut of Hehalutz that the Germans meant to crowd all the Jews into shacks and burn them, his words met with utter disbelief. It was impossible. This was the heart of Europe and the twentieth century, not the Dark Ages.

For every transport the Germans picked twelve or thirteen hundred names out of the general files at their disposal and allowed the community staff to remove the names of its employees and their families, the sick, the old, and the well-connected, until one thousand people remained. The Jews of Prague were in shock. Though there were rumors from time to time of moving, of concentrating Jews in the Protectorate, nobody had thought of transports to the East, nobody was prepared. Fifty kilos per person—what should one take first? Warm clothing? Food? Bedding? What about toys and textbooks for the children, family photographs, fond souvenirs, Rilke's poetry, or drawing materials? There was not a moment to lose, and yet housewives stood in the middle of the room, among open cupboards and drawers, pondering, helpless: how could one squeeze one's entire life into a knapsack? A whole house into a suitcase? The people called for transport—and in keeping with German policy, these included many Polish nationals and welfare cases—ran around like madmen trying to get things together at the last minute. In two days they had to obtain warm boots, a knapsack, and woolen underwear on the black market (Jews did not have vouchers for shoes and clothing); they had to buy flour for rusks, take leave of friends and family, and perhaps slip a valuable item to a non-Jewish neighbor.

Four days before the first transport was due to set out, Heydrich instructed the Zentralstelle to handle all the property of the Jewish emigrants "should the people leaving request this with their own signature," and all such requests would be considered valid documents for the registration of property. Briefly, this meant that all Jewish property fell into the hands of the emigration fund, much to the disappointment of Hacha's government, which, feeling itself shortchanged, even referred the matter to the Ministry of the Interior of the Reich. It was their government, after all, which had suggested isolating the Jews from the general population even before the Germans had issued official instructions to that effect. The Germans prohibited the removal of any household articles prior to departure, but greed was greater than fear of Germans: Czech neighbors not only willingly accepted articles for safekeeping, particularly if they could use them, but sometimes even volunteered their services: this tablecloth, this crystal vase, won't be needed anymore, right? Some Jews feared such transactions. The German orders had been explicit: the entire flat with all its contents was to be handed over as registered. Why take a chance?

The property lists included hundreds of items, recorded room by room: the number of carpets and paper baskets in the living room, irons in the kitchen, jam jars in the pantry; the quantity of coal in the cellar, the numbers of smoking jackets, ties, handkerchiefs in the bedroom cupboard. The deportees were to bring all the cash in their possession, their savings-account passbooks, certificates of stocks and bonds, jewelry, and food-ration slips to the appointed assembly site and hand them in, together with the keys to their flats. The keys were marked with the transport letter and the owner's personal number. This same number was stamped on the cargo, and on a piece of cardboard hung with string around the neck that was compulsory apparel for every deportee.

The youth movements, organized by Hannah Steiner, helped out. The boys ran last-minute errands, the girls sewed, helped pack, and escorted the disabled to the meeting site. The idea of noncompliance with the orders never entered their heads. The passengers on the streetcar saw the numbered bundles, the eyes red from crying, the farewell glances to the beloved city, and averted their eyes. Nobody dared ask where they were going and why. Nobody said, "God keep you." They too feared Heydrich. Friends and family who stayed behind accompanied the transportees as far as they could to the meeting point, where a line of people waited. They had to be strong, not to weep, not to break down, one final kiss and goodbye, and then later, at home, they might give vent to their tears. Where were they being taken? What would become of them, with winter around the corner?

For the assembly point the Germans had chosen the open expanse reserved for the trade fair, which took place in Prague twice a year, in the spring and autumn. The fair was a showcase for Czech industry. Business transactions were negotiated in the modern main building, built only a few years back, and factories catering to the public displayed their wares on the nearby wooden stalls. For children the fair was a paradise where they could collect colorful fliers, watch various devices being demonstrated, and spend an enjoyable day. Now a different and more profitable sort of fair took place here.

The Germans demanded that the Jews turn in any money they had withheld: those who did so voluntarily would come to no harm, but woe to those who were caught with money when searched. With trembling hands, many handed over the last of their money, put aside for emergencies. Others preferred to flush the bills down the toilet rather than give them to the Germans. Most people, however, kept back some money, sewn into a hidden pocket, concealed in a shoe, baked into bread: who knew what awaited them in Poland? The bureaucratic procedures of registration, receiving goods, and endless counting generally took two to three days before I.D. cards were finally returned stamped *ghettoisiert*. At night, everyone, men, women, and children, slept on the floor—if weariness and sorrow permitted sleep at all. People often felt a sense of unreality. It couldn't be true. In the early hours of the morning, before the city had risen to work, the convoy set out for the nearby train station with an escort of German police and Czech gendarmes. The few Prague citizens who witnessed their departure reacted neither one way nor the other. It was better not to take a chance.

The early transports inspired a wave of marriages: if one had to leave for a precarious future, it was better to have someone with whom to share it, come what may. In order to speed up the wedding procedures, all documents were submitted to the general marriage clerk before noon, and if all was in order, the ceremonies usually took place that same day at three o'clock in the afternoon. The ceremony—without flowers, in everyday clothes, in the presence of immediate family only—was confined to several formal questions posed by the marriage clerk. The groom was always called Israel, the bride, Sarah: I hereby declare you man and wife. Mothers shed a tear—not so had they imagined their children's wedding; but it hardly mattered, the main thing was that they would have a companion. Hehalutz members, as in all things, turned to Yekef for advice: was it better to marry one's girlfriend? Would that ensure a common fate? Yekef shrugged his shoulders, turned his palms up in a typically Jewish gesture, and smiled. *Nu,* and what was the great risk in marriage?

On the day that the first transport left, Heydrich held another consultation in Prague: five thousand Jews were being deported from the Protectorate to the Litzmannstadt ghetto; when the entire operation was complete a statement would be released to the press to prove to the public how quickly the Germans had acted. There would then be a break to allow for preparations for further transports. For the time being the Protectorate Jews would be concentrated in a transit camp, and for this purpose all the army units in Theresienstadt had been evacuated and the Czech population told to move. Between fifty and sixty thousand Jews could easily be housed there, and later shipped to the East. The commandants in Riga and Minsk had already agreed to accept fifty thousand each. Following the final evacuation of Jews from Theresienstadt, the Germans would take over the city, and Heydrich promptly devoted the rest of the consultation with the senior SS officers, who included Eichmann, Günther, and von Gregory, to planning the expulsion of the Czechs from their own country and the settling of Germans in their place. Under no circumstances were the contents of the discussion to be leaked to the public. News of the Jewish evacuation would be accompanied by a warning to the Czechs to show the Jews no sympathy unless they too wished to be expelled. The idea was considered of making an example of two or three prominent Czechs who had in the past not concealed their sympathy for the Jews.

The Germans did indeed move quickly: a week after the first transport left, the second official instruction was made public. Fifty thousand Jews from cities in Germany, from Vienna, Prague and Brünn, were to be deported to the regions of Minsk and Riga, and by mid-November the first transport had already left from Brünn, headed straight for Minsk. The deportees traveled in heated compartments and were allowed to have water at the stations; the German escorts behaved correctly, and in general, the atmosphere was fine. When, after a three-day journey, they arrived in Minsk, they were greeted by SS men, whips in hand, and assigned to wooden shanties, where they found the dead bodies of their predecessors— murdered to make room for the newcomers. Within a week, the first Jews to arrive in Minsk from the Protectorate were already dead (out of one thousand, nine returned at the end of the war), but Prague knew nothing of this.

News of the mass transports of Jews from the Reich and the Protectorate soon reached Lichtheim in Geneva, and he reported the fact to Chaim Weizmann: twenty thousand people were transported in October to the Lodz ghetto and further transports were planned, measures that were interpreted as German retaliation against the position of the United States. Lichtheim suggested that Weizmann consider publicizing the facts throughout the world: there might not be much hope of practical results, but statements by diplomats from neutral countries might have some effect, as had been the case with French hostages. Those in Geneva entertained few illusions as to the fate of the German, Austrian, and Protectorate Jews in the East: like most of the Jews in occupied Poland, they would die of starvation, cold, contagion, and epidemics. Only the young would be able to resist, and would be mobilized into the system of forced labor operating in the East. The opinion in Geneva was that the Jews of Central Europe would probably fare somewhat worse than those of Poland, coming as they did into an already overcrowded ghetto; it was not hard to imagine the outcome if they were sent without food, money, or proper covering to the Russian winter in Minsk.

The Jews of Central Europe were lost in the appallingly crowded Lodz ghetto, among veteran inmates who, so long as they were not defeated by hunger or disease, had meanwhile learned the art of survival. The newcomers—bewildered, stunned, penniless, always hungry—gradually sold all the things they had brought with them for food and expired very quickly: their death rate was twice that of the Polish inmates, who in any case died by the thousands.

From the moment that it was learned that transports had been resumed, Dr. Ullman in Switzerland sent off hundreds of letters, almost identical in form, to friends in the Protectorate and relatives of people in the West. "I have not written for some time now. How are you? Please write soon and inform me of any change in address. I'd like to give you an address to write to should you need anything:

Relico, 52 rue de Paquis, Geneva." (Relico was the refugee aid committee.)

Replies started trickling in, one after another, in Gothic lettering, in the precise style of a business letter, in the shaky handwriting of the old, in the courteous form of the cultured:

> Mathilda Weiss and her husband have been sent to an unknown destination.

> We live in a small room as subtenants [announced Karl Kauders]. But it looks as though I may not have to leave, since I have just had two difficult operations and I am still undergoing radiation treatment.

> Despite my seventy-five years and the terrible conditions in which I live [wrote Dr. Ludwig Unger], my spirits have not flagged. I am studying Hebrew in the hope that I will still need it. I have asked my nephew to get me a visa for Cuba.

Some letters were returned marked MOVED AWAY. Bertha Lichtner's reply included a handwritten note from Kahn: "I am still at home. The visas have not arrived yet. You did as you should, but whether it will help, no one can say." No sooner did word come of transports from Prague when suddenly there was money for a Cuban visa for Franz and Olga Kahn, and for Hannah and Ludwig Steiner. The Jewish Congress tried to procure them a visa for Mexico or Colombia, dozens of letters and cables were sent between New York, London, Geneva, and Jerusalem. Through Geneva, Kahn learned of his son's visit to Tel Aviv: he bathed in the sea, had been to a film and a play, and ate various favorite Czech dishes prepared especially for him.

"Kindly inform Dr. Löwenstein," one of the letters to Ullman said, "that Mrs. Ohrenstein is well and still at her old flat. She misses the children and it would be nice if they wrote to her more frequently."

Thank God, the children are somewhere safe, said parents left alone. Thank God, we're all together, said parents whose children had stayed. Thank God, there would be no further transports east from the site of Jewish concentration in Bohemia, said community staff members, as preparations for the ghetto became more intensive.

Edelstein sent Franta Friedmann (who, because he was married to a non-Jew, enjoyed greater freedom of movement) to take a look at Theresienstadt, or Terezin as it was called by the Czechs. The initial report was hardly encouraging: the city was located near the point where the Eger poured into the Elbe, and the level of underground water beneath the fortress was relatively high. Beneath the outside walls, behind stone walls several yards thick, were subterranean cellars with only small apertures for light, and apparently very damp. The army had not used them for living quarters in over twenty years. Northeast of the town, where the river overflowed, was the small fortress whose dungeons had in days gone by served as a prison, and were considered a health hazard even under the monarchy. What the report did not say was that with the onset of the German occupation, the small fortress had reverted to its former purpose: it was the Gestapo's central prison, a substitute for concentration camps, and those who entered it were rarely seen alive again.

As might be expected, the reservations the Jews had about the place made no impression on the Germans: as far as they were concerned, it had all been decided. At the end of October, Siegfried Seidl, a thirty-year-old Austrian national and a member of the National Socialist Party for ten years, who had proved his ability during the transportation of Jews from Warte-Gau to Poland in 1939, was appointed commandant of the future ghetto. According to the instructions about his appointment (received from Eichmann and signed by Heydrich), Seidl reported to Günther in Prague and the next day left for Terezin to discuss the Wehrmacht's evacuation of the barracks with the commander of the garrison army (the small fortress was to remain under the exclusive jurisdiction of the security police and used as its prison). After Seidl saw the place, he voiced his opposition to the Zentralstelle's proposal that eighty thousand Jews be concentrated in the ghetto. Maximum capacity, he felt, could not exceed thirty thousand.

"The ghetto is a sealed-off Jewish settlement established by order of the Center for Jewish Emigration in Prague, and run by the Jewish administration under the supervision of the German authorities' local command. At the head of the ghetto is a Council of Elders and an advisory board consisting of between fifty and one hundred people, representatives of the various productive and consumer branches, a fairly representative cross section of the ghetto population. The appointment and deposition of the ghetto administrator and his deputy are in the hands of the Zentralstelle." So ran the guidelines for ghetto regulations, drawn up by Department G at the beginning of November. The Germans had the leaders of the Prague community submit two tentative lists of the composition of the Council of Elders in the ghetto, one consisting of Czech Jews, the other of Zionists. Weidmann and Edelstein agreed between them to include unaffiliated experts in both lists, so that all the Jews would have some representation on the future council. Edelstein headed one list, and Weidmann the other. The Germans chose Edelstein's list, and so, at the age of thirty-eight, Jakob Edelstein led the Jews of Bohemia and Moravia on their road to the unknown.

The various plans for the ghetto's administrative structure were prepared extremely thoroughly and in great detail. The assumption was that the evacuation of the Aryan population and its replacement by Jews would be effected in stages once the buildings had been adapted to their new function, and during the transfer, local experts would guide the Jewish officials who were to take over from them. The Jews envisioned a city in every respect: a finance department to handle all monetary matters, dispense salaries, and collect taxes; an economic department, whose main functions in ghetto life would be management of production in industry and agriculture, acquisition of raw materials, and negotiating for job contracts from the outside. "The Council of Elders would view its chief task as inducing the Jewish population to be self-supporting through physical labor, but auxiliary institutions would be necessary: old-age homes, facilities for the disabled, hospitals, and public kitchens." The long-standing dream of productivity was to materialize at last, even if somewhat differently from the way the pioneers had imagined.

In the beginning, all able-bodied people were to be employed in building the ghetto; however, once this task was completed, they would be divided into three groups: an auxiliary force, which would work in construction and agriculture in the area; the major labor force, working in the ghetto in important economic fields; and a smaller number who would be concerned with the ghetto's internal maintenance. Larger production groups would work in workshops and smaller ones at home, with the larger production units being preferred. Using already available equipment, it would be possible to set up carpentry shops, metalworks, binderies, optic and drug-packaging workshops. Contract work could be obtained for dry cleaning, the manufacture of wooden toys, brushes, and hand-woven fabrics; a sewing workshop could be opened for linens, hats, and gloves: a factory with seven hundred sewing machines could employ two thousand people.

The community planners thought of everything: during the first

Jakob Edelstein (1903–1944)

All illustrations courtesy of the Terezin Archives, Givat Chaim-Ichud, Israel

All drawings by inmates of the ghetto

Czechoslovakia 1918–1938

Right. A Jewish family before
transportation (transport numbers
around their necks)

Below. Furniture of the deported
stored in a synagogue (for later
German use)

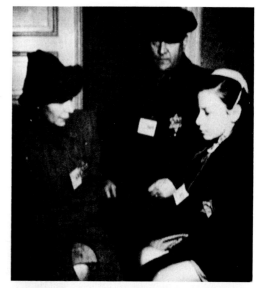

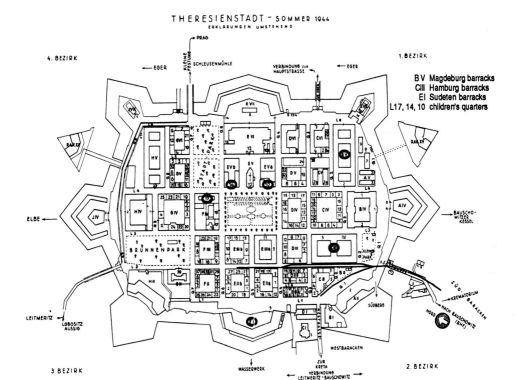

A plan of Theresienstadt prepared in the ghetto, 1944

Fifty crowns in ghetto money (bearing Edelstein's signature)

Right. Dr. Franz Kahn, secretary of the Zionist organization in Czechoslovakia, a man torn between foreboding and hope

Middle. Jakob Edelstein with his wife, Miriam (right), before the deluge

Bottom. Fredy Hirsch, athletic instructor, who cared for the children until their last day

A street in the crowded ghetto (Felix Bloch)

A new transport arrives during the ghetto curfew (Leo Haas)

Right. Women's dormitory

Middle. Every shack and corner used as living space (Leo Haas)

Bottom. No more space—the old from Germany housed in attics (Leo Haas)

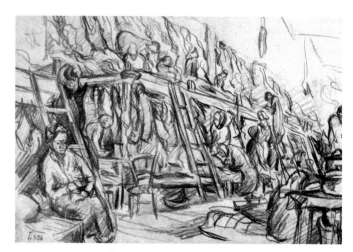

Left. Leaving for work accompanied by Czech gendarmes (Leo Haas)

Middle. Waiting in line for a meal—two potatoes for a long working day (Leo Haas)

Bottom. The last station—a sickroom for the old (Willy Groag)

Nun beginnt der Kampf, dem ghettoisierten Juden beizubringen, dass er trotz Allem arbeiten muss, jede Arbeit, die man von ihm verlangt, ohne Belohnung, ohne Zwangsmittel.

und dafür sollen wir arbeiten?

Right. Clandestine school (Jewish police on guard), drawn by Eva Weiss, aged twelve

Bottom. A theater performance in a barracks courtyard (Otto Unger)

three days, new arrivals at the ghetto would be housed in separate buildings and undergo medical examinations, and those with contagious diseases would be isolated from the rest. All adults were to be inoculated against typhus, all children against diphtheria. A disinfection center was to be opened to purge infested household equipment. At the end of the quarantine period, the arrivals would be taken to hot showers in a central building to be constructed for the purpose.

The ghetto inmates would be subject to general laws unless the German authorities decided otherwise; the Protektor's regulations on removing Jews from economic life would not be valid in the ghetto. All ghetto residents would be equal, would enjoy freedom of movement within the ghetto, and would even be allowed to leave it temporarily on the basis of an exit permit issued by the administration, either to work outside or to perform some other official function. In addition, the ghetto residents would be subject to special regulations to be publicized, if possible, in a local newspaper. All branches of the ghetto's administration would be obliged to perform their functions to the best of their ability and expertise without regard for favoritism or personal interest; they were to keep their work confidential and operate according to accepted rules of conduct; however, their functions should protect them against slander and bodily threat, punishable by law. To enforce its regulations the administration was to have recourse to a legal system and a police force, and have the right to punish delinquents.

The detailed proposal for the structure of the ghetto administration included six major departments and dozens of subdepartments. Edelstein and his colleagues omitted nothing: postal service, telephone and telegraph, savings schemes, dairy farming, restaurants, garbage disposal, fire squad, young people's dormitories, a tuberculosis hospital. A kind of joy of creation caught hold of the planning officials, a sense of mission: they were building a haven to save all the Jews of the Protectorate.

Every day or so, Edelstein, Weidmann, or Zucker met with SS Obersturmführer (Lieutenant) Dr. Seidl (whose doctorate was from the University of Vienna), mostly in order to plan the advance unit, which was to set out for Terezin in the near future. The Jews recorded the discussions after every meeting, turned in one report for Seidl's approval at their next meeting, and kept one copy back for the community. At their meeting of November 10, Seidl decided that the wooden bunks were to be 60 by 190 centimeters, three or four levels high, sturdy, and easy to move. He stressed to Edelstein and Weidmann that families were not to be separated, that officials would be permitted to travel to Prague when necessary, and that they would enjoy separate housing in the ghetto, though he was prepared to listen to other proposals on this matter. The advance unit would take enough food for a few days and the Zentralstelle would arrange for further supplies.

Everyone was fired by enthusiasm at the thought of setting up a Jewish city—not just any city, but a model one, run in exemplary fashion; a city in which Jews would perform all functions and do all the work, where policemen, porters, agricultural laborers would all be Jews—a kind of miniature Palestine. True, it would be under German supervision and the physical conditions would be rough, but the Jews were hardly unfamiliar with trials and subjugation and they had already proved their mettle in the past. The list of necessary skilled workers for the advance unit which Edelstein submitted to Seidl consisted of forty-five specialists in municipal administration, fifteen financial and one postal expert, and fourteen economists, of whom one was a transportation expert. The technicians included one antiaircraft expert and the manager of a motorbike garage. The skilled workers included six drivers and two switchboard operators. The Jewish city was well planned.

Seidl struck off many of the administrative specialists, replaced them with one hundred laborers to do heavy work, and instructed the advance unit to report to Terezin on November 24. The skilled workers—welders, carpenters, electricians, builders, a disinfection expert, a stove-building expert, bakers, cooks—were instructed to come with what tools they still had. Their names were given to Seidl so that their families would meanwhile be protected from transport to Poland, which nevertheless continued. Seidl interfered in the tiniest details. He did not permit a second doctor or a technical draftsman to accompany the advance unit.

Orders had been given to keep the establishment of the ghetto confidential, but this was no longer possible, Edelstein and Zucker pointed out, due to the composition of the advance unit and other preparations. Edelstein requested to leave with the first group, but Seidl felt that for the moment his presence was more necessary in Prague. His departure would be determined later.

The administrators of the ghetto-to-be had to decide the composition of the initial group that would build the ghetto. At a meeting of the Jewish leaders, also attended by Munk and Beneš, Yekef insisted that character was the most important consideration, and the general opinion was that Hehalutz members were to be preferred. As for Edelstein's staff, some argued that it should include various professional experts, but Yekef pointed out that first of all he wanted his friends near him.

Raging debates took place at Hehalutz over whether they should support sending their members in the advance units. The eventual decision to remain with the flock was based on personal experience as well as ideological considerations: the first group of Hehalutz members who tried to steal across the Slovakian border with the help of paid smugglers had been apprehended by the Germans; fourteen of them were hanged. The leadership of Hashomer Hatzair, the left-wing arm with close ties to the communist underground, were mostly from Slovakia or Carpathian Russia; their political and regional ties were different, and it was decided that where possible its members would go underground or escape into Slovakia or Hungary. Their families were outside, and their attitude to the Germans was more sober, perhaps the result of the natural mistrust of all non-Jews ingrained in Eastern European Jewry.

Hehalutz, while disapproving of Hashomer Hatzair's decision to go underground, allowed its members to make their own decisions; but as a body it put itself at Edelstein's disposal. He felt that the shepherd must stay with the flock (of the two thousand Hehalutz members in the Protectorate, only about twenty did not report for transport when the time came). Going underground, among an indifferent, hostile, or frightened population with a very sharp eye indeed for a Jew, was obviously a solution only for those relative few who could make the emotional break from their families, were prepared to endanger the lives of the people who harbored them, and could endure the relentless strain of undercover life for long stretches at a time. Many broke, many were caught—less than five hundred of the Protectorate's Jews spent the war underground and survived.

On November 24, at five in the morning, the advance unit assembled at the train station on Hibernska Street. As instructed, they came with a knapsack containing personal effects and food for two to three days, and a blanket roll. They were told that the rest of their belongings would be sent on later. The building team (*Aufbau-Kommando* to the Germans and *A-K* to the Jews), all of them young men selected from the labor index, were told that they would be permitted to return home on weekends, and to transfer their salaries to their families in Prague, who were to be protected from transports; there was to be a regular postal service, and they would get a week's leave at Christmas. They set out as an ordinary work force, without any idea that their move was final.

The day after they left Edelstein and Zucker reported to Seidl. They said that the departure had gone according to plan, and presented a budget proposal, including working costs and salaries. Seidl informed them that an additional transport of one thousand people, chiefly laborers, would apparently set out for Terezin within a week and would be permitted to include engineers, doctors, and other necessary specialists. Postal service was discussed: letters would be forwarded through the Prague community offices and the ghetto itself would establish a censorship body to ensure that the letters contained no unpleasantness. Seidl further informed Edelstein and Zucker that they would be allowed to go to Theresienstadt to check the conditions but would then have to return to Prague. In a conversation with Günther, some three days later, it was decided that Edelstein would officially remain the deputy leader of the Prague Jewish community, and Weidmann said that he would not appoint a new assistant; instead he would elicit closer cooperation from Kahn and Franta Friedmann.

The conversation with Günther, at which Seidl was also present, resulted in a somewhat modified concept for the Jewish city as envisioned by its planners: for the time being contact between the community and the ghetto would be confined to written communications forwarded through the German command, and for the next four weeks, the ghetto residents would be prohibited all postal contact with their families, including parcels. Following this period, they would be permitted to write letters twice a month. However, traveling back and forth was not feasible at the moment.

Günther approved Munk's appointment as head of the ghetto's medical services, stressing the importance of these and the employment services, and the fact that the sick, particularly those with communicable diseases, and the mentally ill should not be included in the transports. It was agreed to establish a ghetto police force, chosen from among the thousand members of the advance unit awaiting departure at the fairgrounds. The police force was to consist of a chief, two deputies, and twenty policemen. Every policeman would wear a cap and carry a baton (SS Sturmbannführer Günther asked to see several examples of suitable headgear). They would enjoy certain privileges and if they liked, their families could remain outside the ghetto until the final transport left. A large quantity of "Jewish badges" should be sent to the ghetto so that all Jews could be supplied with two stars. Meanwhile requests had come from the ghetto for brooms, typewriters, tools, and kettles: it seemed that conditions there were not quite what had been expected.

The next day Edelstein met with the "boss" alone (as he wrote in a letter to his staff a year later, apparently referring to Günther). This discussion left him shaken. "Even then I did not dare record the conversation, and I told only two or three people what was actually to be the reality of the Theresienstadt ghetto. Perhaps now you will understand my farewell address, which was sad indeed. Was it wrong of me to take my good friends along, to draw them into chaos and calamity? What gave me the moral right to act as I did? Today it may be said that our pioneering outlook taught us always to be on hand when Jewish destiny takes a tragic turn, but also re-creates itself. Who, if not we, were called to this, to give aid in moments of severe anguish and fateful decisions?

"I have never understood nor interpreted the term 'pioneer' in its narrow sense. A pioneer is not merely a worker, but one who implements ideas, finds the good in the bad, lays the groundwork of a new life for all." This was Edelstein's credo, and he took it with him to the ghetto even after he already knew that the plan for a Jewish city was at least partially based on illusion. He also took twenty-two of his close colleagues, chiefly from the Palestine office in Prague: his loyal secretary, Peppi Steif; Otto Zucker as his deputy; Leo Janowitz as his right-hand man; Erich Österreicher, Dittl Ornstein, Seppl Lichtenstern, all Sudetenites who had worked with him since the Munich Pact; Josef Klaber as the police expert, Karl Schliesser as the economics expert, both top men in their own fields, and Harry Tressler as the expert "on Edelstein." Dr. Munk had left a day earlier, accompanied by two other doctors and their equipment.

Edelstein, Zucker, and the staff members (or *Stab,* as they were called in ghetto terminology) journeyed by regular train to the Theresienstadt ghetto on December 4, 1941. They carried small suitcases, had no police escort, and as far as appearances went, might have been ordinary tourists. On the short trip Edelstein was preoccupied with his own thoughts, Zucker told stories, and the general mood was cheerful. Their chief worry was that they would not find their way from the Bohušovice train station, about two miles from Terezin. But Zucker was reassuring and promised to show the way. Nevertheless, the group took several wrong turnings, had to ask directions, and arrived rather tired at the town behind the walls, where the Czech population still went about its business as usual. The administrative staff reported to the Sudeten barracks, where the Jews had all been housed, and when the barracks gate shut behind them, one of the local veterans, a member of the first advance unit, with ten long days of ghetto experience, said to them: "And now, gentlemen, you're in shit." Günther arrived at the ghetto a few days later and summarized the situation in a similar manner when Edelstein complained to him. "Now, Jews, when you're *im Dreck*, let's see what you can do." The Jews accepted the challenge. They'd show the Germans, they'd show the world what Jews were capable of. Despite the obstacles, despite the hardships, despite German domination, here they would build a model Jewish city.

19

A BUFFER BETWEEN GERMANS AND JEWS

EXPULSION CAUGHT the first transportees unawares and threw them in turmoil, torn from their homes before they could fully realize the meaning of departure. Those who followed them, however, already knew what to expect, be it tomorrow, next month, or later in the year, and they made painstaking plans for their departure with a thoroughness typical of Central European Jewry. They prepared knapsacks and sewed jackets lined with cotton padding or down feathers; they made zwieback and roux, durable staples that would last for months; they set aside candles, pocket flashlights, thermoses; they exchanged the white bed linen of the bourgeoisie for the coarser striped sheets of the lower classes; and they stashed a gold or silver ring in a double heel. Hour after hour they pored over lists, deleting, adding, arguing over the contents of the allotted fifty kilos; no item escaped the scale. They procured vitamins on the black market, purchased medicines, copied favorite poetry into notebooks, and removed food and clothing to make room for books, musical scores, and paints. Again and again housewives bade farewell to a Persian rug, a carefully polished table, a cherished house plant. Everyone was living on borrowed time. Sooner or later their turn would come—if the war did not end first.

There were those who left their homes in disorder, lights on, the faucet dripping, crumbs in the kitchen, clothes strewn on the sofa. But others could not bring themselves to do so: they arranged the linen closet in ruler-straight rows, as they had always done, closed the drawers, washed the dishes, hoping perhaps that just so would they find their homes when they returned. There were those who in the weeks of waiting tried to slip some household article for safe-keeping or as a gift to Czech or German friends and acquaintances (there still were some, even if only a handful, who had remained true in the most difficult times when colleagues, employees, neighbors, fellow students, and pupils had turned their backs). Others left their homes intact, whether out of fear or a desire to preserve them whole, an inability to undo what had been built up by years of toil.

The Prague Jewish community (like those of Brünn and other large towns) employed dozens of engineers and draftsmen who drew detailed plans and kept careful records of all the real-estate holdings that the Jews turned over to the emigration fund when they were expelled. In mid-December Heydrich issued instructions regarding Jewish property, including homes and real estate. Appraisals and sales were to be effected from a "national-political" standpoint, i.e., to approved recipients; sales were to be handled in an orderly and irreproachable fashion; records of assessments, sales, and deposit transfers must be able to withstand inspection at all times; it must be borne in mind that the income from Jewish property was public wealth.

Such was the ruling, but in actual fact the Germans vied for the flats that became available, for the furniture, for any article of value. Privileged officials could expect to receive a coveted article on order even before the goods were transferred to warehouses. Under Salo Krämer, the former leader of the Moravská Ostrava community, the Germans set up a "trusteeship" at the Prague office to handle the property from evacuated Jewish homes. Doors were locked, keys were marked with names and addresses and deposited with the *Treuhandstelle*. One team went through the houses and compiled a record of every item; another sorted and crated the goods and had them carted off in trucks and wagons. Warehouses were established in synagogues, the Sokol sports centers (which had long since disbanded), and in vacant Jewish homes. The furniture warehouses also employed Germans, but most of the work was done by the Jews themselves, and it was a popular job, for (so it was said) it ensured one's exclusion from transports as well as the occasional possibility of hiding some small article for personal use. Two years after the start of Operation Krämer, the "trusteeship" warehouses listed hundreds of categories, including almost 700,000 books, 6,060 gas masks, 603 pianos, 55,454 paintings, 21,472 pan lids, 88,074 living-room items, 4,606 pillow cases, and 12 pairs of deer antlers. Inscriptions were obliterated from silver, monograms unpicked from linen, bookplates removed from books. The empty flats were cleaned, painted, and made ready for new tenants.

The rivalry over Jewish property and the pressure exerted on the emigration center for a share in the booty compelled the chief of the Prague Gestapo, Böhm, after six months of flourishing business, to circulate a letter among a dozen different authorities, including the local Wehrmacht, the chief of regular police, and the Reichsprotektor's office. The circular was issued in response to criticism leveled against the Zentralstelle by dissatisfied clients: if the German populace, particularly the officials, were able to move to good homes and acquire furniture at reasonable prices, it was due solely to the Center for Jewish Emigration, which prevented the Jews from disposing of their property to Czechs. It went without saying that the Zentralstelle was willing to help any member of the German nation, but it was not to be regarded as a real-estate agency or a property warehouse. "I have no wish, in light of the repeated unpleasantness, to investigate when the gentlemen who now make claims first became anti-Semitic. It is insolence to demand that the SS, whose distasteful task it is to come into daily contact with Jews, suffer insults from people who openly consorted with Jews in Prague cafés only three years ago. I would ask that in future more understanding be shown of the work done by the Center for Jewish Emigration."

Though fraught with anguish, removal to Theresienstadt did not give rise to the terror evoked by deportation to the East. Terezin, after all, was still the homeland, set in the Bohemian tranquillity of low rolling hills and verdant woods and fields. Many knew it from their army service, others from springtime excursions when fruit trees were in bloom. Visible in the distance were the white houses of Leitmeritz, a town Edelstein had often visited in his salesman days in Teplitz, and which had been included in the Reich since the annexation of the Sudetenland. At the foot of the fortress flowed the Eger River, slow and calm through most of the year. To some the transport orders even came as a measure of relief: at least they put an end to the harrowing wait, the anxiety every time the doorbell rang, the thousand daily minor humiliations. At Theresienstadt waited family and friends, and the sorrow of parting was mingled with the anticipation of reunion.

The first glimpse the transportees had of Terezin was the church steeple, visible from the Bohušovice train station where the transports arrived. The brown brick walls, surrounded by moats, sprang into view only as the procession neared the outskirts of the city. Theresienstadt was no more than a couple of miles from the train station, no distance at all in the eyes of most Czechs, who loved walking. But now, burdened under three or four layers of clothing in an effort to stretch the permitted fifty kilos to their limits, topped by a heavy winter coat, carrying knapsacks on their backs and suitcases in their hands, and with children hanging on to their coattails, it was a laborious procession that made its way to the gates of the city behind the walls. The town was built with military precision: five streets long, eight streets wide, all at right angles to one another with a square in the middle—a ten-minute walk from end to end—and the barracks were also uniform, consisting of an identical number of inner gates and yards.

The town, with its two hundred small, old houses, reflected both the bourgeois spirit of the Austro-Hungarian monarchy and the practical stamp of Emperor Josef II, the "father of the homeland, who, on October 10, 1780, laid the cornerstone of this eternal edifice," according to a Latin inscription on one of the fortress walls. He had named it after his mother, Maria Theresa, who was remembered by Jews chiefly for initiating the mass expulsions of 1744 to 1748. Despite his autocratic rule, the ghetto dwellers of days gone by had held Josef II in affection: he had abolished serfdom and given the Jews a certain measure of freedom. In the words of the poet Friedrich Gottlieb Klopstock, in his "Song of Praise to the Emperor": "You made the Jew a man." The fortress had been built at the height of the Austro-Prussian war for hegemony in Central Europe, to prevent Prussian penetration into Bohemia through the Elbe valley, though no battle was ever fought there—the Prussians had simply gone around Theresienstadt. But Terezin, as the Czechs called it, remained a garrison town even when its fortifications were no longer necessary; first for the Austro-Hungarian army, later for the Czechoslovakian republic's army, and finally for the Wehrmacht. All in all, little had changed over the generations, apart from the barrack names. Three roads cut through Terezin: the road to nearby Bohušovice, the road to the terrifying "little fortress," and the Dresden-Prague highway with its tantalizing signpost: "PRAGUE 63 KM."

When the first advance unit—known as A-K 1 in ghetto terminology—arrived at Theresienstadt, they found the Sudeten barracks in which they were housed empty and filthy. German graffiti covered the walls, scribbled by bored soldiers who called for valor and less glorious deeds. On the ground floor were the storerooms, stables, toilets, primitive showers, and two dark, totally unequipped kitchens. The second floor consisted of two large halls, formerly used as storerooms. The Wehrmacht had left offices without furniture, windows broken, trash in the stables, and filth on the damp, bare cement floors. Here the first arrivals bedded down on those freezing December nights without mattresses or even straw, with only a knapsack beneath their heads and water dripping from the ceiling. Contrary to their promises, the Germans provided no food; the newcomers lived on the provisions they had brought from home and grew more and more hungry. Richard Skarabis, the temporary commandant who had been imported from the Lodz ghetto, addressed the ghetto builders thus: "Today we're on top, tomorrow you're on the bottom." The young men looked at him in bewilderment: what was he talking about?

The Germans had left Terezin, but the town's Czech settlers had remained in their homes, the children attended school, the shops stayed open. On the way to and from work (mostly clean-up operations in the empty barracks), one or another of the Jewish young men managed to evade the Czech guards to post a letter or buy bread. But it was not long before new orders came, one after another: it was forbidden to walk on the sidewalk, it was forbidden to buy anything in the shops, it was forbidden to whistle or sing marching songs while walking, it was forbidden to touch a chimney sweep for luck.

It was camp commandant Untersturmbannführer Karl Bergel, short and squat, who set the early ghetto residents on the firm ground of reality. At assembly in the Sudeten courtyard, he spoke of two hearts beating in his chest, one soft, the other hard; it was up to them, he said, which would predominate, and with that he proceeded to put the group through a lengthy physical drill. A barber by profession, with a facial aspect that conveyed perpetual dullness and inebriation, Bergel cut a comic figure: his words were greeted as a new variation on the famous speech made by Lieutenant Dub to the Good Soldier Schweik: "You don't know me yet, but you will get to know me." Hašek's *The Good Soldier Schweik*, a book that accompanied most Czech-speaking youngsters wherever life took them (if only because literature teachers totally ignored it), was to come to mind again and again: many of the scenes of life at Theresienstadt might have been lifted straight from it.

The chief of Czech police, Theodor Janetschek, whose gigantic head and spindly legs earned him the nickname "Cauliflower," also seemed to belong to Jaroslav Hašek's zoo. Like the officers of the Austro-Hungarian army in Schweik's time, he too tried to atone for his Czech origins by denouncing Czechs as well as Jews to the Germans. In contrast to their chief, however, most of the two hundred Czech gendarmes who were daily in charge of the ghetto residents—escorting them to work, searching their belongings— were reasonably fair. They did not harass the Jews unnecessarily and knew when to turn a blind eye to a suspicious bulge under someone's garments if the SS or Janetschek were not around. Similar origins, sometimes mutual friendship—above all, their common masked hatred for the Germans—and to no small degree their healthy greed, often induced them to help the Jews smuggle in letters or parcels or visit their relatives on the outside—despite the danger, despite the fact that there were informants among the police and the punishment, if caught, was severe (fourteen Czech gendarmes were executed in October 1943 in Terezin's Little Fortress by order of Karl Hermann Frank).

Contrary to the assumption that the Jewish leaders shared with Seidl, that mass transports would begin only after the advance unit had prepared living quarters and basic conditions, two family transports, numbering one thousand people each, were sent to Theresienstadt even before Edelstein and Seidl arrived. According to Heydrich, as stated in a top-secret letter to all relevant authorities, preparations for the Theresienstadt ghetto had advanced far enough to permit mass transports. Another thousand people who had been slated for Minsk arrived at the ghetto a day after the leaders, and within a few days there were over eight thousand people at Theresienstadt—without a thing having been prepared. Everything was rushed, improvised, arbitrary, totally uncoordinated—a far cry from the careful plans on paper. It was the Nisko affair all over again.

The leadership took over a room on the ground floor of the Sudeten barracks and Jakob opened his office out of a suitcase. Meanwhile Seidl arrived and found all his plans equally awry: straw mattresses had to be obtained, medical services activated, kitchen pots procured. A single 300-liter pot catered to thousands of people who had to wait hours in the cold for a black liquid called "coffee" or some soup made from rotten turnips and potatoes. The end of the lunch line received their provisions in the evening—if they received them at all.

The advance unit greeted Edelstein, Zucker, and their aides, with bitterness, rage, even hatred: they had not expected this. They had come to build a city, not to be imprisoned. Most bitter were the Czech Jews: they felt that the entire affair had been concocted by the Zionists out of some misguided notion of Jewish autonomy. Nor was any consolation to be found in the first announcement issued by the leadership: "The management is not empowered to promise the residents anything in advance. It can merely declare that it will do its best and try to carry out its task honestly and fairly. The new leadership faces an exceedingly difficult job which can be done reasonably well and for the common good only if quiet, order, cleanliness, and mutual trust and cooperation can be assured. The new leadership will do all it can to pass on the residents' requests and requirements to the appropriate authorities and will take measures against anyone who disobeys its instructions."

The nature of work became a controversial issue in the ghetto, particularly among the Czech socialists and communists: did it serve German interests or would it benefit the Jews to come? Was it moral to hold a specific function? (In the beginning everyone worked in groups of one hundred at whatever job they were assigned to, with no regard for individual qualifications.) Gradually, however, everyone became caught up in a desire to improve living conditions, for themselves and their families, and on the whole they worked diligently. Work was also a subject of dispute among the Hehalutz people: following A. D. Gordon's theories, Maccabi Hatzair took the position that all work was of inherent moral value, no matter what, no matter where. And the leadership, from the moment it arrived, insisted that everyone worked at the job assigned to him, at the time and place ordered, and asked malingerers who regularly visited the sick clinic to refrain from doing so in future. It took no more than a week for the German command to define tardiness as sabotage.

The bitterness against Edelstein increased sevenfold when, the day after he arrived, the Germans ordered that the men's living quarters be separated from those of the women and children under twelve. The women and children were ordered to remove to a different barracks, and furious, the women descended on Yekef's office. The ghetto police—formed only the day before from among former officers and sergeants in the Czech army equipped with caps, belts, and wooden clubs—was compelled to exercise its authority in this situation for the first time, calming the women, bringing them to order, and appointing a deputation to speak to Edelstein. The women demanded vehemently that he go to the Germans immediately and have the order rescinded, and all Yekef's attempts to explain that it was impossible to rebel against the Germans were of no avail. At their insistence he promised to deal with the matter at once; he rose and left the room. He returned half an hour later and announced that Seidl had refused to see him without an appointment. Only the chief of ghetto police knew that Jakob had never really left the barracks, for he too was forbidden to go out without permission.

The women and children moved in a long procession from the Sudeten to the Dresden barracks. Families could no longer meet unless a man was lucky enough to draw an assignment in the women's quarters and thereby steal a moment with his loved ones. Any men caught by the Germans speaking to the women received twenty-five lashes. The punishment was meted out by the ghetto police in the presence of camp commandant Bergel, and if he felt that the strokes were not vigorous enough he would deliver them himself, to victim and police alike.

The dissolution of the family unit destroyed all the fine planning on paper and brought home the reality of the Jews' position. Theresienstadt was to be run as a labor camp, not a city. The detailed programs for the various departments and subdivisions seemed like a dream from another world. No vestige remained of the proposed liaison office, which was meant to maintain contact with the outside world and represent the Jewish city in dealings with the Zentralstelle, the Prague community office, and in buying from and selling to non-Jewish economic institutions. There was only one type of liaison—and it led straight to German headquarters.

The older children were separated from the adults almost immediately. They were housed in separate rooms, first in the Sudeten barracks and then in all of them, and instructors from the Zionist youth movements were placed in charge of them. The instructors saw their work as a continuation of their former activities in youth dormitories, Youth-Aliyah schools and study groups, and their aim

was unchanged: to continue the children's general and Zionist education as preparation for life in Palestine. Systematic teaching was
impossible during the early chaos, and they occupied the children
with scouting, games, discussions, lectures, and reading. To head
the youth division, Yekef appointed twenty-three-year-old Gonda
Redlich of Maccabi Hatzair, a conscientious and industrious law
student and former vice principal of the Prague Youth-Aliyah
school, endowed with grand ambitions and a formidable will.
Gonda worked in tandem with Fredy Hirsch, who was at first also
responsible for the management of the ghetto buildings, but when
the number of youngsters reached the hundreds and then the
thousands, he devoted himself entirely to the children, especially
their physical education. The instructors were aged between twenty
and twenty-five, which led the parents to mockingly dub the youth
division *kluko-kratiya* (boys' government).

Once a week, in procession, the children were allowed to visit
their fathers and mothers in the other barracks, but otherwise they
were the sole responsibility of the instructors, who worked almost
nonstop. During his first days in the ghetto, Yekef visited the children's quarters and complained about the filth. Gonda tried to
explain how difficult it was to keep the place clean when there were
no brooms, pails, or other cleaning materials, but Yekef also had
other complaints about how the children were cared for and was
generally dissatisfied with what had been done thus far. Gonda
spoke of the difficulties involved in caring for hundreds of children
without normal facilities, but in the middle of the conversation
Yekef suddenly said, "I'm very tired, I must get some sleep." Gonda
realized that he had not heard a word he had said. Fredy, who had a
mania for order, organized a cleanliness competition in the children's rooms and even managed to obtain edible prizes from the
economic division, though he was not pleased when it was Gonda
who presented the children with their prizes.

Soon after they arrived, Edelstein and the other officials were
ordered to move from Sudeten to Magdeburg (no one had yet used
the term "barracks"). The Magdeburg barracks had housed the
cavalry in the days of the monarchy, and two horse heads adorned
its entrance gate; now it was to serve as the administration office and
living quarters for the leadership. Yekef had opposed the change
and requested permission to remain with the others, perhaps because he saw the move as a German attempt to drive a wedge
between himself and the ghetto residents, perhaps because among

the masses he felt safer from German surveillance. Nevertheless he vigorously rejected the German suggestion that the leadership be supplied with special food, a refusal that the Germans promptly labeled communist tactics. "The Germans would have us identify with them, rather than with the other Jews," he told his staff.

In the far-off days in Prague, a newspaper or at least a daily information sheet had been planned to help the leadership stay in constant touch with the people. In the reality of ghetto conditions, the newspaper metamorphosed into "the orders of the day," and the first edition, published ten days after the leaders arrived, announced that at the head of the ghetto stood Jakob Edelstein, assisted by Otto Zucker and a Council of Elders whose names would be released at a later date. The word "elder" to denote a functionary was a legacy from the distant Middle Ages, preserved only in the fraudulent nineteenth-century anti-Semitic document known as the *Protocols of the Elders of Zion*; it was a word rarely used by Jews, nor was it common in either German or Czech, but it was the term the Germans chose because other designations of status, such as "director" or "chairman," were clearly inappropriate for the inferior race. While conditions were radically different from what the employees of Department G had envisaged at their desks in Prague, the administrative structure remained basically the same, and the public learned from "daily orders" that the leadership consisted of departments of administration, economics, finance, and health, as well as a technical office, and that all guidelines would be transmitted to them via the elders of the various buildings.

Each barracks constituted a self-contained unit, with its own facilities for supplies, employment, transport management, census records, and sanitation. The smallest unit in every barracks was the living quarters, and the elders of each room had to present a daily report on the number of occupants and how many were sick, ensure that lights went out as ordered (at first at ten, and later on even earlier), and that water and electricity were not being wasted. For neither the municipal water company nor the small power station could begin to meet even minimal requirements for thousands of additional inhabitants. Every tap was watched by an elderly monitor, showers were prohibited, residents were asked to use a small cup when brushing their teeth, and still the water sometimes ran out. Electric lights often flickered and went out, and yet no prohibition, no threat of punishment was mightier than the temptation to use an electric element or hot plate to prepare some hot soup or other homemade dish from anything at hand—potatoes stolen from KP, green onion stalks smuggled back from the fields.

Seidl, a stickler for military discipline, had the residents learn the German words for common military orders: "*Stillgestanden!*" ("Attention!"); "*Rührt euch!*" ("At ease!"); "*Vorwärts, marsch!*" ("Forward, march!"); "*Kompanie, halt!*" ("Company, halt!"). Inmates were required to salute all uniformed Germans, including the young SS (known as *kindergarten* in ghetto language), the men by raising their caps, the women by bowing their heads. Edelstein never wore a hat, whatever the weather; when Trude Groag asked him why, he replied: "So that I won't have to raise it to the Germans."

The men were ordered to wear their hair no more than three centimeters long, and the women were ordered to adopt men's hair styles. However, except at the beginning, perhaps because of the constant comings and goings the matter was left unsupervised, and no outward change occurred in the appearance of the ghetto residents, unless they took ill. They simply grew thinner. On the whole they wore the clothes they had brought from home and the women took care with their appearance, if only for the sake of that brief encounter with family or friends. When it came to enforcing the nonsmoking rule, however, Seidl was almost insanely fanatic; Jews in the Reich had no cigarette allowance, so that every cigarette in their possession testified to some form of contact with the outside world. In a letter to the Jewish elder, Seidl drew attention to the fact that camp inmates begged the local population for cigarettes or bought them for as much as ten crowns each. Cigarettes, like matches, money, medicine, jewelry, and alcohol, were forbidden from the start. Again and again residents were asked to hand over all contraband, and the penalty for disobedience was heavy. But none was as powerful as that terrible craving for a cigarette, a few drags, even a single puff. Time and again, smokers were prepared to endanger their lives, to risk transport, for a cigarette butt: they longed to close their eyes and inhale deeply, keeping the smoke inside as long as possible, then to savor it a little while longer in their mouths before finally parting from it in sorrow. When someone was caught smoking during one of Seidl's visits to the Aussig barracks, Seidl told Edelstein that in future he would punish not only the delinquent but everyone present as well. The Germans piled prohibition upon prohibition and always attached severe penalties; but life in the ghetto continued to be a never-ending series of infractions.

The Czech population of Terezin started to prepare for Christmas: fir trees could be seen through windows, the fragrance of baking filled the air, and the ghetto residents were overcome by sadness. There was not a Jewish home in Czechoslovakia that in former times had not marked Christmas in some way: a festive dinner—braided bread laden with raisins, fish soup, fried carp— small gifts for the children, a frolic in the snow. Edelstein requested permission for the ghetto's Christian population (Jewish according to the racial laws) to attend midnight mass in the town's church. Permission was refused, but they were allowed to hold prayers in their barracks on condition that it did not disturb the other inmates. On Christmas Eve the Czech Jews sat and sang Christmas carols, longed for home, and consoled one another with the thought that next Christmas they would be home. How much longer could the war last now that the Germans had begun to suffer setbacks? The Russians, contrary to Hitler's declarations, had not collapsed but fought with unexpected obstinacy and weapons the Germans never knew they had, again and again pouring fresh divisions into battle. The autumn rains began when the Germans were forty-five miles from Moscow, bogging down their sophisticated war machinery deep in the mud; and then came the snows. Temperatures fell to thirty below zero. The German forces, weakened, lacking suitable provisions for frost, hungry, and weary to death of the war in the cold, began to retreat, step by step. The myth of the invincible German army was destroyed in that winter of 1941. The Blitzkrieg had met its match.

Hitler was repeating Napoleon's campaign of one hundred and thirty years earlier, the knowledgeable said; the war could not last much longer now. And as if to support the feeling that the war had taken a decisive turn, Japan attacked the American fleet in Pearl Harbor on December 7, taking both Washington and Berlin by surprise. According to the Axis agreement, the Germans undertook to aid Japan if she was attacked, but here she was the aggressor. Nevertheless Hitler saw fit to declare war on the United States immediately, assuming that in the coming months the Americans would be occupied in the Pacific, and that later a victorious Japan would be able to help him against Russia. Hitler was now at war with three major industrial powers, all superior to Germany in manpower and resources, and they could not be beaten—so every last Jew believed. Edelstein, who had been expecting America to enter the war for months, was convinced that the war had been decided (and in this he was no different from Churchill). In the final analysis, money and resources were what counted, he used to tell Harry Tressler, and in both those respects Hitler stood no chance against the United States. Now we must simply play for time.

Hopes were always pinned to specific dates, both Jewish and Christian: Passover, Rosh Hashanah, Christmas—the New Year would bring redemption. The last day of 1941 was celebrated in one form or another in every hall and room of the barracks. The engineers had even managed to smuggle in a bottle of liquor. Happy New Year! We'll be home before the year is out!

But the new year brought an unexpected blow—transports were to continue, including out of Theresienstadt. All Edelstein's efforts, all his ruses, had been aimed at a single objective: to prevent the Jews of the Protectorate being deported to Poland. The Germans had again broken their promise. Theresienstadt was but a way station, not a city of refuge after all.

German headquarters in Terezin did not draw up the list of transportees, as had been the case in Prague, but merely furnished general guidelines for age groups. Doctors decided who was too ill to be sent; members of the two advance units, A-K 1 and A-K 2, administrative staff, doctors and nurses, were exempt. Otherwise, the leadership accepted the task of selection, perhaps for lack of choice, perhaps in the hope of saving the workers, the young people, the teenagers in the name of a better tomorrow. All night long the transport committee labored over the list, subject to dreadful pressure from people who asked that their friends or their relatives not be included. The responsibility was awesome.

As soon as news of the first transport spread, Gonda and Fredy did everything in their power to ensure that the children would not be sent East; they must be kept at Theresienstadt to pursue their studies, continuing the education they had received in study groups and Youth-Aliyah: "Except that there we led the children to freedom," Gonda wrote, "and here we are trying to save them from death." Since it was decided not to send little children, their families also remained in the ghetto. One mother, however, whose ailing sister was included in the transport, insisted on leaving with her small son. Gonda tried to dissuade her: the winter was hard, the journey long. What did people imagine when they spoke of "the East"? A different type of Theresienstadt, foreign soil, more arduous living conditions in some Russian or Polish wasteland, snow, frost, starvation rations, backbreaking work, no contact with home.

No one imagined any system of organized destruction. People sometimes volunteered for transports in the hope of meeting family members who had preceded them, as if "the East" was a single location. One woman, whose husband had been sent to Nisko and had not returned, volunteered for transport to Riga, hoping to find him there; he, meanwhile, had managed to return to Prague and came to Theresienstadt of his own free will to be with his wife. People who had waited weeks, months, to be reunited with their loved ones sometimes arrived at Theresienstadt to find their son, daughter, parents, brothers, friends, gone—deported; conversely, in the ghetto, equally expectant relatives sometimes found that their families were sent East within a day or two after their arrival, scarcely having managed to say hello.

Conceived as a Jewish city, Theresienstadt was no better than the waiting room in a train station. Every transport, both incoming and outgoing, was labeled with a letter of the alphabet until the letters ran out, after which a combination of letters was used. The first two transports, marked O and P, which left the ghetto on January 9 and 15 respectively, were told that their destination was Riga. Afterward, however, they set out with destination unknown. The first transportees left Terezin before sunrise, in frost 23 degrees below zero, so that the townspeople would not see them, and walked toward Bohušovice along the same road they had traveled so recently; only then they had believed they were coming to a haven. The departure of the first transport cast a dark cloud over the ghetto, and Edelstein was doubly disillusioned: it was not just the Germans who had lied to him; the Czechs, too, had broken their promise. He told Dittl Ornstein and other staff members that President Hacha and the Czech government had explicitly assured him that they would not agree to the deportation of the Protectorate's Jews (correspondence after fall 1941 between the offices of the president and Reichsprotektor attests only to the desire to isolate Jews from the general public).

Lest the incubus of transports prove insufficient, another event took place in early January that shattered all remaining illusions as to the true nature of the Jewish city: a gallows was erected. The proximity of the Czech populace, the desire to make contact with families on the outside, the craving for food parcels, the blue mailboxes on the sidewalks, all constituted an overwhelming temptation to disregard the regulation banning postal contact, and all threats of terrible punishment proved ineffective. Even Edelstein and his colleagues maintained underground contact with Prague via a Czech glazier, a citizen of Terezin. Dittl Ornstein (who initiated a sanitation service among the women and later headed the women's employment department) covered the Jewish star on her coat and under the shield of night crept away with another woman to give the glazier a letter for Kahn and other friends in Prague, depicting the true situation in the ghetto. Kahn is said to have wept when he read it. In mid-December, Seidl and Bergel called an assembly in the Sudeten barracks and announced that a Czech citizen had been caught with smuggled letters and arrested. Those who had sent the letters were asked to step forward and were promised that no harm would come to them. Should they fail to do so, however, everyone would be punished. After a moment's hesitation, two young men stepped forward and were immediately apprehended.

On January 9, Edelstein and Zucker were summoned to the German command, where Seidl informed them that several prisoners had been sentenced to death. The Jewish council was to have a double gallows erected in the Aussig moat by nine o'clock the following morning, and to arrange for twenty-five coffins and some sturdy rope. Edelstein called Josef Klaber, the chief of ghetto police, and told him that ten of his men, including Klaber himself, had to take part in the execution (the police drew lots among themselves to decide who would have to go). During the night, a small team of men dug out flat graves in the frozen ground under the watchful eyes of the SS, while another team erected the gallows. At dawn, Bergel appeared, drunk and raging, and sent for Edelstein: he was to produce two Jews to act as executioners, or he too would be shot. Jakob conferred with Klaber: it was not a job one could order a man to do, but perhaps volunteers could be found among the butchers? Klaber went to the Sudeten barracks: one butcher was only seventeen, another was sixty, one had diabetes and was the father of young children. No one was prepared to volunteer. Finally a butcher named Ada Fischer stepped forward, short and broad shouldered, somewhat reminiscent of a hunchback. He had worked at the pathology institute in Brünn and as an assistant to an executioner. He would do the job. He asked only that a bottle of rum and some chewing tobacco be set aside for him, to help him unwind afterward.

Curfew was imposed on all of Terezin, Czechs and Jews alike. In the freezing cold, nine prisoners were brought to the gallows, including the two who had freely confessed to Seidl. Günther, whose office had issued the execution order, arrived from Prague; Seidl was present, as was the entire Council of Elders, who had been ordered to attend. Seidl read out the sentences: by order of the security police headquarters of Bohemia and Moravia, the following were sentenced to death by hanging for offending German honor. The names included a medical student, a glazier, a traveling salesman, two electricians. Their crimes were: writing a letter requesting a grandmother to send food, removing the Jewish star in order to buy honeycake in a shop—an act interpreted as an attempt at escape—a careless wave of the hand which had inadvertently touched the arm of an SS man. One of the sentenced men asked that his wedding ring be given to his wife; one said, "This won't help you win the war"; one sang Voskovec and Werich's famous song "When we will march by the millions, all against the wind." To one, Bergel said, "Come, coward," and the man replied, "I am innocent, not a coward," after which he put the rope around his own neck. At one point the rope broke and the executioner asked that tradition be followed and the man set free. Seidl refused. The Czech gendarmes who attended the execution were as white as chalk (one secretly operated a camera with his foot so that there would be evidence). Dr. Munk was asked to certify the deaths, and when one of the victims still showed signs of life, he asked Seidl to have him shot so as to end his suffering.

After the execution, the elders of all the rooms were assembled in Bergel's presence, and Edelstein, who had returned from the hangings sick in body and shaken to the depths of his soul, announced, as instructed by the Germans, that the sentences had been carried out. He implored the elders to use all their influence and direct all their energies toward ensuring that German orders were obeyed so that similar tragic incidents would not occur. In their rooms, the Jews lit memorial candles, recited kaddish for the dead, and sat in silence. In the Sudeten barracks, some of the young men got together and listened to readings from Heine's "Passional" in memory of their friends: "Thus will German glory pass from the world." Six weeks later another seven prisoners were put to death in similar circumstances. This time, however, Edelstein refused to attend, and he handed Seidl his resignation as Elder of the Jews. The resignation was not accepted, but for the rest of the war no more executions took place within the ghetto. Fischer, who reminded many of the ghetto's residents of the hunchback of Notre Dame, was hot-tempered though kind: he loved children, and devoted himself to orphans, but the adults spurned his company and whispered behind his back: "Fischer the executioner."

When Edelstein, Zucker, Janowitz, and the others returned from the hangings, they were pale, frozen, and in the grip of black despair. The continuing transports, the hangings, were final proof that the hope of a safe refuge until the end of the war had been a terrible mistake. There was nothing to do but look on helplessly as events overtook them. Yekef was the first to revive: No, he said, we must not succumb! We must save anyone we can, anything we can, we must try to hang on here, compete for work contracts from the Wehrmacht, the Aryan firms, display activity, preoccupy the Germans with statistics and diagrams, *play for time.*

As though to lessen the burden and muster the courage to go on living, the most heartening rumors always seemed to spread at the most difficult times. Right after the hangings news spread that the German army had seized control of the government. A bus failed to arrive from Leitmeritz, and rumor had it that rebellion had broken out in Germany. The rumor was discredited only to be replaced by another: Turkey had entered the war. A very reliable source had seen it in the newspaper with his own eyes. Radios were nonexistent, newspapers were forbidden (at first the German paper *Der Neue Tag* had been posted in public places in the ghetto, but with the failure of the German army in Russia, the practice had been stopped). Most people had no access to information and relied on word of mouth, *j.p.p.* in ghetto slang, the Czech initial letters of the words meaning "a woman said . . ."

Official terminology described the ghetto administration as "self-government," and in accordance with the National Socialist concept of central government, it was built like a pyramid, with one man at the top wielding supreme authority. Even here, in this putrid colony, the idea of the *Führer* was upheld. Accordingly, in German eyes, Edelstein bore full responsibility for what went on in the ghetto. Only he or his assistant was allowed to apply to headquarters on behalf of the residents; it was in his name that legal verdicts were issued, and it was to him that the police swore an oath of loyalty: "I swear by Almighty God to serve the Elder of the Jews to the best of my ability and conscience, fearlessly, faithfully, in body and soul, for the benefit of the Theresienstadt ghetto." The Elder of the Jews determined administrative policy—so long as the Germans did not determine otherwise. Had Edelstein had dictatorial tendencies, he might easily have indulged them in this Lilliputian Jewish kingdom.

But Yekef was a socialist by conviction, and sociable by nature; he lacked the passion for order as a cardinal virtue on which all auto-cratic rule is based. He was endowed with sufficient wisdom and common sense not to see himself as a petty dictator. His leadership was invested with a sense of responsibility for the survival of the Jews of the Protectorate, and he had himself assumed the burden of looking out for their welfare.

Every day, except Sundays, Edelstein reported to headquarters. Seidl sat at one end of his spacious office and kept as much distance as possible between himself and his audience. The Elder of the Jews reported on the state of the ghetto, the number of sick, the progress made on previous instructions; he offered suggestions, made re-quests, handed over letters for the Prague Jewish community. He was informed of transports to come and transports to leave, and when he returned to his office he drew up a memorandum, which bound the Jews but not the Germans, and of which one copy was passed on to the Council of Elders. According to regulations, the twelve-member Council of Elders was empowered to make deci-sions on all aspects of ghetto life, but if need be, the Elder of the Jews and his assistant could decide any matter alone and notify the council afterward. In the feverish pace of ghetto life, this practice was not uncommon.

As had been agreed in Prague, the Council of Elders represented all segments of Protectorate Jewry: Czech Jews, such as Rudolf Bergmann, head of the financial department, Karl Schliesser, head of the economic division, Egon Popper, head of the interior depart-ment; Zionists, such as Rudolf Freiberger, head of productivity, Erich Munk, head of health services, Julius Grünberger, head of the technical department; even the communists had agreed, unlike elsewhere, to share communal responsibilities in Theresienstadt, and were represented by engineer Jiři Vogel. Though the members of the Council of Elders received certain privileges with respect to living quarters, supplies, freedom of movement within the ghetto, and exemption from transports, their true power derived not from their position on the council but from the various departments they ran. Karl Schliesser, head of the economic department, was conse-quently one of the most powerful people in the ghetto, and he was the only one, apart from Edelstein and Zucker, who daily reported to headquarters to clarify practical questions.

All threads came together at the central secretariat. This was the focus of activity, where all written information for the Elder of the

Jews or Council of Elders was transmitted, and where the "order of the day" was decided. Its domain included the administrative department and the transport division, which determined who was to be deported. For the position of general secretary, Edelstein chose Leo Janowitz, who had been his secretary at the Prague Palestine office and assumed its management once Edelstein devoted himself to the affairs of the Prague Jewish community. In Theresienstadt, as in Prague, quiet, introverted Leo, with his long and stately face, who had turned thirty the week he arrived at the ghetto, remained Edelstein's right-hand man and the person closest to him.

Edelstein had to navigate a course not only between Germans and Jews, but also among the various Jewish factions, the petty bureaucrats (with a worm's-eye view, as he described them), and the ambitious schemers. If disputes broke out between the Czech Jews and the Zionists, he would sometimes rule against his own people. "I know you are my friends," he would tell them when they complained. "I must ensure the support of the others." In the eyes of those close to him, it was his chief fault: he was a politician to the core, and they hardly considered that commendable.

20

NOT A SHELTER
BUT A TRANSIT CAMP

ON A GRAY DAY in January, Eichmann, now Obersturmbannführer, arrived at the ghetto. Accompanied by Seidl, he inspected the barracks and found everything in order, and checked and approved the two-story wooden bunk beds that were being installed in the rooms. In response to an appeal from the Elder of the Jews, Eichmann agreed to consider relaxing the postal restrictions, and Edelstein was told that the local command would notify him when and how this was to be done.

When, a month later, permission was finally granted, and for the first time people were officially allowed to send thirty-word postcards, they were baffled, and did not really know what to write. Instructions forbade giving a "distorted view" of ghetto conditions; they were not allowed to criticize the Germans, speak of politics, use code, or draw pictures. They were to confine themselves to family news and greetings. What could one say in thirty words? *How are you? I am fine. I am healthy and working.* Veiled hints for food parcels: *Send regards to Mr. Zucker* [sugar], *Mr. Brot* [bread], *Mr. Fleischer* [meat]. *I kiss you all. Write.* Still, the postcards were a sign of life, an address, leaving the recipients with a feeling of permanence—even when they arrived after the writer had already been deported to the East.

* * *

Eichmann did not prolong his stay at Theresienstadt. He had urgent business in Berlin the next day, January 20, 1942: Heydrich had convened a meeting at the defense ministry's recreation center on the banks of the beautiful Lake Wannsee to discuss the solution to the Jewish question. Present were senior officials of all the organizations connected with the problem—the Ministry of Foreign Affairs, the Ministry of Conquered Eastern Territories, the Ministry of Justice, the Reich Security Head Office, the security police, the Polish General-Gouvernement. A consultation on the overall coordination of the Jewish solution had become pressing, since, for several weeks now, transports were already being sent east from the Reich and the Protectorate. Heydrich had wanted the meeting held in early December, but then the Americans had entered the war, and it had been postponed. Breakfast was served, and later cognac, and all in all Eichmann found it a pleasant, congenial gathering, which adjourned around noon.

Heydrich opened by reviewing what had been done so far with respect to the Jewish problem, and noted with satisfaction that, despite the difficulties, more than half a million Jews had already emigrated from the Reich and the Protectorate. What was more, the Jews themselves had financed emigration, in the form of an emigration tax and donations from Jewish welfare organizations around the world totaling $9.5 million. Another solution was now possible by evacuating the Jews to the East, and had been approved by the Führer. Heydrich stressed that this solution would encompass all of Europe, meaning 11 million Jews, including those in countries not yet conquered, such as England, Spain, Turkey, and Switzerland. Europe would be combed from west to east to implement the final solution, beginning with the Reich territories (which included the Protectorate of Bohemia and Moravia).

To begin with, the evacuated Jews would be brought in convoys to temporary ghettos, from where they would be moved to the East for the final solution. Some of them would also be used for manpower: in long labor gangs, with the sexes separated, those fit for work would be made to build roads on their way eastward. There could be no doubt that many would thereby fall away because of natural "attrition." The rest, undoubtedly those with the greatest resistance, who might constitute a nucleus of Jewish regeneration should they be released, would warrant "special" treatment.

In order for the operation to run smoothly, SS Obergruppen-führer Heydrich added, the population to be evacuated must be clearly defined. Jews over sixty-five were not to be evacuated; they, together with seriously disabled people and highly distinguished veterans of the First World War, would be transported to the ghetto for the old at Theresienstadt. This practical solution would simultaneously avoid a good deal of intervention on behalf of one Jew or another. Of the 280,000 Jews in the Reich (what remained of the pre-1933 population of half a million), about a third was to be evacuated to the ghetto for the elderly.

Heydrich proceeded to consider the problem country by country. He noted that apprehending and evacuating the Jews of occupied France was not likely to pose any hardship, as was true also of Slovakia and Croatia, where the local population had already displayed some of their own initiative in the matter. Assistant Secretary of State Martin Luther, of the German Foreign Office, pointed out that a radical solution to the Jewish question might give rise to various difficulties in certain countries, especially in northern Europe, and that the scheme should perhaps be postponed there. However, since in any case those countries contained relatively few Jews, the delay was of no great consequence. Heydrich then turned his attention to the subject of Jews of mixed descent: who would be part of the final solution, and who would not. He spoke of the need to sterilize all children of mixed descent who were not to be included in the final solution so that they could not reproduce; in this way the problem of mixed descent would vanish forever.

Various questions were raised after Heydrich finished his survey. The officials spoke of the influence of Jewish evacuation on the economy, and the secretary of state of the Ministry of the Interior suggested that those Jews who were necessary to the war economy should not be evacuated until they could be replaced. Heydrich had noted in his report that the final solution was to be in the hands of the Reichsführer of the SS and the chief of police, regardless of administrative jurisdiction. Secretary of State Buhler, representing Frank, the governor general of Poland, said that his government would be happy for the final solution to start in their territory; they had no transportation problem, and very few cases of mixed descent. Furthermore, it was precisely in this region that the Jews posed the greatest danger, carrying disease and wreaking havoc on the country's economy with their black-market dealings. And of the two and a half million Jews who would come under the final solution, very few were in any case fit for work. Buhler suggested that preparations for the final solution be gotten under way immediately in the regions concerned, though care should be exercised to avoid alerting the population. Finally, various forms of the solution were discussed, as noted in the protocol. Since official policy was not to record the subject of annihilation, no further details were committed to paper. Eichmann, who was in charge of the protocol, filled in the details some twenty years later: they discussed diverse practical methods of killing.

After the meeting, Heydrich, Müller, and Eichmann stayed behind for a fireside chat to iron out technical details. The protocol of the Wannsee gathering does not mention the word "death."

Three weeks later, Eichmann summoned ten Jewish representatives to Berlin. They came from Berlin, Vienna, and Prague, and included Löwenherz, Murmelstein, and Weidmann. He wanted to inform them of the expected transports to the East and the new function of Theresienstadt as a ghetto for the elderly. He told them that the town's Aryan population was to be evacuated, and that hospitals and other geriatric institutions were to be built and equipped with trained medical staff. The only young people to remain in the ghetto would be those required to maintain it and to care for the aged. In a conversation with local Gestapo officers, Eichmann was more candid: by the summer, or at least the fall, the state police would be rid of all old Jews, who were to be sent to the ghetto for the elderly at Theresienstadt. Czechs were now being evacuated from the city and between fifteen and twenty thousand Jews from the Protectorate brought in "for the sake of appearances," as Eichmann put it. Edelstein had unwittingly become the elder of a ghetto for the elderly, whose chief purpose was to show the world that only young people were being sent east to work—quite legitimate in wartime. Only a few weeks later did the staff at Theresienstadt learn that Reich citizens might also be coming to the ghetto, chiefly those who had been highly decorated in war.

The basic guidelines as to who was to be sent east, as laid down at the Wannsee Conference, were transmitted through Eichmann to local officials and made public in the "order of the day" at Theresienstadt. At the beginning of March exact instructions were given as to who was entitled to submit a written appeal against inclusion in the transports: spouses of Aryans, foreign citizens (apart from citizens of Poland, Russia, and Luxembourg), war cripples with a disability rating of over 60 percent, people with German decorations of honor, those over sixty-five, families of protected persons ("family" meaning parents and children under sixteen). Anyone who wished to leave for the East with his family was allowed to volunteer. Elderly parents volunteered for transports so as not to be torn from their children, brothers went with sisters, sons with mothers; out of love, out of duty, believing that together it would be easier to endure the trials.

German instructions with respect to the composition of the transports varied from time to time, sometimes changing overnight. Seidl had all the inmates of one of the women's barracks included in a transport for heating a room without permission; but he allowed Edelstein to select two to remain with their families. Edelstein refused to make the choice and left it to the women to decide. At the last minute, however, Seidl ordered the Council of Elders to remove 250 women from the transport and replace them with others. In the dark of night, people who had been sure that this time they had escaped the danger were suddenly roused and told to report for transport within hours. The mattress, the bunk, the roommates, the work team, the napkin and family snapshots on the suitcase at the foot of the bed had so quickly become home.

As the number of transports grew, it became impossible to shield parents of young children from deportation. The children left with their parents, and the instructors argued among themselves as to whether they too should volunteer for the East. After all, the children would require some sort of educational framework there too. And what about the moral issue: should they, as counselors, as Zionists, as members of the first A-K units, be protected from deportation while the young and sick left for an unknown future? But the arguments remained theoretical: in the end, family considerations, and the will to cling to Theresienstadt for as long as possible, prevailed.

In mid-February the first child was born at Theresienstadt and named Thomas, but in the ghetto he was known as "A-K One." The order of the day, mimeographed and distributed to all the elders of the rooms, also served as a family chronicle, faithfully recording every birth and death. Three to five deaths were recorded daily, mostly among the aged. An outbreak of scarlet fever took a few young people, however, before the medical services managed to prevent an epidemic by inoculation. Among the dead was a four-teen-year-old boy whom the youth department had some time back wanted to transfer to a dormitory in a different barracks, but whose father had refused to part with him. "What would have happened had we transferred the boy against his father's will?" Gonda wondered. "The responsibility here is sometimes unbearable."

The first dead were brought to burial in the company of friends and family. In the dark of evening, so that the townspeople would not see, the silent procession moved with flashlights in their hands to a grave dug in the frozen ground, where the dead were interred after the rabbi had recited "Merciful God." But it was not long before this ceremony was prohibited too, and the mourners were allowed to accompany the coffin only as far as the warehouse in the city walls that served as a mortuary. There the relatives stood, leaning on one another, their eyes following the horse-drawn cart with the crudely constructed coffin to the cemetery near the river. At first the dead were buried in separate plots in the moist earth, and later in communal graves. But when the crematorium was completed, "with a capacity for 140 bodies per day, the most efficient in Europe," as the ghetto inmates who had built it boasted (never having heard of more efficient crematoria), the bodies were cremated and the ashes preserved in personal cardboard boxes in a "columbarium."

In the early weeks, Yekef's staff used to sit together in the evenings and talk. Yekef told them that in the spring of 1940 the Germans had asked the Jews to act as mediators to prevent America from entering the war on England's side, but that negotiations had stopped after Germany's overwhelming victory in France. Yekef spoke of the German suggestion to establish a Jewish state in Madagascar, Alaska, or Rhodesia, and of the disputes as to the nature of the state: should it be based on industry or agriculture? He talked of the attitude of the different German classes toward Jews. But those evenings together drew to a close at the end of March, when the wives of the leaders arrived at the ghetto—Miriam Edelstein with her mother and son, Fritzi Zucker, Truda Janowitz, and others. They brought with them a great many things, much more than the allotted fifty kilos, and were spared the anguish of checks and confiscation by the German police.

The families of the Council of Elders and other staff members were housed in separate rooms in the Magdeburg barracks, putting the final seal on the status differences Yekef had tried to prevent. Though the rooms were small and gloomy, though they faced inward toward the hallway and were sparsely furnished, they were noble mansions in the eyes of the ghetto inmates, who lived in crowded, and overcrowded, conditions segregated by sex. A private iron stove, an electric hot plate, chairs, a table with a lamp, a place to hang a picture, a separate bed, a mirror, the chance to be alone—all these were luxuries ordinary inmates could only dream about. Gradually, the Council of Elders received special food allotments and eventually also enjoyed the services of the cleaning staff, who washed their floors, laundered their clothes, and fetched coal from the cellar. The Elder of the Jews, as befitted his station, was accorded a two-room flat with windows looking onto the street. Here Miriam ran her home. Arieh, eleven years old now, long legged and thin, did not join a dormitory but continued to live with his parents, which was why he did not participate in most of the activities arranged for his age group. The other children pestered him with questions: were there really carpets on the floors of his home? Did his family receive different food from the rest of the ghetto? When he tried to answer honestly that it was a simple flat and the food they ate was cooked in the communal kitchen, the children did not believe him. For the most part, Arieh, a clever, lively child, studied at home with private teachers, including a chess tutor and an orthopedics instructor (who came to correct his flat feet).

The barracks became increasingly crowded, until the rooms in the fortress walls, eaten through with damp and moss, were also turned into dwelling sites. The ghetto inmates hoped that conditions would improve with the evacuation of the Czech population from the city, which was announced in February 1942 in an official notice that spoke of the establishment of a closed Jewish settlement and the abolition of the local council. The Jewish leadership conferred on taking charge of the city and dealt at length with every detail of life in the Jewish city as worked out in Prague, as though they did not dwell in the shadow of the omnipotent Germans. Even those who were skeptical about implementing the master plan nevertheless consoled themselves with the thought that once the city became Jewish territory, at least men and women would no longer be separated.

The air was clear and caressing, and the blue silhouettes of the mountains were visible on the horizon. The spring sun made it possible to sit in the barracks yards, relieve the crowdedness, dry the laundry. Darkness was late in falling, frost was no longer irksome, and spirits lifted, chiefly because, despite the transports, the productivity plans had begun to be put into effect—the basis of the ghetto's future existence. After two groups, each consisting of a hundred men, were sent to work in coal mines, a thousand young women were called for forestry work in southern Bohemia in the spring. The work in the Křivoklaty forests was not strenuous, the local population was friendly, the Czech police were not overly watchful, and the women returned to the ghetto after two months looking tanned and healthy, as if they had been on vacation. Perhaps, despite everything, Yekef was right: they had to go on fighting.

Little by little the ghetto administration took over the vegetable gardens, the fields, the livestock from the farms around the city. In addition to performing skilled labor, Hehalutz people also worked in agriculture, to continue their practical training for Palestine. However, apart from its ideological virtues, agricultural work had also tangible advantages: the opportunity to leave the ghetto walls, to work in the open air and the sun, in nature, and though the produce was transferred to the SS, there was always refuse, or apparent refuse, that the workers could share. Generally, the agricultural instructor divided the booty equally among the workers and they smuggled the vegetables back to the ghetto, concealing them inside their shirts or trousers. Private pilfering was frowned upon, but only the most principled could withstand the temptation to take something "on the side," a cucumber or a green onion, outside the framework of organized pilfering. Nobody spoke of theft—taking from the Germans was a virtue. The question was how to take without arousing German suspicions or getting caught.

Work was the basis of life, and not merely for Zionist reasons. Production for the war economy could still avert transportation; a vital job could save a life. Within a few weeks of the evacuation of the German army, the *Bauhof* or workshop yard was already operating a metalworks, a carpentry shop started producing beds, and a glazier's shop and paint shop opened up; workshops were begun for shoemaking, dressmaking, and bookbinding. The daily orders called for experts in raising silkworms, milling flour, upholstery, artificial-flower production, ceramics, hairdressing, graphics, raising dogs, and manufacturing synthetic rubber. Sometimes the Germans initiated the call for specialists, viewing the ghetto as an extensive workshop ready to fill their personal orders.

As soon as they arrived, able-bodied newcomers were assigned to the "hundred units," groups of unskilled laborers who did menial jobs. The women were assigned to the *Putzkolonne*, the cleaning division of pails and brooms which in the course of time created its

own subculture. The men pushed hearses, brought from the liquidated Jewish communities at Zucker's suggestion. The hearses were
the chief means of transportation. They delivered bread and potatoes, and drove the elderly to the disinfection center. One hearse
was proudly marked YOUTH DEPARTMENT. Working hours varied
with the seasons, from seven or eight in the morning until five or
seven in the evening, with an hour or two for lunch. Since February
the official day of rest had been Saturday; for many ghetto residents, this was the first time in their lives that they had experienced
the Jewish Sabbath as such, and not as a prelude to Sunday. For
Edelstein, rest was a matter of principle. When his staff worked day
after day, hour after hour, without break, especially during the
initial period, he would stop them and say, "Enough. A man needs
to rest. If we don't rest, if we don't make time to think, we will cease
to be human."

The constant traffic—in the middle of the first year 29,000 people arrived at the ghetto and 14,000 were deported to the East—
sabotaged all production plans: since by German order the elderly
were protected from transport, it was sometimes necessary to send
vital workers instead. Because of the increasing shortage of manpower, people over sixty also worked, as did youngsters over fourteen. They worked as agricultural laborers and as apprentices to
metalworkers, carpenters, and electricians.

City by city, region by region, Bohemia and Moravia were purged
of Jews. Kladno, Budweis, Brünn. The Jews of Moravská Ostrava
were evacuated in four transports in a single month. Two women
ran away before the first transport, and were caught; two others,
inmates of the Jewish home for the aged, Shulamit Vulkan, aged
seventy-seven, and her daughter Miriam, aged forty-nine, took their
own lives. Before the second transport, Susanne Altmann's parents
hid the fourteen-year-old girl in one of the neighboring villages, but
she too was found by the Germans within two days. These were the
only incidents reported by the local police. One hundred and fifty
years of Jewish residence in Mährisch Ostrau, as it was originally
called, drew to an end; the town was once again free of Jews.

The evacuation of Brünn's Jews, the second largest Jewish community in the Protectorate, was conducted by Anton Burger, whom
Eichmann had brought from the Zentralstelle in Vienna. A teacher
by profession, a veteran SS man with cold eyes, Burger, like many of
Eichmann's underlings, was Austrian and hated the Czechs no less
than the Jews. Unlike his superior, however, he was fond of violence.

The transportees assembled at Brünn's former synagogue, and the trains had to pull out of the station in the small hours to avoid attention. Suitcases had been checked by the Germans and were being distributed by community workers to the passengers on the train according to their personal transport number. The distribution took a little too long, and departure was delayed. The hefty Burger shrieked, *"Eine Scheissordnung!"* ("What a screwup!") and slapped Leopold Drucker, the engineer in charge of the technical arrangements, until he fainted. The scene was repeated before every transport left. Burger discovered that Drucker, the former chairman of the Brünn arm of Maccabi and a long-standing Zionist, used to smuggle valuables into his friends' luggage after it had passed inspection. Drucker and three other community workers were immediately arrested and taken to Brünn's Gestapo prison, and a few days later left with the regular night transport from Brünn to Terezin. They traveled in a separate compartment, and the police escort was instructed to transfer them to the concentration camp in the small fortress. During the journey the German police drank themselves into a stupor with the liquor they had confiscated from the Jews, and the four prisoners managed to unlock the door of their compartment and mingle with the other transportees.

When the transport arrived at Bohušovice, Edelstein was there to greet it, as he did every transport. Drucker knew Edelstein well from Zionist activities of old, and he quickly told him why he had been sent. Since Drucker and the other three did not appear on the list of transportees, they never officially arrived at the ghetto. Edelstein instructed the records department not to register them in the files: and so, according to the records, they never existed.

Absorption procedures became more or less routine. Seidl usually informed the Elder of the Jews a few days in advance of an expected transport, but sometimes Edelstein learned of the new shipment only as the train pulled into Bohušovice. The passengers poured out into the commotion of the railway station, physically and emotionally drained, bewildered, the elderly often dazed. Awaiting them were Czech police in green uniforms, Jewish police in train-conductor caps, the SS—including Seidl, who met every transport—Edelstein and the Council of Elders, transportation workers who had come to unload the cargo, and transport administrative staff, including friends or relatives who had managed to wheedle a one-time pass out of Leo Janowitz at the secretariat to come and greet their acquaintances, primarily in order to try to save their luggage from being confiscated.

The Germans urged everyone on: *"Schnell! Schnell!"* ("Quick! Quick!"). Dr. Reines, the Jewish transport physician, decided who could walk to the ghetto and who needed to ride. Transportation was provided on trucks, or platforms towed by tractors, driven by the SS "kindergarten." Arranged in groups of four, the procession set out, the marchers clutching their hand luggage as if it were a lifeline. They were followed by a truck, or "garbage-collector," as the Germans called it, which picked up all the stragglers. While the sight of the ghetto inmates at the railway station was on the whole reassuring—they looked healthy, their heads had not been shaved, they wore ordinary clothes—the entrance into the ghetto itself was forbidding. The Germans imposed a curfew whenever a transport arrived, and the newcomers were marched through deserted streets, here and there catching a glimpse of ghostly shadows behind the windows. Nor was the absorption station any less intimidating.

In ghetto language the depot was called *"die Schleuse,"* meaning "sluice" or "lock." It is not clear whether this was a legacy from Theresienstadt of old, when the moats could be flooded with river water by opening sluices, or whether the Nazis coined the term. Whatever the case, among the Jews the word *Schleuse* became a euphemism for pilfering, and from it derived an entire family of words connected with the art of pinching. Theft was a legal concept only to the authorities. To the ghetto inmates, it was *schleusen*.

The absorption depot was moved from time to time. But for the most part it was located in the damp, dark, subterranean dungeons of the ghetto walls, where new arrivals spent two or three days on soiled floors, waiting for all the procedures—chief of which was plundering—to be completed. After the SS warned the newcomers against hiding money or jewelry, people turned them over voluntarily. Then came the luggage check by Czech gendarmes, sometimes followed by a body check. The women were examined by repulsive German females from nearby Leitmeritz, called *berushky* (beetles) in ghetto language. Every article of value on the official list of contraband was confiscated the moment it was spotted: tobacco, contraceptives, soap, toilet paper. Every transport numbering a thousand people enriched the Germans by several crates of loot weighing hundreds of pounds. Nor did the Czech police leave empty-handed. As for the Jews who worked in the *Schleuse*, they were not above pilfering either: after all, he who steals from a thief is exonerated. By the time the luggage returned to its owners, if it returned at all, it contained only a pitiful remnant of all the articles that had been prepared with so much care, so much thought and deliberation. It took some time to recover from the shock of this loss.

In the summer of 1942, the procedures were simplified: the Germans confiscated everything apart from hand luggage. The junk remained in the ghetto to be distributed; the rest was transferred to the Germans through the Zentralstelle. One of the delightful tasks of the "beetles" was to carry out surprise inspections of the women's quarters. Usually they came while the women were at work and the rooms empty, ostensibly to confiscate prohibited articles. But in fact they took anything that caught their fancy, turned the rooms upside down, mixed up everyone's belongings, spilled sugar, smeared margarine on underwear. Day after day these charming beauties in their greenish uniforms returned to Leitmeritz, laden with parcels. The Council of Elders complained that the beetles were stealing, and Seidl ordered a search of their homes. They were caught red-handed with a good many items belonging to ghetto inmates, including stockings, soap, and alarm clocks, and were tried and sentenced to eighteen months' imprisonment. The verdict did not enrich the ghetto residents, but it made the beetles' successors learn to steal with more discretion.

Permission to enter the *Schleuse* was restricted to those who worked there, the Elder of the Jews and Council of Elders, doctors, and senior employees. Nevertheless, old-timers had their means of gaining access to the *Schleuse* to console friends and relatives: only the beginning was terrible, they said, later everything worked out— so long as one managed to avoid transport to the East. The newcomers all hoped for a miracle: because of their profession, because of relatives who had meanwhile established themselves in the ghetto, because of former connections, friendship with Edelstein, with Zucker, with Schliesser or other ghetto notables. They were registered in the general files and in the employment index, assigned a job and a room, apportioned ration slips, and finally set free—in the ghetto.

Since all life's pleasures—from a moment stolen with one's family to playing the harmonica—were prohibited, existence became a series of attempts to get around rules and regulations. Arrests proved ineffective; time and again people were caught smoking, maintaining contact with the city's non-Jewish population, or smuggling out letters. In a special order of the day, the Council of Elders appealed to the ghetto in an "urgent last warning," the result of a rise in infractions which had elicited a sharp response from the authorities. Furthermore, the council had only recently succeeded, after a great deal of effort, in freeing many prisoners and protecting them from severe punishment: "The Council of Elders will not allow this achievement to be lost because of irresponsible behavior on the part of individuals, and it will therefore take serious steps against anyone who defies the regulations, regardless of his position. The tasks before the Council of Elders are becoming more and more difficult, the working conditions more and more complicated; every disturbance, every setback rocks the organization and life of the entire ghetto. The Council of Elders therefore calls on all residents to behave with the utmost discipline and warns each and every person that terrible consequences are to be expected should this last warning fall on deaf ears."

The ears were not deaf, perhaps, but the will of the heart and belly spoke louder still. When the SS caught one of the Jewish policemen with a large quantity of smuggled letters, a total ban was put on mail again, including the thirty-word postcards. On May 14, in the yard of the Magdeburg barracks, Seidl disbanded the ghetto police and replaced it (temporarily) with an "order guard." The force consisted of fifty men whose distinguishing mark was a yellow armband; no more were they to be equipped with caps and wooden clubs, the symbol of *die Ghettowache*.

Again, people with contraband were pardoned through Seidl's kind offices if they turned in all prohibited articles within a week. These included not only those items in which the Germans might see the spark of an underground operation, such as money, stamps, cigarettes, jewelry, cameras, various drugs and medicines, but, surprisingly enough, also toothpaste, perfume, and hair conditioner. Sometimes the Council of Elders managed to persuade people with contraband to make a symbolic sacrifice and turn in a portion of their treasures, so as not to antagonize the Germans. In such cases, the goods were handed over anonymously through the elders of the buildings as at least partial proof of vigorous confiscatory activity. For this time Seidl had threatened not only severe punishment for even the slightest delinquent, but far-reaching consequences for the ghetto as a whole. He had in mind banning the activities of the youth department, knowing full well that this was where the ghetto leadership, and Edelstein in particular, was most sensitive.

In the children's dormitories life followed the Jewish calendar: for Purim the children prepared a program of fun—chiefly a satire on ghetto conditions. A fete was held, skits were performed, and popular songs sung—much to the dismay of Gonda, who was delighted when someone started singing "Hatikvah" and everyone followed suit. On the 11th of Adar, Gonda gave a talk on Trumpeldor, and on the eve of Passover, a seder was held in all the children's rooms and dormitories. For many of the children this was the first time they had celebrated Passover in the traditional manner, with a festive meal and the reading of the *Haggadah*, the story of the Israelite exodus from Egypt. The Czech Jews sometimes objected to the fact that the children of both Zionists and non-Zionists were receiving a Jewish rather than a Czech national education. But what upset them most was the preferential treatment enjoyed by Zionists and the degree of influence exerted by the "Shalom" people, as they were called. It was enough to greet someone with *shalom*, the saying went, for favoritism to be shown in assignment to rooms and jobs, and in protection from transports.

Even though the ghetto did not know what purpose had been set aside for Theresienstadt, it was clear that it was not a shelter for the Jews of Bohemia and Moravia. In April the ghetto was seriously weakened: orders came to prepare six transports that month, and the leadership, which composed the lists, faced enormous difficulties. In order to safeguard at least the nuclear family of parents and young children, there was no choice but to include the relatives of experts, professionals, and administrative staff, who until now had been protected from deportation. "The Council of Elders is well aware of the great pain it is causing the entire staff by taking this step, but it hopes that they will understand the unavoidable necessity," the order of the day stated, signed by Leo Janowitz.

Represented in the transport committee, which decided the final list of transportees, were the Council of Elders, the general secretariat, and all the departments. The departments competed with one another, often bitterly, to get their people excluded from transports, each claiming that they constituted the most vital sector of manpower. Every council member was permitted to submit thirty names of people close to him whom he wished protected from transport. The fate of all others was decided by chance, pressure, or good luck. The committee deliberated over the preparation of every transport list day and night in room 118 of the Magdeburg barracks, while the members, red-eyed from lack of sleep and ashen-faced with weariness, weighed each and every appeal. Every list was compiled again and again following appeals and last-minute changes; some names were removed, others were added, and new appeals submitted.

The most common grounds for appeal were illness, especially a high temperature, consideration of past activities in wartime or in the community, being of mixed descent, and working in vital jobs. The health department asked that nurse Elsa Kerner be excused, the agricultural department intervened on behalf of Hermann Epstein, one of the top wagon drivers. Every department head had to sign an affidavit stating that all his appeals had just cause and that he knew full well that the penalty for falsifying grounds was evacuation.

Among the hundreds of documents in the file was the record of a telephone call from SS Obersturmbannführer Bergel, the camp commandant, asking that Ladislav Deutsch, born 1896, and Milos Vogel, born 1911, be included in the transport, and that headquarters receive confirmation by phone.

> Paul Meyer attests that he was seriously wounded in World War I and attaches a photograph showing him decorated with all the honors he received for service in the Austro-Hungarian army.

> The youth department requests that Lili and Walter Furth, aged eight and ten, whose father was executed, be struck off the transport list.

> Josefina Marmorstein declares that her two daughters are married to Aryans, one to a Sudeten German, and their children are being raised as Aryans.

> Harry Glassner, aged fifteen, and his sister Herta, aged seventeen, request that their grandmother, Hermina Reich, be removed from the transport: "Our parents died at Auschwitz and we have only our grandmother to take care of us."

> Herbert Furst appeals to Eng. Zucker, thanks him for having saved him from transport when he was caught with cigarettes, and again asks his protection in removing his seventy-year-old father from the transport.

> George Wachtel volunteered for transport because his mother was to be sent. Now his mother has been taken out and he asks to be removed as well.

It is asked that Lotta Salus, who set up the youth department in the Prague community, be removed from the transport (Yekef's list).

The transport committee and the Council of Elders despaired: out of nineteen thousand inmates, about eight thousand were protected by German orders—people over sixty-five, the members of the two advance units A-K 1 and A-K 2, external laborers and their immediate families. Which meant that of the remaining eleven thousand, almost every second inmate had to be sent, even the old-timers, those "on whose heads the water had dripped down" that difficult winter, as they were wont to recall; those who had settled into their jobs and managed to carve out for themselves a niche they called home in the ghetto. The ghetto was small, almost everyone had some connection among the leaders, a friend, an acquaintance, and the pressure exerted on them was enormous. Because of the madcap pace of shipping out one thousand people every two days, people sometimes left on transports within hours of being called, with no chance to retrieve their luggage from the central warehouse, no opportunity to bid friends and relatives farewell. The ghetto never went to sleep. Contrary to the normal blackout rule, spotlights now illuminated the barracks yards, focused glaringly on people packing, people running, people leaving with bundles. Porters worked day and night in the warehouses and at the train station, and over everything hung Seidl's nervousness: Eichmann was expected, and he feared his fury at the chaos and the one- or two-day delays in transports.

Seven thousand people were deported in April; three thousand in May. The departure of thousands of people, mostly young, healthy, and optimistic, who often took leave of their friends in the manner of Schweik and Vodička—"See you at six o'clock after the war"— posed a severe manpower problem for the ghetto, even in those fields of production which had only recently opened. In place of those who left now came the first Jews from the Reich, including a large group of women whose husbands had been arrested after a fire broke out at the "Soviet Paradise" exhibit (aimed at showing the Germans how low the Russian standard of living was). Five Jews had been involved in the arson, as Eichmann informed the representatives of the Vienna, Berlin, and Prague Jewish communities, ushered in to see him after having been made to stand for hours facing a wall. Five hundred German Jews were arrested, half of whom were shot on the spot, the other half sent to concentration camps. Their wives and children were transferred to Theresienstadt without knowing what had happened to their husbands. Here, in the yard of the Cavalier barracks, which was the arrival and departure station for transports, Seidl informed them bluntly that their husbands had been found morally guilty of the fire and had been shot. As a special kindness, the women were to be permitted to remain in the ghetto.

During the last days of May there was suddenly an increase in traffic on the highway from Leitmeritz. Hundreds of SS vehicles raced along the road from the Reich to Prague. There were no newspapers or radios, and conversation with the Aryan population was forbidden. Nevertheless, the ghetto learned within a few hours that an attempt had been made on the life of Reichsprotektor Reinhard Heydrich.

Heydrich had moved with his wife and three children from the Hradčany Castle to an estate in Panenska Brezany, a French-style castle that had once belonged to the Viennese Jew Baron Bloch-Bauer. Heydrich made the fifteen-mile trip to and from Prague almost every day. His Mercedes was open in fine weather, and the only bodyguard was his hefty driver. Unlike Hitler, Himmler, and Goering, who were always surrounded by a bevy of bodyguards and rode in armored cars with bulletproof windows, Heydrich sneered at the possibility of assassination—particularly in the Protectorate, among Czechs, who, in his view, were gutless. In keeping with his methods of breaking and subjugating, the policy of carrot and stick, his initial reign of terror was followed by a period of calm, aimed at mollifying the Czechs. Heydrich distributed shoes to employees of the Škoda factory, increased the size of employee meals in other large factories, received farming delegations at Hradčany, and confiscated food from black-market dealers. Czech radios and newspapers were full of praise for the beneficent Protektor.

More and more, the Czech government-in-exile in London felt that the Czechs were moving toward collaboration, and that unlike other occupied nations—the French, the Norwegians, the Danes—they had initiated very little underground activity. The decision to carry out a daring exploit that would go down in Czech history, even if it invited further repression from the Germans, was taken in the fall of 1941. After Christmas, Jan Kubiš and Josef Gabčik, two members of the Czech underground who had been trained as agents in England, were parachuted into the Protectorate. The local Czech underground, the "Central Committee for Opposition from Home," opposed the plan to liquidate Heydrich for fear that it would lead to mass murder. The underground was connected with the West (the communists operated separately) and was in daily radio contact with London; it suggested that the Czech propaganda minister, a major collaborator, be killed instead. But Beneš was adamant, and in the middle of May final instructions were given to assassinate Heydrich himself.

After lengthy surveillance, the conspirators decided that the most propitious site for the job was in the Prague suburb of Holešovice, where streetcar tracks, the sudden incline toward the banks of the Vltava, and the sharp corner forced all cars to reduce their speed to a minimum. On May 27, Heydrich was to fly to Berlin, and as a result he reached Prague an hour later than usual. As the car approached, one of the conspirators signaled with his whistle and Gabčik tried to fire the sten gun that he had hidden under his raincoat. But the safety catch stuck. His friend Kubiš threw a grenade into the open vehicle, and the two men tried to escape between the moving streetcars. Heydrich jumped out of the car and opened fire at his fleeing assailants, missing by inches. He emptied his cartridge, and then a sudden change came over him: his face turned gray and his legs failed him. A passing bakery van drove him to the Bulovka hospital. There it appeared that steel splinters, leather, and horsehair from the car had lodged in his spinal cord.

Terror descended on the Protectorate. Frank imposed a curfew; all restaurants and amusement sites were closed. A state of emergency was announced and roadblocks set up everywhere. Approximately ten thousand Czechs were arrested, mostly from the intelligentsia, and of these about a hundred, including several well-known writers and scientists, were shot immediately. Thousands of SS and police participated in a massive search for the assailants. Anyone found in a flat where he was not registered was instantly arrested and sent to a concentration camp, to the Little Fortress in Theresienstadt, or executed. Many Jews in hiding were caught, and according to lists the Gestapo had at its disposal, members of Hashomer Hatzair, who had connections with the communist underground, were arrested the day after the assault and put to death at Auschwitz. A reward of one million crowns was offered for information leading to the capture of the assailants, and the

Gestapo received over a thousand reports, mostly from Czechs. Heydrich fought for his life with supreme willpower but finally succumbed to infection on June 4.

The inmates of Theresienstadt learned of Heydrich's death from the lowering of the flag over SS headquarters, and they were filled with fear. In an act of vengeance, the transport marked AAH, consisting of one thousand Jews, including 113 children from Bohemia's provincial towns, was shipped directly to the East instead of to Theresienstadt. The train stopped at the Bohušovice station for a few moments, but the passengers, who had all hoped for a meeting with relatives from the ghetto, were not allowed to disembark. The train pulled out toward the unknown, and the women shed bitter tears (the passengers of the penal transport were all killed, save one who jumped the train and survived). That same day, Seidl ordered thirty young men to travel to Lidice, a small village a few hours away. The men were equipped with spades and pickaxes and escorted by two policemen. An example was to be made of Lidice because one of the villagers was serving in the British army, and all the others were suspected of harboring the parachutists from England. The men of Lidice were all shot, every last one of them; the women were sent to concentration camps, their children taken from them and sent to Lodz. The ghetto men had to dig a pit to bury the 173 dead. They worked a day and a half without food, without rest, under Seidl's personal supervision, at night by firelight from burning furniture, until all the bodies were buried and covered with lime. The SS meanwhile got drunk and had themselves a cookout from food found in the village. Only the sheep, goats, and geese of Lidice survived and were transferred to the care of the agricultural department at Theresienstadt. Together with the young shepherdesses from the pioneering movements, they added a pastoral note.

That same week, on June 16, 1942, all ghetto inmates, including children, were assembled in the barracks yards, shown pictures of a raincoat, a briefcase, and a bicycle, and asked if they could identify these items. Officially the ghetto people had no knowledge of the assault on Heydrich's life or of his death; nor did they know that the items they were shown had been found at the scene of the crime. They signed a paper that they knew nothing, and only a few old women thought the briefcase might once have belonged to them. The mass killings, and the threat that anyone harboring the conspirators would be shot, together with his family, were effective. One of the parachutists turned himself in; the Germans apprehended the other conspirators in the cellar of the Greek Orthodox Church following information received. They were all killed in a shoot-out with the SS. The Czech underground never recovered from the deathblow it suffered after Heydrich's murder, and for the rest of the war there were no more attempts at rebellion in the Protectorate. Heydrich's widow continued to live at the Panenska Brezany estate, where fifty Jews were steadily employed as agricultural laborers. Approximately 23,000 people paid with their lives for Heydrich's death.

21

KING OF THE JEWS

THE EVACUATION committee, comprised of government and municipal representatives, was to expedite the speedy departure of Terezin's Czech population and the transfer of property to the emigration fund. Nevertheless, despite the pressure, the Czechs were in no hurry to leave. Final departure was delayed by two months, and the last of the Czechs left the city only at the end of June 1942. Street names were eliminated and replaced by letters (L for those running lengthwise, Q for cross streets), as is proper in a ghetto, and houses were numbered ordinally. On July 2, the city was officially handed over to the Jews, and four days later, on a stifling summer day, the ghetto rejoiced. It was a thrilling day, filled with excitement and expectation. The Czech gendarmes, who had guarded the barrack gates since the ghetto opened, left in the afternoon, and at 6 P.M. the gates were opened. The inmates were free, free in the small enclave inside the walls. The general feeling, however, was of liberation from prison.

For the first time since November the SS were no longer a regular sight, though, like evil spirits, they still appeared from time to time for surprise inspections. Once an SS driver intentionally ran down and killed an old woman. Once an old man tried to block the blows he had invited by failing to lift his hat and was shot. Another man, Pollak, was shot to death by one of the leaders of the SS "kindergarten" because he refused to release the platform pin from the tractor, a service that passersby were obliged to provide. But most of

286

the ghetto residents had no contact with the Germans, which only reinforced their sense of living in a walled and sheltered haven. People still required a police escort to leave the walls, except for those few who worked in agriculture or transportation, and the Council of Elders, who were issued special permits.

Order and traffic were now in the hands of the Jewish police, and the Council of Elders enjoyed more extensive authority. Night exit permits bore Edelstein's signature and no longer required the consent of the German command. On the day that the gates were opened and the residents walked about in a daze, the Council of Elders issued a moving appeal, urging them to behave with consideration, to put the general good above personal interests, to display maturity, to comply with rules and regulations, to familiarize themselves with, and adapt to, the prevailing circumstances, for the future of the entire ghetto depended on it: and also to maintain high standards of cleanliness in the rooms and on the streets and thereby ensure reasonable living conditions for 40,000 residents.

Even within the small area between the walls, there were still places closed to Jews: the city square and church, command headquarters, the SS club, the policemen's homes, two public parks, the main highway to Prague. But it scarcely mattered. One could now take a walk, indeed walk on pavement, breathe fresh air, meet friends, visit family in their rooms after work. In the evening, couples could meet, parents could be with children; they could sit on a mattress, spread out a napkin, and share a meal prepared from all the hoarded treasures: the potato grandma had gleaned while peeling in the kitchen, the cucumber the daughter had brought back from the garden, the spoonful of beet jam allotted as an incentive for laborers doing strenuous work, the soup made from the concentrate from home, prepared by mother in the small common kitchens in the dormitories. Life suddenly took on a fresh flavor; there was something to look forward to, a reason to mop the floor and wear a clean shirt. At first the visits were limited to three hours, from six in the evening until curfew at nine. But soon all daytime restrictions were lifted and a morning meeting, when the rooms were almost empty, had a special charm to it, reminiscent of the privacy of home.

Each tier of the three-level bunks installed in most of the dormitories had its own advantages and disadvantages. Those on the bottom level could sit fairly comfortably on the narrow bench adjoining the side of the bed and use the bed as a table. They also enjoyed easier access to the toilets. On the other hand, they were smack in the middle of everyone's comings and goings. The topmost level offered much more privacy, and more room to keep belongings or hang ornaments on the wall; and one could sit upright. But the bedbugs also preferred the warmth of the upper level, and on summer nights often forced the upstairs tenants into the yard, to sleep under the open sky. The middle tier, which was at eye level, was akin to a balcony at a free theater: one could watch all the activity while lying down, keep tabs on what everybody did or brought. But because the space between the levels was only about two feet high, it was impossible to sit up on the mattress.

The Czechs had left not a single portable item in the homes they evacuated—primarily to get back at the Germans—and sometimes they had even gone so far as to rip the electric wires out of the walls. Nevertheless, the houses filled up very quickly, and kitchens, storerooms, and shops all became living quarters. Like other labor teams, the members of Hehalutz and the youth movements were allowed to live together, segregated by sex: fifty girls in a three-room flat that had previously housed a single family seemed spacious quarters compared to the barracks. It was an extension of training, of the pioneer hostels, the youth-movement dormitories of the past. One could sing, chat, hold parties, help one's companions. A laundry worker could arrange for her friend's linen to be washed before her once-in-six-weeks turn came up; a carpentry employee could "obtain" boards for shelves; a cook could bring back potatoes and meat-flavored sauce to share with her roommates; and the artistically inclined could adorn the walls. In the women's dormitories, housewives used sheets to sew curtains as a screen for shelves and hanging space, and hung photographs on the walls above the beds. Their personal territory was a private domain, imbued with a sense of home: if only they were not asked to leave now, when life was becoming more bearable, when they could breathe, sit together, and listen to poetry, despite a grumbling belly. One summer evening, Pavel Friedmann, or "Pavliček," as he was called on Hehalutz training, noted for his prominent nose, sensitive soul, and two left hands, read his friends a new poem called "The Butterfly":

> It was the last one, the very last,
> And so content, bitter and bright—
> Which, perhaps, somewhere in the gleam of sunbeam on
> white rock

Seems yellow,
And it spread its wings and upward
Flew to kiss my world's end.

Seven weeks now
That I'm here—
"Ghettoized"—
Here my dear ones found me.
Here too the dandelion beckons,
And the chestnut in white bloom extends its hand,
But I have seen no butterfly here.
That was the last, the very last.
For butterflies don't live in ghettos.

Perhaps more than anyone else, Dr. Erich Munk, the former Youth-Aliyah physician who now headed the health services, was impatient for the Czechs to evacuate. At last he could open a nursery, set up homes for the blind and the elderly, add more clinics. Dr. Munk, proud, meticulous, quick-witted, and endowed with a boundless capacity for work—a man whose reason rather than emotions lighted his way—sometimes came into fierce conflict with Edelstein, opposing, criticizing, and accusing. When Dr. Munk first arrived at the ghetto with fourteen other doctors, he found nothing there: no beds, no mattresses, no clinic. The first sheets for the sick were contributed by inmates from the few they had brought from home. The first operation—an amputation necessitated by gangrene—was performed in a bathroom, using a carpenter's saw. The medical team started with no tools or supplies, but with an abundance of knowledge and skills, blessed with well-known hematologists, pathologists, surgeons, and internists, who had all been sent there.

Little by little equipment began to arrive from Jewish hospitals in the Protectorate which had been shut down, and from community property. Subject to German approval, the ghetto department at Prague's Jewish community office, under Richard Friedmann, was allowed to supply Theresienstadt with vital equipment, taken from the community warehouses or purchased elsewhere. Wagonloads of straw were sent to the ghetto, thousands of mattresses, food, tools, furniture, and large quantities of medicine. Jewish doctors and pharmacists still on the outside combed Bohemia and Moravia, buying up whatever drugs they could, often illegally. Occasionally they managed to procure dry morphine cubes for the operating theater and smuggle them into the ghetto. On the whole the Germans were relatively liberal with the health department, if only because they feared the spread of epidemics to the general population. Dr. Munk was allowed to leave the ghetto in search of drugs in the neighboring towns, and all medicines confiscated from personal stock were transferred to the central pharmacy, where they were sorted and adapted to ghetto purposes. There was still a constant shortage of drugs, because of the high rate of illness.

Despite the claims of favoritism, despite the resentment people felt that their loved ones had been deported while those with pull (perhaps they themselves) remained at Theresienstadt, despite the hatred and jealousy that flared up so easily and were sometimes overwhelming (as in all closed communities), on the whole the attitude of the residents to Edelstein was positive. They believed that he did the best he could on their behalf. Though Edelstein had been appointed by the Germans and his function as Elder of the Jews was to pass on German instructions, the ghetto inmates, regardless of political affiliation, never saw him as a German lackey. He represented them to the Germans and there was sufficient evidence (even from the Czech police) that he did so courageously and wisely, as far as was humanly possible.

Yekef never behaved high-handedly, as did various petty officials whose sudden power went to their heads. In the streets he greeted people readily rather than out of a sense of duty. Always warm, always courteous, he would stop to chat with acquaintances even when he was preoccupied with more pressing matters and could not give them his undivided attention. In Theresienstadt, as in the past, he enjoyed speaking at popular forums, before workers, Zionists, and young people, and even when he avoided meaningful issues, for fear of German ears, particularly at larger gatherings, his talks still contained a grain of hope.

There was nothing in his appearance, his behavior, his home, or his way of life that showed any abuse of the privileges of his position for personal gain—and in this area, the eyes of the residents were very sharp indeed. His two-room flat was modestly furnished and its door was always open. People came and went at all hours of the day and night, in sharp contrast to the tranquillity of his assistant's flat. Zucker had a piano and a fine collection of objets d'art, and his home served as a salon for artists and musicians, people he could feel close to—whether because of his function as head of the cultural department, his own tastes in music and art, or his temperament as a cultured and worldly man. He held chamber-music concerts in his flat, usually on Saturday afternoons, which Edelstein rarely attended. Privately, Edelstein complained of the grating sounds emanating from Zucker's violin when he practiced in the evenings for a concert in which he was to play alongside top professional musicians, a collaboration inspired not so much by his virtuosity as a violinist, perhaps, as by the position he filled and the protection he offered performers. They had to go underground to play their instruments, and they longed for a safe and quiet corner.

Cultural activities had begun spontaneously with an improvised party to celebrate the meeting of friends from the first two transports, A-K 1 and A-K 2. It was held in one of the rooms of the Sudeten barracks during the first month of the ghetto's existence. There was little difficulty in organizing entertainment: among the laborers were poets, actors, musicians, and directors, and the program included songs, skits, and jazz. The orchestra consisted of an accordion, a harmonica, and a recorder (smuggled into the ghetto in defiance of the general ban on musical instruments), augmented by a washbasin which substituted for a drum. The party was a huge success and was followed by two more. There was an evening of readings, including poems by Heine and ballads by Villon, two poets who had also been excommunicated and knew how to laugh at despair. The first cabaret sprang up, founded and managed by Karl Švenk, the sad clown par excellence, the kind of artist who could do everything: write the lyrics, compose the tunes, direct, and play the leading role. Švenk had started his career in the Club of Wasted Talent in Prague, and the cabaret he built up reflected all the irony, all the mockery, all the distortion of ghetto life. It also gave Theresienstadt its anthem: "Everything goes if there's a will," which ended with the belief that "tomorrow a new life starts, we'll pack up our bundles and go home, and laugh on the ruins of the ghetto."

At first it was all improvised, the result of personal initiative and psychological exigency, propelled by the need to master despondency and build up resistance, to affirm life and overcome "despite everything." Cultural activities helped drown one's sorrows, preserve one's human form, bridge the gap between the past and the present, find an outlet for creativity. It was all done without the knowledge of the Germans, or rather with their silent consent. After a few weeks of separate improvisations (since the women were cut off from the men, they started their own activities, set up a choir, and began rehearsals for *Black Lace*, a Jewish play written in Prague in 1760), the Jewish leadership decided to coordinate the cultural activities under the neutral auspices of the buildings administration, headed by Fredy Hirsch, and to camouflage its functions by appointing a young rabbi director. The rabbi, Erich Weiner, was responsible for both prayers and leisure activities. He was given half a desk, a chair, and a pencil in Fredy's office, and Fredy took him on a tour of the barracks, introducing him to the people he deemed suitable for taking an active hand in cultural affairs. All were experienced in artistic fields but totally ignorant of Jewish matters, much to the rabbi's dismay—a situation typical of the Protectorate's Jews. For the most part, the *Freizeitgestaltung* (free time planning), as the cultural activities were called in the ghetto, drew on the general treasures of European culture among which the Jews lived and created before the deluge.

Rehearsals took place at the end of an arduous day's work and as a result were few and short. There was a shortage of musical scores and literary texts (one of the first performances was built around pieces from Chekhov's one-act plays, due largely to the fact that Vava Šenova, a young professional actress, remembered them by heart). The performances were sometimes interrupted when warning was received that the SS were approaching, and applause was sometimes prohibited so as not to attract attention. The audience usually watched while standing, in cellars, in attics, in the cold and wind. Every now and then German headquarters banned all leisure activities as punishment for individual infractions such as attempting escape, smuggling letters, or failure to report for transport. And yet despite it all—or perhaps because of it all—cultural life expanded and flourished regardless of illness, death, or transports. The artists, leaders, and instructors sometimes questioned the suitability of putting on a cabaret or comedy the day after a transport had left, when the atmosphere was melancholy and the grief at separation fresh. They always reached the same conclusion: life must go on. During a performance of Gogol's *The Matchmakers*, news suddenly came that another transport was to leave, and neither the actors nor the audience knew who was to find a transport order when they returned to their rooms. The actors wanted to stop the play; the audience wouldn't allow it, even if it meant losing a precious hour or two from packing and making arrangements. Who could tell when they would have the chance to see a play again?

Ghetto veterans (newcomers hardly knew what planet they had landed on and needed time to acclimate) never hesitated in applying to Edelstein with requests and complaints about the management of the ghetto. They may not have received satisfaction, but their applications were never rejected out of hand, which was why Edelstein responded with a sharp reproof in the daily orders when three anonymous letters of complaint reached the Council of Elders. "Anyone who lacks the courage to speak his mind openly does not deserve a reply." When the ghetto became more established, wooden boxes were posted at various sites through which the residents could lodge complaints with the secretariat. The daily orders advised all residents that they had the right to complain and under no circumstances was anyone who did so to be punished.

From time to time the Council of Elders used the daily orders to express its thanks for work well done under exceptionally difficult conditions. It praised the emergency flood squad, which had been on the alert for two months after the level of the Eger River rose by nearly eight feet; the fire squad, for the fine job it had done in reinforcing the dams when melting snows caused the river to surge and floods seemed imminent. On several occasions the laundry staff was lauded for seeing that the deportees got away on time with clean clothes. The administrative staff, the stewards, the transportation workers, the porters, all were thanked for their exhausting nonstop work through the turbulent days and nights of transports that arrived and others that left simultaneously.

Because of the increasing manpower shortage, the administrative staff was sometimes mobilized for urgent jobs: digging graves, unloading coal from freight trains and storing it in the cellars. The black dust in the barracks basements made it difficult to identify the man who removed his shirt and helped the porters shift the coal from the entrance to the inner store rooms. However, Josef Bondy, in charge of the team, recognized him, and at the end of the shift he led a soot-covered Yekef to the showers at the Hohenelbe hospital, where hot water was available to laborers doing grimy work. Though Bondy was one of the conscientious Czech Jews who objected to the Zionist take-over, above all he regarded Edelstein as the representative of the workers, all workers, whom he protected from the Germans and whose rights he defended, sometimes in the face of opposition from the rest of the Council of Elders.

Many people knew, and those who didn't sensed, that Edelstein would not hesitate to lie to the Germans, to cheat, to conceal, to sabotage, in order to save Jewish life, to cover up smuggling or attempted escapes.

Here, as in Prague, Edelstein served as a buffer between the Germans and the Jews. Again and again he conquered his fear and applied to headquarters to save a ghetto inmate from punishment. One evening the women of the Hamburg barracks put on a chamber-music concert without the Germans' knowledge. It was attended by several men who had exit permits. The two guards posted near the gate suddenly came running: Heindel was coming. Heindel, one of the most despicable of the SS, used to spy on the agricultural workers through his binoculars and pounce through dormitory windows with his great dog to catch smokers. The guests managed to hide in the women's rooms, but the fact that a concert had been held could not be denied. A shrieking Heindel ordered Dittl Ornstein, director of the women's employment service, to remove her hands from her pockets instantly. An uncontrollable rebelliousness took hold of Dittl, as if all her pride, all her self-esteem, lay in the two hands concealed inside her pockets: let him shoot her, she would not remove her hands. That night two panic-stricken women ran to Yekef to tell him of the affair. He was angered by the frivolousness of the incident, the misplaced bravado. Nevertheless, the following day he went to smooth things over with Seidl, on whose desk stood a caricature of a Jew with the inscription DON'T GET ANGRY, ALWAYS TRY TO SMILE.

Edelstein knew fear but was a shield, opposed unnecessary risks but endangered himself. Once, when one of the women workers was absent at the end of the day, the furious SS man wanted to know who was responsible. In keeping with her education, Dittl stepped forward, though she was not directly responsible and had not even gone out with the women to work. Jakob turned pale when he heard her report. "You think you're a heroine? You're an idiot!" Sometimes, when he was suddenly called to headquarters (generally a bad sign), he would wrap himself in his prayer shawl and pray before he went.

The Germans referred to him mockingly as "King of the Jews."

Even before the elderly arrived from Germany the composition of the ghetto population gradually changed, the result of the German policy of shipping out the young people and leaving those over sixty-five at Theresienstadt. When the ghetto opened, the age range of most residents was between sixteen and forty-five; within five months only half the men were fit to work and the burden they shouldered grew progressively heavier. But Edelstein refused to give up his ambition for a productive ghetto, hoping that it could save at least some of the young people from being deported. Accordingly, at his suggestion, a new system of food allotment was instituted. Until then all residents had received equal rations, regardless of age or sex. Now the population was divided into three categories: people who did strenuous work, such as builders, stokers, sewage and extermination workers, and porters, received half a kilo of bread a day; people who did ordinary work received 375 grams a day; and people who were unfit for work received 335 grams a day. Since the Germans did not increase the overall bread allotment, the first category was accorded the increment at the expense of the last category, largely the old. In addition, Edelstein initiated a system of premiums for night work, overtime, exceptionally difficult jobs, and piecework. The employment department calculated the premiums on the basis of a point system; each point was worth 15 grams of bread. From time to time the people doing strenuous work also received extra sugar, margarine, beet jam, and a spread made of meat substitute.

The difference in the daily allowances of the people doing ordinary work and the elderly was only one slice of bread, but under ghetto conditions it was significant, particularly since it was the old people who, if they had no family, lived only on official rations. The difference became even more glaring when the first old people started to arrive from Germany: they had no underground contacts, received no parcels, could not pilfer anything at work, had no children in the ghetto to take care of them, and felt their hunger all the more keenly without work to take their minds off food. The young, who had better uses for their free time, were often prepared to dispense with the long lines for the evening distribution of watery gray soup or ersatz coffee. Not so the old; they waited patiently with small tin containers in their hands, usually downing the liquid on the spot, while it was still tepid. During lunch they waited quietly near the line and asked the young people with their customary politeness, "Is the gentleman taking soup?" for if the gentleman was prepared to forgo his portion of what was officially defined as lentil soup and distributed in addition to the main course, the old people would take it instead. They drank it down hungrily and waited for the next gentleman who was interested only in the main course because he did not live on official rations alone.

22

HERZL'S DAUGHTER IN THE GHETTO FOR THE OLD

THE JEWS OF THE REICH were neither expelled nor transported to Theresienstadt; they simply "changed their address," as official terminology put it. Most of them came to the ghetto on the basis of a "residence contract," apparently signed by both the Jewish Federation in Germany and the candidate for the old-age home. The candidate turned over all his liquid assets—cash, pension rights, life insurance, stocks—in return for lifelong residence at the home, food, laundry service, medical treatment and drugs, and hospital care if needed. The assets were ostensibly deposited in the Jewish Federation's account; however, it was a blocked account, which was transferred in its entirety to the Reich Security Head Office. In this manner the elderly paid the Germans thousands of marks for the right to spend the remainder of their days in a rest home, referred to sometimes as Theresienbad and sometimes as Theresienstadt am See (on the lake). True, further down the contract the management absolved itself of all responsibility, including the obligation to provide a permanent residence, but the elderly read what they wanted: a place of rest and recreation at last. Many imagined a health spa such as they had known in good times, a sort of Carlsbad or Bad

Nauheim with carefully tended accommodations nestling in green-
ery, and with this image in mind they selected the articles they
thought appropriate for their new home: a black suit, a velvet gown,
parasols, hats, mementos for the dressing table. They brought no
spoons, no pots, no towels—life's basic essentials; the management
would no doubt supply those. Upon arrival they asked for a room
facing the lake, a window facing south, sunny accommodation.
Many rejoiced at the thought of common recreation with friends
who had preceded them, and looked forward to the reunion. For by
all accounts, in Berlin and elsewhere, Theresienstadt's hospitals
were excellent, the region was fertile, the farms were run by Jews,
and the first postcards to be sent back from people who had left the
Reich were very positive indeed.

Some of the candidates for the old-age home were never given a
contract, or had it taken from them at the assembly point for
transports. Others, however, guarded it with their lives and used to
produce it as proof that their claims were justified. An astounded
Edelstein notified Seidl of the fraudulent nature of the residence
contracts and Seidl promised to "report the matter to Berlin and get
back to him."

The shock was twofold, both because of the all too terrible reality,
and because of the fraud and deception. After all, most Reich Jews
had been raised in the best German traditions of order, fairness,
and the value of one's word. Many were still proud of the honors
they had earned in the First World War and were careful about
former titles—*Herr Doktor, Herr Professor, Herr Kommerzialrat, Herr
General.* Most of the suitcases, packed with care and attention to
every detail, never arrived. Others arrived empty or half-empty,
and what had not been stolen on the way was confiscated at Theresienstadt. From the absorption depot the elderly were moved to
residences, at first in every corner, every roomlet, every storeroom
of the evacuated homes. Later, when it became impossible to accommodate the surging tide of transports, they were housed in barracks
attics with no insulation against heat or cold, no toilets, no faucets.
In the summer heat the attics were like furnaces, the dust in the air
stood still, and the heavy wooden beams impeded movement.

Thirty thousand people were squeezed into the ghetto, and there
was no room left. Then forty thousand, and not a free corner
remained. The population passed the fifty-thousand mark and the
density was unbearable: 1.60 square meters per person in which to
sleep, to live, to keep belongings. "The transports of the elderly

from Germany and Austria confronted the ghetto leadership with tasks of a dimension they had never imagined during the founding period, and even then there had been no lack of difficulties," wrote Zucker in the *History of the Ghetto up to December 31, 1943* (recorded by order of the Germans). The stock of wood for building bunks ran out, and there were not enough mattresses; the old lay on stone floors, sometimes in their own feces for lack of strength to go downstairs to the toilets. The boiler capacity for cooking was desperately inadequate: in August it fell as low as one third of a liter per person. Lunch was cooked in several shifts, there was no transportation available to deliver food to the ill and incapacitated, and if the food did arrive, it was cold. The young people who were assigned to the old were torn by pity, helplessness, disgust, fear: for the first time in their lives they handled human bodies. The stench was overpowering. There were blind people, mentally ill people, chronically sick people, cripples, ninety-year-olds, all left to their own devices after their children had emigrated overseas. They tended to lose the few articles they had, and sometimes they lost themselves. They could not find their way back to their homes, they forgot the street, the number of the house. A special information service was set up in the ghetto to deal with lost old people. Only a tiny proportion were capable of light work, and the usual job of the gentlemen in dark suits was to keep watch near the toilets and outhouses to see that they were kept clean and that nobody took too long—an indisputable necessity in view of the fact that the ghetto averaged one toilet for every hundred people.

Those who came from the Reich or Vienna did not know any Czech. They had to learn the German peculiar to the ghetto, with its sprinkling of strange words—*Nachschub, Zubusse* (extra food); *cvokarna* (insane asylum)—which they had never heard before. Many of the Czechs resented the old people from the Reich, at least until they got to know them, perhaps because they regarded them as both Germans and intruders responsible for the fact that Protectorate people had had to leave "their" ghetto; perhaps because they viewed with anxiety the transformation of the ghetto from what had been intended as a city of workers into a stockpile of human refuse. The old people were quickly crushed. They shrank down to skeletons, were plagued by diarrhea, struck down by pneumonia. The slightest scratch caused blood poisoning and gangrene; the lack of vitamins led to night blindness. In fall and winter they went for days without removing their clothes. The lice brought to the ghetto by old people from Vienna quickly spread, consumed them, and paraded across their sheets and pillows. The elderly were taken to the disinfection center and died of cold. Many simply burned out, for lack of strength, lack of will to go on fighting.

At the start of the ghetto, the names of the dead were published in the daily ordinance, but as the number of deaths increased, reaching 130 per day, it became impossible to continue this practice. The peak month was September 1943: almost 19,000 people arrived at the ghetto, 13,000 were sent east, and almost 4,000 deaths were recorded. Sometimes the young people tried to preserve their strength by consciously ignoring the old and living in a separate world.

The Germans emptied every Jewish hospital and mental institution throughout the Reich and shipped the inmates to Theresienstadt. When nurse Trude Groag arrived at the ghetto with a transport from Olmütz that included a group of mentally ill people, she asked Edelstein at the train station if there was a mental institution in the ghetto. Edelstein replied that there were a few small ones, but on the whole the mentally ill were sent to Poland. "And there?" she wanted to know. Yekef shrugged his shoulders without elaborating.

One fine autumn day the *Schleusenspital,* the hospital for newcomers, received a transport of sick people from Vienna that included a group of mentally ill inmates from the liquidated Steinhof hospital. Among the latter was a striking woman, relatively young. She caught the eye of Trude Groag, who was on hand as a nurse, and the two started to chat. The elegant woman immediately informed Trude that she was the daughter of Theodor Herzl and asked to meet with the ghetto leadership. Very excited, Trude Groag ran to tell Edelstein and request special treatment for the daughter of the visionary of the Jewish state. But Edelstein was not impressed. He felt that Trude Herzl and her husband Richard Neumann, formerly the owner of a textile factory in the Sudetenland, had behaved disgracefully toward Zionism, and that they had no right to ask the Zionists for preferential treatment now. Nurse Groag knew there was no point in pleading with Yekef; instead she decided to take special care of Trude Herzl herself, with the help of the medical staff.

Trude, Herzl's younger daughter and the only one of his three children still living then, was housed like any other patient on the first floor of the hospital, and because the head of the ghetto did not come to her, she appealed in writing to the ghetto leadership and the "Zionist branch" at Theresienstadt:

> I, the younger daughter of the deceased Zionist leader, Dr. Theodor Herzl, take the liberty of informing the local Zionists of my arrival and asking them for help and support during the present difficult times.
>
> > With Zionist and Faithful Greetings,
> > T. Neumann-Herzl

> Mrs. Neumann-Herzl can no longer endure a dirty nightgown and dirty sheets, and requests clean linens. Thanking you in advance.

> The bearer of this note, Mrs. Malka Hausner, is my dear friend from the Maltzegasse transit camp [in Vienna]. I ask that she be given all possible help, for she has taken it upon herself to fulfill my most urgent wishes. With Zionist greetings and many thanks.

Among other things, Trude Herzl asked for a spoon, a cup, a plate, a glass, a warm bathrobe, and a woollen hat or sweater, and the nurses tried to satisfy her wishes to the best of their ability. Like many mentally ill patients she used to check all the items in her possession over and over again, for fear that something had been stolen, and she spent hours looking for what she imagined she had lost. On tiny scraps of paper she jotted down her experiences in pencil, a kind of diary.

> I have just found a large hairpin. It was on the floor in the corridor.

> A parcel has disappeared with a towel containing the letters T.H. monogrammed in red. Yesterday they gave out jam, which I ate immediately. Last night there was a lovely doughnut for supper. I receive milk every day. Yesterday, twice.

> I get all sorts of extra food from my roommates.

> I've just moved my bowels. My husband was just here. I gave him a manicure.

> Today I washed a pair of stockings. They are drying now. I've begged the kind head nurse to help my husband, his only wish is to place me in a home for the mentally ill, he demands that I come and arrange his belongings. The kind head nurse must prevent

incidents such as has just occurred. If I have been sentenced to be sick, then at least without excitement, please!

Last piece of paper: what will I do when I can no longer write? Riddle.

Trude Herzl grew steadily weaker, due to recurring diarrhea, and died on March 17, 1943, six months after coming to Theresienstadt. The nurse on hand at her death brought her diary of tiny scraps of paper to Trude Groag as a memento. Groag kept some herself, and gave some to Jakob Edelstein. Trude Herzl, like all the other dead, was brought to the mortuary in the city walls, and Rabbi Albert Schön delivered the brief eulogy. He expressed sorrow at the fact that Herzl's words had not found a far greater Jewish following in their time, for had they done so the situation of the Jews would now be very different. He called on the small gathering to remain true to the ideals of the people of Israel, to unite and accept God's will: "Would that the day shall come and suffering shall go out of our lives and Herzl's ideas shall be the lot of all Israel, that we may say: if you will it, it is no legend."

The coffins—crude wooden crates—were loaded onto a horse-drawn farming cart. The cortège stopped at the barrier and the cart continued toward the crematorium. There the ashes of the dead were preserved in numbered cardboard boxes, and arranged shelf by shelf in the recesses of the columbarium, surrounded by grass and red geraniums. The ghetto residents took comfort in the fact that when the ghetto gates would one day open, every family would be able to find the ashes of their dear ones and bring them to burial in the soil of their homeland. (In 1944, the German command ordered all the ashes cast into the river.)

In mid-September 1942, Seidl informed Edelstein that Desider Friedmann, the former president of the Viennese Jewish community, and his assistant, Robert Stricker, would be coming to the ghetto. The two men had been arrested immediately after the annexation of Austria, imprisoned at Dachau, and released only a year later. Edelstein, who remembered the stormy ideological debates he had had with Stricker—founder of the state party—at Zionist congresses, had the engineer Drucker prepare a room for Stricker and his wife and meet them at the train station. The old divisions between socialists and nationalists vanished in the ghetto, or rather were pushed aside because of their common work in the Council of Elders, to which Stricker and Friedmann were appointed.

Stricker, true to his fighting spirit, was convinced that an underground had to be organized to procure arms. Should the Germans decide to destroy the ghetto, there had to be a plan of last resort to defend it in the subterranean corridors of the fortress. Since Stricker himself, as a member of the Council of Elders and later the director of the technical department, feared to take an active part in organizing the underground, an action that could endanger the entire leadership, he delegated the task to Drucker. Drucker formed an underground group, chiefly from former Maccabi people who filled key positions as firemen, police, and transportation workers. One of the group, an electronics engineer, built a radio receiver, which was hidden in the attic of the bakery building, and every evening one of the members who understood English would listen to the BBC news broadcasts. This was how they first learned that Jews were being gassed in trucks (the news appeared in the British press in the summer of 1942, and in October of that year the *Manchester Guardian* and *The Times* gave details of the overall extermination plan). Drucker told Stricker, who in turn told Zucker and Edelstein, who both knew of the underground operation. Yekef asked Drucker to repeat what he had heard on the BBC. His reaction was that it was "British atrocity propaganda." Zucker also felt that there was no point in panicking, while Stricker tended to believe the report—"The Germans are capable of anything."

When the Jewish officials arrived from Vienna and Berlin, Eichmann gave instructions that some of the Protectorate Jews among the leadership should step aside for the Jewish leaders from the Reich and Austria. As before, the Council of Elders had twelve members, but six Protectorate members were replaced by two from Vienna (Stricker and Friedmann) and four from Berlin, including Heinrich Stahl. The former chairman of Berlin's Jewish community, Stahl had been fired by the Germans in 1939 and now became Edelstein's deputy. To some extent, the appointments reflected the Jewish hierarchy in German eyes: the Reich Jews, though Jews, were above the Ostmark (Austrian) Jews, who were above the Slavic Jews. But the appointments were primarily aimed at sowing seeds of dissension and preventing a unified Jewish leadership, a plan which on the whole failed, since Stahl, who had many reservations about the way Edelstein ran the ghetto, died of pneumonia within a month (and in death earned a rare honor in the history of the ghetto, a eulogy in the daily orders).

The Protectorate Jews, the veterans with rights, the functionaries who had built up their departments from initial chaos and harsh beginnings, resented the change in leadership, as might have been expected (and as the SS had hoped), and these feelings only sharpened "Czech" bitterness against the "Germans." Because of them, the privileged Jews from Austria and Germany, Czech Jews were being forced to leave their homeland and go east; because of them, the Czech work ghetto had become a German old-age home; and now, to top it all off, even the fruit of their labors, their positions, were being taken from them.

One of the issues that became more contentious as the composition of the Council of Elders changed was the question of provisions. The members of the original council were unanimous about saving the young people, which meant giving them more food. But when the representatives of the German and Austrian Jews, most of them elderly, joined the second council, the question was reviewed, though the situation remained as before: those who did strenuous work were allocated extra food at the expense of the elderly.

As the population density increased, and the number of helpless and forgetful old people multiplied, so did the rate of theft among the residents. In a concerted effort to stem this tide and maintain at least a minimal standard of honesty among the ghetto population, the leadership announced various measures which it hoped would discourage stealing, such as confiscation of a thief's possessions, including his personal belongings. From the moral point of view, there were essential differences among the various types of theft in the ghetto. From the Germans' warehouse of confiscated goods and vegetable garden it was acceptable to steal without troubling one's conscience, on condition that there was little risk of being caught and endangering everyone else. Stealing from common property such as coal heaps, potato storerooms, the bakery, and the kitchens was frowned on in principle; but it was human, and sometimes the pilfering was even organized (which did not stop "solo" jobs being committed, despite the watch of the economic police). Yeast dough could be hidden in a rubber boot, sauce in a shallow container that fitted bodily contours. But stealing from a roommate, from the personal belongings of a ghetto inmate, was disgraceful and revolting, and the thief was ostracized.

There were two forms of law in the ghetto—the law of the Germans, which covered all areas of life without recourse to appeal, and internal Jewish law, in which the SS also interfered. Since the ghetto was a community by coercion, as stated in the introduction to the collected regulations published at the beginning of 1943, and had no historical legal precedent (the ghettos of the Middle Ages were different in structure, development, and administration), it was necessary to order life in the Theresienstadt ghetto by a series of new laws and regulations, or by calling on general civil law. The ghetto legislators chose a compromise course: in every case where no other law applied, the laws of the Protectorate were valid. The general regulations were formulated by Jewish jurists and approved by the Germans, but the judgments of even the greatest Jewish jurists naturally carried no weight against the intervention of the pettiest SS man.

The law of the Germans was above legal systems. When, following a search, the vegetable cart was discovered to have a false bottom used for smuggling letters in and out of the ghetto, the driver, Weiss, was brought to Camp Commandant Bergel, who dealt with offenders. Bergel was a raging drunkard, suspicious of even his German comrades, and always kept a loaded gun at his bedside. Though brutally beaten, Weiss refused to name his collaborators. Bergel made him sit on a burning iron stove, but Weiss still would not talk. Finally, in a fit of rage, Bergel took the stove and threw it at him, breaking his spine.

From February 1942, camp regulations were somewhat improved and modified, due to the gradually extended authority of self-administration. During the early months of the ghetto, imprisonment was the common German punishment for whatever they deemed an infraction. The two prisons, one for men and one for women, were guarded by Czech police, while the SS dropped in from time to time to bully the prisoners. Punishment was inflicted as the Germans saw fit, and release from prison was often the result of Edelstein's intervention with Seidl. Edelstein spared no effort in trying to take the whole matter of punishment out of German hands and transfer it to the Jews (chiefly in order to prevent headquarters from using deportation as a punishment—*Weisung* in ghetto language). In Jewish hands, punishments could be lighter and prison conditions improved. And in the spring of 1943, the prisons were transferred to the Jews, except for the "bunker" in the basement of SS headquarters where offenders were brought for more serious crimes, such as escape attempts and smuggling

letters, and from where the road usually led straight to the Little
Fortress.

The Jewish judges, all authorized jurists, were sworn in when they
were appointed. Minutes were taken of their deliberations, and
sentences were recorded. A defendant had the right to appeal to a
higher court if the sentence was more than a month's imprisonment.
All legal etiquette was preserved, as if their jurisdiction were not a
ghetto, the very existence of which was an absolute breach of all law
and justice.

> Hermann Gross has been sentenced to ten days' imprisonment
> including one day without warm food, and he has forfeited all
> right to hold any official position in the ghetto, for taking various
> items of food from the Magdeburg kitchen where he worked as a
> cook.

> Rudolf Gross has been sentenced to three weeks' imprisonment
> including two days without warm food. The crime: on March 5,
> 1942, he stole horse meat from camp property.

> Rudolf Fischer has been sentenced to eighteen hours' imprison-
> ment for stealing sugar beet.

> Leopold Kogosch has been sentenced to twenty-four hours' im-
> prisonment for slapping a ghetto resident.

> Erwin Prager has been sentenced to twenty-four hours' imprison-
> ment for disobeying the prohibition of airing sheets out the win-
> dows [one of Seidl's obsessions].

> Alfred Reichmann has been sentenced to three weeks' imprison-
> ment. The defendant forcefully pushed a ghetto resident, causing
> her to fall and injure her ankle.

> Rosa Pollak-Blauweis has been sentenced to three weeks' im-
> prisonment and has forfeited the right to hold any administrative
> position in the ghetto. The defendant stole a pair of gloves from
> the clothing warehouse where she worked.

> Julius Lappert has been sentenced to three weeks' imprisonment
> for stealing a winter coat. The coat has been returned to its owner.

On the whole the judges leaned toward light punishment (though
Seidl outlawed suspended sentences), unless there were explicit

German instructions to the contrary or if the defendant filled a public position: a doctor found guilty of taking a pair of earrings from a deceased patient was sentenced to three months' imprisonment and forfeited his right to hold public office in the ghetto.

According to the form of punishment published in the daily orders, one could tell whether the offender had been apprehended by the Germans, or the Czech police, or whether he had committed an internal infraction: when Milan Seger was sentenced to two months' imprisonment for stealing a few apples and pears, it was clear that he had been caught by the authorities (the ghetto residents passed right by the fruit trees on their way to work, but were not permitted to take so much as the fruit that had fallen off. It was all meant for the Germans). When the sentence stated that Fritz Freud and Jarmila Blazek had been sentenced to two weeks' imprisonment because Freud had left his work without permission and Jarmila had visited Freud during working hours, it was understood that the SS had surprised the couple during the meeting.

Though the prisons were less crowded than the dormitories and the Jewish prison guards were easygoing, imprisonment was nevertheless a frightening prospect, because a copy of the sentence had to be sent to headquarters (briefly formulated, so as not to waste the camp commandant's valuable time), and the Germans were in the habit of emptying the prisons when transports left for the East.

The Czech writer Karl Poláček, a friend of Masaryk's and of author Karel Čapek, was one of the court scribes, and he always tried to have the sentence lightened, particularly when the crime in question was pilfering small amounts of food. Apart from his official function (arranged through friends), Poláček lectured on literature, especially to children, drawing on his light-handed humor and his understanding of human weakness. He could quote entire chapters of works of world literature by heart. Like everyone else, Poláček used to wait in line near the kitchen window with his dish in hand, his ration slips in his pocket, his soup spoon stuck in the lapel of his coat, and among the few things he jotted down in the ghetto were reflections on the art of walking with a bowl of soup: history tells of heroes who could carry iron chains with head erect, but only a slave who has since childhood been taught to bend his back can carry a full bowl of soup. If he walks straight, with his head raised toward the sky, half the soup will spill and he will return home more hungry than when he left.

One of the questions the Council of Elders grappled with in the matter of crime and the heaviness of punishment was the very right of judgment. Is the Council of Elders entitled to judge others? Are they saints? Should someone who receives double rations be allowed to sentence people on single rations?

In addition to the criminal court, a labor court was set up in May 1943. It dealt with labor discipline, failure to report for work, tardiness, and negligent use of tools and materials. Punishment took the form of compulsory overtime added on to the eight-hour workday. The maximum punishment was an extra four hours daily for a period of no more than three days. The administrators of the quarters and the elders of the barracks had the right to mete out punishment for disciplinary misdemeanors in matters of order, cleanliness, or noise. Here too the punishment was additional work or house arrest, and they were no great deterrent. People were motivated to preserve order and cleanliness themselves, insofar as was possible.

Apart from all these regulations the administrative staff of the ghetto was also subject to special rules, and an administrative court deliberated on disciplinary offenses. It consisted of a judge and two members of the court, one of whom worked in the same department as the accused. Punishment included reproofs, loss of perquisites, and, in severe instances, removal from the position for good. According to the regulations, a member of the administrative staff was not allowed to use his position for his own advantage, the advantage of his family, or any third party; nor was he allowed to accept gifts of any kind. But only men of unusual stature could resist temptation. Preferential treatment for family and friends was almost a virtue, and bribes were a common enough phenomenon, especially at the lower levels. With family men it was done discreetly: after the supplicant's visit (seeking a change of residence, a new mattress, a coat), the clerk found a handful of paper-wrapped sugar cubes on his desk, or two cigarettes might be passed in a handshake. Some clerks took the bribes as a matter of course, others took them and despised themselves. At the higher levels, goodwill was won with the aid of gifts from people with means—a cake, soap, a drawing.

As in all proper societies, the ghetto also had a civil court, which dealt with private conflicts—chiefly insults—between ghetto residents. Most of the applicants were older people, mainly from Germany, who were more sensitive about their dignity, more rigid, more miserable, and more humorless; this last had especial impact because humor could often settle affairs of dignity (such as name-calling) outside the walls of the court. But perhaps what these people sought most of all was the reassurance that there was still justice, and a judge, in the world.

The problem was how to educate children about truth in a regime of deception, about honesty in an atmosphere of theft, how to shield them, inure them, and prepare them for normal life in a free society. Children in the ghetto matured quickly. They knew disease: impetigo, enteritis, encephalitis, conjunctivitis, were an integral part of their vocabulary. They learned to cope with hunger—one of the fairy tales told at Theresienstadt went thus: once upon a time there was a king and he was hungry. He went to the kitchen window and ordered the cook to give him a double portion. And indeed, he received a double serving. They met death face to face, saw the mentally ill staring at them from the windows of the Kavalirka, saw old people groping their way through the streets. They were highly critical of the adult world, full of vitality, and realistic. While the adults, with their personalities already formed when they came to the ghetto, were anchored in a different world, the children had no roots in the past. They lived in the present and the ghetto was often the only reality they knew. It taught them that cunning was one of life's basic necessities.

When the Germans allowed the youth department to take sick children out onto the lawns on the walls, the counselors took advantage of this to take healthy children out into the fresh air too. When Gonda, in charge of the youth department, asked one of the boys if he was sick and received a negative reply, he said, "But if the Germans ask you, you must say that you are sick," to which the boy replied, "I'm not a liar."

Formal classes were banned, but the children could be amused by singing, games, crafts, cultural activities. Had anyone bothered to make a systematic check of the lecture series for teenagers, he would no doubt have found that it constituted a curriculum. The Germans turned a blind eye to this, perhaps because they knew that nothing would change the children's future. During classes, pupils guarded the dormitory entrances to give ample warning of SS approach. When this happened, everybody burst into song or started to play games. Thus truth was not an absolute value; deception was often a loftier ideal. As far as theft was concerned, in the children's vocabulary the word *schleusen* had no negative connotations, and for the majority, stealing was a kind of sport: taking potatoes from passing carts, coal from the basement window. Parents, grandmothers, older brothers—all took things for the family. Should a child who tried to take bread from the supply cart for his sick mother be praised or reproved? The idea was after all to raise normal children, who would be able to integrate into society, be absorbed in Palestine if possible: the instructors were torn between the reality they faced and the values they held.

Every instructor educated his class (about forty children) in his image, and according to his world view: graduates of the Zionist youth movements did it in the spirit of Zionism; communists looked toward a socialist revolution; Czech nationalists, toward love of the homeland. The instructor was the decisive figure in the children's lives, much more so than their parents, whose world had disintegrated—particularly since hundreds of children—children of mixed marriages, orphans whose parents had been killed—arrived at the ghetto all alone in the world. Many suffered from the sudden break from home, the separation from parents. Many started bed-wetting. There were almost no material advantages to the instructors' work (as opposed to jobs in the productive sector), only enormous responsibilities. Those who took up education did so out of love, faith, and a sense of mission.

Even if only subconsciously, the children felt themselves privileged members of the ghetto, with respect to living quarters, attention, and food (after the summer of 1943, there was a separate children's kitchen, which from time to time supplied special food: an eighth of a liter of watery milk, made from powder; a small portion of cereal). After the Czech population left, the boys under fourteen were housed in the former school building. Every classroom doubled as a dormitory and playroom: the triple-tiered bunks were built along the walls and in the center of the room was a table and wooden benches. Opposite them was the girls' dormitory, formerly the garrison headquarters, and not far away was the dormitory for German children, who were housed separately partly because of language difficulties, and partly because of educational problems. The German dormitory was coordinated by Sigi Kwassniewsky, a member of Gordonia, and Fritzi, Zucker's wife, was their warm and devoted housemother. Edelstein visited the German children; after all, they had a common language. The children remembered him as a fond uncle who quoted bits of Jewish wisdom and always stressed that they had an important future and must be strong, keep clean, and stay healthy. The Czech and German children at first kept apart from one another, but in time the gap between them closed through common sports activities and courses, and through the love they shared for soccer.

Most of the children liked dormitory life and the wealth of activities: they rose at 6:30 A.M., washed, had breakfast together and then began classes. Some of the teachers at the elementary level were former university professors and lecturers, but an academic degree was no guarantee of success as a ghetto teacher, where good teaching meant the ability to make the material exciting in the absence of textbooks, exercise books, or any other teaching aids. Sometimes a former bookkeeper was better at teaching mathematics than a trained math teacher who clung to his old methods. Paper and pencils were precious, and distributed only for essay writing, dictation, or arithmetic exercises; even then it was either used wrapping paper, bits of cardboard, or the blank sides of old letters. After lunch and a compulsory rest period came sports and hobbies, and in the evening the children visited their parents.

On the whole the children learned willingly and expulsion from lessons was considered harsh punishment. The instructors deliberated at length over the question of punishment: withholding food was forbidden, corporal punishment was not even considered. Giving the children extra work did not seem educational—work was something they tried to instill a love of; it should not be a detestable chore. Punishments therefore consisted chiefly of moral censure within the group, reproofs, and exclusion from cultural activities. When a boy who stole ration slips from a schoolmate was caught, he had to make a public apology in the pages of his group's newspaper, and he almost broke down in remorse.

The focus of identification was not with the Jewish people as a whole but with the group. A very clumsy boy was accepted by his friends in the Shkid home (named after the institution for homeless children in Petrograd, according to the book by Beylik and Panteleyev) only after he was the only one in his class who knew Tolstoy's birthplace. Honza Eisner, his instructor, had made sure that he would know: he had told the boy beforehand in order to reinforce his standing in the group.

We Lead, the children's newspaper, was put out over two years and edited by Peter Ganz, who had arrived at the ghetto at the age of fourteen, without his parents, who were protected from transport because theirs was a mixed marriage. To ensure a continual supply of journalistic material, Peter paid for articles and reports with food he received in parcels from home. And food was the most precious of commodities—almost: "I will not betray my friends, not even for a slice of bread and salami, not even for a quarter of a kilo of real honey . . ." The class group was the all-important framework, and children committed acts of true selflessness for it. When Eli Bachner received a birthday package containing a whole roast goose, a delicacy that Jews had not tasted for years, he carefully divided it into forty-two equal portions, one for each of his classmates.

Most of the day the children lived in a separate world with almost no contact with the old, the sick, the dying. But in 1943 the counselors organized a project called "Helping Hand," in which the boys and girls visited the old people's rooms two or three times a week, cleaned their mattresses, brought food, provided various services, extended birthday greetings, put on performances. Most of the youngsters were repelled and disgusted by the foul sheets and the stench, but a few persisted, formed ties with an elderly person, and took the place of distant grandchildren.

Because of his connections with the camp supervisor, Fredy Hirsch obtained permission to set up a sports field on the wide, grassy fortress walls. In honor of its initiation in May 1943, a sports competition and rally was held in which six thousand children and adolescents participated, some wearing gym clothes sewed from colored sheets. For the Zionists it was a festival in honor of Herzl's birthday, for the communists it celebrated May Day. The festivities ended with the sportsmen spelling out *Cest praci*, meaning respect for work. Dr. Kahn delivered the festive address and everyone was in high spirits: even in the terrible conditions of the ghetto, it was possible to raise healthy youth for a better future. The aim was to instill in the youngsters a sense of Jewish pride and the value of Judaism in a world that treated Jews with contempt. When twelve-year-old Helenka started using dirty words, her mother reproved her. "Children from good families don't speak like that." "What sort of good family?" her daughter wanted to know. "We're only Jews." Her mother wrote the words down in the diary she had kept ever since the child was born, as a memento for when she grew up. "Have you ever heard of a Jewish murderer? Have you ever known a Jewish thief? Kings were born of Jews, even Jesus, and you say 'only Jews'?"

The lecturers tried to impart to the youngsters the moral values that had guided them all their lives. "I told the girls that they must conduct themselves in such a way that they will be able to remember these times with pride," one of the elderly men wrote. "They laughed at first, then they understood my meaning. I told them that self-education toward discipline and accuracy improves first of all themselves. They want to marry one day and raise a family, and then they'll be grateful for their self-education, and after many years have passed they'll say the old man was right."

The ghetto had institutions, dormitories, clubs, for all age groups, ranging from the home for mothers with babies to that for seventeen-year-olds. The youth department also took care of children who lived with their parents (not all parents were prepared to have their children housed in separate dormitories). Well-known educators, such as Professor Maximilian Adler and Professor Hayot, served as consultants to the department. There was an institution for children with learning disabilities and for disturbed children, run by the Baumels, both psychologists and educators. There were instances of delinquency, or what was then termed delinquency: theft, chiefly of food. Two boys stole potatoes and donated them to the commune. How were they to be treated? Should they be judged for theft, or praised for comradeship? In 1943, in order to keep young people out of the general legal system and thus the obligation to report their trials to the Germans, a special juvenile court was set up, presided over by psychologists, educators, and representatives of the youth department, who generally contented themselves with issuing a sharp reproof. However, on occasion they sentenced the young offenders to imprisonment (with maximum sentences being half the term meted out to adults).

The world of the children over fourteen was not as sheltered as that of the younger ones. They were apprenticed to carpenters, metalworkers, or electricians, and though they lived in the common dormitories, they lived the reality of the ghetto, where the strong man was the winner. They dreamt of nice clothes, movies, and ice cream, had their first romance, used bad language, cared for sick parents, and believed that they would come to no harm.

The kindergarten teachers took the little ones on walks through the ghetto within the walls to see a horse in the street or visit the fire station, and the children recorded their experiences in drawings. Some drew scenes from ghetto life: a policeman near a doorway, a barracks, a barred window, the food line; others drew things they had never seen in life: a Dutch windmill, a rural home surrounded by verdant hills, an iris, butterflies. Many of the children wrote poetry, whether they were encouraged by the counselors or because they felt the need to express themselves:

> Small, but full
> Of roses, the garden.
> Along the path walks
> A small boy,
> A sweet boy,
> Pretty as a bud,
> When the bud blooms
> He'll not live, but die
> That little boy.

So wrote Franta Bass in his fourteenth year. He never lived to be fifteen.

23

NEXT STOP PALESTINE

THE JEWS' DREAM of a self-supporting city was almost realized—and then shattered, because the Germans decreed otherwise. In the spring of 1942 it still seemed as if Edelstein's efforts to make the ghetto productive would bear fruit: income from outside work and contract jobs for the Germans covered 84 percent of the maintenance costs of the ghetto (the figure would have approached 100 percent if the expense of feeding the deportees in transit, who stayed in the ghetto only a few days, could have been deducted).

The turning point came in the wake of the transports of the elderly, and in July 1942 the leadership of the ghetto had to admit that the plan for a self-sustaining ghetto based on productive work had failed. The ghetto report for August 1942 stated this openly: "Theresienstadt has become a welfare ghetto, and the ratio of able-bodied manpower to elderly residents is constantly decreasing (11,000:19,000 for the month of July). This change has naturally affected the ghetto's economic structure: whereas in previous months the efforts to achieve economic independence left their mark on ghetto life, since July it has been necessary to bury the hope of realizing this type of scheme." The forestry group returned to the ghetto, income decreased, and earnings covered only half the expense of running the ghetto, despite the fact that the daily food allotments had reached an all-time low (costing 2.79 crowns per capita, as opposed to 3.84 crowns in May).

Nevertheless, the efforts to participate in the war economy were not abandoned, and there was reason to hope; in the summer a new industry was started, employing between 150 and 200 women—separating feldspar, which the Germans used for insulation in arms production. Other industries were set up in shacks; products included leather boots, ladies' clothing, children's books and games, jewelry, souvenirs, artistic postcards, wallets and purses. Various German middlemen, who supplied the raw materials, found the ghetto an excellent source of cheap labor (although there were some who sincerely tried to help the Jews), and ghetto products were in great demand. Professor Sadek and Professor Zadikoff, two artists of world renown, worked in the ceramics industry, and the dolls they fashioned impressed the frequent SS visitors, who enjoyed coming to Theresienstadt; bombings skipped the ghetto, the German command lacked for nothing, and the pleasures were many; abundant food, gifts from confiscated Jewish property, special orders from Jewish workshops (Baldur von Schirach, the Nazi youth leader, ordered four Jewish artistic dolls for his pure Aryan children when he visited the ghetto). Dignitaries sometimes even devised pretexts to visit the ghetto, claiming they needed some report or statistics, a requirement that benefited the bureaucratic paper shufflers and was in the interests of both the German command and the Jewish administration.

The carpentry workshop turned out furniture, mostly on order from SS people and others connected to the ghetto, who found it a convenient source of personal enrichment. It also produced wooden shoe soles, and built parts for shacks for the Wehrmacht. The bindery made cardboard boxes for the army. Bloodstained uniforms were brought from the front and cleaned and repaired in the ghetto. But there were no large orders for vital products for the war economy, and this alone, Edelstein believed, might bring true protection from additional deportation to Poland. Despite the desperate lack of manpower, the army also had to submit to Himmler and the other Nazi ideologues who had made the extermination of the Jews their supreme objective, regardless of the economic or military benefits they might have reaped from using Jewish labor. As Goering explained to the Wehrmacht General Staff in the summer of 1942, the Jews must not be treated as a vital labor force—neither the weapons industry nor any other military sector could keep a Jewish labor force until the end of the war, though some army people had suggested that military victory should be achieved before the complete solution to the Jewish problem was dealt with.

The labor force at Theresienstadt continued to shrink; the young people had to work for the Germans, look after the ghetto, and take care of the elderly. Those fit for work shouldered an enormous burden. In the month of August, transportation workers worked between eighty and a hundred and ten hours per week, including thirty hours of night work. The medical staff and burial team worked between seventy-five hours and eighty hours, twenty hours at night. Kitchen and quartermaster employees worked up to ninety hours a week, about a third of this at night; and craftsmen, sixty-five or seventy hours, ten at night (and all this without the SS at their sides cracking the whip; they did indeed work under duress, but also out of a sense of common responsibility). "Illness among the workers is particularly prevalent," Zucker wrote in his report, "due to undernourishment and the concomitant loss of weight. The body is enfeebled and loses its resistance, and every cold leads to an ear infection, bronchitis, pneumonia. The Council of Elders is doing all it can to order the rationing in such a way that the labor force will benefit at the expense of those who do not work, so as to preserve fitness for work." The dilemma remained almost until the end of the war: how to manage justice in a regime of injustice, how to distribute the starvation rations so that at least some of the ghetto inmates would preserve their strength. After all, few of the elderly were likely to survive in any case, even if they remained at Theresienstadt, and only the young could ensure the continued existence of the Jewish people.

Edelstein tried to induce the SS to change their policy whereby the young and fit were shipped east and the old and helpless remained in the ghetto. The illustration on the working report for August 1942, intended for the Germans' consumption, succinctly captured his feelings on the subject: a giant sieve through which the young fell into the abyss, while the old and sick were caught in the net. Edelstein was well aware of the German weakness for statistics, diagrams, and tables, and supplied them generously with such data, primarily so that they would occupy themselves with paperwork rather than people. Most of the illustrations in the working reports were done by Peter Kien, a gifted artist and poet from the Sudetenland, a member of Hehalutz who had planned to emigrate to Palestine in 1939. But he was found to have a heart defect and compelled to give up training, and so his path to Palestine was blocked.

When Edelstein complained to the camp commandant of the

high death rate among the old at the ghetto, Seidl replied, "The clock is accurate," meaning: all's as it should be. For his own reasons, Seidl did not want the ghetto flooded with old people either. And when a senior German official was expected from Berlin, he ordered (as reported by Gonda), "that all the old and infirm walk about the ghetto, back and forth. He wants the city to look overcrowded to the official. The camp commandant, I think, does not want any more old and infirm to come."

Rather than stop the daily transports of old people to Theresienstadt even temporarily, the Reich Security Head Office solved the unbearable density in its own way: Seidl informed Edelstein that some of the elderly would be transferred to "another ghetto where conditions were similar to those at Theresienstadt," and rumor had it that the place was Ostrovo, near Posen. All old people over sixty-five were first registered in the Magdeburg barracks yard. Jewish administrative employees filled out long questionnaires, and then the elderly appeared before the SS officers, who had come specially from Berlin. After asking a few questions, the SS put an O or T beside each name: O for people going east, T for those remaining at Theresienstadt. The latter category included mostly severely disabled war veterans, people with high German decorations, children of mixed marriages, and well-known names.

During September, ten thousand elderly people from the Reich were sent to the East, ill, feeble, alarmed, bewildered, alone, helpless. The convoy of old people dragging themselves to the train station, some riding on hearses, through the deserted streets of the town they had thought would be a health resort, seemed like a ghostly procession on the road to Hades. In October, orders came to clear the ghetto of ten thousand old people from the Protectorate, but since Theresienstadt did not contain that many, the Germans in the end settled for eight thousand.* Selection was made by the Germans, as reported in the orders of the day, and appealing to the transport committee was therefore impossible—but children were permitted to accompany aged parents.

The dilemma was heartrending: to let aged parents go east alone and perhaps speed their death through starvation, or to give up one's protected status in the ghetto, endanger one's life, and accom-

---

*Three transports, numbering six thousand people, were killed at Treblinka, every last one of them. The last transport of old people, which left October 26, was taken to Auschwitz, the first such transport sent from the Protectorate to Auschwitz. Twenty-eight people survived.

pany them, in order to help them in that mysterious, frightening, and unknown East. Those who decided to stay in the ghetto felt that they had abandoned their parents in their hour of need, and they carried the separation as a scar, an agonizing nightmare.

There were not enough old people to fill the last transport, marked by the letters BY, and so at the last minute the Germans also added young people. In the general confusion, 134 people escaped from the assembly point and hid in the ghetto. There was no time to round up the number to two thousand as required. Seidl raged, imposed curfew on the ghetto with lights out at six in the evening, banned cultural activities, and ordered a general count, room by room. Most of the escapees were caught, imprisoned at headquarters, and beaten, and some were transferred to the Little Fortress. But the general count still did not tally. Edelstein deliberately clouded the issue by adding the names of nonexistent people to the general files, hoping that the calculations would balance in time.

When Trude Groag discovered that her elderly mother was included in the transport, she ran to Magdeburg to ask Edelstein's help, but she was not allowed to see him because his loyal secretary, Mrs. Steif, was permitting no one to enter. Suddenly his door opened and Edelstein appeared, wan and broken. "My mother is dead," he said. "How? Where?" the surprised Trude asked. "In Poland, not of natural causes," Yekef replied. "I'm going to recite kaddish."

Nobody in the ghetto knew how Edelstein had learned of Mattel Edelstein's death, killed in Horodenka's first liquidation campaign on December 28, 1941. On that day half the Jews of Horodenka were shot to death, including Mottel and Mattel Edelstein, Jakob's sister Dora and her husband, and his two uncles on the Koch side of the family. Years later, it turned out that Edelstein had sent his parents a letter from Theresienstadt through Franta Friedmann, the head of the Prague community. The letter had arrived in the spring of 1942, when not a single member of his family was still alive. One of the Jews who had survived, Israel Silber, a member of Gordonia who knew Yekef from his visits to Horodenka and his lectures to Socialist Zionist youth, opened the letter and sent a reply to Friedmann's address. Whether Friedmann wrote a veiled hint about the death of the entire family, and the hint was misunderstood, whether he wrote only of Yekef's mother's death, wishing to spare him too great a shock, whether Edelstein still had other contacts in Horodenka—nobody knows. That same autumn, while

Yekef said kaddish for his mother, the rest of Horodenka's Jews were wiped out at the Belzec concentration camp after a torturous train journey.

Despite the transports, despite the density, despite the lice, the bugs, the undernourishment, the deaths of the elderly, the ghetto inmates did not despair—nor did the doctors, or nurses, or those who transported the sick. They continued their war against death, fighting for every single life. Dr. Richard Stein, an ophthalmologist, performed complex operations to save the sight of inmates as if long life stretched ahead of them. Dentists repaired the teeth of those leaving for the East so that they would suffer no pain on the journey. Nurses rejoiced at the recovery of a child from pneumonia; a week later he was included in the transport for the East.

Apart from the main hospital in the Hohenelbe barrack, into which one thousand beds had been squeezed, there were clinics and infirmaries in every barracks, every block of houses. There was no lack of doctors so long as they were protected from transports east (on average, there was one doctor for every 750 people), but there was a desperate shortage of nurses and people to care for the sick. The registered nurses received help from hundreds of volunteers who knowingly exposed themselves to danger, showing great courage and devotion in treating the old, the dying, and the patients with communicable diseases; they attacked the lice with cold water and soap (composed chiefly of loam) with such ferocity that the lice disappeared entirely within a year.

Anyone who felt he was getting ill informed the elder of the house, and every day the doctor on duty visited all the dormitories and examined the patients in their rooms, issued sick leave from work where necessary, prescribed medicine, or gave orders to transfer the patient to the hospital. Twice a day hospital patients were allowed visits from their families. The visitors brought food saved from their own rations, bought for the price of some garment, obtained at work, or given by friends—an apple, a slice of cake, a candy. There were patients, even among the young people and children, who never left the sick circuit—an infected wound led to pneumonia, pneumonia to some intestinal disorder, then jaundice, mumps, meningitis, and tuberculosis, which found fertile ground in the ghetto because of the crowded conditions. Some ailments became less irksome in the ghetto. Those with ulcers and diabetes felt an improvement (due to the enforced diet), asthmatics recovered. Dr. Weidmann, the former chairman of the Prague Jewish community, who had always been rotund, lost a lot of weight and became very thin in the ghetto, but his chronic asthma vanished and his letters to friends in the community read as though they had been written at a sanatorium.

The greatest emphasis was put on the prevention of epidemics, and the sanitation people waged a bitter war against grime: ushers near the food distribution windows could turn away any person whose dishes were not clean. Ghetto inmates were asked over and over again to wash their hands after leaving the toilet and before eating, and to report to the clinics as soon as the slightest sore appeared, for it might lead to gangrene. Children had to wash every day in cold water, even when it was chilly outside, and the jokers among them included Fredy Hirsch's cleanliness inspection in the list of ghetto afflictions, together with hunger, transports, disease, and bugs. Mercilessly, Fredy would throw below-standard bedding, dishes, or clothing on the floor. Seidl, whose chief concern was for his own neck should the ghetto become a danger to the environment, paid close attention to public spitting, punishing it with two or three days' imprisonment. But despite the care, typhoid fever spread among the children during the first winter in the ghetto and several died.

Dr. Munk had a reputation for rigidity. The notice on the door of his room in Magdeburg read: "Here lives, but does not keep office hours, Dr. Munk," and a sign in his office stated: "I know friendship, not favoritism." But only a man such as he could have coped so unflaggingly with ghetto conditions. In September 1942, nine months after the ghetto was established, there were already 36 clinics, 438 sickrooms, 4,680 sickbeds, and 600 doctors. On average, every inmate was treated four times a month. There were departments of gynecology, urology, otolaryngology, dentistry, ophthalmology, pediatrics, surgery, radiology. Glasses, orthopedic shoes, and trusses were fitted and repaired in the ghetto, several sorts of diet were prepared, test tubes were manufactured, refresher courses were held for doctors and nurses; there was a scientific committee, a central medical library, and a research department, particularly active in the field of communicable diseases. Only against one thing was there no remedy: the horror of eastern transports.

The most depressing site of all was the hospital for the mentally ill, housed in the dark buildings in the fortress walls. While everything possible was done for ordinary sick people, the mentally ill were shoved behind bars, neglected and forgotten on the whole, perhaps because of the instinct for self-survival on the part of those fighting to preserve their own sanity in a world gone mad. There were patients with chronic mental disorders, gathered together from all the Jewish institutions in the Reich, but there were also relatively normal people who simply could no longer bear what was happening—the degradations, the loss of family, the disintegration of their world. Increasing thinness suddenly brought on depression, nervousness, or apathy, compounded by the constant tension (especially among the aged), the eternal lines at water faucets, toilets, and food windows, the lack of sleep, the bugs and fleas, the agonies of withdrawal for bodies addicted to nicotine and caffeine. It is little wonder that they broke down in the ghetto. The wonder is that so many preserved their equanimity, their sense of humor, their vitality, their human visage.

Winter was around the corner, and in the attics, exposed to the cold, there were still three thousand people, mostly elderly. The ghetto leadership appealed again and again to the residents to crowd together even more to make room for the inhabitants of the attics so that they could have the protection of walls. The disparity between these appeals for solidarity and the privileged quarters of the Council of Elders and other functionaries with private rooms did not escape their notice. "I curse the day I moved to Magdeburg," Edelstein often said.

By German order, privileged residents from Germany and Austria received special treatment and added a new term to ghetto vocabulary, "the prominents." They numbered between eighty and a hundred and twenty people, and formed a strange conglomerate of leftover splendor of Central European Jewry and people who merited privileges in German eyes. They included Elsa Bernstein, an old woman, almost blind, known by her pen name of Ernst Rosmer, who was doubly deserving: she was both the illegitimate granddaughter of Franz Liszt and the mother-in-law of Gerhart Hauptmann, one of Germany's great modern writers. At particularly trying moments, Mrs. Bernstein was wont to sigh: "If Gerhard only knew of this!" (At one of his regular meetings with Seidl, Edelstein asked permission to have Mrs. Bernstein's artificial eye sent to the Wiesbaden manufacturer for repairs.)

There were two singers among the honored residents: court adviser Henrietta Beck, who had been highly decorated for her appearances before German soldiers during World War I and who enjoyed the patronage of Goering's wife (also a former opera singer), and the singer Julia Sallinger, whose privileges derived from her two sons, the illegitimate offspring of Prince Hohen-zollern. There was also Ida Steinhuber, the widow of the Bavarian SA chief murdered by the Nazis in 1934; Countess Seyssel d'Aix, whose two sons fought on the German front; Baroness von Bleichröder, the granddaughter of Gershon Bleichröder, Bis-marck's banker and financial adviser; Rudolf von Hirsch, philan-thropist Baron Hirsch's nephew; and Karl von Weinberg, formerly on the administrative board of the A. G. Farben conglomerate.

Also "prominents" were such former senior officers in the Austro-Hungarian army as Johann Georg Franz Friedländer, with the rank of lieutenant field-marshal, as well as various former government ministers: Georg Gradenauer, the prime minister of Saxony; Léon Meyer, France's trade minister; Alfred Meissner, Czechoslovakia's minister of justice; Fritz Rathenau, cousin to Walter Rathenau, Germany's foreign minister during the Weimar Republic.

The privileged residents lived two to five in a room in small houses away from the crowds, received special food rations and permission to write letters frequently, did not need to work (al-though most chose to, as long as they were physically able), had maid services, and were protected from transports—if they were "Grade-A privileged." "Grade-B privileged" received only prefer-ential living quarters, not exemption from transports. The latter category included some collaborators, such as Mandler (owner of the Black Rose travel agency, which had flourished in the days of feverish emigration to Palestine), who had organized transports from various cities in the Protectorate. Mandler, a well-known scoundrel, was subjected to a healthy beating by anonymous ghetto residents who sought to settle accounts with him once he came to Theresienstadt.

In the homes of the "prominents" people still used titles from the past. Women greeted one another as Frau Baronin and Frau Gräfin, and when one of the workers of the commendable *Putzkolonne* (a former writer) tried to give a message to Professor Emil Klein of Jena University, considered the father of naturopathy, he cut her off tersely: "I do not speak to servants." Professor Alfred Philipson, a world-renowned geographer, lived in highly overcrowded quarters along with ordinary mortals, until he received a postcard from the Swedish writer and researcher Sven Hedin, a known Nazi sympa-thizer. As a result of this postcard, Philipson was accorded not only the status of a "prominent" but also the right to bring books and periodicals from his Bonn library to the ghetto.

On the eve of Rosh Hashanah, the Jewish new year, rumor spread among the Jews in the ghetto that Himmler himself was expected, and indeed Seidl ordered several shops to be quickly opened. The tenants of the "shops" were hastily removed, the stores were painted and turned into official business premises, selling cosmetics, food, shoes, clothing, household goods, suitcases, stationery, and books. Ghetto residents were allocated purchase slips, merchandise was priced by points, and points were released in series for various shops. All this was done with complicated bureaucratic procedure and detailed instructions (for shoes and clothing, special approval was required as well as purchase slips), but actually the shops stocked nothing but junk—dilapidated suitcases, old pots, items leftover from the confiscated cargoes after the Germans had taken everything of use. The food shop sold herbal tea, a powder for preparing a liquid that tasted of compote, and a spread that tasted like mustard.

The ghetto prepared to celebrate its first Rosh Hashanah. The Council of Elders sent all residents greetings through the orders of the day and expressed the hope that next year, too, it would be possible to work successfully and ensure the friendly cooperation of the entire population. Ushering in the new year, the Council of Elders thanked all employees in factories, workshops, and other jobs, as well as those who tended the sick, and the office staff for their devoted and responsible work, and took this opportunity to ask, as it was in the habit of doing, that all residents maintain iron discipline and act with all their might to ensure reasonable living conditions for all.

At the central ceremony in honor of Rosh Hashanah, Cantor Goldring sang the hymn Unetaneh Tokef ("We will celebrate the mighty holiness of this day . . .") according to the tune composed by Yossele Rosenblatt, and the kaddish of the Berdichev rabbi. The men's choir, conducted by Otto Fischer, sang the Nineteenth Psalm. Otto Klein, head of the boys' home, read several verses from Micah, and Jeremiah 31:2–14: "For I will turn their mourning into joy, and will comfort them, and make them rejoice from their sorrow." Otto Neumann read the penitential prayer in a Czech translation by engineer Fritz Faustka, who had long ago been a member of Kibbutz Ein-Harod but had returned to Czechoslovakia and worked many years as a Hebrew teacher.

Yom Kippur, the Day of Atonement, was for the Germans a normal working day. But many of the ghetto residents, especially the elderly, fasted, even without having eaten the traditional large meal before the fast. On the eve of Yom Kippur, Edelstein spoke to the workers, the tenants of the Sudeten barracks, and as always with a note of encouragement. "We shall overcome."

On Zucker's birthday a few days later, a party was held for him and the limited circle of ghetto staff, and Yekef gave an "interesting address," as Gonda recorded in his diary in Hebrew: "a privileged ghetto as a cover for the blood and sacrifices of the ghettos in the East, a privileged ghetto where more than one hundred people die every day." The ghetto celebrated birthdays, anniversaries, and other important dates religiously, to have a reason to rejoice, to measure time on its march to the long-awaited end, to ward off fear of the lurking separation. An entire industry for small gifts existed in the ghetto: pictures, songs, mock dictionaries of ghetto life, and pendants made of tin or wood, the most popular of which was in the shape of Old Theresienstadt's emblem: a gate in the wall of the fortress, two turrets, and between them a lion with a sword in one hand and in the other a shield marked with the letters *MT*, an eternal memento of Empress Maria Theresa.

The fearsome scenes of elderly people being shipped east, and the Days of Awe, left their mark on the month of September. There were almost no entertainment performances, and cultural activities were restricted to lectures and holy-day programs. Among other events, Otto Zucker was to give a talk in the Sudeten barrack on the history of the ghetto. A poster of the event was hung up in the entrance to the building and the Jewish policeman who stood guard was instructed to remove it should the SS approach. Suddenly Janetschek appeared, the Czech chief of police who tried to atone for his origins by constantly harassing the inmates and informing on them. He spied the hasty removal of the poster and suspected underground activity. The Jews feared that the affair might lead to the shutdown of the entire department for leisure-time planning, as it was cumbersomely called in German, and as usual Edelstein went to Seidl to smooth things over. Edelstein explained to Seidl that he had intended to inform him of Zucker's lecture but because he had failed to reach him in time, the poster had been removed at the last minute. The camp commandant took note of Edelstein's explanation, and the lecture took place officially two days later. From that time on, the cultural department had to submit an advance list of

weekly events to headquarters, which somehow gave it official recognition and brought it aboveground.

In his capacity as assistant to the Elder of the Jews, Zucker was in
charge of cultural affairs, to which he was by nature and interest
inclined. It was his task to present the weekly schedule to Seidl, after
having changed potentially problematic lecture titles, thereby cam-
ouflaging their true content. During one week (September 22 to 26,
1943), the following events took place in office rooms, basements,
attics, old-age residences, and the school hall:

1. TRAVELOGUES:
   Prof. Federman: Rome and Chicago—from the activities of a
   translator.
   Karl Freiherr von Hirsch: Journey Through France.
   Alfred Sucharipa: Travel Adventures Throughout the World.
2. GENERAL EDUCATION:
   Prof. Werner: Jacob at the Well: Theory and Practice [the origi-
   nal title had been "On the Building of Palestine," but this was
   changed in the version presented to the Germans].
   Prof. A. Sadek: On Jewish Art.
   Otto Brod: The Importance of Voltaire: One Man's Contribu-
   tion to Civilization.
   Prof. Dr. Steinhertz: Brief Chapters from Jewish Life in Bo-
   hemia.
3. GENERAL LECTURES:
   Construction Consultant Eng. Schönberg: The Development
   of Electricity.
   Maurice Polak: Tales from Theater Life.
4. ARTISTIC PERFORMANCES:
   The Švenk Troupe: Entertainment.
   The Grab-Kernmayer Troupe: Songs Written at Theresien-
   stadt.
   The Klinka Troupe: Popular Songs and Arias.
   The Stark Troupe: Songs and Recitals.

All this took place on top of the regular courses in Czech, English,
French, Spanish, and Hebrew for beginners and advanced; the
reading evenings; the Sabbath parties in the children's and young
people's dormitories, the old people's living quarters, and barracks
courtyards, which provided an almost natural Shakespearean theater for afternoon performances.

Cultural events were performed voluntarily, out of a sense of
need, and outside working hours. But once the cultural department

was officially recognized, lectures and theatrical performances were considered overtime and every now and again the performers received payment, in the form of a supplementary spoon of beet jam or twenty grams of margarine. When Patia Fischel, a member of Maccabi Hatzair whose heart was in the theater, asked Vava Šenova to teach him acting, he said with pride, "I am not asking for free lessons," and produced a cucumber from his pocket as payment.

The Germans never laid down guidelines with respect to performances, but an internal censorship operated regarding the choice of plays and lecture topics, so as not to antagonize the Germans. For the same reason many activities were masked beneath innocuous covers. In fact, works that nobody would have dared perform outside the protective walls of the ghetto were performed at Theresienstadt: in some respects, it was the most liberal stage in all of occupied Central Europe.

In October 1942, a Hehalutz convention was held in the ghetto, accompanied as usual by lengthy debate: the younger members had serious complaints about the old guard (that is, against those members who were approaching or even past the ripe old age of thirty), and vice versa; there was harsh criticism about the lack of a clear program, the minimum of deeds, as had always been the case at Hehalutz conventions, both in freedom and in bondage. The practical outcome of the deliberations was the decision to unite the diverse movement streams in youth education, and, after liberation, to bring tidings of a united kibbutz movement to Palestine. In more limited forums, the Hehalutz people discussed the question of physical labor in Palestine: did they honestly want to be laborers? Would they not be leaving the ghetto somewhat deficient? Would they be able to live in a kibbutz? And what about the married women—would they be able to live in a collective? "Every woman likes to command some personal property, to cook, to organize; and children's education is also important to them," Gonda recorded in his diary.

Hehalutz in Theresienstadt lacked a dominant personality (the true leader was in fact Yekef Edelstein, but he was too busy with general ghetto affairs). Still, the leadership, composed of people from Kibbutz Hameuhad and Maccabi Hatzair, as well as representatives of the pioneers who had come from Germany, were dedicated, and conscious of the responsibility they bore: in their hands lay the future of the movement, and of the next generation.

There were several hundred pioneers in the ghetto, and in order to ascertain the precise figure, a census was held in the spring of 1943: every member had to deposit forty grams of sugar in a common kitty as a sign of membership. In this manner, one thousand members were counted and the kitty amassed a treasure of forty kilos of sugar to aid sick members. As an extension of the mutual aid activities, there was also a permanent fee: twenty grams of margarine or thirty grams of sugar per month. Considering the fact that the weekly ration was seventy grams of sugar and forty to sixty grams of margarine per person, this fee was a not insignificant measure of one's readiness and sense of sacrifice. The members who worked in the food line—the kitchens, the food stores, and the bakery—were also taxed separately for the Hehalutz general store, which packed food parcels each week for members who were sick or chronically ill, especially with consumption, and prepared parcels of provisions for those who left on transports east.

"If we can only save the young people under thirty-five," Edelstein repeatedly told his friends, "the Jewish people will have biological continuity." In the efforts to save the younger generation for the regeneration of the Jewish people, the members of Hehalutz and the Zionist youth movements played an important role; justifiably or not, they considered themselves an elite: there was substance to their deeds, purpose to their stay in the ghetto. Through key people on the staff of the employment department, Hehalutz members were assigned to productive jobs and the care of youngsters after they had completed their stint of unskilled work in the groups of a hundred. They were permitted to room together in separate halls in the barracks and dormitories, and, most important, for a long time many of them were protected from transports, whether by virtue of their jobs, or through Leo Janowitz in his key position as general secretary. Idealistic motives were in play here, together with personal considerations, but there can be no doubt that the Hehalutz people sincerely tried to prepare themselves and their young charges for a future life in Palestine.

Because they were far away and isolated, Palestine symbolized freedom and justice, a kind of Jerusalem-on-high in secular terms, almost totally divorced from reality. There was a slender mail connection with Palestine through Budapest and Bratislava, via members of Hehalutz who were still in Prague, mostly underground, and from them in letters smuggled to the ghetto, or through clandestine meetings with labor groups outside. But for security reasons only a handful of members of the Hehalutz leadership knew of these contacts. For everybody else, Palestine and liberation went hand in hand, the realization of all their longings, and very few were as aware of concrete reality as Gonda Redlich: "I will come to Palestine without vain hopes. I know that there, too, there are only people with human weaknesses and open to error; but I know, too, that the idea of justice is real and exists."

Hehalutz Day took place on Laag Be'Omer in May 1943, on the lawns of the walls under the open skies. It included competitions and addresses, and ended with a massive assembly where Yekef gave a talk. He reviewed the value of pioneering activity and asked that the intensive work continue. Finally, in the best of old-time tradition, everyone danced an enthusiastic hora. The important Hehalutz work, however, took place in small forums, in the rooms of the pioneers, the teenage dorms, in lectures, Sabbath get-togethers, and programs organized for holidays, Herzl Day, and a Bialik festival. For this last a speaking choir prepared Bialik's "The Dead of the Desert," and the youth-movement youngsters studied and learned the difficult Hebrew words which they barely understood.

> So rise, wanderers, leave the wasteland!
> But raise not your voices, tread firmly in silence.

Hebrew study was compulsory among the pioneers, but everyone interpreted this obligation in his own fashion, according to his nature and diligence, and very few were as dedicated as Gonda. "I've been studying Hebrew for three years now, and I still come across new words I don't understand. Hebrew is a difficult language. I keep at it, but I can't say that I know it. And what will those people do who only start to study Hebrew in Palestine? They'll never learn it. I'd like to be fluent in Hebrew before I get to Palestine—and be able to read newspapers, books, speak."

The advanced students studied with Professor Kestenbaum and Professor Voskin-Nahartabi, a former lecturer at Halle University who fled to Prague after Hitler's rise to power and opened a seminary for rabbis. In the course of time, a nucleus of Hebrew speakers formed in the ghetto who proudly displayed their emblem, the Hebrew letter *ayin*. In the certificate that went with the emblem, and was headed by the motto "Speak Hebrew and be healed," recipients were asked to fulfill their obligations toward the language and respect the emblem. "The Jewish people cannot be revived if the language is not revived. A memento of Hebrew Week, There-sienstadt Exile." But the vast majority of youth-movement members failed somewhere along the way, whether because of illness, worry over sick relatives, the burden of work, the fear of transports, or lack of staying power.

One of the child-care institutions opened in the ghetto was a Hebrew-speaking kindergarten, where seventy children were taught by a kindergarten teacher from Palestine (there were several former kibbutz members in the ghetto, who had returned to Czechoslovakia either because of illness or disappointment with Palestine). In the children's houses, where Hebrew study was not compulsory, several classes were organized, a Hebrew library set up, and workbooks issued to students. A Hebrew committee, led by Jacky Wurzel and Professor Voskin-Nahartabi, even invented new words for terms necessary in the ghetto. Exams were held—and all this under the constant shadow of incoming and outgoing transports, which swept away teachers and pupils alike.

From time to time small handwritten glossaries were put out, with useful words for day-to-day life in the ghetto: bugs, roster duty, private property, nail, board, mattress, peel, caraway soup, ersatz fat. The severance from Palestine left its mark, and the glossaries included strange inventions as well. But people continued to learn, to copy, to study.

Among the Hehalutz committees in the ghetto, which included those for Hebrew, education, and mutual aid, was also a security committee, composed of members who filled key positions. Its major function was to acquire information from the outside world and draw up plans of the barracks and passageways in the walls should the Germans attempt to liquidate the ghetto before they retreated at the end of the war—which was getting ever closer. But there was no practical plan for an uprising or armed combat, and the only weapons that the security committee possessed were a few sets of brass knuckles. The Maccabi people and the communists had their own underground, but the chief concern of all was for the chaos that would undoubtedly precede the end of German rule. There was no practical preparation for an uprising because the danger of death did not seem imminent.

There were openings onto the outside world. Ghetto labor gangs came into contact with railroad workers and Czech chimney sweeps who worked in the ghetto. Aryan relatives came to the wooden fence that separated the ghetto from the main road, once the time and place of meeting had been determined through a go-between, in order to exchange a few words with relatives, even if they could not see their faces. The agricultural workers were left in the fields unsupervised from time to time. They could see the passing cars on the Dresden-Prague highway, but did not flee, out of loyalty to their families in the ghetto, out of ignorance of the death that awaited them in the East, out of certain knowledge that without Aryan papers and contacts there was nowhere to flee except straight into the arms of the Gestapo or the first informer; and also because there were no forests in the vicinity to offer cover. Some of the fields were opposite the Little Fortress, and the agricultural workers could see the prisoners forced to run up slopes with stone-filled wheelbarrows, hour after hour; they saw the SS standing over them, and felt compassion: compared with them, the ghetto inmates lived almost as free men. To the Little Fortress were sent political prisoners, Jews who had broken the anti-Jewish laws, and their accomplices. The SS guards had a reputation for brutality and sadism. Thousands of prisoners of the Little Fortress (where the murderers of the Austrian crown prince Ferdinand had been held during the Hapsburg monarchy) were tortured, beaten, and murdered inside its walls, and the SS brought their bodies in coffins to the ghetto crematorium to burn them. Compared with the SS, the Czech guards and gendarmes were almost angels.

Rarely did prisoners make the trip back from the Little Fortress to the ghetto alive. One of the few who reached the ghetto, after terrible torture, his spirit unbroken, was Slavek Lederer of Pilsen, forty-two years old, a former officer in the Czech army and member of the Czech underground. Caught by the Gestapo, he was transferred from the Little Fortress to the ghetto with instructions to ship him out in the first transport east. Since firemen were exempt from transport, Edelstein and Zucker appealed to Leo Holzer, head of the ghetto fire brigade, to employ Lederer with his men until he had recovered from the horrors of the Little Fortress.

At first it was not difficult to escape from the ghetto, especially for people who worked on the outside. All one had to do was take off the Jewish badge, buy a train ticket at Bohušovice, and disembark a few hours later in Prague. But it was almost impossible to escape capture on the outside. One of the escapees made a mistake and got on the bus to the Sudetenland instead of Prague. He was caught at the border and hanged. Another couple was caught after forgetting to remove the numbers painted on their luggage. In April 1943, the order of the day announced that due to the disappearance of six ghetto inmates (three of whom had been caught escaping), Seidl had forbidden people to leave their quarters except for work, official duty, or to get food, and had prohibited lights in the residences. All cultural activities were stopped, and the curfew was lifted only a month later (with the threat of renewal if garbage were found in the streets). In the ghetto's first two years, twenty-eight people escaped, of whom eleven were soon caught; it is not known if the others, who included two women, survived the war.

24

MONEY ON SHOW

IT SEEMED as if Jewish order had superimposed itself on the initial German chaos. Repair shops were opened for watches, fountain pens, orthopedic shoes, and even socks and underwear could be given to mend: one torn pair paid for the repair of three. There was a sense of permanence in the long lines for handing in laundry or buying at shops which, even though they stocked very little, still added a certain variety to life. A spark of illusion: *going shopping*. The people who ran the depots for collecting dirty laundry were mainly former merchants, owners of large businesses who retained the courtesy of their former life: they greeted the clients with their soiled bundles warmly, and returned their clean laundry to them as if it were merchandise bought with money.

Provisions gradually improved. Officially the ghetto residents received the same daily ration of calories as the Czech population (1,600 in 1942), but this included no butter, eggs, fat, vegetables, or dairy products. Even if hunger could be borne, the chief hardship was the total lack of all fresh protein and vitamins, apart from the vegetables the agricultural workers managed to lift from the gardens. Beginning in the fall of 1942, the diet included meat once or twice a week, the remnants of necessary slaughter, a spoonful of guts, sometimes called goulash, sometimes hash. In the mornings, a coffee substitute made of herbs was distributed—unsweetened, as sugar was distributed separately, seventy grams or seven flat tea-spoons per week. But it was a pity to waste it on a lukewarm liquid whose only resemblance to coffee lay in its dark color. People ate sugar sprinkled on bread and margarine and considered it cake. For special occasions—birthdays, anniversaries—women prepared cakes that were almost real: bitter bread soaked in coffee and drained, spread with a cream made of sugar and margarine, topped with another layer of bread and garnished with beet jam (one teaspoon per week).

For lunch there was a grayish liquid called soup, and a ration of potatoes—sometimes in their skins, sometimes rotten, sweet-tasting, and acrid—supposedly weighing three hundred grams. The cooks did the best they could. They added sauce to the potatoes, varying the flavoring with mustard, caraway, and dill. Once a week the potatoes were replaced by a dumpling made of flour and yeast, or a yeast cake with a cream made of the ersatz coffee, a sweetener, and margarine, which to the inmates tasted of heaven. In the small kitchens in the residences, the women prepared dishes from leftover bread, stolen potatoes, the roux they had brought from home, and the herbs they picked at work, and in the evenings they exchanged recipes: "I used to add a few tablespoons of sweet cream to my mushroom sauce."

Considering the various stages of total war, the food supply was comparatively regular, due chiefly to the fact that Himmler's SS kingdom had priority with suppliers. But from time to time there was a shortage of salt and the food became entirely tasteless. Coal failed to arrive and heat in the rooms was permitted only when temperatures fell to five degrees below zero (centigrade). Sometimes the orders of the day would contain such announcements as that the supply of glass had come to an end and that therefore broken windows could not be repaired, or instructions to economize on office paper, because no new shipment was expected in the near future.

A talent for inventiveness and technical know-how overcame most situations: the electricity supply grew from 405 to 651 kilowatts, the water supply gradually improved and eventually averaged one hundred liters per capita per day, which meant that everyone could wash at the faucet daily and do dishes and a bit of laundry—if only with cold water and no soap—after a lengthy wait on line. The boilers of the beer brewery (one of Terezin's few industries when it was a city of gentiles), now furnished enough steam for the kitchens, the carpentry, the hospitals, and the disinfection center. The sewage system was repaired, the number of toilets increased to 1,500, 60 percent of which had water, the fences between the inner court-yards were dismantled to make the living space outdoors more open. The old military bakery was expanded and could now turn out 50,000 buns at a time, to be distributed on festive occasions, including Passover, as a special delicacy. A noodle factory was set up that consumed 700 kilos of flour daily; its output went mainly to the ill, the children, and the diet kitchens.

In certain respects life in the ghetto seemed freer than before, when the Jews had been ostracized within the general population. On the outside, all synagogues had been shut down, whereas in the ghetto, even if explicit permission had not been given, there was no ban on public prayer, and one after another, synagogues opened up in the various barracks, the attics, the office rooms, and the perfor-mance halls. Edelstein prayed regularly on Sabbath eve in the Mag-deburg synagogue, and after several rabbis came to the ghetto he used his authority as Elder of the Jews to appoint Rabbi Sigmund Unger of Brünn Theresienstadt's chief rabbi. Rabbi Unger and his two deputies together constituted a rabbinical court, though offi-cially they worked for the burial department. There was no lack of cantors in the ghetto, nor holy-day prayer books, nor sacred ob-jects—the only thing impossible to obtain was wine for the benedic-tion, and black coffee (a substitute in itself) was used instead. The rabbis mostly worked according to a duty roster in the mortuaries and purification rooms (preparing the bodies for burial), but they also gave religious instruction, prepared boys for their bar mitzvahs, and officiated at weddings.

Despite the fact that they could not live together and civil mar-riage was impossible, couples sometimes sought a formal bond any-way, whether out of a desire to share their fate with someone come what may, or in the hope of being saved from transports east by virtue of a protected mate. Following the wedding, either with a rabbi or without, couples could declare their life partnership at the records department, which meant that they would leave together for the East or stay together in the ghetto. In 1942, 142 couples declared that they were married; in 1943 the number rose to 233. Sometimes the couple asked for a ceremony beneath the wedding canopy just before they were deported. Instead of taking a honey-moon tour they journeyed toward death.

Sex—beneath a blanket in a room full of people, on the grass of the ghetto walls, in offices that emptied toward evening, in the private rooms of the privileged, out of love, a need for comfort, a desire to crowd into life everything possible, in return for food or status—was not without its consequences. Contraceptives had been confiscated at the start and were banned, and a young man found with a condom was tried by the Germans for sabotage.

When Seidl told Edelstein that all pregnancies, whether in single or married women, must be terminated, Yekef said to Dittl Ornstein, "They want to crush the Jewish people." Because of undernourishment, women did not menstruate regularly, and as a result pregnancy was sometimes discovered too late to abort. There were girls who refused to have abortions on principle, even if it meant expulsion to the East, and they gave birth covertly. Because the Germans had at first allowed pregnancies to run their course, if the woman had arrived at the ghetto pregnant, records were falsified from time to time, by order of Edelstein or Janowitz, to allow women who had become pregnant in the ghetto to give birth. In this way two hundred and thirty children were born in Theresienstadt, some after the general ban on births which came into effect in July 1943, and under the shadow of the German threat to send the father, the mother, and the baby on transports to the East.

Abortions were performed by doctors in the hospital, and after a few hours' rest the women returned to their rooms. Following German orders, Dr. Munk, head of the health department, sent a circular to all doctors asking them to report all cases of pregnancy without delay and warning that any doctor who failed to do so would be considered an accessory to the crime. And yet babies still saw the light of day, sometimes by special dispensation from a German high official. Among the proud fathers were also some Hehalutz people, including Gonda Redlich, head of the youth department, who kept a diary in the ghetto for his son Dan. The diary concluded with the following words: "Tomorrow we too will go. Would that the hour of our redemption were near." The entry was dated October 1944, when Gonda, his wife, Gerti, and their baby were sent—in a locally manufactured wooden carriage—to the gas chambers at Auschwitz. Twenty-three of the children born at Theresienstadt survived the war.

There was no way to get a legal divorce in the ghetto, but a couple could ask to be recorded separately in the general files, which meant separation for purposes of transport. Some marriages grew stronger in the ghetto. Others broke under the pressures, the separation, the constant strain, the temptation to form liaisons with the "nobility"—the cooks, the bakers, the butchers, the stockmen. In the summer of 1943, a man came to Edelstein and told him that after twelve years of marriage his wife had just become pregnant. He was not prepared to have the child aborted. Later his wife came to Yekef and told him that her husband was not the father of the child; she asked for an abortion.

Hope for the future was stronger than the anguish of the present. People clung to life, for the sake of someone or something, for the sake of life itself. True, compared with the rate among the general population in Czechoslovakia, suicide and suicide attempts were high (336 per 100,000 as against 30 per 100,000), but considering the level of personal distress, the figure was very low: out of 120,000 people who arrived at the ghetto in the first two years, only 768 tried to commit suicide, and only 246 succeeded. The others were saved—for a different sort of death. Among the Czech Jews, the chief reasons for suicide were transport orders and fear of them or of separation from family. Among the aged from the Reich, the chief cause was simply the reality of the ghetto: there seemed no point in living such a life. People committed suicide by swallowing poison, cutting their veins, jumping from the third floor of the barracks, hanging themselves. One form of suicide, however, escaped the statistics because it was caused by omission rather than commission: the will to carry on simply burned out.

In the early days of the ghetto, the main causes of death were pneumonia, consumption, and execution. But after August 1941, with the start of transports from Germany and Austria, old age became the chief cause. Though most of the elderly had left their homes in relatively good health, the ghetto broke them and disappointment knocked them down. Their shock at what they found in the ghetto in place of the health resort they had been promised, the undernourishment, the frequent intestinal infections, took their toll. Despite the overcrowding, communicable diseases took only fifth place in the causes of death (at Theresienstadt everything was recorded). Few of the young people and children feared death, which in the ghetto was mainly the lot of the aged. In the first two years, in fact, only eighty children under ten died (as opposed to almost 15,000 people between the ages of seventy and eighty for the same period).

Postal contact with the outside world remained intermittent, despite all the German promises. Only in the spring of 1943 was a regular routine achieved, with permission granted on a roster system and letters restricted to those same frustrating thirty-word postcards. The censor (usually a jurist, who had tackled more difficult tasks in his time) collected the postcards from the homes, checked to see if they complied with regulations, and returned those that did not. From the censor's office the postcards were transferred to the ghetto command, from there to the Central Office for the Solution of the Jewish Problem (as the Zentralstelle was called after the summer of 1942), and from there to community representatives in Prague, Berlin, and Vienna, who saw that they were forwarded to their destinations by regular mail. The procedure often took weeks, sometimes months, and the cards often reached their destination long after the writers had been shipped east or had already departed this world. But they left the recipients with the illusion of life in a normal location—an address, even a street number.

The members of the Council of Elders and senior functionaries were permitted to write more frequently, and sometimes the restriction on the number of words was even lifted. In the fall of 1942, Edelstein was allowed to write to Geneva for the first time. When his letter, dated October 19, 1942, reached Dr. Ullman, it had been stamped "opened by the Wehrmacht" and had apparently taken almost three weeks to reach the postal service from the Reich Security Head Office in Berlin. There was no doubt that Edelstein had chosen his words with care.

Dear Ully,

Letters are not philosophical treatises but an expression of daily life. Whether we live, how we live, and to what purpose—those are the interesting questions. You needn't worry, we are alive and well.

Miriam, in addition to her duties as a housewife, is working in the garden, a job that she likes and finds satisfying. As is her nature, she takes her work seriously and will no doubt become a skilled gardener after proper training. Our son has developed nicely; he is comparatively knowledgeable and has proved himself a good student, both diligent and quick to learn. Perhaps my proud paternal heart judges the child too indulgently; nevertheless our Arieh is a wonderful boy and you would enjoy him.

As for myself, I am swamped with work; as director of the entire organization I carry a heavy responsibility. Physically and mentally I am under much tension, but the belief that I am doing my job devotedly and that my efforts are successful gives me true joy. Work for the common good, no matter how difficult, always gives one the strength and courage for new beginnings and deeds.

Organizing public life is no simple matter. It is unnecessary to describe how complex such work is. Everything must be arranged so that all things will be coordinated and fit together like cogwheels. The administrative network, technical achievements, economic enterprises, sanitation measures—everything must be arranged and created, suitable experts chosen and placed in the right jobs—this, too, is no light task. If I can summarize these efforts as successful, you can understand my feeling of satisfaction and share my happiness in these achievements. Our people work together, relations are good and everyone is always prepared to help. You would marvel at the achievements of our friend Dr. Munk: a hospital to be proud of, the latest sanitary installations, baby nurseries, dormitories for children and the elderly, all sparkling clean and carefully tended, all an endeavor one can contemplate with satisfaction.

In other areas too organization has not failed us. A well-organized economic department enables well-planned work and ensures fair distribution and a supply of necessary goods to all. In every area there may be imperfections, but always there is goodwill and the ability and necessary conditions for development, expansion, completion. Nothing can be achieved without energy and effort and if we fail on the first try, we start again from the beginning.

Zucker and Janowitz are with me and they play a considerable part in all endeavors; their families are also well and send regards. Even my secretary Steif followed me here and fills her former function; she too sends warm regards.

I would be so happy to get a letter from you. Is Lotte well? Is Lichtheim still in Geneva? If so, give him and his family warm regards. Do you have any news of our Max [Miriam's brother]? My mother-in-law, who is also here with me and well, would be glad of a letter from him.

I await news from you, I am interested in every detail of your activities.

> I greet you and Lotte in friendship,
> Yours,
> Jakob

Whatever doubts there may have been as to how accurately Edelstein's letter reflected the situation, especially considering the opening lines of his letter, his satisfaction at what was being done in the ghetto rang true. Ullman answered in a similar vein, speaking of various achievements and praising the devotion of Edelstein, Zucker, Munk, and Janowitz in their never-ending work. "Your letter

339

was the most precious sign of life from all contemporary friends." Ullman wanted to know if Jakob had received the small parcel he had sent as a test case, to see if it would get there.

Gerhart Riegner, the delegate of the World Jewish Congress in Geneva, gave a copy of Edelstein's letter to, among others, Karl Burckhardt, the chairman of the International Red Cross, and both men were particularly struck by the opening lines, which they read as a hint of the true situation. At a meeting on November 17, 1942, which dealt with the question of International Red Cross aid to the Jews who had been expelled, Burckhardt noted that his organization had repeatedly appealed to the German Red Cross about German treatment of the civilian population, the Jews, and the execution of Polish, French, Czech and Dutch hostages. But the representative of the German Red Cross had told him openly that as far as the Jews were concerned, nothing could be done. Burckhardt said that the International Red Cross had considered lodging a formal protest with the German government. They had not done so, however, for fear that it would not only achieve nothing but would also adversely affect the activities of the Red Cross on behalf of other citizens under German occupation; and he, Burckhardt, as a realist, preferred practical help to vain protests.

The issue was debated rather heatedly, and Riegner pointed out that protests should be made only if it was certain that there was no other hope for the Jews. Ever since Hitler's order to destroy all the Jews by 1942 had become known, it seemed the Jews were doomed. But recent political events had changed the situation at least somewhat. Opposition might be growing among the Germans themselves, and they would perhaps look for an alibi to use after the war. If a protest was not to be lodged, then some other action at least must be undertaken beyond merely drawing up statistics on transports. Burckhardt said he was prepared to request official permission from the Foreign Office in Berlin for a Red Cross delegation to visit the ghettos in Poland, at Theresienstadt, and in the Transnistria camps in the Ukraine. This request proved to be a decisive turning point in the history of the Theresienstadt ghetto: no longer was it to be a labor camp for the Protectorate Jews, nor an old-age home for the Jews of the Reich; it was to be a showpiece for the world, a stage set to hide the truth.

The first tangible result of the request made by the International Red Cross was permission to send collective parcels to Theresienstadt containing food and medicines, and gift parcels for individuals. The first shipment, addressed to Jakob Edelstein, containing 100 crates of preserved milk, 1,000 kilos of prunes, and 2,000 kilos of powdered soup, was sent in May 1943. It is not clear how much of the shipment was confiscated by the SS and how much reached the Jews (nobody in the ghetto ever saw prunes), but the Red Cross continued to send collective shipments, financed by Jewish institutions, following approval from Theresienstadt. During 1943 a total of fifty-four tons were sent, for the most part containing milk and dried fruit and vegetables. After notification was received that medicines were sorely needed, eighty-six crates full of medicines and body-building materials such as malt extract and calcium were dispatched as well.

In the telegram Riegner sent to the World Jewish Congress in New York, he noted that the test parcels sent to individuals in Theresienstadt had reached their destination and that new letters had been received from the ghetto. Riegner asked for a special allocation of funds for the activities of the Red Cross and according to the decision taken by the Congress in March 1943, £1,000 was allotted monthly for the purchase of food and medicine to be sent to the Council of Elders, and £4,000 for the purpose of food shipments to individuals. Since parcels could not be sent from Switzerland to countries under German rule, one-kilogram parcels, usually containing sardines and dried figs, were sent from Portugal.

Among the first few hundred people to receive parcels, on the basis of a list drawn up with Ullman's help, was the entire Zionist leadership. One of the first recipients to confirm receipt of the parcel from Lisbon was Zucker. A letter written on January 15, 1943, contained, apart from the usual assurances as to the ghetto dwellers' well-being and regards to friends and relatives, two allusions to his forced restraint: "I assume that you have no great interest in the details of our management, which are of course adapted to local conditions." Zucker remarked on the friendly relations with Desider Friedmann and Robert Stricker from Vienna, "who now work with us here. They have already written to you themselves, and it goes without saying that we continue our work with their support. You would enjoy seeing how, even under different living conditions, people find a way to work constructively, adapt, change their professions, all by applying themselves, and with moderately successful results. Former attorneys and businessmen become laborers, even do strenuous physical work, and prove themselves in their new occupations. Despite the hard work, they are still able to listen attentively to a lecture in the evening, or attend a play, of which there is no lack here." To Zucker's letter, Edelstein added brief handwritten greetings.

In honor of the ghetto's anniversary, the members of the employment department prepared a gift for Yekef—a history of the year in the ghetto, told in drawings by the artist Leo Haas, and presented in a heavy wooden binding, as a sign of love and appreciation. They received a letter of thanks from Edelstein in which he again spoke of his fateful decision of December the previous year, after his talk with Günther, when he had wondered if he had the right to take his close friends with him into chaos and catastrophe. If at the time he had answered in the affirmative, he had done so in the spirit of the wider sense of the word *halutz*, the pioneer who translates ideals into action, who must take his place wherever the fate of the Jewish people is to be decided. At the end of one year, Edelstein could summarize the situation thus:

> I believe that you share my feelings, and I am happy to say that on this crucial point, I have not been disappointed in the least.
>
> The year at Theresienstadt has not passed without leaving its mark on us all, as I am even better aware than the rest of you. The consciousness that I am doing a historic job, and the constant fear that I will not be able to cope with the immense task, have shaped my attitude. More than once I have learnt humility, and I have realized how little we know and how few are our creative and original talents. Under the pressure of these feelings, I have grown more nervous and less confident in myself, a fact that onlookers interpret as signs of weakness, or lack of courage to execute things we planned. At Theresienstadt I have grown more serious, and, surprisingly enough, also more obstinate and stiff-necked.
>
> If I were to review the past year, I would have to admit that all the things I really wanted and which were worth fighting for have gradually been realized. But it is a system that takes its toll on my personality. I have become less candid and honest, sometimes even with my friends. I would like to assure you today, that despite everything, I have never strayed from the path of fellowship and true friendship.
>
> I wanted to say these things to you in order to express my satisfaction at the choice I made on December 3, 1941, to tell you

that a beneficent destiny has fashioned our lives better than I had then imagined and feared, and that despite the changes in my personality, I have remained your true friend.

Sincerely,
Yekef

The ghetto's first anniversary was marked in all departments, institutions, and barracks. Zucker, who was in charge of cultural affairs in his capacity as assistant Elder of the Jews, received a present from the cultural department of poems written or translated in the ghetto, including translations from German into Czech of Maurice Rosenfeld's "Song of the Ghetto" and Goethe's "Sorcerer's Apprentice."

Edelstein spoke to the workers on the self-administration of the ghetto. Josef Klaber, chief of police, addressed the policemen and reviewed the ghetto's development in the past year. He mentioned the many achievements, including the surprising fact that in the appallingly overcrowded conditions, where 58,000 people lived in an area that had previously housed only 7,000, there had not been a single case of murder, no incidents of violence, no rape, robbery, or physical injuries committed by Jews. In that one year the Jewish police had recorded 5,200 violations, of which 72 percent were thefts. The rest had been offenses against ghetto regulations and the inheritance laws (all the possessions of the dead were ghetto property and next of kin could take only a wedding ring, a personal memento, and vital items owned in common). Only 2 percent of the offenses had been squabbles, 2 percent breaches of faith, and one percent affairs of honor. These dry statistics, perhaps more than the lofty words of readiness for sacrifice and devotion that were voiced on the first anniversary, testified to the true caliber of Theresienstadt's Jews, human frailty notwithstanding: despite the hunger, the density, the personal agony, the disease, Jewish life among Jews was safe for as long as it lasted, and people preserved their humanity. Most of the speeches, like Klaber's, ended on an optimistic note: for the first time in the history of the fortress, a breach had been made in the southern walls to enable the laying of railroads into the ghetto—a road which would lead also to a new life.

Christmas was once again celebrated in the ghetto and now there were several priests among the residents, Catholics and Protestants, defined Jewish by race. They included Father Heinrich Kohner from Vienna and Pastor Goldschmied from Berlin. The two held mass in the Jewish ghetto near an altar drawn on paper, in an attic, where a small fir tree stood decorated with candles. The children of mixed marriages, who had become Jews as a result of the Nuremberg laws and did not understand what had happened to them, sang Christmas carols. The year 1942 drew to a close, and in retrospect the optimism of New Year's Eve 1941 appeared to have been premature, but now the situation was entirely different: now, if people said, "By the end of the new year we'll be home," their words were based on knowledge of the facts, not simply desire. Now that Rommel's army had suffered defeat at El Alamein, now that Anglo-American forces had landed in North Africa, now that the Russians had counterattacked on the Don and near Stalingrad—now the war could not last much longer. And when, a month later, rumor spread through the ghetto of the defeat of the German Sixth Army near Stalingrad, where almost one hundred thousand German soldiers were trapped—hungry, flayed by the cold, numb, and broken—there was no doubt left in anyone's mind: Hitler's fate had been decided. They had only to hold out until then.

Strange things began to happen in the ghetto. Cameramen came from Berlin and began filming local life. "They're making a film. The Jews are the actors, happy and content. They're happy in the film, but only in the film," Gonda recorded in his diary on November 9, 1942, and that same day Gonda had a meeting with Jakob. It was very frank, but instead of discussing the Germans, they discussed Hehalutz. "I don't think that anybody has talked like that to Jakob for a long time," Gonda wrote. "I may have harmed my own position. But what should we do? We must fight against the attitude of many of the members, who think their job consists of sitting on the Hehalutz council and making demands. In my opinion, no new movement can be created like that. The only remedy is for people to really work physically."

The propaganda film was completed. It was based on a rather shallow screenplay about a Jew named Holzer and his wife passing through all the stages of ghettoization, from being registered in their local community up to their arrival at Theresienstadt. The filmmakers left and the film itself was canceled by order from Berlin, but the show went on. At the beginning of December, by German order, a café was opened in the city square where there had once been a pub. Admission to the café was on the basis of slips and a roster system, with preference given to the "prominents" and disabled veterans. The slip entitled the customer to sit in the café for two hours, have a cup of ersatz coffee or herbal tea, and listen to popular concerts performed by ghetto musicians. All of a sudden, as if someone had waved a magic wand, musical instruments were permitted again, and permission was given to reclaim instruments from confiscated Jewish property. The café was open all day long until curfew, waiters in dark suits were in attendance, and it had a daily turnover of five hundred customers, mostly from among the elderly population of the Reich, who for this festive occasion donned whatever finery was still in their possession. There they sat, lost and fragile, nodding their heads to the sound of *Tales from the Vienna Woods* or tunes from *Carmen*.

Within a few weeks an explanation was finally given for the changes—the café, the orchestra, the sham shops. A group of SS visited the living quarters of the "prominents," found them overcrowded, and ordered them enlarged: a delegation was expected from Berlin. "The Germans want to build Potemkin villages," Gonda decided. "We are to be a showpiece," Yekef told Dittl Ornstein. "They are apparently expecting an international delegation." "You don't even begin to grasp how good you have it," Seidl said to Edelstein. "Theresienstadt is being turned into a ghetto of paradise."

The fact that money was to be introduced into the ghetto was made public in the fall of 1942. The German command asked the artists' studio to prepare several proposals for bills, and this was done by Peter Kien and engineer Heilbron, who used various Jewish motifs, such as a seven-branched candlestick. However when the bills finally arrived at the ghetto in the spring of 1943, in seven denominations ranging from one crown to one hundred and differentiated by color, the same eagle-nosed Moses stared out from each, his forehead creased in thought, his side curls extending to the Tablets that he held near his left ear. The bills, or vouchers as they were officially known, bore the date January 1, 1943, a Star of David, and the signature of Jakob Edelstein as the Elder of the Jews of Theresienstadt.

The treasure of 53 million crowns that arrived from Berlin was stored in the former municipality building, which served as a bank for all purposes, and Desider Friedmann from Vienna was appointed its director. Because of the delay in issuing the vouchers, the monetary system went into operation only in May of that year: deductions were made from salaries to pay for living quarters, food, medical care, public services; employees received a small sum in cash, and the balance was recorded in blocked individual savings accounts in the bank. Nothing could be bought for the money, but the vouchers were in great demand with collectors on the outside, and the bills were smuggled out in large quantities. In one month, out of the five million crowns issued, only two million returned to the bank. In order to increase the flow of money back to the treasury, payments were gradually introduced for the café, the plays, for receiving parcels. To buy merchandise in the ghost shops, the cracked clay vases and rhinestone bijouterie, money was now required as well as purchase slips (between fifteen and sixty crowns for a battered suitcase, between five and twenty for an old towel, depending on size). An employee's average wage was twenty-five crowns per month. Every ghetto resident had a savings passbook and the entire mechanism of recording salaries (at one's place of work) and welfare payments (through the residence administrators) employed a huge clerical staff. But there was no lack of former bank clerks, and as an attraction for visitors from the outside a visit to the bank could not be topped. Those who left for the East had to return all their money to the treasury before their departure—it could not be exchanged for any currency in the world.

Under the regular symbol of his office, denoted by the letters Z/L, Zucker dictated a memo to his secretary, Mrs. Lind, on October 29, 1942, to SS Obersturmführer Dr. Seidl, pertaining to the establishment of a lending library and reading room at Theresienstadt. The store of books in the ghetto, Zucker said, was relatively small, a total of four thousand volumes which had been brought from liquidated communities or confiscated by the German authorities from suitcases. The number of books could be significantly increased if books were brought from vacated Jewish homes, once they had been checked and sorted. The Germans considered the proposal and a month later the orders of the day announced that a library was to be opened in shop number L/304. Due to lack of space, however, only people who had a particular interest could visit the library, on the approval of Prof. Dr. Emil Utitz, its director. Everyone else was to receive books through the residence administrators. The mobile library moved from building to building, in cardboard boxes, thirty books to a box, absorbing germs and soup stains, here and there shedding pages, ripped out for other purposes in moments of supreme need. But the mobile library could not quench the thirst for reading: it was an incidental collection of Judaica containing many volumes of Jewish history by Dubnov or Graetz, as well as other reference books, while the number of novels in the collection, especially in Czech, was negligible. For two hours, twice daily, anybody who had ever been somebody could come to the shop stocked ceiling-high with old books, feet dragging, shoes tattered, nose running, hands trembling, to satisfy his hunger for the written word.

The Germans agreed to transfer to the ghetto the libraries of the liquidated Hehalutz training centers and Jewish academies of learning, as well as books from empty Jewish flats that had been completely stripped of their contents. In one year the library expanded to fifty thousand books, a fifth of which were Hebraica and a fifth Zionism; there were thousands of volumes of old Jewish newspapers, philosophy books, Greek and Latin classics, thousands of volumes on the history of art and music, rare editions from the sixteenth through the eighteenth centuries, and only about five thousand books of fiction, mainly old German novels.

The Germans started collecting books on Jewish subjects at Theresienstadt, and rare editions from the pillaged communities. Jakob would go into the central warehouse from time to time, located outside the ghetto walls, to draw strength. As he used to say to Berl Herschkowitz of the Hehalutz leadership, "Look, what spiritual treasures the Jewish people have!"

The central library had branches in various areas—medical, technical, and youth sections—and in addition some books had been kept privately: a book or two of favorite verse, a beloved author, brought to the ghetto in people's personal cargoes at the expense of food or clothing. Many of the books lent out never returned to the library; people transported to the East took them with them for the journey (losing their deposit of fifty crowns in ghetto money). If the library staff, mostly academics, regretted the loss of a book from their shelves, they consoled themselves with the thought that it would serve its purpose elsewhere. After all, in the East too people would need reading material.

Above the library, in the same small building, was the artists' studio, considered in ghetto terms a "German enterprise," meaning that it came directly under German supervision and worked according to orders, sometimes for individual requests. Its staff never knew when the SS was likely to drop in. Officially the artists may have drawn for German tastes, but privately they also drew ghetto life and figures. Sometimes the drawings were done on the back of

347

good cardboard on which architectural designs from some community or other had been drafted, sometimes on library property, and the library stored the drawings away from watchful German eyes. The center for the ghetto artists, both as a studio and a shelter, was the drafting room of the technical section in the Magdeburg barrack. Officially, the artists—Otto Unger, Frita (Fritz) Taussig, Peter Kien, Leo Haas—were supposed to be busy with technical designs for construction and various other graphic work for the ghetto, but in fact they drew a running chronicle of ghetto life, a pictorial testimonial of the hangings, of old people scrounging in the garbage, convoys leaving for unknown destinations, sickrooms, living quarters with no space to breathe. The drawings were hidden in a hollow wall, in a tin box buried in the ground, and some of them were smuggled out of the ghetto, to the Czech underground, to serve as evidence and indictment. From the underground, according to the contact man, the drawings even left the borders of the Reich, a fact for which most of the artists paid with their lives after terrible torture. Some of the drawings fell into German hands in 1944, and following an investigation by Eichmann, who had come to the ghetto specifically for the purpose, the artists, together with their wives and children, were sent to death in the Little Fortress or other concentration camps. Otto Unger, whose right hand was crushed in the Little Fortress so that he could never draw again, always kept a piece of charcoal with him, even in Buchenwald, and tried in vain to sketch lines on paper.

25

THE ELDER
OF THE JEWS
LOOKS FOR A JOB

THE GERMANS seemed to be plotting something. At the end of September 1942, Seidl informed the Council of Elders that Karl Löwenstein, who had been chief of police in the Minsk ghetto, was to take over the police command of the Theresienstadt ghetto. Until that time the police had not stood on pomp and ceremony and their relations with the ghetto inmates had been friendly, based on the trust felt by the residents that the ghetto police would not inform on a Jew who had defied one of the many German regulations. The arrival of the chief of the Minsk police was shrouded in mystery: he was brought to the ghetto in May, held under private arrest for four months, and accorded preferential treatment, with special food rations and the right to receive a newspaper every day—a right not even the Elder of the Jews enjoyed.

Löwenstein, a former naval officer who was a half-Jew and Protestant by religion, had served as adjutant to the German crown prince during naval maneuvers at Kiel in 1910 and had kept in touch with him afterward. In November 1941, Löwenstein, who had been decorated three times for saving life, was sent from Berlin to the Minsk ghetto and put in charge of organizing the regular police. Wilhelm Kubbe, the general commander of White Ruthenia, intervened with Hitler over this and instructions were received to return Löwenstein to the West. He was sent first to Vienna and from there to Theresienstadt.

Löwenstein did not reveal the details of the liquidations he had witnessed in Minsk, but his words left no doubt as to the dire situation of the Jews there. Ghetto inmates turned to Löwenstein for information about friends and relatives who, as far as they knew, had been sent to Minsk. Löwenstein would reply, "They're fine," but after they had left the room, he would bow his head and tell the leadership, "They were killed before my eyes," as Gonda recorded in his diary, adding, "Everyone fears him."

Löwenstein, who had direct access to the German command, was proud of his special relationship with Seidl and other SS people which enabled him to have women who had stolen spinach from the fields released from prison even when the efforts of the Elder of the Jews had failed. He credited himself with getting punishments by lashing canceled at times, and when Seidl ordered the old people to move quickly out of the cars at the train station "or I'll shoot your asses full of blue beans," Löwenstein told him in private that it was not fitting for the commandant of the ghetto to speak in such a manner.

The attitude of the veteran leadership to Löwenstein was one of utmost suspicion, especially after the rumor spread that he was to replace Edelstein as Elder of the ghetto. For his part, Löwenstein found no common language with the ghetto leaders either. The inflated administrative mechanism, staffed by people who viewed it as life insurance, the system of "pull" and connections, the theft, with or without complicity, were not to his liking. Löwenstein wanted to impose order in the ghetto, primarily by consolidating his own position, and in time not only the regular police passed into his hands but also the orderly police, the firemen, the economic police, and the antiaircraft unit. The ghetto police, comprising 150 men when he arrived, all of Czech origin, were in Löwenstein's eyes no more than a band of thieves and smugglers. He fired a large part of them and replaced them with former German and Austrian officers, imposed iron discipline and military exercises, and issued terse and strict orders. Some people felt that the Germans meant to reinforce the small SS contingent that ruled the ghetto with a trained Jewish police force which would do their work for them, instilling fear in the inmates.

The crowning feature of the improvement in the image of the police, whose numbers under Löwenstein rose to 420, was a festive swearing-in ceremony in the best military tradition, attended by the Council of Elders. When Edelstein, in his capacity as Elder of the Jews, was asked to review the ranks, he went over to a policeman wearing one of the new gray shirts sewn from dyed sheets, felt it like a textile merchant checking quality, and said, "Very nice, very nice," a small gesture that suddenly brought the whole grandiose performance down to earth.

Löwenstein soon earned himself many enemies, whether because of his arrogant behavior, his German officer's air, his mysterious relationship with the Germans, or his war against corruption, in the course of which he set up a special economic unit in the police force which was meant to prevent theft from the storerooms and kitchens and to ensure proper administration and fair distribution. The economic department, mostly of Czech origin, may never have heard of the maxim "Thou shalt not muzzle the ox when it treads out the corn," but they nevertheless conformed to it: it was unrealistic to expect people who worked in the bakery, the noodle factory, or the kitchen to stick to official rations. The practice of added rations had been institutionalized to prevent pilfering, and the increments employees received by virtue of their occupations were sometimes gargantuan by ghetto standards: bakery staff received one loaf for each of their long and arduous shifts, while cooks received seven dumplings per shift compared with the single one rationed out to ordinary mortals.

From time to time a small square yeast cake was handed out at lunch instead of the dumpling (on this point there was no disagreement among the various nationalities in the ghetto: the Czech cooks managed miracles with the limited ingredients at their disposal). When Löwenstein discovered that a large quantity of the cakes were being distributed among the food staff, he demanded a written statement of the additional amount involved and insisted that this be restricted to a specified maximum, as published in the orders of the day. Löwenstein managed to tread on many toes simultaneously and his heavy foot made him foes everywhere, even among those who sought a more egalitarian society, and even among the German and Austrian residents on whose behalf his campaign was based.

Despite the basic disagreements between them, Löwenstein did not come into open conflict with Edelstein, as he did with members of the economic department. In his memoirs, Löwenstein even mentions the cooperation between them, noting Yekef's courage in dealing with the Germans. When Janetschek, chief of the Czech gendarmerie, said on one occasion that the Jews actually had it good, since they were protected and did not need to go to the front, Edelstein replied with a thin smile: "Herr Hauptmann, you can always convert." The main point of issue between Löwenstein and Edelstein revolved around one matter: the preferential treatment accorded young people at the expense of the elderly, particularly with respect to food. When Löwenstein brought up the matter of hungry old people from Germany, the Elder of the Jews replied that the camp commandant was opposed to the elderly. Löwenstein lost no time in clarifying the point with Seidl who, according to Löwenstein, told him, "I'm not against the aged, I'm simply not interested in them because they don't work."

More than 21,000 of the ghetto inmates were old and infirm; 2,500 were chronically ill, 600 were blind, 2,000 were war veterans, hundreds were deaf-mutes, retarded, or mentally ill, and against all these stood the will of Seidl and Edelstein for a productive ghetto, each for his own reasons.

Löwenstein admired Edelstein's caution in rarely going to head-quarters alone but generally in the company of Zucker or some other member of the Council of Elders. In January 1943, however, Edelstein was removed from his post by German order, and Paul Epstein, who had headed the Reich Union of the Jews in Germany in recent years, was appointed in his place. Epstein arrived at the ghetto after the liquidation of the Berlin, Vienna, and Prague Jewish communities left a Jew-free Reich, completed as a birthday present for the Führer.

The replacement came as a surprise. On January 27, Edelstein and Zucker were summoned for a talk with Seidl in the presence of Obersturmführer Ernst Möhs from Berlin, who regularly visited the ghetto on business for Eichmann. They were told that the following day would bring new arrivals, including Leo Baeck from Berlin, Löwenherz and Murmelstein from Vienna, Weidmann and Richard Friedmann from Prague, and that the administration of the ghetto would henceforth be in the hands of Epstein, Löwenherz, and Edelstein, with the chief responsibility being Epstein's. Möhs said that SS Obersturmbannführer Eichmann had asked him to express his recognition of the work done by the Elder of the Jews, Jakob Edelstein, and convey his thanks, and Edelstein was not to take the change personally. A new ghetto, styled after Theresienstadt, was being considered, Möhs said, and the Germans had Edelstein in mind to run it, but the final decision had not yet been taken.

In response to a question from the SS, Edelstein admitted that after fourteen months of pioneering work he could not view the change with equanimity. Edelstein said that he did not feel strong enough physically to assume the organization of a new ghetto and Möhs assured him that the matter had not yet been decided and his feelings would be taken into consideration. Möhs felt that Epstein should be given two rooms as living quarters and that both he and Löwenherz should enjoy double rations, as had been the case all along with members of the Council of Elders. The other newcomers should also be given preferential residences but there were no special instructions regarding their functions in the ghetto: that would be left up to Epstein and Edelstein. Dr. Seidl noted that he would intervene should people like Murmelstein try to pose difficulties for the new leadership because of thwarted ambitions (and from the minutes of the meeting, which were signed by Edelstein, it was clear that neither looked forward to Murmelstein's arrival).

So much for the documentation. It is said that Edelstein, following Epstein's appointment, asked to be released from all official duties and work as a common laborer, but his request was turned down. It seems that the Germans did in fact consider setting up a new ghetto like Theresienstadt, because of the overcrowding, and Edelstein was asked to submit a list of the manpower necessary to do so. But in the end the Germans gave up the idea and solved the problem of overcrowding by the proven remedy of extermination. It is possible that the whole idea of a new ghetto was from the start no more than a grand bluff.

Seidl, too, was wary of the changes, for his own reasons: he had managed to arrive at a modus vivendi with Edelstein and Zucker, who were both aware of his ambitions and helped him impress his superiors. In a conversation with Epstein and Edelstein the next day, Seidl insisted that the established work patterns continue, and that people who had proved themselves capable would not be pushed aside—and he referred in particular to Zucker, who was to relinquish his post as assistant Elder of the Jews. Seidl noted that the thanks expressed by his superiors to Edelstein had not been idle talk, but a sincere reflection of their feelings, and he even added that he might move with Edelstein to the new ghetto, should it actually be established. Seidl expressed his hope that Edelstein would help his new partners in the leadership, and that the ghetto population would accept the change with understanding, and said that Edelstein should speak to them to this effect. That same evening Yekef, at two meetings, one in the men's barracks and one in the women's, announced the imminent changes. The people from the Protectorate listened to him anxiously, and regarded the changes as another sign of their displacement.

The changes were based on the German view of the Jewish hierarchy: German Jews were of higher status than Protectorate Jews. Ghetto veterans understood the significance: their existence was in danger. "Never have Edelstein and Zucker been as popular as they are today," Gonda wrote in his diary, "but there is also envy of those who for fourteen months have lived in relative quiet." This was precisely the German purpose: to undermine the position of the Jewish leadership by promoting internal intrigues over the question of leadership among the various nationalities and turn the leaders into pawns in German hands. In his memoirs (there are no documents on this matter), Murmelstein mentioned several other possibilities for the changes: fear of contact between the Czech underground and the Jewish leadership, headhunting for those who had caused the failure of the ghetto for the aged, and German suspicions that one of the reasons behind this failure was Edelstein's preferential treatment of the young. Murmelstein even suspected that someone had informed on Edelstein to the Germans. Edelstein had never hidden his position; he felt that the young Czech Jews had not only the right but the duty to remain where they were in order to defend the ghetto population from the danger of liquidation. And furthermore, without the young people to shoulder the maintenance of the ghetto, the old could not last.

Edelstein was hurt by the change in function: he regarded it as dismissal. When Harry Tressler asked him why he was so worried, he said that he did not trust Epstein's staying power. "I know the man. It's a disaster for the ghetto," he said again. Yekef had met Epstein in the first half of 1939, at a meeting with Eichmann in Berlin. When he had returned to Prague, he had told Harry that he had doubts as to Epstein's ability to hold out. It was clear that the Germans would be exerting more pressure, and one had to know how to resist. During their meeting in Berlin, Epstein had been a shadow of himself (this was also the impression he made on Gertrude Tijn, the head of the Dutch refugee committee, when she visited Berlin). The Gestapo had arrested Epstein on the pretext that he had abetted illegal immigration to Palestine and released him four months later, having subjected him to severe torture.

In many respects, Epstein was the complete antithesis of Edelstein: a son of Western culture, highly educated in philosophy, sociology, and political economics, Epstein had at the age of twenty-five already held the title of assistant professor at the university. When his scientific career was halted by Hitler's rise to power, Epstein was called to Berlin to assist the Reich Representation of the Jews in Germany, especially in money matters. Little by little, in the wake of the emigration and liquidation of the Jewish leadership, Epstein became the central figure in Jewish life. The administration of welfare affairs brought him into constant contact with the Gestapo's Jewish department, and his work in occupational training and guidance led to close cooperation with the Hehalutz people in Germany, and to his unequivocal support of the efforts on behalf of illegal immigration.

Edelstein liked having people around him; Epstein was by nature a loner, reticent, unreceptive. He loved music and was a skilled pianist. He brought his grand piano to the ghetto and the top musicians used his apartment for concerts before a select audience of music lovers. While Yekef's flat always bustled like a train station, Epstein preferred to stay away from the madding crowd, and the orders of the day informed the ghetto residents that Dr. Epstein received the public in his office in the Magdeburg barracks between 1600 and 1700 hours.

Edelstein showed courage and resourcefulness, and did not hesitate to falsify records, quietly sabotage German instructions, lie. Epstein was by nature a man of truth, whether because his Prussian correctness would not let him lie, even to the SS, or because he lacked the necessary impudence. Edelstein set no store by clothes, and his appearance was far from impressive. Epstein was always dressed impeccably, his hair neat, his appearance exemplary. He was precisely the right type of man to greet outside visitors should they come to the ghetto.

Edelstein was by nature disorderly, a man of improvisations. Epstein was organized and methodical, and it is hardly surprising that he complained of the corruption, the irresponsibility, and the lack of conscientiousness in work he found in the ghetto. It is even less surprising that his efforts to remedy the situation did not win him a great following. Whereas Edelstein never went to headquarters alone, always preferring to have a witness with him, Epstein usually preferred to meet the camp commandant on his own.

Since his arrest in Berlin, Epstein had always carried a dose of cyanide, ready to end his life should the Germans try and force him to act unacceptably. In private conversations with Bertl Simonson, one of the Hehalutz leaders in Germany, he did not hide his pessimism as to his own fate: "I know that the time will come when I'll no longer be able to say yes, if I wish to live with my conscience and face the Jewish public."

The Germans had also promised Epstein that he would remain the head of the Reich Union of the Jews in Germany (as the central organization was called since 1939), and be permitted to return to Berlin for consultation. They had also deceived him.

> Elder of the Jews seeks employment:
> 14 months' experience, good references;
> address offers to the editorial board for "Jakob."

This ad appeared in the humorous newspaper *Friday Greetings* as a result of the change in leadership. The newspaper appeared in only one copy, but it had over two hundred avid readers whose names were signed on its cover. They came to read it in room 248 of the Magdeburg barrack where its editors lived. *Friday Greetings* was a satire of ghetto life from a Czech Jewish point of view (among the lecture titles it proposed were "On Men and Jews," "Zionism and Pull." The warning on its cover read: "Kindly refrain from spilling soup on this issue. Do not waste soup").

Edelstein had to swallow yet another pill: since Löwenherz of Vienna did not come to the ghetto but was permitted, thanks to Eichmann's protection, to remain in Vienna with his wife until the end of the war, Murmelstein took his place as one of the three leaders. As Seidl announced, the leadership hierarchy would be as follows: Epstein, Edelstein, Murmelstein.

Dr. Benjamin Murmelstein, a native Galician proud of his Viennese accent, fat, round faced, pug-nosed, with small eyes, was a doctor of philosophy, and ordained rabbi. He had a phenomenal memory and a mind that was both sharper and wittier than that of his two partners in the triad. He had served as a rabbi in Vienna and in time lectured at the Vienna University, publishing various studies, including one on the influence of Jewish thought on early

Christianity as well as selected commentaries on the writings of Josephus Flavius (on which he also lectured during his stay at the ghetto).

The general attitude toward Murmelstein, both of the Viennese residents whom he had represented on the community committee since 1937 and the Prague Jews, was one of suspicion, despite the fact that he was the only one of the newly arrived community officials for whom the Germans had not demanded special treatment. He felt that the reason for this was that Eichmann bore him resentment for his study on the idea of a Jewish state, which Eichmann had asked him to write. In the study, Murmelstein stated that a solution to the Jewish problem was possible only in Palestine, and he had not presented Germany's victory and dominion over the Mediterranean (including Palestine) as an indisputable outcome of the war. Nevertheless, in the end he was appointed deputy Elder of the Jews with the concomitant benefits afforded by the position, but Seidl was quick to announce that Murmelstein's personal presence was unnecessary at headquarters and that he need not report daily to the camp commandant as did the Elder of the Jews and his assistant.

Because of the distance between the new Elder of the Jews and the public, many people continued to view Edelstein, even in his capacity as deputy, as the sole repository for appeals, requests, complaints, clarification of problems, and the door to his flat was never locked, even now. When nurse Trude Groag sent him a letter in honor of the anniversary of their meeting at the Bohušovice train station, complaining of the few opportunities they had had to talk since then, Yekef replied somewhat bitterly, "Your remarks strike me as entirely incomprehensible. I showed your letter to Miriam and she feels that you actually ask too much: in the sixteen months we've been here together, I have certainly not spoken to Miriam even twice without being interrupted. This has never been my fault. The reason lies in the nature of my work and shows without a doubt that people in public office have almost no opportunity to live as they would like or spend their free time according to their inclinations." Friends who came to play with Arieh at the Edelstein flat knew that Arieh's mother was a very quiet person, and though his father may have been amiable toward children he never had time for his own son.

Contrary to German expectations, most of the tension did not derive from the relationship between Epstein and Edelstein—

chiefly thanks to Yekef's flexibility and wisdom in human relations—but between Epstein and Löwenstein. They were both rigid, Prussian in nature, and ambitious for authority. When Löwenstein asked the people who did strenuous physical work to forgo their added food rations at least once a week in favor of the constantly hungry elderly, he did so behind Epstein's back and incurred his anger. Epstein felt that Löwenstein had overstepped his authority to the detriment of the division of labor, while Löwenstein accused Epstein of trying to shift responsibility for the elderly onto German shoulders—and the correspondence between them smacks of mutual loathing.

Their cultural background, their common love of music, their planned and organized work patterns, served to draw Zucker and the new Elder of the Jews close together. In a letter he wrote on the day of his mother's death, Zucker informed Ullman in Geneva of the changes that had taken place in the ghetto. "I am happy to inform you that I have managed to form friendly personal relations with Epstein, and our cooperation is in all respects satisfactory. The work jurisdictions have obviously been narrowed, since more people are involved in the ghetto's administration. I work in the area left me more intensively for the common good." Zucker wrote that in future he would also look after youth affairs and that he had assumed the supervision of the employment services, which involved close cooperation with Dr. Österreicher (two fields that had always been Zionist strongholds). In addition there was also close cooperation with Kahn, whom Zucker had brought into the circle so that he could "bring to bear his talents and special knowledge"—that is, in the framework of the Zionist movement.

Kahn arrived at the ghetto at the end of January 1943 when the Prague Jewish community was liquidated. He had been arrested together with Richard Friedmann in the community building and both had been brought straight to Theresienstadt without being allowed to stop at home first. Their wives and belongings arrived at the ghetto the following day. Richard Friedmann looked at the ghetto with the eyes of an outsider and was deeply shaken that Edelstein had not been able to prevent the moral degeneration of the ghetto clerical staff, particularly at the lower levels. Friedmann was astonished that, contrary to the practice in Prague, the leaders had agreed to compose the lists of people transported east and in so doing, decided matters of life and death. On this issue, as he told his wife Cecilia, he waged an ongoing dispute with Yekef. Friedmann was no longer interested in an official position and at first he worked as a laborer in sanitation jobs, transportation, and agriculture. Later, under pressure from Epstein, he was coopted into the employment department.

Nor was Kahn prepared to accept any central function in the ghetto; he agreed only to head the lecture section of the cultural department, as the center for Zionist activity. But in the ghetto he also remained a leading background figure who gathered around him a faithful following, chiefly from among Hehalutz people. While courting one of the members of the Council of Elders might have been prompted by some element of material consideration, the grouping around Kahn, who held no official position, derived solely from his personality and from people's need for moral support in times of fear, doubts, questions of conscience, and the search for faith.

26

OPENING NIGHT

As ALWAYS, decisions were made over the heads of the Theresienstadt population. In December 1942, Müller, the head of the Gestapo, notified Himmler that 45,000 Jews were to be sent to Auschwitz in January, including 10,000 from Theresienstadt. Müller asked Himmler's permission to include 5,000 old people in the transport from Theresienstadt. But this was not granted and in January 1943, 7,000 ghetto residents were sent to Auschwitz, all under sixty (apart from fifteen elderly parents).

Ostensibly, the young people were transferred to Auschwitz as part of the efforts of the SS head office for administration and economy (led by Oswald Pohl) to ensure a supply of manpower, particularly in the Buna factories near the camp, which manufactured synthetic rubber. But despite the fact that the transports from Theresienstadt included more than six thousand men and women of working age, only one fifth remained in Auschwitz after the selection, and the rest were sent straight to the gas chambers. The commandant of the Auschwitz camp explained to the office for administration and economy that this was due to "the feeble health of the men and the high percentage of young girls among the women." But the truth was otherwise: most of the people from Theresienstadt were fit for work. However in the struggle between those who favored using Jewish manpower in the war effort prior to extermination (as did Pohl), and those who wanted the Jews entirely stamped out regardless of economic considerations (as did Kaltenbrunner, Heydrich's successor in charge of the Reich Security Head Office), the latter, seeking an overall and immediate final solution, held the upper hand. Himmler himself, who outranked both Kaltenbrunner and Pohl, was undecided on this issue. Indeed he wanted both things at once: the maximum use of manpower and the immediate annihilation of the Jews.

In February 1943, Kaltenbrunner applied to Himmler with a new request. On behalf of Eichmann's department, he asked that the elderly be transferred from Theresienstadt to Auschwitz. According to Kaltenbrunner's figures, which were not entirely accurate, only 6,000 of Theresienstadt's 46,000 residents worked in productive jobs, paving roads and laying railroad lines. The rest of the population was involved in the maintenance of the ghetto, including 4,000 people who tended the sick and the old. The severe overcrowding, he pointed out, demanded the expenditure of large quantities of medicine and considerable manpower in order to care for the sick and the old and prevent epidemics from spreading and harming the surrounding Czech and German population. Kaltenbrunner mentioned the old-fashioned structure of the city, the difficult sanitary conditions, and the danger of an increase in typhus in the spring, and he asked, meanwhile, for permission to send 5,000 Jews above the age of sixty to Auschwitz, obviously with special consideration for well-connected Jews and those who had been highly decorated.

The answer he received, which emanated from Himmler, was surprising, to say the least: the SS Reichsführer refused the request because it interfered with the general policy of allowing the Jews in Theresienstadt's ghetto for the old to live and die in peace.

It was typical of the situation in the ghetto: one could never be sure what was good, what was bad, what served as protection from transports, what prompted expulsion. At times the sick were protected from transport, at other times they were shipped east in groups. At times old age was the reason they stayed behind, at other times it was the reason they were deported. Policemen, veterans of the ghetto, appeared to be exempt—until they were transported on special orders from the Germans. Everything—place of work, origin, family ties, state of health, age, date of arrival at the ghetto—was fateful, but nobody knew how or when this fate would prove decisive.

The efforts of Dr. Munk, the medical staff, and the sanitation services proved ineffective: overcrowding triumphed and typhus started to spread through the ghetto, among the children as well. A frantic attempt was made to locate the source of contamination; a high-level German doctor arrived from Prague and in his honor the Jewish doctors were asked to don clean white coats (a very rare commodity indeed). On January 20, 1943, Eichmann visited Theresienstadt and ordered the typhus epidemic stopped, or there would be dire consequences. All residents under sixty-five were inoculated—three injections at one-week intervals—and a vigorous information campaign instituted. Signs posted throughout the ghetto read:

NACH DEM STUHLGANG
VOR DEM ESSEN
HÄNDEWASCHEN NICHT VERGESSEN

Over and over again people were told to wash their hands after going to the toilet and before eating and to make sure that the toilets and outhouses were kept as clean as possible. The smell of Lysol and Carbol was everywhere. On February 1, at their daily meeting with Seidl, Epstein and Edelstein reviewed the state of the ghetto and the state of the sick, and presented a report on the incidence of typhus. Seidl asked them not to submit the report formally. He agreed to the expansion of the special typhus hospitals but expressed the hope that the epidemic would end soon. He too feared the consequences of Eichmann's displeasure. He requested and received a report on the employment situation which stressed the serious deficiency in manpower, but he found the report unsatisfactory: it was not convincing enough. Here, for instance, it said that 570 people are required in agriculture, when actually 800 were necessary. Seidl clearly wished to keep the manpower at the ghetto.

During this conversation, the name Birkenau was mentioned for the first time. Epstein and Edelstein asked Seidl if it was possible to maintain direct postal contact with the Ostrovo camp (to which the Germans claimed that the elderly who had left the ghetto in the fall of 1942 had been transferred) and the Birkenau labor camp. Seidl felt that postal contact with these camps was possible only through Berlin, but he promised to make inquiries about sending mail there outside the regular postal circuit. The Jewish leadership did not know the true nature of the Birkenau labor camp, whose lyrical name conjured up an ideal setting abundant with green birches—

and they preferred not to know. On one of their walks through the ghetto, Berl Herschkowitz suggested to Jakob that he ask the Germans for permission to visit one of the labor camps in the East where the Theresienstadt people had reportedly been sent; Jakob had contacts with the Germans and would no doubt know how to put the question. After a moment's silence, Jakob said: "If I raise the matter with the Germans, they'll kill me. As soon as I voice any doubts, I won't survive."

The transport that left the ghetto on February 1 with 1,001 people was the last of these for six months. Days of calm had come to the ghetto.

In deciding to give the town a face-lift and display it as a model ghetto, the Germans did not ignore the propaganda value of Theresienstadt's cultural life, and for their own purposes, they permitted theater and music to flourish almost unimpeded (so long as performers and audience were not swept away by transports). With the establishment of the café orchestra, calculated to please local customers and impress outside visitors, the ban on owning and playing musical instruments was virtually lifted. (Concerts had been held before, in the residences and particularly in the Magdeburg barrack where the leadership lived. One performance in April 1942 had included Dvořák's American Quartet and the world premiere of the Theresienstadt Symphony, composed and conducted by Karlo Tauber. Musical instruments had been brought into the ghetto via the underground: a cello had been smuggled in, wrapped in a sheet like a corpse, and a piano with amputated legs had remained in the former Sokol building after the local population had been evacuated from Terezin.) Now there were far greater possibilities: musical ensembles could be set up, and trios, quartets (the best of which was led by Egon Ledeč, formerly the leader of the Czech Philharmonic Orchestra) and concerts could be prepared for the entire ghetto.

After Zucker was compelled to relinquish his post as assistant Elder of the Jews because of the changeover in leaders, he assumed the day-to-day management of the cultural department. He instituted changes, established subdivisions for chamber music, vocal music, and light music, obtained rooms for rehearsals, enabled musicians to devote more of their time to practice and study, all for the sake of offering a wide audience a varied musical program, including Weiss's jazz quintet, Meyer and Sattel's piano duo, the Ghetto Swingers troupe, Fischer's liturgical choir, Ledeč's quartet, piano soloists such as Alisa Sommer-Herz, and a string orchestra conducted by Karl Ančerl.

There were numerous fine musicians in the ghetto, young and old, from all regions of the Reich; and there was an enormous thirst for music, which opened a window into another world, different from the reality of the ghetto. Listening with closed eyes to Bernard Kaff playing Chopin, one knew oneself to be above all the degradation suffered at German hands, to be a man. Soon after the ghetto began, the conductor Raphael Schächter, who had acquired his stage experience at E. F. Burian's Progressive Theater in Prague, had formed a men's choir, and now, with instrument-playing officially permitted, it was only natural that the first opera performed in the ghetto should be Smetana's *The Bartered Bride,* considered the Czech national opera in their struggle against the Hapsburgs. The opera opened in November 1942 at the former school gymnasium, which now served as children's home L-417. Only a fraction of the audience had seats; everyone else stood shoulder to shoulder, listening. The true meaning of the choral words seemed to be clear for the first time: "Why not be merry, if God has granted us health"— and if not full health, at least life. People were moved to tears, the performers were called back again and again by an emotional audience who would not let them leave.

The Bartered Bride was performed thirty-five times, and the children of L-417, who repeatedly crowded into the gymnasium to hear it, learned entire scenes by heart. The school became the center of musical life: there the musicians met after work, copied scores, discussed interpretations, and gave children lessons; there music lovers came to hear Gideon Klein, who worked as an instructor in the boys' dormitory. At twenty-three years old, a tall, slim young man with black hair on a pale forehead, Gideon was a superb pianist and a master of languages, philosophy, and composition. He who should have been one of the world's great musicians sat at the old piano, supported on crates, and burst out of the confines of the ghetto, conquering the darkness and shedding light all around.

The Bartered Bride was followed by *The Marriage of Figaro,* then Smetana's *The Kiss* and Bizet's *Carmen,* premiere after premiere on the ghetto stage, in Czech and in German. The performance schedule for a single month (February 1943), in a ghetto which knew nothing of extermination, reflected the attempt to crowd an entire world into each day:

CONCERTS: Jewish liturgical music; opera arias; *Journey Through the Land of Music* (premiere), Raphael Schächter's Hebrew Choir (premiere)—20 performances altogether.

OPERAS: *The Bartered Bride; Rigoletto* (premiere—the cultural department's anniversary performance); *The Marriage of Figaro* (premiere)—10 performances altogether.

THEATER: Wolker, *The Grave* (premiere); a revue, *Youngsters Not Admitted* (premiere), a cabaret within the framework of the *Stolen Stage;* Cocteau, *The Voice;* opera evening; Thoren's Cabaret with Skits; Evening of Songs from Erben's *Flower Bouquet;* puppet theater; *Women's Dictatorship*—50 performances altogether.

Tickets were distributed free or for a nominal payment of ghetto vouchers, largely according to a key worked out among the various labor units, with some tickets reserved for dignitaries and "prominents." There was always a line and never enough space for people who wished to laugh, to lose themselves in their past, confront the present, believe in the future.

On the whole the German theater was conservative, perhaps because the actors from the Reich were mostly elderly, experienced, and set in their artistic ways, perhaps because the use of the German language necessitated greater caution. The Czech performers, on the other hand, were mostly young. Some were amateurs and many were socialists, influenced by Prague's progressive theaters, by Voskovec and Werich, by E. F. Burian. Unshackled by tradition, they had excellent instructors, such as Gustav Schorsch, who, like Stanislavsky, strove to capture the audience entirely and ruled out improvisation. They were daring, they experimented, they searched for new expressive forms, and they wrote new plays, allegories of ghetto life: *The Bedridden Prince,* who awoke one day to find himself incapacitated; *Emperor Atlantis,* about a kingdom where dying was impossible; *The Last Bicycle Rider,* about a government of insane people who attributed all blame to bicycle riders (inspired by the popular saying that everything was the fault of Jews and bike riders).

At first the actors performed without special lighting or props in ordinary clothes, with the yellow badge. As time went on they obtained costumes from the general clothing warehouse or sewed them from sheets, sacks, and paper. The dust-filled attics with their thick wooden beams sometimes provided natural settings, enhanced by a few atmospheric props. Every group centered around a director, and, as in the theater world, there were intrigues and jealousy; actors moved from director to director amid the creative tension, the ghetto tension, and the tension of people who never ate to their fill but still tried to achieve as much as possible for as long as possible. Many plays never had a premiere: in the middle of rehearsals the leading actors were deported east.

In his own way, everyone tried to see Theresienstadt as an extension of his former life, his areas of interest, his hobbies. Clara Karo, a rabbi's wife from Cologne whose husband had turned down immigration so that he could stay with his congregation, was sure that there must be other women in the ghetto who, like herself, longed for Jewish and Zionist cultural activities, and she went to Edelstein's office in Magdeburg to speak to him about it: the trying times the Jews were now experiencing, she said, should also be a time of test and preparation, a time of spiritual growth. It was up to the Jews alone to make any blessing come out of the curse that the Nazis had cast on them. Edelstein agreed with her, and through Drucker referred her to the WIZO women from Brünn. At first, at Yekef's request, they met in a small forum, no more than twenty women at a time, usually on Saturday afternoon. But after Hannah Steiner came to the ghetto, in January 1943, the activities of the WIZO women donned new proportions.

Hannah was allotted a small room of her own almost entirely filled by a double-tier wooden bunk: her sister and brother-in-law slept on the upper level, she and her husband below. The remaining space was taken up by a narrow wooden bench along the wall, and here the WIZO women sat huddled together and were served like guests as in the days of yore, except that now, instead of coffee and cakes, they were given herbal tea and a piece of bread with margarine the size of a stamp. They listened to lectures, held discussions, spoke of what had been and what would be. From time to time Hannah organized larger meetings, which were attended by over one hundred women at a time. She held an oral magazine in which the guest speakers were professional women: a juvenile court judge and the only woman in the ghetto who was an ordained rabbi. After work, the WIZO women generally visited the elderly or read and sang to sick children, and they viewed the meetings at Hannah Steiner's as a festive occasion: they wore their Sabbath clothes, carefully tidied their hair, and felt something of the flavor of days gone by. Like Hannah, they were filled with faith that all this was a preparation for departure for Palestine when the long-awaited day arrived.

The cultural department kept a card file on the Zionists in the ghetto (catalogued under "Interested in lectures on Jewish topics"), and the Zionists used to meet on Jewish holidays and remembrance days for Herzl, Bialik, and Trumpeldor. On the 21st of Tammuz, a fine summer day, the Zionists gathered in the yard of the Hanover barracks to hear a lecture by Robert Stricker, one of the founders of the radical faction and state party at the Zionist Congress. Stricker spoke of the generation that had forgotten Herzl and of the future Jewish state, and the meeting finished with Hebrew songs and the "Hatikvah."

Ever energetic, Hannah Steiner organized agriculture and gardening training for the younger WIZO women, and they all studied Hebrew. Under Dr. Kahn's guidance, an intensive course on Zionism was given once a week in the department for the chronically ill at the engineer's barracks so that the paralyzed Fritz Baum, one of Czechoslovakia's veteran Zionists, could participate.

As soon as news came of Dr. Kahn's expulsion from Prague to Theresienstadt, his sister Stella Korda in Chicago intensified her efforts to obtain American citizenship for him and his wife Olga on the grounds that his father had emigrated to the United States and had been an American citizen. At the initiative of friends in Palestine, who took care of Kahn's children, his son Raphael (Titus) wrote a letter to Mrs. Roosevelt:

> I learned English in order to write you this letter. It is terribly important. I must save my father and mother from Hitler. You are good, but perhaps you do not understand letters in Hebrew and so I started to study English three months ago and now I will explain everything to you in your language.
>
> I am a pupil at the Mishmar Ha'emek school in the Jezreel valley. My sister and I were sent from Prague to Mrs. Szold in Palestine when the war broke out, but my father is a Zionist leader and he decided that he must stay where he is for the good of the Jews in Czechoslovakia, and he was president of the Jewish community in Prague. He was a hero in the First World War and lost an arm in the battle. Why am I writing you this? My grandfather is American.

Rafi recounted his aunt Stella's efforts to obtain American citizenship for his parents, and her appeals to the state department:

> But many months have passed and she has heard nothing. And one day a letter came that my father had been expelled from

Prague to the Theresienstadt ghetto, and we cried a lot. I am full of fear. Will he travel the dark road to Poland? And I asked myself: why doesn't the clerk at the state department give him a passport? Maybe it's even been lying on his desk for a long time already but since he has so much work because of the war, he hasn't had time to sign it, etc. But what if the president himself told him that the matter was very important?

Now you understand why I am writing to you, and I ask you with all my heart: please, please, ask Mr. Roosevelt to phone the man and tell him: deal with the matter today! And my parents will be saved and will always be grateful to him and so will we children.

The reply was a meaningless, official, and brief note received through the American legation in Palestine, but the American consulate in Brünn informed the state department that Dr. Kahn had always been a Czech citizen, meaning there was no room for intervention. Nevertheless, hope found another outlet: "The Germans are apparently showing some restraint with respect to the Jewish leaders," Dr. Ullman wrote to Palestine. "They probably wish to improve their image in the eyes of the world press. Let's hope that Franz and Olga will live safely through the expected difficult period—before the Nazis are finally defeated."

Dr. Kahn had long since resigned himself to his fate, but Hannah Steiner, who had sought ways to leave the Reich while still in Prague, during the expulsions, did not give up even in the ghetto. In the fall of 1943 she sent a postcard to Ullman in Geneva, asking that all her friends be notified of her change of address and year of birth: 1894, so as to avoid error arising out of identical names. "We are fine, we have adjusted well," she wrote, "and without difficulty, because we are hopeful and if I may say so, at peace with ourselves."

Attempts were still being made to get people out of the ghetto— all in vain. When a representative of the Vatican intervened with the German Foreign Office on behalf of an elderly couple, Jakob and Esterika Lucas, Eichmann's office informed Eberhard von Thadden, the director of the German department in the Foreign Office which dealt with Jewish affairs, that they had both died in early 1943 in Theresienstadt. "However, it would be wise to inform the nuncio who expressed an interest in them that the emigration of the Lucas couple is out of the question at the moment."

In April the ghetto was treated to a sensational event: the arrival of the first Dutch Jews. The fate of the Jews in Holland under the Nazi regime had followed the same course as that in Czechoslovakia, just as Edelstein had warned when he visited Amsterdam in the spring of 1941: they wore the yellow badge, were stripped of their property, concentrated in the Westerbork transit camp, and from there sent to Auschwitz. The more privileged for the most part came to Theresienstadt, where those among them who were well known or decorated were protected from transports east.

The Reich Jews were no longer the new and strange arrivals. There were newer and stranger than they, but the deception had not changed. Holland's Gestapo had promised also the Dutch Jews a vacation resort with self-administration, freedom of movement within a twenty-five-kilometer radius, playgrounds, gardens, theater, cinemas. So rosy had the German descriptions been that one of the mothers included in the first transport had decided to bring with her her small son, who had been hidden with a Christian family (unlike the Czechs, thousands of Dutch people risked their lives and sheltered Jews). The Dutch Jews brought butter and chocolate in their suitcases, items that had long since disappeared from the Protectorate, and the Germans, as might have been expected, confiscated the lot. The reality they encountered—the separation of couples, the searches, the wooden bunks, the outhouses—was a tremendous shock for the Dutch Jews, but for the Germans their advent was valuable for propaganda purposes: they arrived in ordinary passenger trains, since they were simply "changing addresses," not being deported, and one Dutch couple was even photographed on arrival: he in a dark suit, tie, and hat; she in white gloves—ready for the theater.

27

CODED MESSAGES

THE GERMANS achieved their objective: the comparative unity of the ghetto leadership was disrupted. The Magdeburg barracks, seat of the Council of Elders, swarmed with intrigue, suspicion, and mutual recrimination. Relations at the top were worsened further by personal antagonism, and differences of ideology and background.

Josef Klaber, the former chief of police who continued in the police force as Löwenstein's deputy, accused Löwenstein of informing the Germans about his talks and disagreements with Epstein, Edelstein, and Zucker. He claimed that he had got hold of a letter from Löwenstein detailing the disputes of the ghetto leaders, and he was convinced that Löwenstein was motivated, not by any desire to help the Jews, but by personal ambition and the debt he owed the Germans for saving his life. The fear that what was said at their meetings was being transmitted to the Germans only increased the mutual suspicions among the Council of Elders.

To Löwenstein, the ghetto police were the pride of Theresienstadt. Children imitated them in games, and residents flocked to see the musical *Girl of the Ghetto,* which portrayed the police in a positive light. It was therefore a heavy blow to him when in May 1943 the police force, as he had built it, was disbanded and reduced to 150 men, all over the age of forty-five. Löwenstein blamed the change on a remark Edelstein had made to Seidl at the swearing-in ceremony attended by the SS, the Czech gendarmes, and the Council of Elders. "Look what a fighting force our police present," Edelstein had reportedly said as the men in gray uniforms marched to the sound of a brass band in imitation of the German army. But the accusation was unfounded. The police force was disbanded shortly after the revolt of the Warsaw ghetto, which made the Germans firmly resolve to extinguish all underground organization in all the ghettos. A well-trained police force of 450 men could easily constitute the nucleus of a future revolt.

Who in Theresienstadt even knew of the revolt in the Warsaw ghetto or the transports to the gas chambers that preceded it? Nobody even considered the possibility of rebellion, since everyone was hopeful: now that the bare tip of the war's end was in sight, logic said, the Germans would want to preserve a model ghetto more than ever. In May 1943, German journalists visited the ghetto and reviewed the stage set in its entirety: the "prominents," a theater performance, the bank with its ghost money. They dropped in at the courthouse, where the case to be heard had been determined in advance (though at one of the hearings when the guests were present the defense lawyer pleaded hunger as the motive for stealing food—he was dismissed by the Germans). According to Gonda, while the journalists were in the ghetto, "only young people were sent to the showers. People were forbidden to answer the committee's questions unless they had no alternative, in which case they were to reply slowly so that the camp commandant could have a chance to answer for them." The reports of the journalists, if they were written at all, were never published in the German press.

Epstein waged a fierce battle against smoking in the ghetto. This was not only because the Germans had punished anyone caught smoking—or even witnessing the infraction—heavily (though some of the SS themselves took part in the profitable trade of smuggling cigarettes into the ghetto), but because the discovery of large quantities of cigarettes necessarily confirmed German suspicions of Jewish contact with the outside—and as far as they were concerned, if cigarettes could be smuggled in, so could ammunition. For this reason, Epstein sought wider authority in security matters, a fact which brought him into direct conflict with police headquarters. Klaber was dismissed and sentenced to six months' imprisonment, and forfeited all his special benefits. The orders of the day of June 19, 1943, stated that Klaber had confessed to smoking, borrowing money, and giving it to his wife to buy food. In so doing, he had broken camp regulations, a particularly serious crime in view of the fact that he had been deputy chief of the security services and his behavior was thus a flagrant breach of trust. At the end of September, Löwenstein was also dismissed, on the charge of possessing extra food-ration slips. He was sentenced to four months' imprisonment; but sometime later he was absolved of all guilt by an arbitration committee composed of former senior military officers.

A month after the journalists came, some much more important guests visited the ghetto. On June 28, accompanied by Obersturmbannführer Eichmann and two other members of the Reich Security head office, two representatives of the German Red Cross and one from the Foreign Office came to Theresienstadt. For the first time, representatives of the Red Cross were permitted contact with transported Jews, and their impressions, despite the attempts at camouflage, were exceedingly negative. As reported by Hartmann and Neuhaus of the German Red Cross to de Pilar, a member of the mixed committee of the International Red Cross in Geneva (who in turn conveyed the content of the conversation to Gerhart Riegner, the delegate of the World Jewish Congress), the population at Theresienstadt suffered from severe undernourishment. Medical services were totally inadequate and living quarters were disgraceful—a conclusion they reached after having visited the residences of the "prominents," where only four or five people lived in a room, including the Bleichröder family.

The two representatives of the German Red Cross pointed out that the internal administration did the best it could: there were public kitchens, children's dormitories, hospitals; a monetary system had been instituted, gift parcels from Portugal had arrived and been handed over to their recipients, and the larger shipments had also reached their destination. However, the fact that there were trains marked JUDENRAT THERESIENSTADT had been brought to the attention of several Nazis in Vienna, and in future one should exercise more discretion. To the question as to whether the people in Theresienstadt stayed where they were or were sent on, de Pilar could not give a definite reply. The gentlemen of the German Red Cross had received the impression that the people would remain there: these were after all Jews whom the Germans wanted to protect, and they had therefore been sent to a preferred ghetto. As to the situation of the Jews in the territory of the General-Gouvernement, de Pilar did not know much; he had heard only of a revolt in the Warsaw ghetto. The ghettos in Poland had apparently been liquidated, and where Jews had survived, they seemed to be in labor camps adjoining industrial complexes. The Red Cross suggested that some of the provisions intended for Theresienstadt be sent to other camps in Upper Silesia, particularly to Birkenau, which was also defined as a labor camp.

There were people in the ghetto who knew the truth about Birkenau. Among the last Jews to arrive from Berlin in January 1943 was Dr. Leo Baeck, the chief rabbi of Berlin and president of the Reichsvertretung, the representative body of the Jews in Germany. Before he left his widower's apartment, Dr. Baeck took care of two pressing matters: he wrote a farewell letter to his daughter in London (Baeck had frequently accompanied groups of Jewish children from Germany to England, always returning, however, because he was resolved to remain with his congregation until the very end) and two checks, one for the gas bill and the other for the electricity bill of the apartment being taken from him.

Dr. Baeck was also allotted a small dark room in one of the houses of the "prominents," but during the first few months of his stay in the ghetto he worked in general services like everyone else. He pushed hearses laden with bread or potatoes and refused to accept any official function. He had brought with him to the ghetto the manuscript of his book *This People* and information which he kept to himself: in the summer of 1941, a Christian woman married to a Jew had come to see him. She had voluntarily accompanied her husband to exile in Poland and later returned to Berlin. She told Dr. Baeck that after the SS had separated her from her husband, she had seen hundreds of vehicles resembling buses leaving full of people and returning empty. According to rumor, the vehicles were fitted with devices for gas poisoning.

Dr. Baeck, who was seventy when he came to Theresienstadt, with a white beard and a high forehead, was an authoritative figure who commanded respect even pushing a cart. Even those who did not know that he was one of the great scholars of his generation— learned in Judaism, philosophy, mysticism, Christianity—sensed his inner strength in the serenity he radiated. After three months of physical labor, Dr. Baeck began to serve as a rabbi, dividing his time between the dead (his three sisters who had preceded him to Theresienstadt died before he arrived, the fourth soon after), the sick, and those greedy for knowledge. Among other things, Dr. Baeck gave a series of lectures on the history of philosophy, each of which drew over seven hundred people (including most of the members of the Zionist leadership), who came to hear his views on Plato, Kant, and

Spinoza. In one of the more restricted forums, Dr. Baeck told his audience that the plight of the Jews was frighteningly difficult, but must be borne with the faith that the Jewish people, who had weathered all the storms of the last two thousand years, would withstand this trial too.

In August 1943, a Czech engineer called Grünberg came to Rabbi Baeck and asked to speak to him privately. The man told Baeck that he had been awoken in the night by a good friend whom he had not seen for years. Grünberg knew that his friend had not been sent to Theresienstadt, and he asked him how he had come there, but the friend cut him off. He was greatly agitated and made him promise not to reveal to anyone what he was about to tell him: because he was half-Jewish he had been sent to Auschwitz, where he had passed selection and been forced into labor. All those who did not pass selection were sent to the gas chambers. He knew this for a fact. Everyone in Auschwitz knew it. The friend had managed to escape from the labor camp and get to Prague, and from there, by bribing a Czech policeman, he had stolen into Theresienstadt in order to warn him, Grünberg, and save his life.

Baeck listened to Grünberg in horror: so it was not just a rumor, the fantasy of a sick imagination. As he stated in his memoirs, Baeck waged a difficult struggle with himself as to whether or not he should persuade Grünberg to repeat what he had told him to the Council of Elders (of which Baeck was an honorary member), and in the end he decided against it: once the Council of Elders knew, it would become common knowledge in the ghetto within hours. To live in the expectation of death was, in the rabbi's eyes, harder than the death itself. Nor was it sure, after all, that everyone would meet their death this way: there was selection for work, and perhaps not all Theresienstadt's inmates would even be sent to Auschwitz. And so Dr. Baeck's decision was not to say anything to anyone, but to keep the truth to himself.

Others had received word of mass extermination too. Viteslav Diamant, an electrician, learned from one of his colleagues, a nationalist Czech Jew who had contacts with workers on the railroad lines, that transports from Theresienstadt had been sent to Lithuania and Latvia, where they were shot to death. Some time later he was told that the trains were going to Auschwitz and there the people were gassed to death. Diamant relayed this information to his friends at work and those members of the Council of Elders whom he knew personally, but according to him, nobody believed it.

During his trial in a Viennese court ten years after the war, Seidl claimed that, much to his surprise, Edelstein had asked him one day if it was true that one of the transports from Theresienstadt had been stopped somewhere and its passengers killed by gas. "I answered him truthfully that I had no idea," Seidl declared. "A few days later, in reply to my query, Eichmann gave me his word of honor that such a thing was impossible. Since postcards started arriving from the people sent east soon after, I never gave the matter another thought."

Edelstein was in the habit of turning to Seidl for verification of rumors rampant in the ghetto. According to the minutes of their meeting of February 1943, Seidl was asked about the rumor that Jews still in Prague had been concentrated in barracks and a Council of Elders had been appointed there too. Seidl could give no answer. On the same occasion, Seidl asked the Elder of the Jews and his assistant to submit a report on the general mood of the ghetto (apparently following the changeover in leadership).

After the war, when the few people who remained in the ghetto until the very end considered Dr. Baeck's decision, they decided that his silence had been justified. "We knew that transports meant severance from family, exile to the unknown, starting all over again, more arduous conditions. Had we known what they really meant, we would not have been able to endure." Those who went to the gas chambers not knowing were unable to give their opinion.

The Jewish community in Palestine knew of the extermination of the Jews—and did not want to know. There was sufficient information in the West on the systematic slaughter: it was brought by fleeing refugees, supplied in reports smuggled to Switzerland, described in the British press from the summer of 1942 onward. But only when a group of eighty-four people, mostly women (all of them citizens of Palestine who had been exchanged in an agreement with the Germans), arrived in Palestine in November 1942, only when they told of the death camps, of the daily mass murder of Jews, were the national institutions prepared to consider the information genuine and issue a public statement. The Jewish community was stunned. Until then, for the same reasons Edelstein and the ghetto inmates had discounted the stories of atrocity, they had tended to reject the rumors of what was happening under German occupation as unreliable—and also, perhaps, because of the unbridgeable gap between the economic prosperity which the war had brought to Palestine and the fate of family and friends across the sea.

In the aftermath of the shock, which was followed by meetings and demonstrations, a rescue committee for the Jews of occupied Europe, headed by Itzhak Grünbaum, representing the Jewish Agency and all Zionist parties, was set up at the end of November 1942. His aim was to raise funds for operations and find ways to save the Jews in Europe and stop the slaughter. One of its practical measures, apart from asking the democratic powers to take steps to halt the extermination and organize demonstrations of solidarity with the victims of Nazism, was the establishment in Istanbul of an offshoot of the rescue committee, headed by Haim Barlas, the director of the Jewish Agency's immigration department. Its members included Viniya Pomerantz, an emissary of the Meuhad kibbutz movement and the Mapai political party, and Menachem Bader, an emissary of Hashomer Hatzair and the Ha'artzi kibbutz movement.

From the start, the leaders of the rescue committee in Jerusalem did not believe in the possibility of rescue, or in the practical benefit of "noisy operations in the free world, such as strikes and demonstrations." They viewed negotiation with the Germans to save Jews in return for money as German extortion. Grünbaum assumed that there was no point in spending huge sums of money on rescue operations—the money could be put to better use consolidating the Jewish community in Palestine with understandable pessimism— like many others he saw the extermination of European Jewry as a fait accompli: it was clear that neither the Allies nor the neutral countries were really prepared to do anything to stop the slaughter. The legation in Istanbul, however, made up mostly of young people who had been involved in illegal immigration, believed in the value of action, if only limited, and began to try to make contact with Zionists in the camps and ghettos to ascertain directly what practical help could be extended.

The first attempt to establish direct contact between Istanbul and Prague was made in December 1942. In the name of Sharka Mandelblatt, a Jewish woman of Turkish citizenship who allowed the rescue committee to use her address in dealing with German-occupied countries, a letter was sent to Lazer Moldavan, one of the last Hehalutz people still in Prague. The letter, written in transparent code, informed him of the rescue committee's establishment in Istanbul under the auspices of the Jewish Agency:

The family is thinking of you. Ivri, Gordon, Kolodny, and Mizrahi have met. They were invited to dine with Dobkin. I will remain here some time. We would like news of the whole family.

The Meshek [economy] and Taassiya [industry] families in Palestine are fine. Our friend Giyus [conscription] is also well. I was asked by Aunt Moledet [homeland] to mention little Ezra [aid]. He is fine and would like to visit you.

Moldavan, who was the chief liaison between Prague and Budapest, replied with a letter telling of Hehalutz's shrinking numbers in Prague. Nearly all of them had been sent to Theresienstadt and were well, according to reports from there, but there was no news from the General-Gouvernement in Poland. In March 1943, after several weeks, a German wearing a swastika paid a call on Heinz Schuster, who was in charge of the community's employment services and another of the last Hehalutz members remaining in Prague. The German told him that he had greetings for him from friends across the border and for friends in Theresienstadt. Schuster feared a trap and at first refused to accept the small parcel, but eventually he took the risk and opened it. It contained $7,000 and a brief coded note.

The bearer of this note will bring regards from Caspi [money] and Zayinelef [seven thousand]. Please tell us how Ishur [confirmation] is. Write too if you managed to give Edel regards from Caspi.

A letter was attached for Jakob Edelstein and other friends at Theresienstadt:

We are happy to write to you. We worked hard to reach you with these greetings. They are being brought to you by a man with one of the following names: Andre Greiner, Rudolf Schultz, Erich Werner, Fritz Stron. He is very good at his job, since he has reached you on his own resources.

Rudy Schultz was a handsome Viennese, a safecracker by profession. He fled to Paris when the Austrian police got on to him and there the German occupation caught up with him. Like all citizens of the Reich, he was conscripted into the army, but because of his professional background and connections with the Paris underworld, he was made a Gestapo agent in the war against insurgent movements. It was in this capacity that Rudy went to Budapest (among other places) where he met a Jewish typist who worked for the local rescue committee and fell in love with the Austrian "businessman" who traveled frequently. Schultz hated the Nazis, and when the girl told him of the underground contacts with Jews in the ghettos in Poland and other areas of German conquest, in an effort to save lives, he offered his help on condition that he would receive no payment.

Fearless and impressive in his elegant suits with the swastika on his black coat, Rudy traveled a great deal. At the Kolomea ghetto his composure and resourcefulness saved an entire group of young activists in the underground youth movement from being arrested by the SS, and he managed to bring them all safely to Budapest. It was Rudy who brought the surprised Schuster news of the free world. The people in Istanbul asked for as much detailed information about the situation as possible, as well as names of people and addresses to send parcels. "We also have in mind financial aid on a greater scale. We would like to do all we can to help you until the day when you will be able to come to us." The letter reflected the mood of the Jewish community in Palestine.

Dear brothers and sisters,
    In anxiety and pain we start this letter to you. We know only too well how often resentment must have filled your hearts against the family in Palestine, and throughout the world, for not having flown to your side sooner. . . . We could not help you and we cannot excuse ourselves. We managed to get to this place with great difficulty and we are trying to reach you through this narrow aperture. Let us hope that the day will come when we will meet in Palestine and much will be told on both sides. But what is the point of self-justification when our road was blocked and we were prevented from speeding to your rescue? Our hearts ache that we have been saved without you.
    News of your plight and the situation in the wretched Diaspora has shaken the Jewish community in Palestine, our common home. For months now Palestine has been restless and the sound of her cry has reached the world at large. The response so far has been slight considering the extent of the disaster and people's needs. In recent weeks the Jewish Agency has received permission to bring thirty thousand Jews, mainly children, to Palestine from all over the world, including your country. In the last group that came from Hungary, however, there were also members of pioneering youth movements under cover of Youth-Aliyah. The problem we're up against is how to get people out. Perhaps your connections with the administration could find a way to permit the depar-

ture of the younger among you. Otherwise, as things are today, only people who can reach Hungary can be brought to Palestine. We do not know if it is possible for you to try this. If it is a question of means, we will find the money immediately, for the Jewish community in Palestine is shocked and large sums have been placed at the disposal of the Jewish Agency and the Histadrut for the purpose of rescuing what can be rescued.

The letter told of the manpower shortage in Palestine, the new enterprises being built with a view to the time "when you will be with us," the plans for new settlements throughout the country, from the Dan region in the north to Beersheba in the south, for the hundreds of thousands of Jews who would find security and livelihood in Palestine. The authors of the letter, Viniya (Pomerantz), Menachem (Bader), and Zeev (Shind), requested a prompt reply and promised that the emissary would soon visit again.

The emissary did not manage to reach Edelstein personally, and the letter (or its contents) was smuggled into the ghetto through Heinz Schuster, who had used the money from Istanbul to buy food for Hehalutz members in the ghetto. The parcels were sent through the Prague community to Erich Österreicher, who, as head of the employment services (the Hehalutz stronghold), was permitted to receive shipments of materials required by his department. Gretl Wiener, who worked for the employment services, dealt mainly with Hehalutz affairs, and it was she who distributed the parcels, chiefly among the sick. No more than a handful of people knew of the connection with Palestine; even people in Yekef's close circle had no idea.

The emissary returned to Istanbul, bringing a letter from Heinz. He told of their meeting, and of how he had had difficulty even persuading Schuster to speak to him before he would accept the letters and money. In June he again set out for Prague, with money and the usual note about "the gentleman bearing this letter [who] will give you regards from Caspi [money] and Vavelef [six thousand]. Please write of the situation of Ishur [confirmation] and a few lines." He also brought a long letter to Schuster, Moldavan, and others, who were asked if possible to pass on most of the money to Edelstein. "In the event that none of you can travel to Yekef, the emissary is prepared to try." The Istanbul group wrote that the emissary was to stay in Prague a day or two, and they asked that he be given letters from friends, including those who were with Yekef.

They promised larger shipments of gift packages and wanted to know if it was true that the recipients in Theresienstadt had to pay duty on the parcels to avoid confiscation—how could this obstacle be overcome? (It was true that the Theresienstadt people had to pay, but only in ghetto money, of which there was no lack.)

The letter writers sent a message to Dr. Kahn from Teddy Kollek (the future mayor of Jerusalem), who had recently visited his children: they were well, indeed positively flourishing. They spoke of the fear of deportation in Hungary, and of the attempts to make contact with "Zivia," i.e., the Warsaw ghetto. "The question of the Diaspora is of crucial concern to all of us in Palestine. The editorials in the press deal with it daily, it is discussed at meetings, and the inability to breach the wall between us casts a tragic shadow over all gatherings." Only in two areas could something be done—transferring some money and preparing settlements—"so that we can carry on on a larger scale when you all come."

> You cannot imagine how we long for news from you. If we cannot be with you, we would at least like to have as much detail as possible so that we may picture your situation, even if only somewhat. A true description is no doubt impossible.

In July 1943 Heinz Schuster and Lazer Moldavan were sent to Theresienstadt, and Hehalutz no longer had a contact man outside the ghetto walls. On his third trip to Prague, the emissary brought a letter addressed generally to "friends and colleagues" without mentioning names, since the Istanbul group did not know whom it would reach. This time the letter was signed by Haim Barlas. The two letters from Heinz and Lazer which reached Istanbul had told something of the situation in the Protectorate. "Nevertheless, we would like to hear more and in greater detail. There are many conflicting reports about your and Jakob's situation, about the number of Jews, the conditions, the children, the elderly. There is also the oppressive and gnawing anxiety and fear that Jakob's place is only a transit site. Please write us whatever you know about this; tell us how we can help and if there is a way to escape for you and Jakob. If money is the key to locked doors and gates, we will get it to you. In view of the world situation at present, there will perhaps be avenues of rescue. Perhaps the new situation, which is bringing those fighting for the freedom of the world nearer you will knock down the stone wall built by enemies all around. Or a breach will be found.

Perhaps this breakthrough will be achieved by means of funds and we will be able to save at least some of the children and bring them to Kraus [i.e., Budapest] or even further."

Barlas wanted to know if the large packages from Istanbul and Lisbon had reached Jakob. "Those fighting for world freedom are coming closer to you, and among them are many of our friends. The will and determination to avenge our spilt blood urges them forward and speeds them on their way. Sometimes it seems that they would like to come to you even on wings, and if you lift your eyes toward the stars, your thoughts will recognize them among the clouds hastening relentlessly eastward and toward you."

The only hint that this letter did in fact reach Edelstein was a surprising question he posed during a conversation with his friends. "What would you do if parachutists from Palestine landed here one day? How would you ensure their safety?"

This time, since Schuster and Moldavan were no longer in Prague, the emissary gave the money to Franta Friedmann, who now led the remnants of the Prague Jewish community: Jews like himself, who were protected by mixed marriages, or those who were only half or one quarter Jewish. Friedmann sent Istanbul a short note. "There is no need for cash anymore and it would be better to continue sending gift packages straight to the ghetto," which meant that Friedmann was not prepared to endanger himself through underground activity. All contact with Prague was broken.

28

COMPLICITY IN ESCAPE

IT WAS ONE almost happy spring. There had been no transports since February 1943, conditions had improved, the typhus epidemic was under control, and the end of the war—after the German army's staggering defeat near Stalingrad—seemed very real. To mark the eighteen-month anniversary of the ghetto, in May, a large celebration was held in the potato-peeling hall of the Sudeten barracks, with Edelstein sitting in the front row, and the date was marked by a soccer match between the two vanguard teams, A-K 1 and A-K 2, with an enthusiastic crowd on hand. Due to the size of the main playing field, in the yard of the Dresden barracks, soccer teams at Theresienstadt consisted of seven players rather than eleven. The game was not particularly brilliant and A-K 1 won.

Soccer, which was very popular in Czechoslovakia among Jews and non-Jews alike, took on a professional form in the ghetto in the spring of 1943. It had always been popular, played by children and workers in every available corner, and there was no lack of good players or devoted fans. But that spring a league was organized according to official rules, with two adult divisions, A and B, and a juvenile division; and teams were formed according to occupation—cooks, gardeners, electricians, butchers, police—or former loyalties: the Prague Hagibor, the Terezin Hagibor, SD Vienna. The sports department reported that in the first nine months of the league's existence, 144 games took place on the main soccer field in the Dresden barracks, attended by 300,000 spectators, and the figures were not inflated for the Germans' benefit. Children, teenagers, workers, every soccer fan of days gone by made an effort not to miss a single game—they watched in excitement, shouting and cheering on their teams.

Apart from the spring league and the autumn league, there was also a summer cup (the butchers beat the warehouse workers 4–3 in a great game in the cup final), a winter cup, and exhibition games. In the finest match of the year, Moravia beat Bohemia 5–2. It was no accident that the most profitable professions were on the whole also the ones who excelled on the field: they could supply their players with the necessary calories and could thus attract promising soccer players. Payment was not in ghetto money but in items of true value: sugar, margarine, bread, meat. Transports came and transports went, epidemics broke out and died down, but soccer continued to be played, occupying the children and turning Saturdays into holidays.

The Allies had won the war in North Africa, and the front moved to southern Italy, drawing nearer to the territories of the Reich: a little resistance, a little patience, a little cunning, a little luck, and it would be possible to hold out till the end. Gift packages were coming into the ghetto, changing the way of life, whether because people were better fed, or because of the hope they engendered, or because they widened the gap between the haves and the have-nots. Every few months a twenty-kilo package could be sent from the Protectorate, using a special stamp depicting the ghetto's scenic surroundings which was greatly coveted by collectors on the outside. Parcels from Germany were limited to one kilo in weight, the same as for soldiers on the front, but they could be sent once a month. The packages contained all the delicacies of paradise: bread from Aryan relatives or brave friends, potatoes, noodles, onions, jam, dried vegetables, sugar, margarine, soup cubes, even sausages. Much of it had obviously been procured on the black market, but surprisingly enough, the Germans showed absolutely no interest in its origins.

The recipients of the packages were suddenly wealthy, but the less fortunate benefited too: the riches were spread around in the form of payment for services rendered, for laundry, mending, or building shelves; they made gifts to friends and neighbors or were pilfered in

the mails. The Jewish postal workers who helped the Czech gendarmes and "beetles" open the packages in the search for contraband were at first permitted to eat to their heart's content, on the
assumption that you could not expect hungry people to handle
food for eight hours without taking something. But the pilfering
did not stop there: their families also shared in the bounty, so that
sometimes the packages reached their destination half empty, leaving the recipients with a bitter sense of loss. People transported to
the East sometimes authorized those who stayed behind to claim
their packages on their behalf, while unclaimed packages were
usually distributed among the children and the sick.

It was Ullman's idea to attach a confirmation slip to the parcels
sent from Lisbon so that at least some direct sign of life might be
had, either through the recipient's signature on the slip or information as to his fate—whether he had died or been sent elsewhere. In
June 1943, the orders of the day announced that following an
appeal from the Elder of the Jews, the camp commandant had
agreed that slips confirming receipt of packages could be sent in
addition to the regular postcards. The confirmation slips, which
said, "I confirm with thanks receipt of the gift package dated . . ."
and sometimes had the word "dear" or "love" added to them,
reached the free world and reinforced the hopes of friends and
relatives that they would be reunited with the ghetto inmates after
the war, especially when reinforced by the occasional postcard,
which even bore an address—Lake Street, Garden Street—and
conjured up the image of a tranquil town.

The wording of the postcards was also reassuring: "I work as a
graphic artist in the bijouterie department, and see our friends
frequently"; or "I am continuing my practice as a pediatrician." "We
work in our professions and have a lot of opportunity for construc-
tive and organizational work," wrote Dr. Karl Fleischmann, Munk's
assistant in charge of the elderly. Fleischmann, who was an artist
and a poet as well as a doctor, added, "I wrote you some time ago but
received no reply." "You see," said Ullman in a letter to Dr. März,
chairman of the Czechoslovakian immigrants' association in Palestine, "not all the letters get through. We must not despair, even if
no sign of life has been received." Ullman received thousands of
signatures including those of Edelstein, Kahn, Zucker, and Hannah
Steiner, and all were a source of optimism: the work involved in
organizing the packages and keeping an up-to-date list of addresses
had not been in vain.

In the end, Edelstein's aspirations were also realized. Theresienstadt had become part of the war industry, not merely through the small workshops that manufactured leather boots and safety goggles, sewed and mended uniforms, produced cardboard boxes for ammunition, repaired jute sacks, and separated feldspar, but also through an enterprise that had real operational value. In April 1943, the orders of the day announced a general call for manpower at a work site denoted by the letter *K* (the initial letter of *Kisten*, "crates") which would employ one thousand people. The finished boards came from the Lodz ghetto, the metal parts from Germany. In Theresienstadt protective crates were assembled on a conveyor belt and fitted with insulation material to prevent the engines of German vehicles from freezing on the Russian front. The conveyor belt sometimes stopped for lack of parts, and to avoid embarrassment, in case important visitors came (particularly from the Reich), a stock of ready crates was always kept on hand and dismantled when necessary so that the production process could be displayed before the distinguished visitors. The original order had been for 120,000 crates, to be completed within three months, but actually the K factory continued to operate until November 1943.

The ghetto worked at full speed. The dream of productivity had become reality, at least partially. Apart from chimney sweeping, all the work was done by Jews. Jews laid water pipes, paved roads, cleaned sewers, drilled wells, made sausages, washed the Germans' laundry, changed electric wires, baked bread, swept streets, wove baskets, made furniture, drove wagons, milked cows, raised silkworms, grew cucumbers in hothouses, and built steam boilers for the kitchen.

With great ceremony, a rail line was inaugurated between Bohušovice and the ghetto, built by about three hundred Jewish laborers over a period of ten months ("When the line is opened, we'll be home already," the optimists had said at the start of construction). Now trains came right into the ghetto and those coming and going would be spared the exhausting two-mile walk. Seidl ordered an especially fine coach from the railroad authorities and opened the line in the presence of several SS visitors. At night the SS celebrated the event by drinking themselves into a stupor, as Gonda recorded in his diary. One of them sent for the members of the ghetto administration and made them stay with him all night.

Two days after this event, Seidl (who later became camp commandant at Bergen-Belsen) was suddenly replaced by Anton Burger.

The Council of Elders viewed the change as a bad omen: they knew Burger—violent, suspicious, devious—from the days when he was head of the Zentralstelle in Brünn. Seidl suddenly appeared the lesser of two evils: during his twenty-month rule in the ghetto he had settled personal accounts with only one Jew, an Austrian tax collector called Müller who had arrived on one of the transports from Vienna and who had, according to Seidl, reduced his father to ruin after the latter had gotten into financial difficulties. Müller, by then an old and frightened man, was taken directly from the train to the cellar at headquarters and beaten and starved for weeks, until pneumonia and diphtheria put an end to his suffering.

Burger, who was Austrian and had once been an elementary school teacher, now bore the rank of Hauptsturmführer, or captain, and could look back with pride on his career in the SS, the role he had played in the Anschluss, and the honors he had received for his activities on behalf of National Socialism. As a start, he forbade the SS to use Jewish doctors or domestics, as had been common under Seidl. It was obvious that the Protectorate Jews and Edelstein were his prime target: he hated them both as Jews and as Czechs.

At the end of August, instructions were issued to close off the area that bordered the new railroad line, an unusual security measure which aroused a good deal of curiosity among the cognizant. A train arrived at Terezin's temporary station, but the doors remained locked and no sound was heard from inside. On Burger's orders, food was brought for 1,500 people, and the doors opened only after those who delivered the provisions had left the station. Mad-hungry children, scarcely more than skeletons, fell on the food before being returned to the train cars. That night, a convoy of children with young bodies and old faces, barefoot or in wooden shoes, wearing rags and tatters of adult clothing, was led through the deserted ghetto streets to the disinfection center. At the sight of the signs POISON and CAUTION, the children cried out in terror. They huddled together and tried to flee, and the older children pushed the younger ones under the showers first. "No, no! Gas! Gas!" some called.

The disinfection of the lice-ridden children was carried out in the presence of the camp commandant and the SS in order to prevent conversation between the children and the staff of the disinfection center. The latter tried to reassure the youngsters by standing under the showers themselves to show them there was nothing to fear; they did not understand the children's panic. One of the staff workers managed to draw one of the older children aside in a dark corner, and the boy told him in Yiddish that they all came from the Bialystok ghetto, which had been destroyed, that some of their families had been shot before their eyes, and some had been taken to a place that bore the sign SHOWERS, where they had been gassed to death. Those who spoke to the children were in no hurry to publicize what they had learned for fear of incurring German wrath when the latter discovered that they had defied regulations. The few who did learn the story interpreted death by gas to mean that the families had apparently been taken to showers and from there to some unknown destination, which was why the children associated death with disinfection.

The children were allotted clean clothing and taken to new barracks in Kreta, a suburb of Terezin outside the walls erected by laborers who were totally ignorant of its purpose. Nobody was allowed to approach the barracks behind the barbed wire, not even the Elder of the Jews or his assistant. Two doctors, fifty-two nurses, and instructors from the ghetto—including Otla, Franz Kafka's beloved sister—were permitted to join the children, having volunteered for the task, but they were forbidden all contact with their families in the ghetto. Dr. Blumenthal, a noted pediatrician from Berlin, was in charge of the staff and took cheerful leave of the nurses in the ghetto before being transferred to the children's barracks; he told some of them that the children were to be sent to Switzerland. Another rumor said that the children were to be exchanged for German citizens and their destination was Palestine. The best of the youth-movement instructors went to the Bialystok children, inspired by the challenge of returning these frightened souls to humanity, ethics, and values. Later, after the barracks were evacuated, they found the minutes of an open trial, led by Aharon Menczer, the former principal of the Youth-Aliyah school in Vienna and one of the leaders of Austria's Hehalutz. Under his guidance, the children had pondered the meaning of theft.

The Germans told the children with contagious diseases that they were being quarantined for treatment, and the next day the SS carried out several undersized coffins from the Little Fortress, still dripping blood. They brought them to the crematorium and burned them themselves. But the rest of the Bialystok children gradually gained weight, the fear disappeared from their eyes, their behavior improved, and after six weeks in the ghetto, on October 6, dressed in new clothes without the yellow badge, they left for the free world in the company of the nurses and instructors. Before leaving, the latter had to sign a document stating that they would not tell the world anything about the ghetto.

Among the instructors walking toward freedom was Lazer Moldavan, the contact man between Prague, Budapest, and Istanbul. The Zionist and Hehalutz leaders gave him a confidential and detailed letter for friends in Budapest and Palestine, signed by many people, including Edelstein, Kahn, Zucker, Österreicher, and Dittl Ornstein. Sometime after the Bialystok children left, Österreicher was summoned to German headquarters and questioned about the smuggled letter, and in this way the leadership discovered that their greetings had never reached their destination. Nothing was ever heard from those who accompanied the Bialystok children, led by Aharon Menczer (who had at one time passed up a certificate to Palestine because he was not prepared to leave the young people). It was as if the earth had swallowed them up.

Only after the war did it become known that the Bialystok children and their escorts had been taken straight to the gas chambers at Birkenau. The entire affair had been an offshoot of negotiations between the German Foreign Office and various elements in the West over the question of allowing Jewish children to leave the conquered territories for Palestine. In March 1943, Eichmann quashed an attempt to take one thousand Jewish children out of Rumania through Istanbul. To the repeated requests from the Foreign Office about this, he replied on behalf of Himmler in May 1943 that the emigration of Jewish children must be rejected on principle. There was some willingness to consider Britain's proposal that 5,000 "non-Aryans," 85 percent children and the remainder escorts, be allowed to leave the occupied countries in the East in exchange for 20,000 young fighting men incarcerated in Allied countries. In response to this proposal, which was transmitted to the German Foreign Office through the Swiss consul in Berlin, Eichmann pointed out that the Reich government "could not help such a brave and noble people as the Arabs to be dispossessed of their homeland by the Jews," and that negotiations were possible only if the British government was prepared to shelter the Jews in Britain rather than in Palestine. Should this proposal be rejected, Himmler felt, it would have a positive effect on Arab nationalists; should it be accepted, it was safe to assume that an additional 5,000 Jews in Britain would exacerbate anti-Semitism there. Either way, Germany would profit. One of the letters to the German Foreign

Office about this from Eichmann's department emphasized that the negotiations must move quickly, for it would soon be "technically" impossible to accomplish the departure of 5,000 children, "as a result of the implementation of our activities against the Jews." The plan failed because the British could not accept the German conditions. The Bialystok children, who had been kept alive in reserve, were no longer necessary.

Epstein, Edelstein, and the heads of the youth department were denied access to the Bialystok children during their stay in the ghetto. But Fredy Hirsch ignored the prohibition and stole into the barracks to find out what the children had been through. He was confident that his good relations with the Germans, especially with Camp Commandant Bergel, would protect him from punishment if he were caught. He was caught—and imprisoned and included in the transport to the East. There had been no transports out of Theresienstadt to the East for six months, a state of affairs which ghetto inmates had hoped would continue until the end of the war; but it was the war itself which brought an end to this period of relative calm.

As the bombings over German cities increased, the Germans needed more and more safe places for factories, institutions, and property. Since the English and American airplanes had till now passed over Theresienstadt, the Germans assumed that the Allies knew of the concentration of Jews at Terezin and would therefore not bomb it. One summer day in 1943, Günther appeared at the ghetto with a large contingent of senior SS officers. They made a thorough inspection of the various buildings, and a few days later the Jewish administration was ordered to evacuate three of the larger barracks and some of the residences. In one day, 6,500 people had to be moved, and place found for them in a ghetto already jammed to its limits (the density had reached 130,000 per square kilometer). With no working time lost, and the orderly distribution of food continuing, almost 5,000 laborers were moved out of the Sudeten barracks, including the A-K groups, the two vanguard transports for whom Sudeten had been home for a year and a half. The barracks yard resembled a feverish anthill: thousands of people toted bundles, pushed wagons, dismantled bunks and threw boards out the windows: the evacuation was completed within twenty-four hours, without clashes or fights of any kind.

The buildings were cleaned and painted, and stood empty for

three weeks. Then a new form of transport started arriving at the ghetto: crates full of documents. It was the central archives of the Reich Security Head Office. Together with five million files came dozens of SS people with their families, who were housed in the evacuated homes. The streets that served the staff of the Reich Security Head Office were separated from the ghetto by a wooden fence and bridge. The ghetto shrank, the overcrowding worsened, with the Jews almost stepping on one another. The optimists saw the transfer of the archives as an encouraging sign: the end of the war was nigh. The pessimists feared deportation.

The barracks evacuated by the Bialystok children were immediately occupied by Jews from Denmark. From the moment they arrived, it was clear that the Danish Jews were different from those of the Reich and the German-occupied territories, who had been sent to the ghetto after their host countries had readily yielded them up and delivered them to the Germans on a silver platter. Behind the Jews of Denmark stood their king. As soon as he heard of the intended action against the Jews of his country, he dispatched a memo to the German Foreign Office:

> Out of human concern for citizens of this state, but also out of anxiety for the future relations between Germany and Denmark, I must point out that the adoption of special measures against a group of people who have enjoyed full civil rights for more than one hundred years will have the most serious consequences.
> Christian

At the same time, in a planned campaign, dozens of protest letters were sent to Germans of all rank, and when the Jews of Denmark were threatened with expulsion, Danes from all walks of life helped take their Jewish countrymen in boats to Sweden, beyond the reach of the Germans. Out of eight thousand Danish Jews, fewer than five hundred failed to escape, and these came to Theresienstadt, where they enjoyed special status.

The first group of Danish Jews was received by Burger, Haindl and other SS people, and was welcomed by Epstein. The Germans behaved like gentlemen, allowing the Danes to smoke, seating them at laden tables, giving them postcards and asking them to write home about their fine reception. Only afterward were their effects searched, as was customary, and a few days later they were moved from the barracks to the town. Because the Danes came straight from their normal lives at home, with no Jewish badge, into the reality of the ghetto, they found it particularly difficult to adjust. But the provisions they lacked were sent to them, the keys to their homes had been deposited with the Danish authorities, and their belongings waited for them undisturbed when they returned at the end of the war. Danish Jews were permitted to write letters more often than other inmates, and, some weeks after their arrival, they began to receive a regular stream of parcels, including vitamins, especially prepared for the residents of the ghetto, thanks to a joint effort by various organizations and the Danish government. Above all, the Danes were protected from transports east on Eichmann's orders, which just goes to show that the attitude of the local population to German persecution of the Jews had a crucial effect on the Nazis' subsequent behavior toward those Jews.

Immediately after the expulsion of the Danish Jews, the chairman of the Danish Red Cross, who was believed to be a collaborator, asked the German authorities to permit representatives of his organization to visit the Danish Jews at Theresienstadt. He pointed out that such a visit would quiet the Danes at home, who had raised a clamor about the deportation of the Jews. The request was not rejected out of hand, but the visit was postponed to some later date, certainly not before the spring of 1944—by which time the necessary setting could be staged.

The summer heat was oppressive. The bugs and fleas were merciless and made sleep in the rooms and attics impossible. Many people preferred to bed down on the floor in the halls, or outside in the yards. Living space shrank, it was difficult to breathe: some of the Sudeten evacuees had been squeezed into other barracks, some found room in attics and converted them into living quarters with partitions of tar paper, wood, and Heraklit, a wartime insulation material made of wood shavings and plaster. The attics were renovated partly with official approval and help from the technical department, partly out of private initiative, with materials stolen from ghetto property.

It was not just the unbearable overcrowding that caused the renewal of the transports to the East. The revolt in the Warsaw ghetto had put the Germans more on the alert for young Jews with organizational ability, especially those who maintained contact with a nonhostile surrounding population. It was therefore decided to deport from Theresienstadt all Protectorate Jews of working age, much to the satisfaction of Burger, who hated the Czech Jews both as Czechs and as Jews and preferred, if he had to deal with Jews at all, to do so with Jews from the Reich and Austria. Burger called an assembly of all the A-K members, who until then had been exempt from transport, causing great agitation in the ghetto: these were the builders of the ghetto with priority rights, Edelstein's people. While they stood on line to be registered, word got out that Burger and the SS were checking everybody's hands to separate those who did physical labor from those with sedentary occupations, with the express purpose of transporting the soft-handed to the East. The more resourceful of the youth instructors rushed to don soiled clothing as evidence of physical labor and rubbed the palms of their hands against the bark of a tree to roughen them; and, indeed, they were not included in the transport.

In a single day—September 6, 1943—five thousand Protectorate Jews of working age and their families were deported to the East, including Fredy Hirsch and Leo Janowitz, the general secretary of the Council of Elders and Edelstein's right-hand man. He had been charged with possession of census documents found in a search of his home, and arrested; but it was clear that his deportation was no accident. Rumor had it that he and Fredy were meant to head a new labor camp and Janowitz himself sent confirmation of this to Geneva. Riegner, the delegate of the World Jewish Congress, wired London: a new labor camp had been built at Birkenau, to be administered by Leo Janowitz, the former director of the Palestine office and a close colleague of Edelstein's in Prague and Theresienstadt. "Fredy Hirsch, the director of the youth department in Theresienstadt, has moved with Leo. Leo Janowitz hopes to organize Birkenau well, on the basis of the experience he gained working with Jakob Edelstein, and asks me to keep in touch and help wherever possible. He is urgently awaiting packages both for individuals and general consumption." The news from Janowitz came from the Reich Union of the Jews in Germany in Berlin. The address gave neither a street name nor a block number, only a prison number and his date of birth. In the last months of 1943, through the aid committee and representatives of the Czech government-in-exile, 2,420 packages of food were sent to 500 people in the same way as the collective packages to Theresienstadt. Confirmation was even received that the shipments had reached their destination. The news of a new labor camp at Birkenau also reached Theresienstadt and was greeted with relief. At least it was not Auschwitz or some other concentration camp.

The image of Birkenau in Geneva as described in letters to Palestine, was of a large camp in Upper Silesia, not far from Katowice, "where there are apparently 35,000 people; it includes adjoining towns as well as the town of Birkenau. Near Birkenau is the Auschwitz camp, which is believed to be a concentration camp, where conditions are exceedingly difficult. At Birkenau the Jews work in mines, metal industries, and the manufacture of synthetic rubber. Nourishment is appalling, there is a lack of vitamins and scurvy is rife; appeals reach Switzerland through Slovakia for packages of onions, oil, and meat. But until now all attempts to obtain permission from the German authorities for a delegation of the International Red Cross to visit Birkenau have failed—nor has the visit to Theresienstadt yet materialized."

Ullman's office, which served as the communications center for all Jews from Central Europe, received thousands of postcards from occupied territory, some of which hinted at fire and death. Despite all the information collected in Geneva, even Ullman did not know that Birkenau and Auschwitz were in fact one and the same place, and that Birkenau was the real extermination camp, just as the people in Theresienstadt did not know.

Again and again Ullman tried to renew direct contact with Edelstein, but his postcards and letters, sent through ordinary channels, remained unanswered, even if they did reach their destination. Edelstein was no longer allowed to write to the free world. The Germans knew of the open and covert contacts between the Protectorate people and Geneva (the Gestapo in Budapest sent a message to Eichmann that an agent—with good contacts in informed Jewish circles in Switzerland—had said that a Jew called Nathan Schwalb and a Dr. Silberstein received a lot of news from Theresienstadt, and these same sources had even shown him letters and postcards from there), but they also knew that the visit of the International Red Cross to Theresienstadt kept being postponed because of the need for far-reaching changes at the ghetto.

The Istanbul group again tried in September to send a contact man straight to Terezin, without success. They repeated the attempt a few weeks later, as can be seen from the letter to "Dear Jakob, dear friends," written in Istanbul on October 25, 1943. They told of three vain attempts to reach the ghetto.

With this letter, we are again trying our luck. Perhaps we'll succeed this time, since the messenger is able, and our hope, our
desire, our longing for you, must finally breach the wall.

We've been here with Barlas almost a year on behalf of the
Jewish community in Palestine, the Jewish Agency, and the Histadrut, and our efforts have been aimed at alleviating somewhat the
disaster that has befallen our wretched people. Perhaps we have
achieved something with the £170,000 that the Jewish community
in Palestine has set aside for this purpose. We dare not do a
reckoning, for the disaster is not over and those who have been
extricated from the ghastly snare have not yet reached safety and
are not yet here or in our country. Believe us, we are trying
everything, and our chief sorrow is that so many things are beyond
our reach. . . .

The messenger will bring you some money. We know that you
need funds to pay duty on the parcels we send. Let the messenger
have a receipt. Perhaps you need money for other purposes as
well? Write and we'll be only too happy to receive a request we can
fill. Write of your situation, your lives—we read every official letter
from you over and over again, await all signs from you, and fear
and worry that all is not as you write.

The attempt failed this time too—the contact man could not
penetrate the ghetto. Whether the letter reached Theresienstadt
remains unclear. Berl Herschkowitz, the only member of the
Hehalutz leadership at the ghetto who survived, remembers two
letters from Istanbul that were successfully smuggled into the
ghetto and one that was intercepted by the Germans.

The Hehalutz people felt that Yekef's life was in danger. Through
the window of the bakery where he worked, Berl Herschkowitz saw
Eichmann and Edelstein on the street and heard Eichmann threat-
ening to have Edelstein shot, his voice raised in anger. Berl told his
friend Yenda Kaufmann and they decided that the Hehalutz secretariat must meet with Yekef. At the meeting the next day the
Hehalutz members suggested that Yekef and his family escape from
the ghetto. One of the sewage workers, a valiant Czech Jew, knew all
the underground passageways leading out of the ghetto and was on
friendly terms with Bilina, a Czech policeman. Hehalutz had at its
disposal large sums of smuggled money and gold which could be
used to find Jakob, Miriam, and Arieh a hideout. Edelstein rejected
this suggestion quite definitely; he felt that his place was among
those who trusted in him. He did sense that some plot was afoot, but

he would not abandon the ghetto. "I don't know if I'm helping the ghetto with my contacts with the Germans or not; but even if not, I'm not running away."

The war had already dragged on for four years. Even the worst pessimists had never imagined it could last so long. Seasons changed, hope flared up and died down. The advance of the Russian army in its counterattack on the Eastern front seemed incredibly quick to the ghetto—as opposed to its real progress—and the comedians quipped that the Allied general staff had broadcast a message to the ghetto that said, "Stop the rumors. We are unable to keep up with you." The days grew shorter, and in mid-September, when permission was given to wear overcoats for work outside (inside the ghetto, people could dress as they pleased), the ghetto inmates knew that a new winter—their third—was approaching. In summer it was completely dark only between about 11 P.M. and 3 A.M.; in winter, the nights were long and depressing, because windows had to be kept shut if a light was on, even if it was only one 40-watt bulb in a room for forty people. The Jewish New Year came and the ghetto was still there. The Council of Elders sent holiday greetings to the public, as was its custom, thanking all for their devoted work and expressing the hope that in future everyone would continue to work together out of a sense of common responsibility. A series of lectures was given on the Days of Atonement: Dr. Baeck gave an address at the New Year's ceremony for German-speaking youngsters, as did Rabbi Feder for the Czechs. On Yom Kippur itself the Kol Nidre was recited before both groups at a combined gathering, and the men's choir sang "Open Thy Gates to Me." The prayer rooms in the attics of the elderly residents were packed, the old women put on their hats, leftover from days long gone, and the entire congregation prayed for one thing and one thing only: for the war to finish quickly, for the end to be in sight.

It was clear that some of the people in the September transport, particularly several of the A-K members, had been sent east in order to undermine Edelstein's position. Among the last of the Prague community staff members to arrive at the ghetto in the summer of 1943 was Bedriška Hostovska, who knew Edelstein from his work in the community education division. Hostovska worked in one of the groups of a hundred and lived in an attic, far from the ghetto's leading ranks. But one day she was called to Edelstein's office in the Magdeburg barracks and after she had gotten past the barricade erected by his loyal secretary, Mrs. Steif, Edelstein took her into his room and asked a strange question: what did the ghetto veterans tell newcomers like herself about him? The surprised Hostovska replied that she had heard nothing but good about him, that people believed in him and depended on him. It seemed to her that Edelstein was relieved by her words. He said something that she did not understand at the time but which remained engraved in her memory for years: "You must know that I would never sign anything that could harm my people." The embarrassed Hostovska felt that the main thing had been left unsaid and that Yekef was disturbed by something. Soon after this conversation, on November 10, Edelstein was arrested, after being interrogated until noon the previous day at headquarters. A few days before his arrest, he had bumped into Dittl Ornstein (one of the staff members who had come to the ghetto with him) in the dark corridors of Magdeburg. Yekef pushed Dittl into one of the small rooms and closed the door behind him. He asked her if she had seen anyone at the other end of the hall. Dittl had seen no one, but Edelstein, who seemed extremely nervous and tense, said, "I know that I am constantly being followed."

The Germans accused Edelstein of complicity in the escape of Jews, since the population records did not match the facts. They were right—there were discrepancies in the resident files. It had begun accidentally, without any premeditation, when Leo Janowitz had mistakenly entered the name of a dead man in the list of people to be deported, and the matter had gone unnoticed. In the commotion of departure at the train station, it was not always possible to count every single person, and the overall figure was based on the lists. For this reason, in the course of time, other names of dead people were entered in the lists in place of living people who remained in the ghetto; several dozen were thereby saved. Furthermore, some disappeared, escaping with the help of relatives on the outside and by bribing the Czech gendarmes. If a young man (only the young tried to escape) failed to report for work and his bed remained empty, it was obvious that he had run away. In order not to alert the Germans, he remained registered in the records. Several of those who escaped deportation in October 1943 were never discovered, while those who joined transports at the last minute to be with their families were not recorded. In time, there was a total deficit of fifty-five people, covered up at Edelstein's orders by the records department and with the knowledge of engineer Foltyn and two or three others who worked there.

The records department had faced a difficult task from the start, due to the constant comings and goings, the people who were never registered so the Germans would not know of their presence, the babies whose births in the ghetto were never reported to the Germans. In some cases two people with the same last name died on the same day, and only one of the names was removed from the records.

As early as October 1942, Seidl had imposed curfew, ordered a census, and threatened heavy punishment for anyone obstructing the count, which was carried out by the elders of the rooms. There was no lack of irony in this emphasis on accuracy: as a human being the Jew had absolutely no value; as a statistic, he was important. Alive or dead, the main thing was to be recorded. It is not clear just how Burger found out about the irregularities in the files. According to the version accepted by those close to Edelstein, two Jews who had escaped from Theresienstadt were caught by the Gestapo in Prague; after their arrest it came to light that they were still registered in the ghetto files and the local commander knew nothing of their escape. Murmelstein, the only member of the leadership who survived, had an entirely different version: Alfred Goldschmied, the records director of the Dresden barracks, was named to go on the September transport. When he appealed to Epstein, the Elder of the Jews, and pleaded to be allowed to remain in the ghetto, he pointed out that he had risked his life in the course of his work. A year before, on instructions from Edelstein, he had falsified the barracks records and added fifty-five people who were not in the ghetto to the list. An astounded Epstein discovered that the daily report he handed in to headquarters on the state of the ghetto, which bore his signature, was in fact false.

In the ensuing investigation, Epstein located the root of the problem in the general pandemonium during the departure of the transport that left on October 26, 1942, when 134 people failed to report for their deportation. Instead, people who were not even on the list had been pushed into the compartments. Following this oversight, a census had been taken, but it was still not clear who had left and who remained. To balance the accounts, Edelstein instructed Foltyn, the director of population records, to register fifty-five names of dead people in one of the barracks, and for a year the matter had been kept confidential among everyone involved. Now that Goldschmied had opened his mouth, Epstein feared that Burger would soon learn of it as well. Epstein had tried to gain Burger's trust from the beginning; now he feared that news of the affair might reach Burger's superiors in Berlin, who were liable to interpret the falsification as evidence of an underground organization. According to Murmelstein, he therefore decided to bring the matter to the attention of the Germans himself.

Foltyn, Goldschmied, and Egon Deutsch, another clerk in the records department, were arrested along with Edelstein. They were held in the basement of the bank building under blinding lights twenty-four hours of the day. Edelstein's arrest, which took place on the fifth anniversary of Kristallnacht—a popular date for perpetrating acts of vengeance against the Jews—dealt the ghetto a stunning blow. Dittl Ornstein managed to smuggle two cleaning women into the prison with letters for Yekef from his friends and partners saying that they wished to leave with him, no matter where he was sent. The women told how Jakob wept when he read the note, but he forbade his friends to volunteer to join him. The message he sent them remained engraved in Dittl's memory: "Beware of Murmelstein."

Edelstein's arrest remains a puzzle: did the Germans act simply on the basis of their own desires and plans, unmotivated by their relations with the Jews? Was he really arrested because of the irregularities in the files? Or had they sought an excuse to get rid of him? There are no answers.

Gerda, Deutsch's wife, managed to sneak into prison with the cleaning women. Her husband had been brought to jail straight from the hospital, where he was being treated for an intestinal ulcer. He told her that he had been interrogated for seven hours, facing a German police dog the entire time, its paws on his shoulders. After the investigation, he had lain faint with weakness for two days.

Yekef's flat, which had always been filled with guests, visitors, and people seeking favors, now attracted only a handful of friends. On Sabbath eve, Miriam lit candles and as always was quiet and reserved. She was not permitted to see Yekef, but every day she walked slowly by the cellar where her husband was being held. She could not see him, but she assumed that he saw her through the window near the ceiling of the cellar.

The day after Edelstein's arrest, Burger ordered a general census taken in the ghetto. The entire population, including small children and old people, was to assemble outside the walls in a large field which in the past had been used for military maneuvers. Only the bedridden, mothers with babies, and the prisoners remained in the ghetto. According to the marching plan set down by Epstein, almost 40,000 people walked out of the ghetto, street by street, in groups of one hundred, five abreast. It started at six in the morning and by nine-thirty everyone was in place. Instructions had been given to wear warm clothing and bring food, but some people also took along the necessities they would need while traveling, just to be on the safe side. Some wrapped themselves in blankets against the chilly weather.

At first the ghetto residents regarded the census indulgently, almost an excursion. They were allowed outside the walls for the first time in many months. They saw trees, moving buses, people passing on the road. There was still an outside world. But as time dragged on, their spirits fell, children cried, and old people fainted, and since it was forbidden to break ranks, people relieved themselves where they stood, in front of everybody, and were ashamed. All around stood Czech police, armed with rifles. Machine guns were in position, the SS rode through the ranks on bicycles, Burger rode a black horse, military aircraft flew overhead, and for a moment people wondered: did they plan to kill them all? But the thought was immediately rejected by logic: why would they do it outside the ghetto, in full view of the world?

The task of counting fell to Mandler, who had been accorded "prominent" status because of his experience in organizing Jewish transports from provincial towns to Theresienstadt. But despite his experience Mandler was unsuccessful. Everybody counted: Epstein, his face wan and anguished, and the SS, and the more they counted, the greater the muddle. People stood patiently. They stood and waited. It grew dark and still they stood. Maybe they would stand all night? Maybe they would be exterminated under cover of darkness? At around ten o'clock at night, rumor finally spread that they were returning, and they started homeward, streaming in through the one narrow opening the Germans had left in the ghetto walls in order to add to the torments of the day. Forty thousand people returned in the dark, along a narrow path, having stood on their feet for twenty hours under terrible stress. Nobody was trampled to death, but several hundred old and sick people paid for the census with their lives. Never had the feeling that Theresienstadt was home been as strong as when they returned from the census. The last of the lines got to bed at midnight, frozen, hungry, exhausted—and happy to be home.

Statistically the census was a failure, and a new count was required, this time with the help of personal documents and a new index. When the calculation was finally in order, transports were renewed. On the day of Edelstein's arrest, instructions were given to remove the top tier of the three-level bunks built in all the dormitories, particularly from residences that outside guests were likely to visit. The ranks were obviously to be thinned out. There was no point in trying to improve the ghetto's appearance as long as everything smacked of unbearable overcrowding. The production of crates for the German army came to an end; the thousand employees and their families were dispensable, as were others whom Burger considered undesirable—those close to Edelstein, including most of the staff of the employment services, regarded as Edelstein's stronghold, and composed chiefly of Hehalutz people, because of the supreme importance Edelstein attributed to work as the key to the ghetto's survival.

The daily ordinance for December 13 announced that by order of the authorities, a transport of 2,500 people would be leaving on Wednesday, December 15, for regions of the Reich. The people leaving would be advised that very morning. Anyone who tried to evade or otherwise violate transport instructions would suffer the most severe punishment. Three days later another transport of the same number would leave. According to Burger, the five thousand transportees, including more than 500 children and many Hehalutz people and youth instructors, were being sent to another labor camp.

When Honza Brammer, the director of the juvenile employment services, packed his belongings for the December transport, his roommate, Avraham Fixler (who had acted as the liaison between the Prague Jewish community and the Zentralstelle and had arrived with the last newcomers from Prague), said to him somewhat cynically and pessimistically, "When I leave for the East, I won't take a thing with me." Nobody tried to get to the bottom of his words. Friends brought Hehalutz people vitamins, families donated food from their emergency stock, Hanukkah candles were packed within reach at the top of the knapsacks. Among Edelstein's people expelled from Theresienstadt was Harry Tressler. During their long conversations on the future of Palestine and Europe after the war, Edelstein had often told Harry very matter-of-factly, "I won't live to see it, but you young people will." As to his own life, Edelstein had no delusions, but he firmly believed that his only son Arieh would survive, for he was destined for greatness.

Miriam Edelstein, her mother, and Arieh were included in the first transport, made up entirely of people from the Protectorate.

Until the very last moment, when they had already been herded into the cattle cars, Jakob's family did not know if he was being sent too. Word was that Edelstein would join his family and would also hold a central function at the new labor camp, and this was what Miriam believed. "How disappointed she must have been when she saw the police leading him toward the train, but to the last car, the prisoners' car," Gonda wrote in his diary. "Terrible. One train; in one car the wife and child, journeying to an unknown future, in the last car the husband, being taken to a concentration camp." En route the train passed through the outskirts of Prague. Packed eighty to a car, the passengers who managed to press against the small window caught a glimpse of the familiar sights along the Vltava, so near, so far.

Following Edelstein's departure, the composition of the Council of Elders changed: Otto Zucker became the first assistant to the Elder of the Jews in place of Edelstein, and was now considered the main spokesman of the Czechoslovakian Jews. Life in the ghetto continued as usual. A large Hanukkah party was held, Hebrew Week took place as planned; every evening a Hebrew program was held for the public, including an oral newspaper, and on the last night of Hanukkah the more advanced students received the emblem with the Hebrew letter *ayin*, which obliged its bearers to speak only Hebrew to one another. Immediately afterward came the Christmas parties and a week later the end of the year was celebrated. There was no longer any shadow of a doubt: the war would end in 1944.

The working reports for 1943 noted the ghetto's achievements with satisfaction, especially in the cultural field. During the year, 410 theatrical performances in Czech had taken place, including thirty-seven premieres: Chekhov's sketches; Cocteau's *The Voice*; František Langer's *The Camel Through the Needle's Eye*; Molière's *Georges Dandin*; Karel Čapek's *The Fateful Love Game*; four cabarets, including Švenk's *To Life*; various poetry readings, including Jiři Wolker, Rimbaud, Villon, Erben, Neruda, and Macha; two plays for the puppet theater; six children's plays, including *The Legend of the Drop of Water, The Fireflies, The Flowery Horse,* and the greatest hit of all, the children's opera *Brundibar,* written in Prague but denied performance there (except in the Jewish orphanage) because its composer, Honza Krasa, was a Jew and the authorities in the Protectorate had banned it. The story of the wicked organ grinder, Brundibar, who did not allow children to sing in the streets to raise money for milk for their sick mother, ended with the organization and victory of the children, and also contained a moral for the children of the ghetto: united, the strong man could be defeated. The finale, "Sound the drums—we have won, we were unbeaten, unafraid," fired the children, and Honza, the child who acted Brundibar, was the star of the ghetto. But when the wicked man was finally defeated in the adult world, neither the actors nor the children's audience were still alive.

It was time for the crowning musical event in the life of the ghetto: Verdi's *Requiem,* conducted by Raphael Schächter. Three times Schächter had been compelled to start anew—each time musicians and choir members had been shipped east. It was a daring choice: a Christian requiem in a Jewish ghetto—but it was also a claim for a share in humanity's cultural heritage, a cry against injustice: when the 150-voice choir sang "Dies Irae," it was also a verdict against the Germans.

Since art brooks no compromise, even in ghetto conditions, the cultural department also had a criticism section. Kurt Singer, the music critic, noted that the performance of the *Requiem* lacked consistency, even by the same performers during the same program; uneven quality was the result not only of undernourishment, excitement, and weariness, but also because between five and eight hours of daily rehearsals were required for such an ambitious production, and the cast had no more than an hour or two a day. Singer called the production a great artistic accomplishment for the ghetto and an achievement by conductor Rafi Schächter. But why Verdi's *Requiem?* Why not one of Handel's oratorios—*Judas Maccabbeus, Elijah, King Solomon*—which had a Jewish content? This was the place to perform them; and if a Christian requiem, why not Brahms's, which is at least based on the Bible and mentions the verse "How goodly are thy tents, O Jacob . . ."? The Christians in the ghetto would no doubt rejoice, Singer concluded, since "art for art's sake has triumphed."

Kamil Horn, the theater critic, was much more harsh in his criticism of *The Golem,* a rhymed play by Georg Kafka, cousin to Franz, who wrote German poetry: the figure of the Golem was childish, tasteless, weak; "Mr. Kafka's talent, if he has any, does not lie in plays."

The History of the Theresienstadt Ghetto, a report on the ghetto's two-year existence which bore the date 31/12/1943, was ordered by German headquarters and recorded by Otto Zucker. It expressed satisfaction at achievements to date: Theresienstadt had become a modern city. There were now 2,000 water faucets, 500 meters of dishwashing sites, and 1,500 toilets, 60 percent of which were equipped with flushing devices. The three large kitchens and several other enterprises were now supplied with steam from the former beer brewery, two new large kitchens had been built, the central laundry had been expanded and reorganized more efficiently, the bakery used modern techniques such as time-and-motion analysis. There was a much wider legal base for self-administration, and all employees had periodical medical checkups. The medical department had managed to wipe out the lice epidemic using Zyklon gas, and had eradicated typhus as well. Production had developed in the first nine months of 1943, and had adapted itself to the war economy: instead of ready-to-wear clothing, the central sewing workshop turned out uniforms; instead of decorative items, a workshop now made ammunition cartons. Looking back, one could see that tens of thousands of Jews of different ages, occupations, and ways of life had managed through self-administration to carve out a life for themselves within the given framework, within confined territory. Looking forward one could say: "We must aspire to a better balance between caring for the old and increasing productivity of the labor force."

Jakob's friends, who had worked with him during the feverish days of the Palestine office, and in the Prague community, and from the difficult beginnings of the ghetto, felt bereft after his departure. Nobody had been given an opportunity to take leave of him and only stories remained of his last days in the ghetto. In the style of hasidic tales, Gonda wrote one down in his diary:

> Jakob, how he suffered and how great was his anguish. On the night of the count in November, he could not sleep for thought of the whole ghetto passing the night outside, beneath the skies. He could not talk to the guard, for this guard was a foe of Israel. In despair he began to put on his phylacteries. Witnessing the strange scene, the guard was moved, for at first he thought that Jakob was committing suicide. He burst into the cell, and Jakob explained to him that he was not considering suicide, and that putting on phylacteries was a religious rite. And pity stirred in the heart of the guard and a wonderful thing happened in the twentieth century—an enemy of the Jews learned to love the Jews. A miracle which came to pass through the donning of phylacteries.

In early January, Itzhak Grünbaum, chairman of the aid commit-tee for the Jews of occupied Europe, notified the Czechs and Aus-trians in Palestine:

> On Terezin: several thousand have been moved to the Birkenau labor camp. Otherwise there is no change in the security situation. We must consider whether it is worthwhile publicizing the matter. Perhaps it is enough to tell the newspapers that according to information received, until this month there had been no general expulsion of Theresienstadt inmates. It might however be better not to mention the matter.
>
> Through Budapest, Istanbul received information that Jakob too is no longer at Terezin. We don't know if he has been moved to Warsaw, as reported, or if it means that he's dead, for there are no longer any Jews in Warsaw.

29

DON'T TOUCH THE FENCE

THE DOORS of the train cars were thrown open forcefully, and voices shouted, "Quick! Quick! Everybody out!" But when the passengers—frozen, petrified, thirsty, stunned from the journey in the packed cars with only a single pail in which to relieve themselves in full view of all—tried to take their bundles with them, the strange men in striped jail uniforms ordered them coarsely to leave everything behind and get out onto the platform. Before the Theresienstadt people knew where they were or what was happening, they were loaded onto trucks under glaring spotlights, and driven in the dim dusk to empty barracks where the doors were locked behind them. Only a handful had had the presence of mind to exchange a few words with the locals during the general commotion, and what they had heard was puzzling indeed: it seemed as if Auschwitz and Birkenau were one and the same place, equipped with a gas factory where everybody died. However, since the locals had at the same opportunity asked for cigarettes, money, and any articles of value, claiming that in any case everything was to be lost, the Theresienstadt people treated these revelations with skepticism. They would have to wait for what the morning would bring. With relief, they stretched their legs out for the first time in three days and nights, and lay down in families to sleep.

The next day the men and women were driven separately to showers, called "saunas" by the locals. Arieh Edelstein went with the men, Miriam and her mother with the women. Like everyone else, Miriam was ordered to deposit all valuables for safekeeping in exchange for a signature, and then the women were told to roll up their left sleeves to the elbow. Women prisoners sat at a table and tattooed a number on every arm. "Does it hurt?" one of the newcomers wanted to know. "Idiot," came the derisive reply between quick stabs. "Be happy that you're getting a number, because a number means life." The women were numbered from 71,000 to over 73,000; the men from 165,000 to 168,000.

Next came the anguish of separation from all personal articles: wedding rings, snapshots of distant parents and children, the last remaining mementos of home. Naked, the women were hustled into the showers and emerged to stand shivering in the cold until clothes were issued to them—threadbare, grimy garments, allotted with total indifference to size: a child's vest and linen skirt, a black silk dress, a tattered coat without buttons. Within an hour all the women resembled scarecrows. "Lucky, lucky," the veterans told them. "You're staying alive." On the way back from the sauna, led by SS men with fearsome German shepherds along a path between two high wire fences which had been cleared of snow, the convoy of women and children from Theresienstadt met up with another convoy of women prisoners coming from the opposite direction, Polish-speaking women wrapped in rags who burst into tears at the sight of the children. "Poor, sweet little children!" they whimpered, and tried to kiss the hands of the frightened youngsters until an SS man chased them off. What had happened to them? the newcomers wondered, not understanding the feelings of veteran women prisoners who had also once been mothers and sisters and had not seen a healthy living child for a long time.

Only after they entered the camp (B/II/b according to the official designation) and met the people from the September transport, who had preceded them by three months, did they slowly begin to grasp the nature of the place they were in. Even here, only a few hundred meters from the chimneys of the crematoria, there were many who still refused to believe, who could not bear the thought, that thousands of people were killed by gas every day. But they understood immediately that this was a terrible place from the appearance of friends and acquaintances from the September transport who had undergone a radical change in their brief period at Birkenau: thin and transparent, or swollen with starvation, huddled inside tattered garments and in their eyes a look of sadness, of vulnerability, of being party to a terrible secret; or else hard, hostile, and violent.

The arrival of the September transport had apparently caused great excitement all over Auschwitz: for the first time in the history of the extermination camp there had been no selection on the railway platform between those destined for immediate death and those permitted to live—temporarily at least—in order to provide manpower. Instead, they were all allowed to live—men, women, children, old people—and housed together in one camp (though men and women lived in different blocks), the first Jewish family camp in all the thirty-nine camps of the Auschwitz complex. (The only other family camp was that of the Gypsies.) Their heads were not shaved, and they were not sent out of the camp to work in mines, foundries, or agriculture, like all other camp prisoners. They worked within the camp where building had not yet been completed because the pace of building never caught up with the pace of transports. The SS in charge of the family camp had been instructed to treat these prisoners differently: there was to be no torture, no executions for amusement's sake, no violent beatings, and no selection to weed out the sick and dying. However, the head of the camp was a sadistic German criminal called Arno Böhm, who proudly wore his number 8 and green triangle, the mark of criminal prisoners (political prisoners wore a red triangle, members of Christian sects a purple triangle, homosexuals a pink triangle, and Jews were marked by two triangles, one red, the other yellow, which together formed a Star of David). For the first time in the history of Birkenau, administrative posts were filled by new Jewish prisoners, and even the heads of the residence blocks and their assistants, who were generally particularly brutal specimens drawn from the ranks of non-Jewish prisoners, were now appointed from among the Theresienstadt people.

News of the Czech family camp spread throughout the entire Birkenau complex and remained a riddle. Rumor had it that it was meant to be a model camp for display should a delegation of the International Red Cross visit. Soon after the establishment of the family camp, Eichmann arrived, the only outside visitor authorized to move freely through the camps, unescorted by the camp commandant. Eichmann notified the secretariat of B/II/b that prisoners of the family camp could receive mail and parcels, and this too was highly unusual for Jewish prisoners. Eichmann ordered the *Schreib-stube* (as the secretariat was called in camp language), headed by Leo Janowitz, to ascertain how many people wished to send post-cards and how many postcards each person desired. Every block submitted its requests and the total came to about 2,500 (many people no longer had anyone to write to, for their families had preceded them to that same East shrouded in mystery). The matter was pressing, Eichmann said, and indeed he returned two days later with the requisite number of postcards of the type used in Theresienstadt. He gave them to the secretariat together with the injunction that the prisoners were to write to friends and relatives in Theresienstadt and other regions of the Reich saying that they were well and could receive packages.

The postcards achieved their purpose: in Theresienstadt, in Prague, in Switzerland, and in Palestine, everyone assumed that Birkenau, near Neuberun, was a new labor camp, led by Leo Janowitz and Fredy Hirsch, and packages started to arrive for those still fortunate enough to have a relative outside, Jewish friends protected by mixed marriage (for only they could maintain contact with Jews in camps or ghettos without having to pay the consequences), or their names on the list of package recipients from the free world through Geneva. The packages could not prevent the death of hundreds of those who arrived on the September transport who succumbed to typhus, dysentery, malaria, or starvation with any of its concomitant ailments, but they sufficed to give the residents of the family camp the feeling that they enjoyed a special status in this kingdom of death, only forty-five miles from the Czech border and yet a different planet, far from human earth.

The September deportees occupied the camp before construction was completed. The barracks—thirty-two windowless stables from the surplus equipment of Rommel's campaign in Africa, with a small airhole near the ceiling—were all in place, but there was no water yet, and when the water was connected, it was so foul that the Germans were prohibited from washing their dishes in it, let alone drinking it. The blocks were still empty and it was some time before the characteristic three-level bunks were built. Two rows of bunks lined the entire block, separated by a low concrete wall with a pipe connecting the two heating stoves at either end of the building.

The September people set up the camp from scratch, and it differed from all other men's, women's, and Gypsy camps in Birkenau because of the special conditions laid down by the Germans and the sense of togetherness and identification felt by the inmates. All the prisoners hailed from Czechoslovakia, all had passed through Theresienstadt, all had been raised in an environment foreign to cruelty—although some people in official positions were changed by Birkenau, their latent instincts exposed. When a *kapo* in one of the blocks, a former member of a youth movement, slapped an adult and shouted at the newcomers: "You should know where you've come to; nobody leaves here alive," his conduct caused widespread astonishment: how was it possible to degenerate to such a degree? But there were few people like him. The majority of the functionaries of the September group—Leo, Fredy, the doctors and nurses in the sick block where the ill and dying lay almost on top of one another, the youth counselors—continued, as they had in Theresienstadt, to bear the responsibility for common existence; still men, still abhorring brutality.

To be an elder of a block was to be almost a god: while each ordinary resident of the blocks had a living space 60 centimeters wide, the elder had his own little room near the entrance, and he knew the meaning of hot water, eating his fill, and clothes that were intact, warm, and clean.

Among the officials was Ada Fischer, Theresienstadt's executioner, who in Birkenau enjoyed the position of kapo, head of a labor gang. Fischer, who was short, with long arms extending almost to the ground, a stick in his hand, and a bellowing voice, instilled fear all around. Children recoiled when he patted their hair, and waited, petrified, until he left them alone.

When the new prisoners—men and women—met, after a separation of only one day, they were already different people. The sudden changes were especially noticeable in the men. Most wore trousers too short, torn coats with elbow-length sleeves, unmatched shoes, and hats with the rims cut in back so as to deprive them of any resemblance to civilian headgear. With the perpetual drip at the tip of their noses (the mark of prisoners who had nothing with which to wipe it away), arms crossed over their chests, hands thumping shoulders in a vain attempt to generate some warmth, shivering from head to toe after hours at roll call with the cold penetrating into every bone, into the blood, the teeth, the brain, they resembled storks—sad, forgotten, lost. The chill was worse than the hunger: a cold, bitter liquid in the morning; for lunch about half a liter of turnip soup with rotten potatoes, cold before it even reached the blocks in open wooden casks; a blanket of textile wastes, thin and saturated with damp, the only cover at night; and shoes, which were never dry, as the pillow. Once, just once, to feel warm, and then to eat to one's fill—just once.

With the arrival of the December transport, ten thousand people occupied the family camp, which covered an area of 150 by 750 meters, sorely straining its capacity. At the two outhouses—six rows with twenty-five holes per row—there was always a line of people, legs crossed, trying with all their might not to soil their only underwear. The air in the barracks hovered like a cloud; it reeked of four to five hundred people, of damp and urine and nightmares and death (corpses were removed only once a day and piled up behind the block), and still it was preferable to the desolate cold outside. Only the young, those with iron principles, had the stamina to strip at least partially at the faucets and wash in half-frozen water, when there was nothing with which to dry themselves; only the young were prepared to wash some articles of clothing and wear them wet, for there was no way to dry them.

In pairs, women dragged the large wooden casks by means of a thick wooden beam laid across their shoulders, with the heavy cask suspended between them on two iron rings, for the privilege of scraping the sides of the barrel after distribution. They volunteered to remove the dirty pails from the blocks to the outhouses, from evening to morning, when going out was prohibited, in return for an added half-portion of soup, which they divided with children and husbands. Once a day the men and women could meet for a brief moment on the way to the washrooms or outhouses, since visits in the blocks were absolutely forbidden and were punished with the lash.

During the first few days the children remained with their parents, until they joined the children's barracks, a project initiated by Fredy Hirsch, and his domain. Arieh Edelstein also joined the barracks which stood at the back of the family camp. Behind it was the electric fence and to the right, on the horizon, was the silhouette of a large chimney. Block 31 was like every other block, a stable without windows, cut in half by a concrete step, but without bunks. At first Arieh and the other children slept with the men, but after some time the boys and instructors were housed in a separate block, near the children's barracks. The children spent the entire day in the barracks, mostly sitting in circles on low stools, group next to group, on either side of the heating pipe. During the peak period, there were six hundred children between the ages of five and fourteen in the barracks, which came under the direct supervision of the health department, headed by Mengele, Birkenau's chief doctor.

Officially Fredy retained his position as elder of the block, a post which in other camps controlled life and death. But to the children, Fredy remained what he had always been, the instructor. Everyone—children, counselors, parents—knew that it was only through his efforts that the barracks had been opened at all. Soon after the arrival of the September transport, Fredy and Leo Janowitz had reported to the camp commandant and pointed out the burden that the children constituted, dispersed as they were throughout the camp, hindering parents from obeying orders, making discipline difficult, constituting a nuisance during roll call. The best solution therefore was to concentrate them in one place and teach them, first of all, the necessary German terms for camp order. Whether these arguments indeed convinced the SS, whether approval for the children's barracks was given out of propaganda considerations in the event of a visit by the Red Cross commission, or whether Dr. Mengele wanted his future guinea pigs concentrated in one place— nobody knew. But one thing was clear: Fredy was a tower of strength. The SS talked to Fredy differently from the other prisoners. There was unspoken respect in their voices, perhaps because, to a large extent, Fredy personified their ideal: tall, erect, and athletic, his black boots were always polished, his German pure and forceful.

Fredy Hirsch did not change, even in Auschwitz: as always he was a fiend for cleanliness and order, and the children had to wash themselves with half-frozen water even in the Polish winter, which crept into the very marrow of one's bones, with one towel for between six and ten children. Cleanliness to Fredy meant health, and health meant hope of survival. The day in the barracks began with morning exercises and cleanliness inspection, and the older children used to help the smaller ones, check their hair, and pull out lice, the carriers of typhus. "A single louse means death" was a favorite motto of the Germans, posted at the entrance to various camps, and indeed life at Birkenau was a never-ending battle with lice, which found themselves a warm haven in clothes that were never removed.

Fredy, who looked after the Edelsteins from the moment they came, made Miriam one of the housemother's assistants in the children's barracks, which meant primarily protection from filth and cold. The housemother was Hannah Epstein, the former direc-

tor of a nursery in Prague. Even here Auntie Hanka, as the children
called her, retained her energetic gait, her talent for organization,
her maternal heart. She had never married, and for her the children's block at Birkenau was a direct continuation of her past life.
Children needed caring, and more so here than anywhere else in
the world. Auntie Hanka, still wearing an apron, showed the new
girl instructors how to turn wooden twigs into knitting needles and
knit sleeves or gloves using the wool ripped from rags, and how to
pull threads out of a blanket and use them to repair holes in
clothing. Helplessness and despair did not exist for her.

The children received the same food rations as the adults, a black
liquid twice daily, and a quarter of a loaf (250 grams) of glutinous
bread and soup once a day; the children's soup was thicker. In some
groups, each child contributed a spoonful of soup so that at least
one child, in turn, could feel a semblance of fullness every now and
again. Some children ate their soup with small spoons to make it last
longer. From time to time the children received extra rations: a
small portion of cooked noodles, white bread, a meager portion of
cake from an unclaimed package, soup prepared in the barracks
from ingredients in the packages. Fredy, who was responsible for
obtaining the benefits, insisted that the children eat in their own
block so that no one would touch their rations, while parents feared
that the instructors might pilfer from the children. The instructors
were hurt: were they to be suspected of stealing from children in
their charge? At most they took the liberty of scraping the sides of
the pot after distribution, quietly, with feelings of shame. Sometimes, as a sign of love, the children forced the instructor to swallow
a spoonful of their thick broth, but Fredy forbade this too. When
one of the instructors had a birthday, the mothers of her group
prepared a "cake" from black bread and coffee, which she divided
equally among twenty-five children, leaving one portion for herself.
On Friday night, after the children were bedded down, the instructors ushered in the Sabbath. They all donated their daily bread
ration and the girls prepared a Sabbath feast: four small thin slices
per person with a hint of margarine on them and a tiny piece of
cheese out of the official ration, half the size of an infant's hand
(every prisoner received forty grams of margarine three times a
week, a tablespoon of beet jam twice a week, a small semicircle of
cheese once a week. Once they got half a slice of solid foodstuff
defined as sausage).

There were no teaching aids, no notebooks, no pencils, and no textbooks, apart from what the craftsmen from the other camps brought as gifts: Avi, the instructor of the group of older boys, had at his disposal a Russian-language textbook, a geometry book, and a Bible. The counselors taught from memory, and drew on personal accounts from the past. A favorite speaker with the boys was an athlete who had participated in the 1932 Olympics. It was sometimes difficult to teach the children—particularly the younger ones who did not remember any other sort of life—concepts from yesterday's world; to speak to them of money, when the only means of payment they knew was cigarettes or bread; to tell them of a famous athlete who came from a family so poor that they had lived only on bread and potatoes, things which at Birkenau were signs of wealth. Best of all, the boys liked tales of valor, courage, the struggle of the few against the many, cowboy stories, stories about Eskimos, the wars of the Greeks against the Persians, the battle at Thermopylae. Because the groups sat so close to one another, the children sometimes absorbed three lectures simultaneously. Sometimes there were sing-alongs, with Czech and Hebrew songs, but the children's favorite, oddly enough, was the French song "Alouette."

For the Sabbath, every group prepared something—a song, a scene from a play, a skit, pieces from *Manon Lescaut* in Czech translation, *Robinson Crusoe, Snow White and the Seven Dwarfs,* with topical texts set to music from the Walt Disney film and the block walls decorated with drawings based on the cartoon. Fredy's instructions were that there were to be no discussions about the gas chambers with the children, but they knew of their existence, from the messenger boys who moved freely through the camp and worked as the personal servants of the elders of the blocks. Sometimes they spoke among themselves of the chimney through which they too would pass. In a skit written by one of the children, a patient called Stephan, aged fourteen, was brought in an ambulance shouting, "I don't want to ride, let me walk," eliciting laughter from children and counselors alike. For they had all understood the hint: in Birkenau vehicles led to the chimney.

Due to the success of *Snow White and the Seven Dwarfs,* performed in German before the SS, Fredy was permitted to open a second home in the adjacent block, for children aged five to eight. The children spent most of the day in the block; it was very difficult to occupy them for hours at a time with games and stories. There were

413

no toys, no auxiliary aids. The smaller children, who had never known any life other than the ghetto and the camp, imitated the adult world, acted out roll call and the approach of an SS man, played at being sick and dead.

In this godforsaken neighborhood, abounding in bogs and polluted water, with heavy fog in autumn and blazing heat in summer, winter temperatures sometimes dropped to 35 degrees (Celsius) below zero. When it was bitterly cold, however, the children did not stand outside at roll call, as did their shivering parents, but were counted in the barracks—which was heated—by an SS man. For those members of Hehalutz and the youth movements who were not counselors, the children's block was heaven: you could lean your back against the heating and feel warmth. When the snows melted, the children played ball on the field between the last two barracks in the row, but the game had to be restrained so that the ball would not hit the electric fence or fly over it into the neighboring camp. The children knew that under no circumstances, not even for the sake of a ball, were they to touch the fence: they had seen the scorched bodies of adults who had ended their lives when their endurance had failed them. Toward evening, the children went to their parents, lay beside them on the bunks where there was no room to sit, warmed one another beneath the thin blanket. Parents spoke of home, of the family which had scattered, of what had been. Only one subject was not mentioned: the crematoria.

The prisoners of the other camps, those fortunate few craftsmen who were permitted to wander about, liked to come to the children's block to forget the reality of Birkenau for a few moments, and the SS were also frequent visitors. On the eleventh anniversary of Hitler's rise to power, the SS entered during an activity when Avi, one of the counselors, was demonstrating how different people read a newspaper, though he held no newspaper in his hands. Mellowed by wine, one of the SS took that day's newspaper out of his pocket, an item the prisoners had not seen for years, and said, "Take it, to make it more real."

Arranged in rows, the kindergarten children sometimes went for walks, from one end of the camp to the other. The highlight of their outing was a visit to the kitchen where the cooks kept a raven in a cage, and in the spring there was an added attraction: a small fruit tree, the only tree at the other end of the camp, started to bloom. None of the counselors questioned the point of teaching and educating the children, the purpose of their endeavors in the shadow of death. As long as the children lived, they had to be taught, just as if long life stretched ahead of them. For the children it meant occupation, for the counselors the joy of doing, and for everybody together, a way to forget. The choice was between helplessness and despair, or ignoring the future. Even at Birkenau, the children knew moments of happiness.

30

NOTHING BUT CHIMNEY SMOKE

EDELSTEIN and the three employees of Theresienstadt's records department who had been arrested together with him were taken off the train before the other passengers and brought directly to Auschwitz's main camp, the center of the giant realm of camps. The two-story stone buildings were originally military barracks during the era of the Austro-Hungarian monarchy, and the physical conditions here were better than in the Birkenau camp, less than two miles away. Auschwitz Camp 1 housed the headquarters of the entire concern, which included all the Birkenau camps and Buna, A. G. Farben's industrial complex, which produced synthetic rubber, medical products, and ammunition. It was the home of the political department, as local Gestapo headquarters was called in camp language. The first prisoners in Auschwitz had been German criminals, brought from the Sachsenhausen concentration camp to fill internal administrative positions; Polish political prisoners; Slovakian Jews; and starved Russian prisoners of war, the first guinea pigs for death by gas in the cellar of block 11.

Now, in the winter of 1943, the extermination center was in adjoining Birkenau, where up to a quarter of a million prisoners were packed in, and the inmates of the main camp at Auschwitz—mostly non-Jewish veteran functionaries—were considered an elite, except for the prisoners of the punishment block, number 11, where Jakob Edelstein was taken. From the outside, block 11 looked just like all the other camp buildings. It contained several types of prisoners: those slated for transfer to other camps, a few who expected to be released, those punished and sentenced to death. The tenants of the first floor for the most part worked in the Buna factories, the mines in the region, and in the special commando which operated the crematoria. At the start of their stay there they did not even know that beneath them was a cellar with thirty cells where political prisoners awaited sentencing, generally execution. The bunker residents slept on the bare ground; some shared cells, others were kept in isolation cells so small that they had to sleep standing. They were completely cut off from the rest of the camp prisoners and were taken out into the yard only before they died.

Between blocks 11 and 12 was a yard surrounded by a black wall four meters high and eighty centimeters thick. It was built of plaster and fiber, to prevent bullets passing through, and in front of this wall individuals were executed—partisans, political prisoners honored by a verdict of personal death, or small groups of Jews: people who had been found in hiding, or remnants of liquidated camps. In Auschwitz terms, a small group could mean between two and three hundred men and women, for whom it did not pay to operate the gas chamber.

During executions, the prisoners of block 11 whose rooms faced the yard were moved to the other side of the building, and the windows were hung with blankets. The prisoners sat in the dark, heard the sound of the approaching SS cars, and waited for the work to be done. In the yard, a kapo undressed the prisoners sentenced to death and, if need be, held them while the SS shot them in the back with a revolver fitted with a silencer. After the execution, the bodies were removed and sand was scattered in the yard to cover up the bloodstains. The blankets were taken off the windows and the prisoners returned to their rooms. The windows of block 10, which also faced the yard and wall of death, were permanently boarded up, for it was the only women's block in the men's camp. Its four hundred women residents were kept as guinea pigs for the lethal medical experiments aimed at developing sterilization methods through chemicals, radiation, and surgery.

The cellar prisoners sat in the dark, their only opening into the outside world a small aperture under the air vent which led to the ground of the yard. If the prisoner had friends on the outside who

417

knew exactly where he was, they sometimes managed to push food or notes through the grate. Edelstein spent most of the time in an isolation cell in the bunker, and his only contact with the other prisoners was by knocking on the walls. He was interrogated by the political department and charged with abetting the escape of inmates from Theresienstadt.

Rudolf Gibian, also from Theresienstadt, who had been sent to Auschwitz in January 1943, had passed selection and worked in transportation. He saw Edelstein being led by the SS to block 11 in the main camp. Edelstein was wearing civilian garb and glasses, a fact that Gibian particularly remembered because one of the first things the Germans generally did while torturing prisoners was to break their glasses and thereby what little confidence they had left. But he got no chance to speak to Edelstein.

Among the few from Theresienstadt who passed selection and survived was also Otto Fabian, expelled to Auschwitz in October 1942 and tattooed with number 71072. Fabian worked transporting corpses and could therefore move freely between all the blocks of the main camp at all hours of the day. One day his friend Honzik Weiss of Bratislava, a clerk in block 28, told him that Jakob Edelstein was in their hospital. Fabian rushed over and managed to exchange a few words with him in the small operating room of the hospital, unattended by the SS. Edelstein impressed him as calm and showing no fear. Because there was little time to talk, the first thing Fabian asked was something that had troubled all the Theresienstadt people at the extermination camp: had he known the truth about Auschwitz when he was Elder of the Jews in Theresienstadt? Had he known where the deportees were being sent? Had he known of the gas chambers? Edelstein replied that he had neither known of, nor ever imagined, such horror.

Edelstein told Fabian that he had been ordered to write several letters and he had also written to his wife in Theresienstadt. Jakob knew that people from the ghetto were at one of the camps in Birkenau, but neither he nor Fabian were aware of the fact that both Miriam and Arieh were among them. It seems that Edelstein had been taken to the hospital clinic for treatment, but he was not allowed to remain there as a patient, and after the treatment he was returned to the bunker in block 11. When Edelstein returned for further treatment, Fabian again managed to have a few brief words with him.

A few steps away from Edelstein's bunker, across the yard, worked

Otto Heller, the Zionists' great rival in the faraway years of the Czechoslovakian republic. Heller was a devout communist, author of *The Decline of Judaism*. He had been brought to Auschwitz as a political prisoner, having been sentenced to death by the Gestapo, but a different Otto Heller had been executed in his place by mistake. The physical distance between communists and Zionists had shrunk, but the ideological distance remained unchanged. In Auschwitz Heller was still active in the communist underground, firmly believing in the victory of the forces of progress, led by the Soviet Union.

As far as the residents of the family camp were concerned, Jakob Edelstein had disappeared somewhere en route, and nobody in Birkenau or Theresienstadt knew where he was. However a copy of a letter from Dr. Munk to Edelstein has remained, dated January 23, 1944: "I am happy to have this opportunity to let you know that I am well, I have completely recovered and am working at full speed. I work in radiology three times a week—I have returned to my old love." In his reply of January 27, Yekef wrote that he was pleased that Dr. Munk had returned to work and was well.* Because Yekef's reply was written within four days, and because of the general nature of the letter, it is safe to assume that an SS man served as the go-between without revealing Edelstein's whereabouts.

Munk's reply to Edelstein's letter was written at the beginning of March. "You have no idea how happy I was to receive news from you and I hope that much more will follow. From your letter I see that you are strong in spirit and full of faith." Munk gave Edelstein news of the ghetto—who had married whom; he wrote of the establishment of a central medical library and the expansion of a nursery school, and he told Yekef that Miriam and Arieh had confirmed receipt of packages sent from Geneva. At about the same time, Munk sent a postcard to Dr. Ullman in Geneva, telling him that he had received a card from Leo Janowitz and adding, "Jakob Edelstein says that he is well and in strong spirits," from which Ullman understood that Edelstein was with Janowitz in Birkenau; he even assumed that Jakob would return to Theresienstadt.

At the end of February, a delegation of senior SS officials from Berlin, led by Eichmann, appeared at the family camp, bringing

---

* A copy of the letter was kept at Terezin, brought to Prague, and from there to Jerusalem, where it disappeared.

with them Neuhaus, the director of the external department of the German Red Cross. The commission showed great interest in camp life, especially the children's barracks, block 31. Eichmann even praised the attempt to set up a cultural center at the camp and told Fredy to prepare a report of its activities to be submitted to the International Red Cross. At the camp offices, Eichmann called in Miriam Edelstein and asked her if she had any special request and if she had had any news of her husband. Miriam answered truthfully that she had no idea where he was and asked Eichmann's permission to write him a letter. Eichmann agreed to accept a letter for Edelstein, and promised to consider her request for a meeting with her husband; Miriam understood from his words that Jakob was at one of the camps in Germany. After the entourage left, Janowitz, with the voice of experience, said, "Eichmann means transport, his visits at Terezin never boded well."

When Neuhaus returned from Birkenau, he wrote to the Reich Security Head Office, emphasizing the importance of allowing the prisoners to receive food packages and medicine sent from the International Red Cross; so that the organization's delegate in Geneva could see for himself, when the planned visit to Theresienstadt and another Jewish labor camp materialized, that they had in fact reached their destination. In light of the growing number of queries from the world regarding the Jewish camps, the planned visit, which had often been discussed, was of the utmost importance.

A few days after Eichmann's visit, on March 4, the prisoners of the family camp were given postcards to send to friends and relatives. They were instructed to date the cards March 25, and those who questioned this were told that the post might be held up because of censorship. The cards were collected for mailing, and two days later SS Obersturmführer Schwarzhuber, the commandant of the Birkenau camps, ordered the administration to prepare the September prisoners for transfer to a new camp called Heidebreck,* with instructions to record the numbers of the functionaries leaving on the transport list, so that the command at the new camp could utilize their administrative experience.

But rumor said otherwise: the transport was slated to be gassed. On March 3, Katerina Singer, a clerk in the women's camp, learned

---

* The name was not fictitious: one of A. G. Farben's factories was at Heidebreck. There was a grain of truth in the transports of manpower to the West: in early 1944, some young Auschwitz prisoners began to be sent to work in the Reich.

that Eichmann's Berlin office had ordered "special handling" (the German euphemism for murder by gas) for transports DM and DL, which had arrived in Auschwitz at the beginning of September 1943, numbering 5,000 people. The figure was now less than 4,000. The others had died in the last six months of "natural causes"—starvation, cold, weakness, and typhus.

Erich Schön-Kulka, one of the veteran Czech prisoners in the men's camp, who worked as an electrician and could therefore move relatively freely among Birkenau's various camps, told Fredy the destiny that awaited the transport, corroborating what Fredy had already heard. Fredy, Leo, and some of the people close to them who had been in the September transport met to confer in Fredy's room. According to hearsay, they decided to rebel if the Germans did take the September people to the gas chambers. The actual discussion cannot be confirmed, since no witness to the meeting survived. The barracks counselors of the December transport were not party to the secret, and it therefore seems likely that Fredy and Leo were not considering a large-scale rebellion, or any serious preparations. According to another version, Fredy was asked to lead the rebellion; he was to be joined by the *Sonderkommando*, the men who operated the extermination facilities, after the September people had been moved from the family camp to the adjoining quarantine camp. This proposal was apparently made to him by roof repairman David Shmuelevsky, a member of the communist underground in Auschwitz. Either way, it is clear that in so short a period it was impossible to organize a rebellion, except as a final act of despair that contained no real threat to the SS and no chance of saving the prisoners.

There could be no illusions as to the outcome of rebellion: it too spelled death. Every camp was surrounded by an electrified wire fence, and all around the camp complex was a great protective chain of electric fences, watchtowers manned night and day, ditches, trained watchdogs, and SS armed with machine guns. There was no civilian population within a twenty-five-mile radius of the camp complex. The entire area was closed off, flat, and exposed, and any movement could be seen for miles. In wooden sandals, threadbare clothing, without documents, without money, without help on the outside, and in the midst of a hostile, collaborationist, and frightened population—who could hope to find shelter? At best, perhaps ten men would be saved. The women and children were sentenced to death, one way or another.

Most of the inmates of the family camp refused to believe the rumors of approaching extermination: Schwarzhuber himself had explicitly said that they were being moved to a labor camp called Heidebreck. Gassing them now seemed to defy all logic: why should they have been kept in special conditions for six months, permitted to write postcards, receive packages, set up a children's barracks, if not for some specific purpose, if not for the fact that they were protected by the International Red Cross? If the Germans wanted to murder them, they would have done so immediately, when the transport arrived. The general opinion was that they were still needed for propaganda purposes. Schwarzhuber came to the family camp again, spoke to the women, and restored calm: at Heidebreck there were better living quarters, the barracks had windows, sanitation conditions were superior to those in Birkenau, and the old and sick would receive medical treatment and regain their strength.

In honor of the farewell between the September and December groups, Lagerältester Böhm ordered a soccer game to be held, which the September people won.

The instructions were to report for transfer with all one's effects—and like hoarders, despite the bans and confiscations, the prisoners had stockpiled private treasures even at Birkenau: a towel, a needle and thread, a spoon, a pot without holes. The instructions also said that those with contagious diseases were to be left behind. There was the proof, reasonable people said, that they really were going to a labor camp. German cities were being bombed day and night, manpower was needed to remove the rubble and rebuild.

For the older children in the barracks, March 7 was a double holiday: it was President Masaryk's birthday, which had always been a national holiday in Czechoslovakia, and it was the second anniversary of the founding of the children's dormitory in Theresienstadt. The children prepared a program, but Fredy, who never missed the parties and happy hours in the dormitory, was not there. The children discussed what was happening. Did it mean that they were going to the chimney? "I will be a fire stoker up above too," said one of the boys whose task it was to tend the stove in the dormitory. "I will be a trumpeter up above," said fourteen-year-old Čupek. Two days before he left, Fredy appointed the new leaders of the children's block from among the December transportees: Seppl Lichtenstern, who in the far-off days of freedom had managed illegal immigration at the Palestine office, was put in charge of education;

Honza Brammer, an experienced instructor, who had been in charge of the boys' employment service at Theresienstadt, took over the organizational side; and Miriam Edelstein became house-mother.

One of the SS suggested to Truda Janowitz, Leo's wife, who was in charge of the women's block, that she remain behind. He'd find a way to leave her at the camp. Truda hesitated and discussed it with her friends while packing in her small room at the entrance to the block: should she let Leo leave alone or go with him? What would you do? And you? "I," said the friend, "would go with my husband." Truda concurred. She would go with everyone else.

Fredy asked those who stayed behind to pass on his regards to friends in Palestine, should they be fortunate enough to get there. The girl counselors told Auntie Hanka to send them news of Heidebreck. "Watch the chimney the day after tomorrow," she replied. "I'll wave to you with my apron."

At first the September people were concentrated in some of the blocks in the family camp, everyone clutching his last bundle of possessions. After all the numbers were checked, the prisoners were transferred to the neighboring quarantine camp, which had been evacuated.

The old and the frail, who were unable to walk the short distance, were carried by employees of the auxiliary detail. Some consoled themselves with the thought that there couldn't be anything worse than Auschwitz anywhere in the world. Among the last to leave were Auntie Hanka, her walk as brisk as ever, and Fredy Hirsch, who took his whistle with him, the symbol of his position. For the time being, it seemed that the optimists had been right: the first day in the quarantine camp passed without incident. The Germans took everyone to the "sauna," the showers, as was customary before leaving the camp. People could be seen moving between the blocks, and the daily roll call took place as always. In the late afternoon sounds of singing could even be heard from the quarantine camp. Suddenly the half-empty children's barracks learned that Fredy was very ill. Miriam made him a pudding and one of the boys smuggled it into the camp through the fence. But Fredy was not sick. He was dead. At the age of twenty-eight, he had taken Luminal and ended his life. Why, nobody knows for sure. Perhaps he sensed the utter futility of rebellion, perhaps he did not want to witness the death of his young charges, for whose lives he had fought.

In the evening, Schwarzhuber came to the men's camp and took forty of the toughest and cruelest male kapos. They were instructed to equip themselves with clubs for a special assignment. Total curfew was imposed on all the Birkenau camps. For the first time in the camp's history, an armed SS man was posted beside every block to prevent anybody from leaving. In the blocks of the family camp, people lay on their bunks in coats and shoes, tense, waiting, trying to gauge what was happening from the sounds they heard.

They heard dozens of truck engines roaring, the SS giving orders, dogs barking. Through the openings under the ceiling the light from the blinding spotlights filtered into the rooms. Suddenly the air was split by wild cries. One of the men from the September transport, a hefty elder of a block called Honza Bondy, had apparently shouted to the people in Czech not to get on the trucks, for they drove to death. The SS attacked and killed him on the spot. The people got on the trucks, with the SS shouting, and those left in the family camp waited in the dark with pounding hearts to hear what direction the trucks would take: north to the railway line, or south to the gas chambers. The trucks turned north, toward the train—toward life. But suddenly the screech of brakes and the sounds of a sharp turn were heard in the distance: at the end of the railway shack, the trucks turned back and headed south, toward the crematoria, and all along the route stood a chain of armed SS men, in an unprecedented call-up. Some of the September people were taken to crematorium number 2, some to number 3, and here at last everyone finally understood: the Germans had deceived them for the last time.

The first to arrive, and to alight from the trucks under a spray of blows, had to wait in the cloakrooms near the gas chambers on the basement level of the crematorium until the trucks returned with a second load. While they waited, one of the men of the *Sonderkommando* who operated the crematorium, Philip Miller, a twenty-two-year-old Jew from Slovakia, had a chance to speak with the people waiting to die. Unlike all the other deportees, who found themselves in the gas chamber before they realized what was happening, the people of the family camp knew exactly what awaited them. Husbands and wives parted, mothers embraced children, weeping soundlessly. There was no point in telling them to remember their hanger number so that they would be able to find their clothes after disinfection, as the commando unit usually told new victims.

When the gas chamber—a long hall with bare walls, lit up by electric light, which contained nothing but several openings in the ceiling, shower heads without water, and perforated iron poles—was half-full, a few SS officers appeared, including Dr. Mengele. Almost in chorus, the people called out to them: "Let us live! Let us work!" When their appeals fell on deaf ears, several men tried to make a run for the exit and were shot on the spot. The rest were brutally assaulted by the SS, beaten over the head with clubs that drew blood, and shoved back into the rear part of the hall. By now almost everybody was weeping and sobbing, and one of the SS in charge of the crematorium, Oberscharführer Voss, tried to silence them: what was the point of all this commotion? Their final hour had come. No power on earth could save them. They would do far better to remain quiet and not make their children's last moments more difficult.

The people grew still and began to undress slowly, as if to prolong their last moments. But now the patience of the SS ran out. With murderous blows they pushed the people into the gas chambers, whether they had managed to undress or not. The dogs went mad, the SS shouted, and suddenly singing was heard from the people about to die: first the notes of the Czech national anthem, "Where Is My Homeland?" and then "Hatikvah."

Philip Miller, who had seen it all many times before—the doors of the gas chambers opening after about twenty minutes when the SS doctor gave the signal that everyone was dead, the men and women hugging one another in death, the children clinging to their mothers so fiercely they had to be torn apart, the extraction of gold teeth, the clipping of women's hair—felt that he could not bear any more. He had seen in the gas chambers Jews from the Drancy camp in France, the Jews of Saloniki, the Jews of Holland, the Bialystok children who had come from Theresienstadt, the people of the Polish town Bendzin who had understood what was happening and had begun to recite kaddish for themselves. He had seen it all and borne it. But now, at the sight of the pretty, healthy girls from his own country, who spoke his language and walked toward death, he felt that the time had come to put an end to his torment: he would join them, and die with them. "No, my friend, you mustn't," the girls said when they realized his intention. "You must live to tell the world what happened to us . . ." The girls pushed Philip out and the last thing he heard in the empty cloakroom was "Avenge our death!" From the chamber were heard sounds of weeping, coughing, choking, isolated screams, and then silence.

Miller described the last moments of the Theresienstadt people

425

to his friends Erich Schön-Kulka and Otto Kraus. He even brought Kulka a farewell letter from his wife which she had written before she died. And one of the girls had shoved a paper into his hand, containing three poems that she had written while waiting to die.

No, there are no crosses on our graves
No tombstones mark our dead
No wreaths or ornate latticework
No angels with bowed head

No willows or gold-beribboned wreaths
No fire of eternal flame
We rot in ditches caked in lime
In our bones the wind's refrain

Skulls whitened in despair
Quiver on barbed wire
Swept away from countless urns
Our ashes soar ever higher

We form a chain around the world
Seeds scattered by the wind
We wait and count days, months, and years
For us time has no end

And our numbers down here multiply
We swell day by day
Already now we bloat your fields
And we'll burst your earth one day

Then we'll set out, an awesome convoy
Skull to skull and bone to bone
And we'll rend the air before mankind:
We the dead accuse!

In one night, 3,791 Czechoslovakian Jews were put to death in the gas chambers, including Leo Janowitz, Auntie Hanka Epstein, the youth counselors, the barracks children. The only survivors of the September transport were the employees of the sick block, doctors, a pharmacist, nurses, and a small group of patients and twins whom Dr. Mengele needed for his experiments on behalf of the speedy propagation of the Aryan race—all in all, about thirty-seven people. The next morning the inmates of the family camp saw high flames and heavy smoke rising out of the crematoria, as was usual after a hard night's work; specks of soot flew in the air and landed in the camp, a last farewell from their friends who only two days ago had sung with them, learned with them. "Look," said the children left in the barracks when they saw the smoke rising out of the chimney opposite the camp, "that's Heidebreck. There's Auntie Hanka's apron."

The half-empty family camp resembled a cemetery: the remaining inmates, the December transport, were unable to speak to one another for hours, days, until their taste for life revived. There was more sleeping room, more blankets to cover themselves with against the chilly night, more coffee in the morning and evening. Desirable jobs became available—cooks, potato peelers, block elders. In the children's barracks life returned to normal. The groups continued to sit on both sides of the stove, to play games, hear songs, prepare programs for Sabbath parties. The Germans agreed to bring children's clothes from the central clothing warehouse to replace garments that had fallen apart or been outgrown, and the children with a flair for barter sold what they received for bread and returned for a second allotment. From time to time packages arrived for Leo Janowitz's transport and were distributed among the children: dry cakes, bread, and sometimes, inside the bread, a note with greetings or a piece of sausage.

Miriam Edelstein was housemother now, meticulous and reserved as ever. In the evening, after roll call, the counselors would sit in Seppl Lichtenstern's small room and talk. One evening, after rumors spread that the December people could expect the same fate as the previous transport, and the date for "special handling" had been set for June 20, 1944, the counselors asked Miriam: "Now tell us the truth. Did Yekef know what awaited the people transported to the East?" Miriam swore on all that was dear to her that Yekef had not known, and not a person there doubted her sincerity. In the family camp people began to count the days. Each day that passed brought the end of life nearer.

31

I AM MASTER OF MY
LAST MOMENTS

THE POSTCARDS written by the September people who went to their death, and the December people who were given a reprieve, reached their destinations in the course of April and announced "I am fine" and "I am well" about people of whom nothing but ashes remained in the marshland of Birkenau. "I sometimes see Miriam," Truda Janowitz had written; "I work for Fredy," Seppl Lichtenstern had said. Some, feeling that death was imminent, had tried to warn friends and relatives in Terezin either by hints or by some prearranged code. Codes were among the popular games played in the Scouts and youth movements, and most Hehalutz members knew at least one. The most common code used three types of print and a numerical value for all the letters of the alphabet, denoted by various combinations of the numbers 1, 2, and 3.

When Dolfa Beneš in Theresienstadt received a postcard from a friend in Birkenau who had written "We'll soon see your brother"— a brother who had been arrested in the early days of the Nazi regime and taken to the Mauthausen camp, from which notice came after Heydrich's assassination that he had committed suicide—he went to Dr. Kahn so they could decipher the meaning of the words together. Dr. Kahn's opinion (or so he said) was that Beneš's brother was not dead, but alive at one of the camps in the vicinity of the

Birkenau labor camp near Neuberun. When the postcards said "We're following Dr. Lieben," that humanitarian doctor from Prague who had been killed by the Germans at Dachau, the recipients at Theresienstadt found this encouraging: it must mean that Dr. Lieben was still alive.

The messages from Birkenau were so very oblique; what did they mean by "If you come here, don't ride in vehicles, walk"; or "Don't come here, people die of unnatural causes." Avi Fischer, one of the instructors in the children's barracks, had arranged a code with his brother in Theresienstadt, using Hebrew for the decisive message: "Arrived safely. Kol Lakach [all have been taken] behaved well. Sack Anna [danger] has grown. Sofie [my end] is near." The Hebrew teacher who was asked to decipher it decided that it was meaningless. Some had started their postcards with the salutation "Moti Hayakar" [my dear death], or closed with: "And with this, Moti Hayakar, I end." Gonda received a card from Fredy Hirsch which said "Doda Mavet [Aunt Death] is with us," which was simply taken as further corroboration of the difficult conditions in Poland. If the code read "Gas, fire, and death," the recipients assumed that their friends at Birkenau apparently worked in coal or sulfur mines and that the work was very dangerous. Nobody could conceive of mechanized death.

Miriam Edelstein wrote three postcards (for herself and on behalf of Arieh and her mother, Mrs. Olliner). Two she sent to the son of one of the last community workers in Prague, Heinz Prossnitz, who had single-handedly organized an entire network for sending packages to the camps. Heinz, a member of Maccabi Hatzair, even stole articles of clothing from his parents and bartered them for food destined not only for friends in Theresienstadt and Poland, but also for people he did not know but who had appealed to him because they no longer knew anybody else outside the dominion of death.

Thank you very much for the parcels, which made us very happy. We—mother, Arieh, and I—are healthy, which is the main thing. If packages should still come, we would be very pleased. But we don't know where Jakob is or what he's doing or how he is, and this causes us great concern. Have you any idea? I am sure that you won't forget him either. Heartfelt thanks and warm greetings to you and your family and all friends.

Yours,
Miriam Edelstein

One postcard was sent to Dr. Ullman in Geneva. It too bore the date
March 25, 1944:

> Dear Ully!
> Mother, Arieh, and I are here with Leo. We are well and that's
> the main thing. Unfortunately I have no news of Jakob. Perhaps
> you will have more luck. I am sure that you will do all you can for
> Jakob's family (exchange). Help them, if possible.

Dr. Ullman immediately telegraphed Dr. März in Jerusalem to do
all he could to help the Edelsteins by issuing certificates within the
exchange framework, and also applied to Istanbul on the same
matter. The British had in fact agreed to issue over one thousand
immigration permits for women and children in Nazi-occupied
territories, families where the father was in Palestine, and they had
even reached an exchange agreement with the Germans for German women in Palestine whose husbands were in Germany or in the
German army. But it appeared that the German women in Palestine
were not overly eager to be exchanged, and legally they could not be
compelled to return to Germany against their will. The rescue
committee tried to find German women in other regions of the
British empire to be exchanged. Copies of the immigration permits
for the Jewish women and children who were candidates for exchange were sent to the occupied countries, once from Istanbul,
according to the addresses that the rescue committee had, and
again through the International Red Cross. Six hundred copies
were returned to Istanbul without reaching their destination; from
five hundred and thirty others there was no response; and for
seventy, confirmation was received, including a list from Theresienstadt with twenty-four names of certificate bearers. However, all
efforts through the German delegates in Switzerland to obtain
approval from the Reich Security Head Office for getting the people out of Theresienstadt were fruitless. Since copies of the immigration permits had been sent in the early summer of 1943, it is safe
to assume that Miriam knew of the exchange while still in Theresienstadt, even if she herself was not included in it.

Dr. Ullman was optimistic, and on June 15 he wrote to Heinz
Prossnitz in Prague, "Doda Aliyah [Aunt Immigration] feels fine
and often thinks of Jakob and his wife." The exchange scheme was
in fact implemented, at least partially, and in July 1944 a group of
284 women and children arrived in Palestine from German-
occupied regions; but not one of them came from Theresienstadt or

Birkenau. Efforts to get Dr. Kahn and his wife out of Theresienstadt continued, but despite repeated appeals to the American state department, no passport reached Berlin for him. Only an application form for a passport arrived—and even in the smoke screen that hid what went on in Theresienstadt, it was clear that the Germans would not forward it to the ghetto.

Because the end of the war seemed very near in the spring of 1944, Dr. Ullman thought it more reasonable to stop the attempts to get certificates to Theresienstadt (which he felt might endanger their bearers) and instead make all the necessary preparations for transferring the maximum number of certificates as soon as the German regime collapsed. Meanwhile the package service to Theresienstadt and Birkenau should be expanded to include shoes and clothing as well as food and medicines. In early June, through the Red Cross, a shipment weighing one thousand kilos was sent to Birkenau containing a body-building preparation made of oats and malt. Whose body it built up, nobody knows.

The Germans suddenly became generous. After the deportation of the last staff members of the Prague community in July 1944, they agreed to forward a shipment of lactose and Ovaltine, originally intended for Prague, to the Protectorate Jews at Birkenau, knowing full well that no one was still alive at the family camp. Heinz Prossnitz was also sent directly to the gas chamber. Shortly before this, Heinz had written: "I am eighteen, I would like power, money, influence, and to be somebody. I cannot be a pioneer, I'm too much of an individualist for that—and the collective would not overly enjoy having me." Before his banishment, Heinz transferred his address files for sending packages to Edith Brezina. "Have you perhaps heard anything of Edel's family?" she wrote to Geneva. "Robert Mavet [death] was moved there too."

On April 5, three weeks after the extermination of the September people, the scream of sirens was suddenly heard throughout Auschwitz, signaling an escape attempt. This time a prisoner from the family camp had run away. Among the SS who habitually frequented the children's block was Rottenführer Victor Pestek, a German from Rumania who had been seriously wounded on the Eastern front and transferred after his recovery to an easy job in the rear: guard service at Birkenau. When Fredy was in charge of the children's barrack, Pestek used to go to his room from time to time. Sometimes Fredy left and Pestek remained inside, and to the children, ever watchful, it was a riddle: what did Fredy and Pestek have in common? It appears that Pestek had belonged to the anti-Fascist underground and had tried in vain to convince the prisoners of his sincere desire to help them escape: they suspected a trap. Pestek, whose task it was to confirm the daily count in the family camp, fell in love with one of the Czech prisoners, a beautiful girl called Renee Neumann, and because he knew the date of the "special handling" which had been set for June, he wanted to get Renee out of the camp. But she refused to leave her mother. For lack of choice, Pestek decided to find a hideout where both women could remain until the end of the war. Pestek and Renee met secretly in Fredy's small room, where Pestek met also with Slavek Lederer, formerly an officer in the Czech army and a member of the Czech underground, who had been imprisoned and tortured at length by the Gestapo in the Little Fortress. He finally arrived at the Theresienstadt ghetto, where his work in the fire brigade protected him until he was caught smoking and sent to Birkenau in December 1943. Pestek revealed himself to Lederer while escorting him to the main camp, where he had been summoned by the political department for interrogation.

Lederer was firmly resolved to escape from Birkenau, find shelter with the help of his underground contacts, and warn the Theresienstadt inmates of what awaited them. Lederer offered to help Pestek find shelter for Renee and her mother if he in turn would help him get out.

Pestek got Lederer an SS uniform and military documents, told him that day's password, which was *Tintenfass* ("inkstand"), and opened the gate of the family camp for him when he was on duty at the camp headquarters barracks, near the entrance. Soon after, when his replacement took over, Pestek left his post and he and Lederer bicycled to the train station of Auschwitz town. At the last minute the two managed to get on the train bound for Prague and from there, with the help of friends from the Czech underground, they managed to find shelter in Pilsen, Lederer's hometown. Meanwhile the prisoners of the family camp stood for hours at roll call as punishment; their legs gave way, but their hearts were with the fugitives.

With the help of a Czech barber who shaved policemen (and whose assistant Lederer had been), Lederer went first to Theresienstadt. To a small circle of friends, including Leo Holzer, the chief of firemen, he revealed the true meaning of the word "East," to which the transports were sent. He told them of the extermination of the September transport, and of the death factory at Auschwitz. His audience found it difficult to believe. They had proof that the September deportees were alive after the extermination night of March 8: postcards in their own handwriting, dated March 25. Lederer met also with Karl Schliesser, director of the economic department, and with Rabbi Leo Baeck, who was shocked; but he too, like Holzer and Schliesser, was convinced that the information must be kept secret. If everyone found out, it was likely to come to the attention of the Germans and invite immediate reprisals against the inmates, whereas otherwise they might be able to hold out in the ghetto until the longed-for end of the war. Lederer returned to Theresienstadt twice more, bringing letters, weapons, and radio parts. After he learned that the confidential Gestapo archives had been moved to Terezin, he acquired documents that said he was a mechanical engineer called Friedrich Walker, called to work in Germany, and he journeyed to the German-Swiss border, to the town of Constance on the shores of the lake. From there, with the help of the family of a friend of Pestek's who had fallen on the Eastern front, he forwarded a report, through a sailor, on Theresienstadt and Auschwitz to the International Red Cross in Geneva. Pestek meanwhile waited in Pilsen.

When Lederer returned to Bohemia, Pestek pressed for the implementation of the second part of their plot—getting Renee and her mother out of the family camp—because the extermination date for the December transport was approaching. The plan was to use a forged letter from the Reich Security Head Office, ostensibly summoning the two women to Gestapo headquarters in Katowice for questioning. During the journey, Pestek decided not to get off the train at Auschwitz, but to continue to the nearby village of Mislovitze, where he had left the valuables he had collected while working in Birkenau, which were meant to fund the two women until the end of the war. However, at the Auschwitz train station, the appointed meeting place between Pestek and Lederer, an SS unit suddenly appeared and surrounded one of the train cars. Shots were fired, a grenade exploded, and a bleeding Pestek was led from the station. Lederer took advantage of the general commotion to grab the nearest motorbike, and for two hours he rode nonstop to the Czech border. There he boarded a train and hid with friends in Theresienstadt, where he wanted to plan together with them an uprising in the event that the ghetto was to be destroyed. To Lederer's pleas not to believe the Nazis, the answer of the ghetto officials was that now, when the Germans were suffering defeats on all fronts, they would need them for an alibi. It was madness to rebel now, when the International Red Cross had finally taken an interest in them. When rumor spread through the ghetto that an armed partisan was hiding in the town, Lederer had to leave. He stole across the border to Slovakia and joined the partisans. Pestek, after a month of terrible torture in the punishment block 11, was shot to death, but he did not reveal the names of the members of the Czech underground who had helped him hide.

A week after Lederer's escape, the sirens at Birkenau wailed again: two Slovakian Jews, Walter Rosenberg and Alfred Wetzler, had escaped from the men's camp. They reached the Slovakian underground and wrote a forty-page report describing the systematic annihilation of 1,760,000 European Jews at Auschwitz. The report gave an exact description of the camp, including the location of the gas chambers and crematoria. It was smuggled into Budapest, from there transferred to the representative of the Czech government-in-exile, and from there to the commission for war refugees in Geneva. In June, it was brought to the attention of the U.S. government, together with a request to bomb the railroad line leading to Auschwitz in order to slow down the transports, which at the time were coming mostly from Hungary.

For four months there was no reaction from the United States, and when it finally came, it was negative: the bombing of Auschwitz and the rail lines leading to it might push the Germans to adopt even greater retaliatory measures—though nobody bothered to specify what could be worse than systematic murder by gas. Excerpts from the report on Auschwitz were published in the press in the free world. "I have received information from the Jewish underground which confirms the fact that thousands of Jews from Theresienstadt were gassed to death at the end of March in the Auschwitz slaughterhouse. The information includes an appeal to warn the nations and call on the world to prevent transports," Ignacy Schwarzbart of Geneva telegraphed the Jewish Agency in London on June 18, after speaking on the telephone to Chaim Weizmann. On the same day, Reuters published a report on the death of Czechoslovakians at Birkenau, and the Czechoslovakian government-in-exile warned the German government to avoid any further mass extermination or "the Germans [would] pay with their blood for the blood shed."

* * *

Life at the family camp became easier: Arno Böhm was dismissed as head of the camp and replaced by Willy Brachmann, his assistant, a sailor from Hamburg. Willy had been sent to Auschwitz for negligence leading to the sinking of a boat, and he was accorded the special status enjoyed by criminals. But unlike Böhm, Willy still had a human spark in him; he was neither a sadist nor given to inflicting violence. For his mistress, he had chosen Lotte, one of the Jewish girls from Prague—a lovely, slender girl with honey-colored skin who was striking even in the rags she wore at Auschwitz. (Much to everybody's surprise, Willy truly loved her. After she was sent from Birkenau to a labor camp in Hamburg, he escaped from Auschwitz and followed her, finally reaching Bergen-Belsen in her wake, in order to protect her should the Germans try to destroy her in the last dying breath of the Nazi regime.)

The Germans speeded up the pace. In the middle of May, along railroad tracks which had been extended all the way to the crematoria, the first Jews started to arrive from Hungary (occupied by the Germans in March 1944), and thereafter train followed train, bringing thousands of people every day. The death factories achieved their peak output. The gas chambers in the two large crematoria could accommodate three thousand people at a time. Each crematorium had fifteen furnaces, each furnace three compartments, and the whole procedure, including the removal of the ashes, took fifteen minutes. In one day, the two large crematoria (the two small ones were found to be inefficient and worked only partially) could destroy up to four thousand bodies—but the gas chambers supplied more still. To keep pace with the rate of transports from Hungary—between three and five trains a day—the surplus corpses had to be burned in ditches, using wood and rags soaked in benzine, and the odor of scorched flesh spread throughout the camp in the summer heat.

The young Hungarian women who passed selection were housed in the camp next to B/II/b. The inmates of the family camp saw them across the fence, heads shaved, wearing thin gray prison dresses, bewildered, standing for hours at roll call, heard their voices—"*Lani! Lani!*" ("Girls! Girls!")—and pitied them: they were still unable to grasp that their families, with whom they had arrived only yesterday on the train, had been reduced to smoke and ashes. The sudden shock was too great. The Theresienstadt people had had time to get used to the idea of approaching death.

The children's barracks continued to attract prisoners from all over the camp, those who were allowed to move about by virtue of their occupation. It was a window into another world, long-forgotten, suppressed, obliterated, and because of the many visitors, the block was a hotbed of information: it was not long before news came from one of the workers in central administration that confirmed the vague fears: the December transport was also slated for "special handling," to take place six months from the date of their arrival (as had been the case with the September transport), meaning June 20, 1944.

The children also knew; sometimes they knew even more than their parents, who shut their eyes, who could not bear knowing. The boys ran errands, moved among the officials, heard what was going on, and told their peers. And despite their knowledge, the children drew pictures, danced horas, exercised, learned, joked, put on plays. Once the stream of Hungarian transports started, the chimney emitted heavy smoke by day and high flames by night, and the inmates of the family camp hoped that the surplus candidates for death would cause their own extermination date to be postponed, forgotten.

Meanwhile, in the latter half of May, another 7,500 people from Theresienstadt arrived at Birkenau. They too were spared selection, their heads were not shaved, and all of them—men, women, children, old people—were brought to the family camp. The newcomers had exciting news: Theresienstadt was preparing for a visit from the International Red Cross commission. In February, Burger, the commandant of the ghetto, had been replaced by Karl Rahm, a close associate of Hans Günther, director of the Central Office for the Solution of the Jewish Problem in the Protectorate. Rahm, a mechanic by profession, was to supervise the ghetto's face-lift, begun under Burger immediately after the departure of the December transport. The inmates painted, cleaned, and plastered; laundry was banned from windows and yards during the daytime; street numbers were replaced by picturesque street names: Lake Street, Hunter Street, Mountain Street. But it soon became apparent that no superficial repairs could mask the true situation. A thorough cosmetic job was required to transform the crowded ghetto into a model Jewish city.

The May transport to Birkenau was a direct result of these endeavors. It included a large group of consumptives whose presence was unseemly in a model ghetto, and many orphaned children whose parents had either been murdered by the Nazis or had died in the ghetto. What was a child to say if one of the distinguished visitors asked him where his parents were? It was safer to have the orphans out of the way.

The temporary buildings in the city square which had housed the production for the German army were removed, and grass and rosebushes were planted in their stead. The word "ghetto" became obsolete: the ghetto library became the central library; the ghetto police, the local police; the ghetto itself was called the Jewish colony. The transport numbers, which served as the basis for registering the inmates at the ghetto, were now called identity numbers.

The newcomers heard the truth about Birkenau from the December transport; they heard of the extermination of the Theresienstadt transport on that night in March and they refused to believe it. It was technically impossible; how could thousands of people be burned in a single night? The veteran children in the barracks told the new children about their friends and said that they too would one day leave through the chimney. The newcomers laughed: how could corpses leave through such a high chimney? The new children asked their parents about the things they had heard and were reassured: they were just stories, it was better not to think or dream of such terrible things. The family camp was unbearably crowded, the meager food rations became even smaller, there was a shortage of water, at every outhouse people had to wait an hour and more. It was eminently clear that this situation could not continue.

In May 1944, following repeated appeals from the Danish Red Cross, which above all wanted to see how its compatriots were being treated, Himmler finally agreed to permit a commission of the International Red Cross to visit Theresienstadt and a Jewish labor camp. The visit to the ghetto was set for June 23.

Three days before the commission's visit, all the Danish Jews were transferred to small rooms with two or three beds, pretty bedspreads, a table, chairs, a pot with a real plant, and on the door a nameplate with the tenants' names. In the presence of the camp commandant and Eichmann's emissary, Möhs, Epstein, the Elder of the Jews, spoke to the Danes and warned them not to tell the truth. Those Danes for whom better rooms could not be found were locked up in the offices of the Magdeburg barracks for the duration of the visit, so that the commission would not bump into them.

In the interest of the grand display, Eichmann permitted the rescue committee in Budapest to officially transfer $10,000 to the Protectorate Jews. The ghetto leadership received new stationery headed by an idyllic scene of Theresienstadt, and the leaders of the Zionist movement—Kahn, Munk, Zucker, Epstein, Österreicher—wrote letters to Joel Brand in Budapest thanking him for the many shipments of packages from Lisbon and Istanbul: "Our food supply is totally adequate and there is no need whatsoever for you to worry about it, but we are glad of the packages as a sign of your friendship."

The letter stated further that "Theresienstadt is in all respects a Jewish city; all the work is done by Jews, from street cleaning to the most advanced medical treatment, from all technical work to cooking in the communal kitchens, from manning the fire brigade and police force to staffing the legal system and postal service, from running a bank with its own currency to organizing cultural programs, lectures, plays, concerts, a library with 50,000 volumes, children's houses, old-age residences. The good general state of health is in no small part due to Theresienstadt's excellent climate, but also to the doctors' tireless efforts and the regular supply of medicine.

"We sometimes think of friends and the possibility of immigration. As we see from your letter, you too hope to achieve this solution, and not on a small scale."

Franta Friedmann, the Elder of the Jews in Prague, where only half-Jews and a handful of Jews of mixed marriages remained, sent a letter that same week in the same saccharine-sweet tone. He too told of the rich and proud Jewish life in the ghetto, despite the fact that he had never been permitted to visit Theresienstadt. The similarity in content and date showed that both letters had been written on instructions from above.

The Germans spared no Jewish money, effort, or manpower to improve Theresienstadt's image. A modern children's home was built of wood and glass, with new beds, adjoining showers, and a playground with a swimming pool. A villa, till now occupied by one of the German citizens, became the (temporary) infirmary for sick children. Painted signs were hung in the streets. The residences along the route mapped out for the commission were literally whitewashed to cover up all telltale signs of grime visible at a superficial glance. The bank director's office was furnished in keeping with his position. The former cinema, which had served as living quarters for masses of old people, reverted to its former purpose as an auditorium. The former Sokol building, which had housed the chronically ill and those with communicable diseases, was masked as a social center, with a performance hall and synagogue, and café tables with gay umbrellas were set out on its veranda.

The program for the visit was worked out to the tiniest detail, with mounting tension. Epstein prepared written answers to any questions the visitors might ask and submitted them to headquarters for approval. Sidewalks were scrubbed with soap and water, the food staff was issued white gloves, the disabled were ordered not to leave their quarters, rehearsals were held for athletic shows and plays to be put on for the visitors. Rahm, a skilled organizer who was better than his predecessor at putting on a friendly face, checked every point along the route with Möhs: the show must pass without incident. On a fine summer day, the distinguished entourage appeared: Dr. Franz Hvass, representative of the Danish Foreign Office; Dr. Yuel Henningsen, representing the Danish health commissioner on behalf of the Danish Red Cross; Dr. M. Rossel, commissioner of the International Red Cross; the commissioner of the German Red Cross; the heads of the Gestapo in the Protectorate, the head of the department for Jewish affairs, representatives of the German Foreign Office, the Czech propaganda minister Moravec, all in civilian clothing. Epstein received them dressed in a black suit and top hat, as befit the head of a Jewish city during a royal visit. A car was put at his disposal, a carpet had been laid in his office, and there he gave the visitors an introductory talk on the ghetto, complete with figures, few of which matched the facts.

The visit lasted from the morning till seven in the evening, with a break for a long and festive lunch. The guests saw a group of suntanned agricultural women workers pass by, as if by chance, hoes on their shoulders, laughing and singing. At food distribution they heard the dormitory children ask, as primed: "Uncle Rahm, are we getting sardines again?" They saw a performance of the children's opera *Brundibar.* They did not see the mass residences, the quarters of the old or mentally ill, the transport files, the thousands of cartons containing ashes, the Czech police on guard. Like obedient children they walked along the route laid out for them, and their general impression was exceedingly positive, as revealed in their reports, written on their return to their respective countries. Most impressed was Dr. Rossel, the representative of the International Red Cross in Geneva, who in a confidential report wondered with surprise why the Germans had postponed the visit for so long: they had nothing to hide after all. Theresienstadt was in all respects an admirable Jewish city, unifying the various elements of the Jewish population, who had come from different countries and diverse economic levels. There was no shortage of furniture, carpets, curtains. The living quarters were comfortable, though somewhat crowded: one flat was shared by two or three families. The nutrition appeared adequate and ghetto residents even received items that had long since disappeared from the market outside. The dining rooms were spacious (they had been set up for the day with waitresses in white aprons).

The tone of the report by the two Danes was somewhat more restrained, but it too confirmed that the situation was better than they had expected. They had been given free access and were allowed to talk to the local residents unhampered, though with "discreet supervision." The relatives of all the Danes at Theresienstadt could rest assured: this was not a transit camp, and none of the Danes had been shipped further on. Pregnancy was permitted, contraceptives were available, food rations were similar to those in all parts of the Protectorate except that margarine was distributed instead of butter. The city was clean and its residents did not suffer from undernourishment. The houses were painted and had small gardens around them where vegetables were grown for the residents. Food could be cooked at home or meals taken in the communal dining room. The buying power of the Theresienstadt crown was in fact greater than that of the ordinary crown, and shops in the town offered secondhand shoes and clothing for sale. The dormitories were equipped with electricity, heat, and running water; all that was missing were radios, newspapers, tobacco, and alcohol. Theater, opera, an open-air orchestra, chamber concerts, a court of law, a soccer field, a swimming pool were all laudable features of the Jewish city.

The residents worked eight hours a day; those in the free professions—engineers, doctors, lawyers—continued to work in their respective fields. As far as health was concerned, there were no epidemics, due to systematic inoculations, and no fleas, bugs, or lice, for every ten days the residents washed with warm water. The central hospital looked like any ordinary hospital in any provincial Danish town, and there was no lack of drugs. The death rate was between five and ten people a day, all elderly.

The Danish representatives were aware of the fact that part of what they'd seen had been prepared for their benefit, but they assumed that these improvements would continue after their visit.

When the visitors left, Epstein told some close friends from the former Reich Association of Jews in Germany that he did not believe that the committee had been duped—they had seen through the cosmetic job. The children enjoyed their new home for exactly twenty-four hours.

Hvass and Henningsen also reported to the Danish embassy in Stockholm and to the aid committee for deported Danes, and their report was published by the committee for occupied Europe, albeit under the ironic title "Jewish Paradise on Earth." The article said that, according to other sources, six Gestapo people had been present at all of the committee's conversations; nevertheless the heartwarming description was encouraging. The words "autonomous state" were adorned with quotation marks, but the overall impression was that conditions in Theresienstadt were infinitely better than in Poland. From the German viewpoint, according to Neuhaus, the visit had passed satisfactorily in all respects. Since the representatives of the Danish Red Cross were satisfied that all the Danes had remained in Theresienstadt, and their chief worry after all had been for the Danish Jews, they did not insist on a visit to an additional labor camp and there was no longer any need to keep the stage set with the family camp at Birkenau. It no longer served any purpose.

On June 20 an SS car pulled up before punishment block 11 in Auschwitz. Its passengers went to the bunker cell that Edelstein shared with a few other prisoners and told him that he had been sentenced to death. Edelstein shook hands with his cellmates, including Yossel Rosensaft, and when Hössler, the commandant of the women's camp, pressed him, saying "Quickly, quickly!" he said, "I am master of my last moments." The car drove to crematorium number 3 and deposited Edelstein. Then it drove to the family camp to collect Miriam Edelstein, her mother, and Arieh. That day Miriam was in the sick block, ill with diphtheria, but when she was told that she could see her husband she was ready immediately. The doctor refused to release her, however, and the car drove back empty. But a few minutes later the SS returned with explicit instructions to take the whole Edelstein family, sick or well. Miriam was brought on a stretcher to the gate where the car waited. Meanwhile Mrs. Foltyn and Mrs. Deutsch, whose husbands had worked in the records department at Theresienstadt and had been arrested with Edelstein, were also summoned. Gerda Deutsch ran all along the road between the two rows of barracks, calling radiantly: "I'm going to see Egon!"

The family camp waited for the return of the Edelsteins in vain. Only a few days later did the counselors of the children's block learn from a Polish roof repairman called Zosek that the Germans had killed them all. At the end of the war—in June 1945—a Polish prisoner from Auschwitz arrived at Theresienstadt where the sick, the homeless, and the administrative staff still lived. In his hand he held ghetto currency and he asked the members of the administration, including Dittl Ornstein, if they had known the man whose name appeared on the notes. When they replied that they had, he said, "I saw him just before he died." It seems that the man had served as an executioner at Auschwitz (one of his jobs had been to hang two girls for trying to blow up a crematorium), and he had witnessed the end of the Edelstein family. Making derisive remarks throughout, the Germans had first shot Miriam, Arieh, and Mrs. Olliner before Jakob's eyes, and only then did they shoot Edelstein himself. The man said that Edelstein had asked him to give his regards to his friends in Theresienstadt, should he get out of Auschwitz alive.

A prisoner called Kalman Furmann, whose functions in the *Sonderkommando* included holding prisoners still during execution if they were unable to control themselves, told Yehuda Bakon, one of the few boys from the children's barracks to survive, that Edelstein and his family had stood very quietly and did not cry. Srulek Zukerman, who worked at crematorium number 3, was delegated to burn the bodies. Foltyn, Deutsch, and Goldschmied were also killed that day.

Edelstein was given the honor of individual death. The time had now come to liquidate the family camp as a whole, this time through Birkenau's approved channels, by selection. Dr. Mengele, elegant in gleaming boots, erect and slim, with a whip in his hand, appeared at the family camp with an SS escort. All the inmates between the ages of sixteen and forty, the men and women segregated, had to parade naked before him. Sometimes the prisoners were ordered to run, sometimes they were asked their occupation. The instructors, the Hehalutz people, mostly defined their occupation as agriculture, and the girl counselors said that they were gardeners, hoping that physical labor would bring salvation. One of the girls, who replied truthfully that she was a physical education teacher, was ordered to exercise, naked, on the raised stove while the SS watched and laughed, until finally she too was told to join the group which according to the Germans was being sent to work in the Reich.

Again the same question was raised: did the Germans truly intend to take the young and strong for work as they claimed, or was it a ploy, an attempt to separate the weak from the strong in order to prevent all possibility of rebellion? If there was hope that more than two thousand young people would leave this hell alive, then there was no point in rebelling, which in the best of circumstances would enable only a few individuals to escape; on the other hand, leaving for work meant abandoning the others—the old, the children—knowingly leaving them to the gas. Mengele left the decision to the mothers: they could leave for work—if they left their children in the camp. The mothers of small children, all young women, were in a dilemma. Hope of life lay in leaving, but it was unthinkable to leave their children. "What would you do? Tell us," they asked Ruth, the kindergarten instructor. "Why ask me? I have no children." Still, they wanted to know, still, what would you do? "I'd stay with my child." The mothers nodded their heads in agreement. They too thought so. They simply wanted support for their decision. Most of the parents who did not pass selection themselves urged their older children to leave, but there were some who asked them to stay: in hard times the family must stick together.

This time practical plans for revolt were made in the family camp: bottles of kerosene, matches, razors, wooden clubs, caches of benzine were collected and hidden in various blocks. An underground network was set up in which each person knew only the one who passed on instructions to him and the one to whom he transmitted them. The plan was to set fire to the barracks and break through the gates with a steamroller used for paving roads in the camp. And then? A shrug of the shoulders. There was nowhere to run to in wooden-soled shoes and tattered clothes marked as prison outfits, without money, documents, or contacts. To the left was the quarantine camp, to the right the Hungarian women's camp; further on was a men's camp, with the Gypsy camp opposite; across the road was the SS camp, and on the other side the road led to the gas chambers and the train—and all around the great chain of concentric circles of sentries.

There were more agonies of doubt: news came from the clothing warehouse that orders had been given to prepare clothing for prisoners who were leaving. Maybe this time the Germans did mean what they said. The communist underground, which planned the

443

revolt with the counselors of the dormitory, estimated that out of twelve thousand camp inmates, perhaps thirty or forty would get away, whereas the chances of survival were far greater for any leaving the camp to work. Opinion was divided in the men's camp, too, which was party to the plot. If only the family camp was threatened with immediate death, the others were better off not taking the risk. Now, in the summer of 1944, the front was drawing nearer. Liberation was close in any case. Hugo Lengsfeld, who had served in the international brigade in Spain and who, with Růžena Lauscher, was in charge of the communist underground at the family camp, ordered that one of the prisoners, suspected of collaborating with the Germans prior to his deportation, be killed. Not a whisper of rebellion must reach the SS. (As it turned out, the revolt of the *Sonderkommando* of Birkenau did not take place until October; the uprising was brutally quashed and three hundred prisoners were killed.)

Between the twentieth and thirtieth of June, SS officers kept coming and going in the family camp. The order came on July 1: one thousand men who had passed selection were to leave for work in Germany. It was decided to postpone the revolt and wait and see what happened to them. The men spent their last night with their families, their farewells near the gate were brief and tearless. They left torn between feelings of shame at abandoning the others, and hopes of life; between fear of a trap and impatience to put as much distance as possible between themselves and the crematoria. They walked in the direction of the sauna, and their families and friends waited in agonizing suspense at the far end of the camp. From there they could see the railroad junction, which now reached into the heart of Birkenau. A few hours later, they could make out the silhouettes of a long procession in striped jail garb, heads shaved, waving toward the family camp, boarding the train, and pulling out. In the family camp, people wept and embraced: they had left! To live!

Four days later, one thousand women were taken out and given gray prison dresses, and they too got on the train. Then another group of five hundred men, another of two hundred and fifty women. After the work force left, the family camp seemed to be forgotten. There was no more roll call, no one was counted, no one recorded. Everybody just waited. A few days later, Mengele and Schwarzhuber appeared and took away eighty-nine children between the ages of twelve and sixteen. They were taken to the men's camp to serve as runners for the various officials. Mengele reassured the mothers at the shrinking camp that they and their children would be transferred to a barracks with brick walls and left in peace. The mothers had no illusions about what to expect, but all of them, except for four, out of almost six hundred—chose to stay with their children. A life haunted by thoughts of their children going alone to the gas chambers was not worth living. One of the mothers tried to leave with her baby, born at the camp and bundled up in a blanket to resemble a parcel. One of the SS pierced the bundle with a bayonet.

Between July 10 and 12, the remaining inmates of the family camp, numbering over six thousand, were sent to the gas chambers. Kalman Furmann, prisoner number 80810, twenty-four years old, who worked in the special commando, said after the extermination that the children had not cried.

The SS were struck by the beauty of one of the children, and wanted to remove him from the lines of people waiting to die and include him in the group of boys who were to serve as runners. But the child refused to leave his mother, knowing exactly what that meant. One of the girls whose mother told her that she would soon see her grandmother again broke into a joyous dance, while the other mothers watched her wordlessly.

The family camp was emptied, the children's barracks, with their drawings of Indians and Eskimos, Snow White and the Seven Dwarfs, was orphaned. The children did leave through the chimney, just as they had always said.

Out of almost three thousand prisoners who passed selection and were sent to concentration camps in Germany, seven hundred and fifty were alive at the end of the war—the highest survival rate of all the sixty-three transports that had left Theresienstadt for the East.

After the distinguished Red Cross visitors left the ghetto, the Germans decided to use Theresienstadt for a propaganda film before dismantling the pleasant setting they had built for the benefit of outside guests. The film was to include scenes of bathing in the river, amusements at the café, and a soccer game. It was called *The Führer Gives the Jews a City* and was completed in September 1944, at which time the show ended and the model ghetto became dispensable. In the second half of September, the Germans announced that five thousand men of working age would be leaving. According to headquarters, they were to build a new industrial complex in Upper Silesia, and when the work was finished, they would return to the ghetto. Until that time, they would be allowed postal contact with their families in Theresienstadt every week or two. They were permitted to take only a few personal effects; the rest of their belongings would be kept in the ghetto for their return. Otto Zucker was to be in charge of the new labor camp, and he could choose the men under fifty whom he would need for the job. Among others, he took a large group of Hehalutz people and Karl Schliesser, director of the economic department. The Germans sounded convincing, as always. Only a few months before, two hundred and sixty men from Theresienstadt had been sent to the Zossen camp to build barracks for evacuees after the heavy Allied bombing of Berlin. They wrote their families regularly and their reports had been reassuring.

Two transports of laborers, with 2,500 men in each, were brought straight to Birkenau. The last anyone saw of Zucker and Schliesser was of them being escorted in handcuffs along the Auschwitz train platform. The wives and girlfriends of the men in the "labor transport" were allowed to follow them, and more than four hundred women volunteered, including Fritzi Zucker, whom Günther promised that she would see her husband the very day she left. Once the young and strong men had been disposed of, work at the ghetto could proceed without fear of revolt. On September 27, Epstein was arrested and accused of attempting to escape because he had gone to one of the warehouses outside the gate without permission (it was he who signed the passes). He was taken to the Little Fortress and shot in the back. The next day the SS brought four coffins from the Little Fortress to the ghetto crematorium. Three contained wood and weighed about as much as a man, the fourth contained a corpse.

According to Benjamin Murmelstein (who now became the third Elder of the Jews of Theresienstadt), following the participation of Jewish partisans in an armed revolt in Slovakia in the summer of 1944, and because of rumors that there was an underground network at the ghetto (there were still 30,000 people there, including thousands of young fighting men, former soldiers of the Czech army), the Germans had decided to wipe the ghetto off the face of the earth by means of aerial bombing which could be blamed on the enemy. Epstein was asked by the Germans to speak on German radio, broadcasting from Dresden, and protest the cruel Allied bombing of the ghetto to the world, providing the Germans with the endorsement they sought to destroy the ghetto. But Epstein, who had long told those close to him that "I know the day will come when I'll no longer be able to say yes," refused.

Theresienstadt was not bombed but liquidated in the usual manner, through transports to Auschwitz. In a single month 18,400 people were deported, and this time the transport lists were composed by the SS, led by Möhs himself. On explicit instructions from the Germans, these transports included the entire Zionist leadership: Franz Kahn, Gonda Redlich, Erich Österreicher, Erich Munk, Hannah Steiner, and their families; Desider Friedmann, Robert Stricker; members of the Council of Elders, representatives of the Czech Jews; the actors, singers, musicians; Gideon Klein, Rafi Schächter, Peter Kien; the poets, the writers; Karl Poláček; the athletes, instructors, children and their parents. Eleven thousand people over sixty-five remained at the ghetto: the war-disabled, the half-Jews, all the Danes, some of the Dutch, the "prominents," the Jews of mixed marriages, and women.

The last transport from the Theresienstadt ghetto was also the last transport to be put to death in the gas chambers of Birkenau on the eve of October 28, the national holiday of Masaryk's republic. The following day, by order of Himmler, the gas facilities ceased operations.

Out of the 118,000 Jews living in Bohemia and Moravia when the Nazis occupied the region, 26,000 managed to get away. Out of the 92,000 who remained trapped in the Protectorate, 85,000 were deported to the East, either directly or via Theresienstadt; 3,250 of these returned from the camps at the end of the war, walking skeletons. Out of 15,000 children who passed through the ghetto, about 150 survived—one in a hundred.

It is impossible to end with dry figures. Somewhere in all this there must be a lesson for the coming generations. I have not found it. I know only one thing: humanity has not learned a lesson and perhaps is incapable of doing so. As for the Jews, they have merely lost their innocence—perhaps not even that. Perhaps they simply became more vulnerable. I would like to be able to say that Edelstein and the children died for something, for a Jewish state, for a better future. But in all honesty, I cannot do so. They died because they were not allowed to live.

447

BIBLIOGRAPHY
AND SOURCES

Archives

CZA	Central Zionist Archives, Jerusalem
YVSA	Yad Vashem Archives, Jerusalem
ILR	Institute for Labor Research, Tel Aviv
OHD	Oral History Department, Hebrew University, Jerusalem
WA	Weizmann Archives, Rehovot
BTA	Beth Terezin Archives, Givat Chaim-Ichud
GFHA	Ghetto Fighters House Archives, Lochamei Hagetaot
MA	Moreshet Archive, Givat Chaviva
ETD	Eichmann Trial Documents, Jerusalem
LPA	Labor Party Archive, Beth Berl
(H)	in Hebrew

THE JEWS OF CZECHOSLOVAKIA UNTIL 1939—
GENERAL BACKGROUND

Society for the History of Czechoslovak Jews, New York, The Jewish Publication Society of America, *The Jews of Czechoslovakia*, 1–2, Philadelphia, 1968–1971;
Gesher (Review), "The Jews of Czechoslovakia," Tel Aviv, September 1969 (H);
Weltsch, Felix (ed.), *Prag ve Jerushalajim*, Jerusalem, 1954 (H);
Yahil-Hoffmann, Chaim, *Memoirs* (manuscript), A 382, CZA (H);
Gold, H., *Die Juden und Judengemeinden Böhmens in Vergangenheit und Gegenwart*, Brünn-Prague, 1934

Zionist Federation of Czechoslovakia:
Die Selbstwehr (SW), 1926–1938;

Židovské Zprávy (ZZ), 1926–1939;
Jüdischer Almanach, 1934–1938

THERESIENSTADT GHETTO—GENERAL BACKGROUND

Reznicenko, Yehuda (ed.), *Theresienstadt,* Tel Aviv, 1947 (H);
Adler, H. G., *Theresienstadt 1941–1945—Das Antlitz einer Zwansgemein-schaft,* J.C.B. Mohr (Paul Siebeck), Tübingen, 1946;
——, *Die Verheimlichte Wahrheit—Theresienstädter Dokumente,* J.C.B. Mohr (Paul Siebeck), Tübingen, 1958;
——, "Die Rolle Theresienstadts in der Endlösung der Judenfrage," *Aus Politik und Zeitgeschichte/Das Parlament,* B XXII (6/1/55);
Council of Jewish Communities in the Czech Lands, *Terezin 1941–1945,* Prague, 1965 (anthology);
Feder, R., *Židovská tragedie—dějství poslední,* Luck-Kolín, 1947;
Lagus, K., and Polák, J., *Město za Mřížemi,* Naše Vojsko, Prague, 1964;
Lederer, Z., *Ghetto Theresienstadt,* London, 1953;
Murmelstein, B., *Terezin—Il Ghetto Modello di Eichmann,* Capelli Editore, Rocca San Casciano, 1961;
Starke, K., *Der Führer schenkt den Juden eine Stadt,* Berlin, 1970;
Utitz, E., *Psychologie života v terezinském koncentračním táboře,* Dělnické nakladatelství v Praze, 1947;
Tůma, M., *Ghetto našich dnů,* Saliva, Prague, 1946;
Hyndráková, Franková, "Die Jüdische Selbstverwaltung im Ghetto Theresienstadt," *Judaica Bohemia,* VIII, Prague, 1972;
Kárný, M., "Terezinský K.Z. v plánech nacistů," *Acta Occupatione Bohemiae,* Prague, 1966; and *Československý časopis historický,* (12/5/74);
Löwenherz, J., Bericht 1938–1942, Wien 1945, 0–30/5, YVSA;
"I Never Saw Another Butterfly": Children's Drawings and Poems, Terezin 1942–1944, London, 1962;
Taped testimony, 376–397, OHD;
Testimonies 02/47, 02/584, 02/217, 02/1103, 02/443, 03/1598, 02/237, 03/89, 01/293, 02/453, 02/534, WL/157, 02/244, 07/6–3, 01/280, YVSA

CHAPTER 1

HORODENKA–BRÜNN

Crankshaw, Edward, *The Fall of the House of Hapsburg,* London, 1963;
Meltzer, Shimshon (ed.), *The Book of Horodenka,* Tel Aviv, 1963 (H);
Mauthner, F., *Prager Jugendjahre,* S. Fischer Verlag, 1968;
Stölzl, C., *Kafkas böses Böhmen,* Munich, 1975;
Čapek, Karel, *Hovory s T. G. Masarykem,* Prague, 1946

CHAPTERS 2–3

TEPLITZ-SCHÖNAU

Weihs, F., *Aus Geschichte und Leben der Teplitzer Judengemeinde 1782–1938*, Jüdischer Buch und Kunstverlag, Brünn–Prague, 1932;
Wanie, P., *Geschichte der Juden von Teplitz*, Verlag Vinzenz Uhl, Kaaden, 1925;
Samel, L., *Eine Teplitzer Judengeschichte aus dem Jahre 1803*, Verlag Adolf Becker, Teplitz-Schönau

Zionist Youth Movements:
Interviews 870–916, OHD;
Hehalutz files 111/38 (437), ILR;
S. H. Bergman, *Bamish'ol*, Tel Aviv, 1963 (H)

Socialist Zionists:
101/6 (ČSR, 1934–1938), LPA

Kahn's letter:
5/2/33, WA

CHAPTERS 4–5

The Bernheim Petition:
Färber, M., *Dr. Emil Margulies, Ein Lebenskampf für die Wahrheit*, ATASA, Tel Aviv, 1949

E. Margulies's letter:
S 25/9033, CZA

Arlosoroff's death:
Edelstein, Jakob, "Erwiderung," *SW* (5/7/34)

Zionist Congress, Prague:
Protocols 1933, CZA;
Sokolow, Florian, *Nahum Sokolow, Life and Legend*, London, 1975

E. Bachner's story:
S6/2954, CZA

Refugees:
Maria Schmolka Society, *Maria Schmolka*, London, 1940

Palestine Office, Prague:
S6/1633–36, S6/1552–59, CZA

Fictitious marriages:
S6/2954, CZA;

Maimon, Ada, *Lorech Haderech*, Tel Aviv, 1972 (H)

Hehalutz, Prague:
Diary of A. Ofir, 111/38 (437), ILR;
Kugel, H., "Brechet die Macht der Finsternis," *SW* (9/21/34)

Edelstein on Ben-Gurion:
Edelstein, Jakob, "Zur Vereinigung der Sozialistischen Zionisten in der Tschechoslovakei," *SW* (8/27/36)

CHAPTERS 6–8

Arab riots:
Diary of A. Ofir, 111/38 (437), ILR

Emigration to Palestine:
Edelstein, Jakob, "Alijá není emigrace," *ZZ* (1/21/36)

Appeal to Jewish Czechs:
Edelstein, Jakob, "Slovo o dorozumění," *ZZ* (5/15/36)

Edelstein in Palestine:
Youth-Aliyah S6/3362–63, CZA;
Edelstein, Jakob, "Jüdische Jugend lernt," *SW* (2/11/38)

Burgenland:
Abeles, E., Testimony, Eichmann Trial, Jerusalem, 1974, p. 690 (H);
Edelstein, Jakob, "Emigrationschiff auf der Donau liquidiert," *SW* (8/12/38)

Political situation:
Hoffmann, Ch., 101/38, LPA

CHAPTERS 9–10

MUNICH—GENERAL BACKGROUND

Benes, Eduard, *Demokratie dnes a zítra*, ČIN, Prague, 1946;
Brod, Max, *Streitbares Leben*, Munich, 1960;
Mastný, V., *The Czechs under Nazi Rule*, New York–London, 1971;
Kennan, George F., *From Prague after Munich (1938–40)*, Princeton, 1968;
Höller, F., *Von der SDP in die NSDAP*, Gaupropagandaleiter der Sudeten, 1939

In Teplitz-Schönau:
Schmiedt, Shlomo, 02/596, YVSA;
Weihs, P. M., 02/117, YVSA;
Kulka, Otto Dov, "Veidat München ubajat hayehudim be Czechoslovakia," *Yalkut Moreshet* 3, 1964, (H);
Yahil, Chaim, "München—Tragedia Velikcha," *Davar*, September 1970 (H)

Runciman's mission:
Stoppard Report, A/341, CZA

Jan Masaryk:
A/145, A/341, A/288/5, CZA;
Weizmann, Chaim, *Trial and Error*, London, 1949

Jews in Germany:
S 25/9703, CZA;
Roth Kirchen, Livia, "The Czechoslovak Government in Exile," Yad Vashem Studies 9, Jerusalem, 1973

EMIGRATION

Barlas, Chaim, *Hatzalah bijmei hashoah*, Tel Aviv, 1975 (H);
Avriel, Ehud, *Open the Gates!*, London, 1975;
Kugel, Chaim, 104/111, ILR;
Edelstein, Jakob, "Beratung des Mittelstandes," *SW* (7/29/38)

Planned assassination of Hitler:
Shimkin, J., 03/3279, YVSA

THE FINAL SOLUTION—GENERAL BACKGROUND

Eichmann Trial:
Testimonies, Jerusalem, 1974 (H);
Verdict, Jerusalem, 1961 (H);
Hapitaron Hasofij: Documents, Beth Lochamei hagetaot, Tel Aviv, 1960 (H);
Shirer, William L., *The Rise and Fall of the Third Reich*, London, 1962;
Dawidowicz, Lucy, *The War against the Jews 1933–1945*, London, 1977;
Friedmann, P., *Aspects of the Jewish Communal Crisis: Essays on Jewish Life and Thought*, New York, 1954;
Hilberg, R., *The Destruction of the European Jews*, Chicago, 1961;
Kogon, E., *Der SS-Staat, Kindler*, Munich, 1974;
Lukacs, J., *The Last European War*, New York, 1976;
Morse, A., *While Six Million Died*, New York, 1968;
Poliakov, L., *Harvest of Hate*, London, 1960;
Reitlinger, G., *Die Endlösung, Colloquium*, Berlin, 1956;
Trunk, J., *Judenrat: The Jewish Councils in Eastern Europe under Nazi Occupation*, New York, 1972

CHAPTERS 11–13

THE PROTECTORATE—LAWS AND EMIGRATION

Jüdisches Nachrichtenblatt–Židovské Listy, Prague, 1939–1941;
Friedmann, F., "Rechtstellung der Juden im Protektorat Böhmen und Mähren," 6/30/42, 064, YVSA

Children's education:
Diary of Anna Faltyn, 2/216, GHA

Contact with Gestapo:
Reznicenko, Yehuda (ed.), *Theresienstadt,* Tel Aviv, 1947 (H);
Interview with P. März;
Yahil-Hoffman, Chaim, *Memoirs* (manuscript), A 382, CZA (H)

Illegal immigration:
Yahil, Leni, "Select British Documents on Illegal Immigration to Palestine,"
Yad Vashem Studies 10, 1974

Polish citizens:
Report Jewish Community, Prague, ETD, 06/1323–32;
Interviews with P. März, A. Tarsi

Money transfer:
S6/3363, S6/1571, CZA

Contact with Switzerland:
A 320/41–42–43, CZA

Rescue of Zionist leadership:
P1/205, S6/1636, CZA

Edelstein in Palestine:
S6/1571, CZA;
S.D. Prague to RSHA Berlin, Schwalb Collection, ILR

Jewish community in Prague:
06/1323–32, ETD;
Kulka, Otto Dov, "Magaim bein kehilat Prag veha S.D.," *Yalkut Moreshet* 18,
November 1974 (H)

Jews in Protectorate:
Moshe Baumgarten, 8/23/38, WA;
Emigration files 1939–1940, Report 9/10/41, Dokumentationsaktion /064,
YVSA

CHAPTERS 14–16

Nisko settlement:
06/1135–36, ETD;
Eichmann tape 3/124–26;
Burger, M., testimony, ET, p. 125 (H);
Kratky, H., testimony, ET, p. 134 (H);
Zehngut, J., Report, *Věstník ŽNO,* M 27/71, YVSA;
Rat der Jüdischen Kultusgemeinden in der Tschechischen Sozialistischen
Republik, *Nazidokumente sprechen,* YVSA

Edelstein in Trieste:
A 320/25, CZA;
to Weizmann, 11/30/39, WA

Youth-Aliyah:
L 17/2441, S 6/3363, CZA;
M. Baumgarten, 347, OHD

Edelstein in Geneva:
Moshe Sharet, diary, S 25/192–198, A 320/4113, CZA;
Goldmann to Weizmann, 2/9/40, WA

Edelstein in Berlin:
E. Frank, 01/227, YVSA

Weizmann in Washington:
2/8/40, WA

CHAPTERS 17–18

Madagascar Plan:
06/172/1054, ETD;
Yahil, L., "Madagascar—Phantom of a Solution for the Jewish Question,"
Yad Vashem Studies 11, 1976;
Friedmann, P., "The Lublin Reservation and Madagascar Plan," *Annals of Jewish Social Science,* VIII/C (1953)

Meeting with Eichmann:
06/1143, YVSA

Contacts with Benes:
12/4/40–1/7/41, WA

Legal problems:
Jewish Community, Prague, files, 064, YVSA

Edelstein in Holland:
Pinkhoff, M., "Reshit hamachteret hachalutzit be Holland," *GFH Bulletin,*
1/13, 1956 (H);
Melkman, J., testimony, ET, p. 451 (H);
_____, "The Controversy Surrounding the Jewish Council in Amsterdam,"
Yad Vashem Studies, 1979;
Friedmann, S., testimony, Dokumentationsaktion, 064, YVSA

Isolating the Jews:
06/503, ETD

CHAPTER 19

PREPARATIONS FOR THE THERESIENSTADT GHETTO

Heydrich conference:
06/1143, ETD, Eichmann Testimony, 111–115, ET;

Král, V., *Lessons from History—Documents*, Orbis, Prague, 1961;
Memos on Dr. Seidl's instructions, Oct.–Nov. 1941, 064, YVSA;
Transport to Minsk, L. Herzog, testimony, Dokumentationsaktion, 064, YVSA

Ghetto leadership:
J. Bor to author, 10/12/76

Education underground:
Diary of an unknown child, MA

Jewish property:
Recht, E., testimony, ET, p. 606 (H);
Documente Treuhandstelle, Dokumentationsaktion, 064, YVSA

Hehalutz decision:
Interviews with R. Friedl-Ben Shalom, Berl Hershkowitz

CHAPTER 20

Tagesbefehle, BTA;
Redlich, Gonda, diary, BTA;
Zucker, O., Geschichte des Ghettos Theresienstadt zum 31/12/43, 02/385, YVSA;
Seidl, S., testimony at his trial, 06/109, ETD

Gestapo letter on property:
Adler Dokumente, p. 54

Edelstein comes to Theresienstadt:
Ornsteinová, E., "Vzpomínka na Jakuba Edelsteina," *Věstník ŽNO*, Prague (7/3/45);
Tarsi, A., "Gevurat nefesh bejn chomot haghetto," *Lamerchav*, 5/27/65 (H);
Interview with J. Klaber, head of ghetto police, 064, YVSA;
"Jak vznikl Terezín," *Věstník ŽNO*, Prague, 11/XVIII (Nov. 1956);
Friedmann, H., "Kunstführung durch Theresienstadt" (Nov. 1943), 07/64–2, YVSA;
Plan zum Aufbau des Ghettos, 12/2/41, SC

CHAPTERS 21–22

Wannsee Conference:
T/74, T/734, 06/1104, ETD

Transports to the East:
Appeals, 064, YVSA

Heydrich's assassination:
"Lidice," *Věstník ŽNO*, Prague, XXXIX (June 1977);
Kraus, T. R., "But Lidice Is in Europe," *Terezin 1941–1945* (anthology);
Wiener, J., *The Assassination of Heydrich*, New York, 1971

Health:
Fleischmann, K., "E. Munk der Schattenriss einer Persönlichkeit," 064, YVSA;
Springer, E., "Health Conditions in Terezin," *Terezin 1941–1945* (anthology)

Culture:
Yearly Report, 1943, Freizeitgestaltung, Report R. Weiner, 1941–1944, 064, YVSA;
Šormová, E., *Divadlo v Terezíně 1941–1945, Památnik Terezín*, Ústi n.L., 1973

CHAPTERS 23–24

Herzl's daughter:
HNI–H/25, CZA

Crime:
Court sentences—Tagesbefehle, BTA;
Klaber, J., Ein Jahr Theresienstadt 5/12/42, 02/581, YVSA;
Stux, R., "Denkschrift über die Ausübung einer Gerichtsbarkeit im Gebiete von Thereseinstadt," 07/1–5, YVSA

Youth:
Ansbacher, M., testimony, ET, p. 503 (H);
Children's newspapers published in the ghetto: *Vedem, Kamarád*, BTA;
Klein, O., *Vliv koncentračního tábora na etický charakter židovské mládeže*, Symposium, Prague, 1969

Mortality:
Die Morbidität in Theresienstadt 21/11/41–30/6/43, 064 YVSA;
Selbstmorde in Theresienstadt 1941–1943, 064, YVSA

Hehalutz:
Schmiedl, S., "Hehalutz in Theresienstadt," Yad Vashem Studies 7, 1963

Pregnancies:
Letter of Dr. Munk, 064, YVSA

CHAPTERS 25–26

Letter from Edelstein, 12/6/42, 064, YVSA

Contacts with Geneva:
P1/220, P1/217, P1/191, CZA;
Istanbul Archive, GFHA;
Löwenstein, K., "Aus der Hölle Minsk in das Paradies Theresienstadt," *Mahnung*, Berlin (1958);
_____, "Minsk," *Schriftreihe der Bundeszentrale für Heimdienst*, 02/595, YVSA

Edelstein's dismissal:
Adler Dokumente, pp. 131–140

CHAPTERS 27–29

Dr. Kahn:
A 320/30, A 306/37, CZA

Jews from Holland:
T 624/ETD, 03/392, YVSA

Underground connections:
Morgenstern, A., "Vaad hahatzalah sheljad hasochnut hajehudit," *Yalkut Moreshet* 13, 1977;
Istanbul Archive, GFHA, CZA, MA;
Avriel, E., *Open the Gates!*, ch. 16

Rumors of destruction:
Diamant, V., testimony, ET, p. 616 (H);
P 1/98, CZA;
Boehm, E., *We Survived,* Yale University Press, New Haven, 1948;
Friedländer, A. G., *Leo Baeck—Teacher of Theresienstadt,* New York, 1968

Edelstein's arrest:
L. Lederer to P. März, 3/20/61;
Murmelstein, B., chapter from his book sent to author, 1978;
Interviews with A. Tarsi, D. Ornstein, B. Hostovská

CHAPTERS 30–33

AUSCHWITZ-BIRKENAU, GENERAL BACKGROUND

Kraus, Ota, and Erich Kulka, *The Death Factory,* Oxford, 1966;
Broszat, M. (ed.), *Kommandant in Auschwitz: Autobiographische Aufzeichnungen von R. Höss,* Munich, 1963;
Langbein, H., *Menschen in Auschwitz,* Vienna, 1973;
_____, "Rebellions and Escapes in Auschwitz," *Yalkut Moreshet* 11, 1969;
Rücker, A., *NS Vernichtungslager im Spiegel deutscher Strafprozesse,* Deutscher Taschenbuchverlag, 1977;
Testimonies 398–511, OHD

The family camp:
Taped interviews with A. Ofir, E. Bachner, G. Ben-Zvi, Y. Bakon, D. Barnea, H. Fischl, O. D. Kulka, A. Karni, OHD;
03/1202, 03/2636, 03/6233, 03/2896, YVSA;
Kárný, M., "Terezínský rodinný tábor v Birkenau," *Sborník historický,* 26 (1978)

Punishment block:
Testimony 1625/GFHA

Meeting Edelstein:
Taped interviews with R. Gibian (401), A. Fabian (400), A. Radvansky (408), OHD

Postcards from Birkenau:
Prossnitz Archive 07/18–19 YVSA; Prossnitz file, BTA; A/320, CZA; Interviews with A. Benes, W. Groag (with author), D. Kraus, E. Müller, OHD

Letter from Edelstein:
Dr. Munk, 3/12/44, 064, YVSA, interview with A. Tarsi

Gassing of September transport:
T/1498, T/1424, ETD;
P. Müller, 405/OHD;
F. Müller, *Sonder-Behandlung*, Munich, 1979;
Testimony of Two Escapees from Auschwitz-Birkenau Extermination Camps, WA Office of Strategic Services, Field Memorandum, 225/425

Escapes:
Kulka, E., "Five Escapes from Auschwitz," *Yalkut Moreshet* 3, 1968 (H); Interviews, 402, 403, 411, OHD

Red Cross visit:
Letter to J. Brand, 5/23/44, Istanbul Archive, GFHA;
Report in Stockholm, S 26/1304, CZA;
Report of Swiss representative, Adler Dokumente, 312–316

Execution of Edelstein and family:
Sheck, Z., "Shenatajim Lehirazho shel Yaakov Edelstein," *Haaretz*, 6/10/46 (H);
Interview with Y. Bakon, OHD;
Interview with D. Ornstein (with author);
Y. Rosensaft, *Bergen-Belsen Book*, 1957, p. 51;
L. Lederer to Dr. März, A/371, CZA

Epstein's death and the mass transports:
K. Rahm at his trial, 04/20/16, YVSA;
Murmelstein, B., "Stellungsnahme eines Beteiligten," *Die Welt* (1/14/64)

PERSONAL INTERVIEWS WITH THE AUTHOR

Horodenka:
I. Zohar, P. Fleschner, M. Fleschner, I. Streit—Tel Aviv

Brünn:
D. Itzhaki—Shaar Hagolan

Teplitz-Schönau:
M. Olliner—Haifa, C. Glassberg—Jerusalem, M. Tauber—Jerusalem,
U. Fluss—Givat Chaim Meuchad, A. Reich, M. Scheuer—Tel Aviv

Youth movement:
A. Ofir—Afikim, J. Erez-Reznicenko—Givat Chaim-Ichud, D. Ornstein—Tel Aviv, A. Givoni—Cholon, H. Grünberg—Ein Shemer, J.
Tuvin—Beth Zera, J. Pfenniger—Givat Chaim-Ichud, W. Zur (Feuerstein)—Merchavia, Moshe Zippor (Vogel)—Sarid, S. Rosen—Sarid

Zionist movement in Czechoslovakia:
D. Biegun—Tel Aviv, R. Löwy—Ramat Chen, E. Moller—Naharia, P. D.
März—Jerusalem, U. Naor (Lichtwitz)—Jerusalem, I. Pollák—Tel Aviv,
E. Propper—Tel Aviv, R. Rabinowitz—Jerusalem, D. Rufeisen—Lehavot
Habashan

Palestine:
Y. Yaari—Jerusalem

Prague during the occupation:
B. Amir (Spitz)—Naoth Mordechai, S. Enoch—Naan, M. Bitan (Baum-
garten)—Tel Aviv, R. Ben-Shalom (Friedl)—Haogen, A. Benes—Cholon,
Ch. Barlas—Jerusalem, M. Golan (Goldzeil)—Haifa, A. Dagan (Fischl)—
Jerusalem, A. Tarsi (Tressler)—Hachotrim, V. Zimmet-Cohen—Tel Aviv,
E. Schultz—Jerusalem

Holland:
J. Melchmann—Jerusalem

Theresienstadt:
D. Ornstein-Rauff—London, D. Barnea (Brammer)—Beersheba,
J. Bakon—Jerusalem, A. Glaser—Tel Aviv, W. Groag—Maanit, Tr.
Groag—Tivon, L. Drucker—Ramat Gan, H. Hahn—Kiriat Motzkin, B.
Hostovská—Haifa, D. Hershkovitz—Ashkelon, R. Stein—Tel Aviv

Birkenau:
I. Genczi—Haifa

INDEX